SEA OF THE CALIPHS

SEA OF THE CALIPHS

The Mediterranean in the Medieval Islamic World

CHRISTOPHE PICARD

Translated by Nichols Elliott

THE BELKNAP PRESS OF HARVARD UNIVERSITY PRESS

Cambridge, Massachusetts London, England

2018

Printed in the United States of America

First printing

LIBRARY OF CONGRESS CATALOGING-IN-PUBLICATION DATA
Names: Picard, Christophe, author.
Title: Sea of the caliphs : the Mediterranean in the medieval Islamic world / Christophe Picard ; translated by Nicholas Elliott.
Other titles: Mer des califes. English.
Description: Cambridge, Massachusetts : The Belknap Press of Harvard University Press, 2018. | "This book was originally published in French as La mer des califes: Une histoire de la Méditerranée musulmane, VIIe–XIIe siècle, copyright (c) Editions du Seuil, 2015"—Title page verso. | Includes bibliographical references and index.
Identifiers: LCCN 2017025099 | ISBN 9780674660465 (alk. paper)
Subjects: LCSH: Mediterranean Region—History—476–1517. | Islamic Empire—History, Naval. | Sea-power—Islamic Empire. | Abbasids—History, Naval. | Shipping—Mediterranean Region—History. | Navigation—Mediterranean Sea—History. | Muslims—Mediterranean Region—History.
Classification: LCC DS37.8 .P52813 2018 | DDC 909/.0982201—dc23
LC record available at https://lccn.loc.gov/2017025099

To Manuela, Benjamin, Alexandre

My profound gratitude to Annliese Nef, Françoise Micheau,
and Patrick Boucheron
for their support and advice

CONTENTS

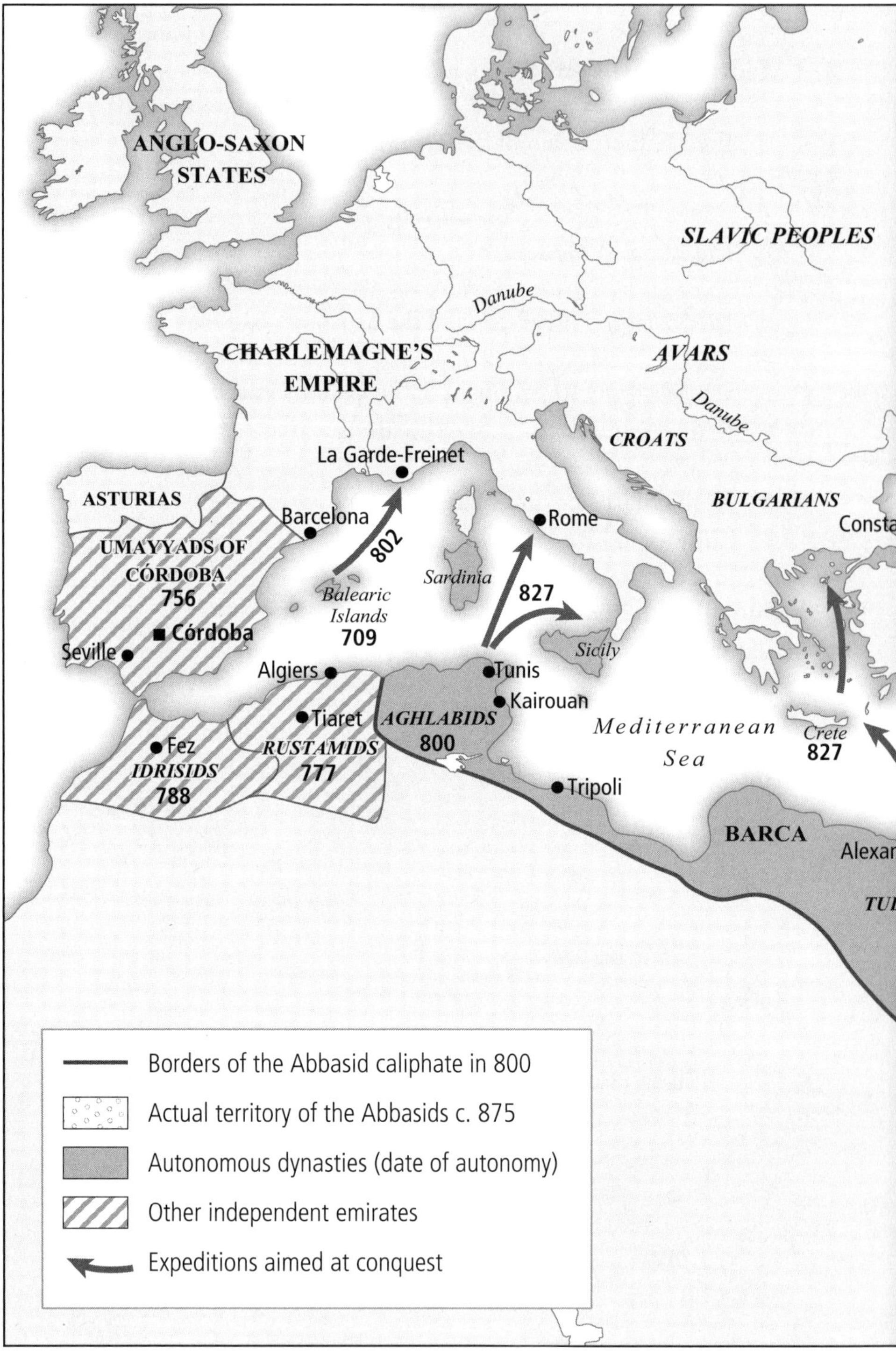
ANGLO-SAXON STATES
SLAVIC PEOPLES
Danube
CHARLEMAGNE'S EMPIRE
AVARS
Danube
CROATS
La Garde-Freinet
ASTURIAS
BULGARIANS
Barcelona
Rome
Consta
UMAYYADS OF CÓRDOBA 756
802
Sardinia
827
Balearic Islands 709
Córdoba
Seville
Sicily
Algiers
Tunis
Kairouan
Tiaret
AGHLABIDS 800
Mediterranean Sea
Crete 827
Fez
RUSTAMIDS 777
IDRISIDS 788
Tripoli
BARCA
Alexan
TUL
Borders of the Abbasid caliphate in 800
Actual territory of the Abbasids c. 875
Autonomous dynasties (date of autonomy)
Other independent emirates
Expeditions aimed at conquest

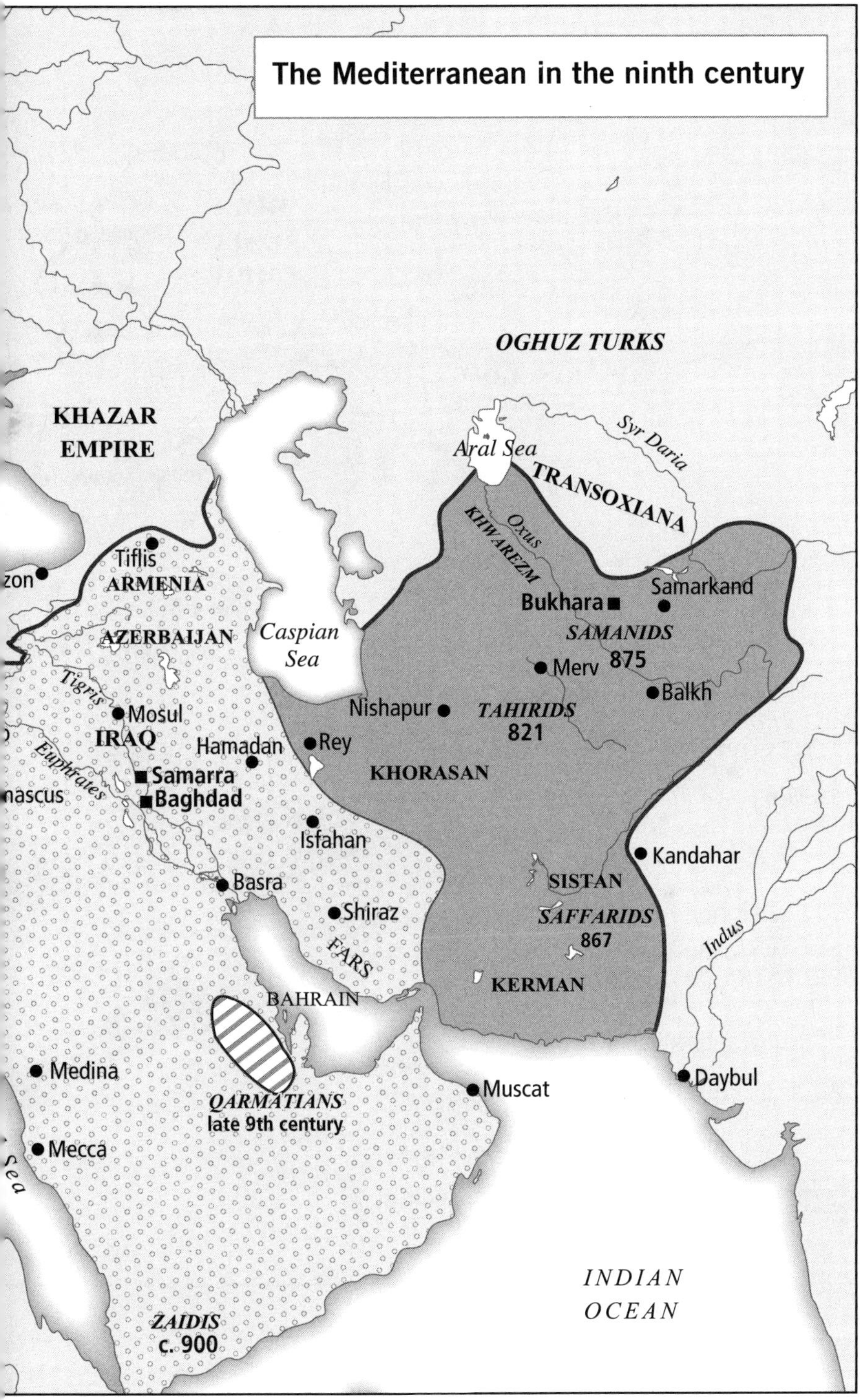

The Mediterranean in the ninth century
OGHUZ TURKS
KHAZAR EMPIRE
Aral Sea
Syr Daria
TRANSOXIANA
Oxus
KHWAREZM
Tiflis
zon
ARMENIA
Samarkand
Bukhara
SAMANIDS
875
AZERBAIJAN
Caspian Sea
Merv
Balkh
Tigris
Mosul
Nishapur
TAHIRIDS
821
IRAQ
Hamadan
Rey
Euphrates
Samarra
Baghdad
KHORASAN
nascus
Isfahan
Kandahar
Basra
SISTAN
Shiraz
SAFFARIDS
867
FARS
Indus
KERMAN
BAHRAIN
Medina
Daybul
Muscat
QARMATIANS
late 9th century
Mecca
Sea
INDIAN OCEAN
ZAIDIS
c. 900

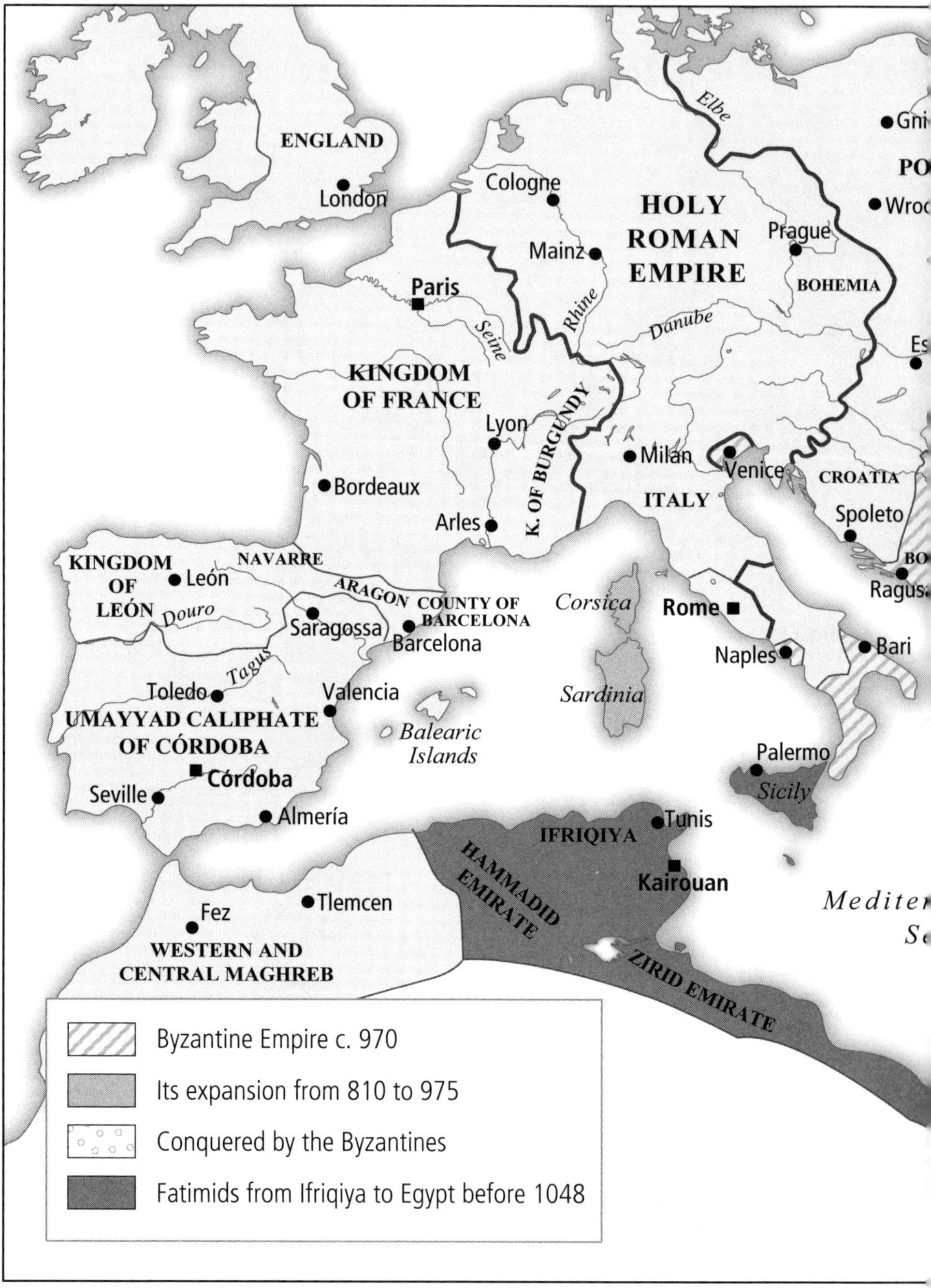
ENGLAND
London
Cologne
HOLY ROMAN EMPIRE
Elbe
Prague
Mainz
BOHEMIA
Paris
Seine
Rhine
Danube
KINGDOM OF FRANCE
Lyon
K. OF BURGUNDY
Milan
Venice
CROATIA
Bordeaux
ITALY
Spoleto
Arles
KINGDOM OF LEÓN
León
Douro
NAVARRE
ARAGON
COUNTY OF BARCELONA
Saragossa
Barcelona
Corsica
Rome
Naples
Bari
Tagus
Toledo
Valencia
Sardinia
UMAYYAD CALIPHATE OF CÓRDOBA
Balearic Islands
Córdoba
Seville
Almería
Palermo
Sicily
Tunis
IFRIQIYA
Kairouan
HAMMADID EMIRATE
Tlemcen
Fez
WESTERN AND CENTRAL MAGHREB
ZIRID EMIRATE
Byzantine Empire c. 970
Its expansion from 810 to 975
Conquered by the Byzantines
Fatimids from Ifriqiya to Egypt before 1048

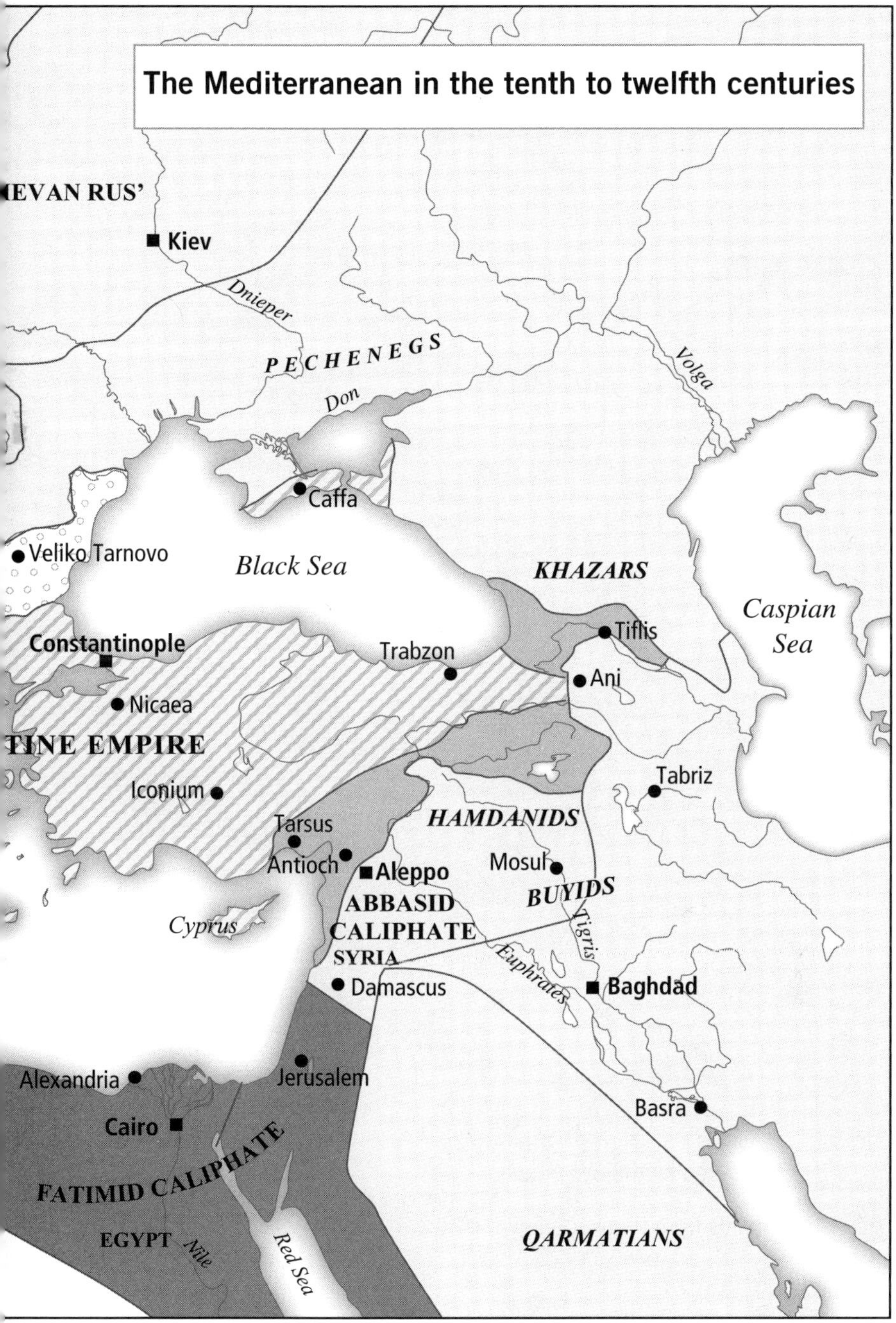
The Mediterranean in the tenth to twelfth centuries
Kiev
Dnieper
PECHENEGS
Don
Volga
Caffa
Veliko Tarnovo
Black Sea
KHAZARS
Caspian Sea
Tiflis
Constantinople
Trabzon
Ani
Nicaea
Tabriz
Iconium
Tarsus
HAMDANIDS
Antioch
Aleppo
Mosul
BUYIDS
ABBASID CALIPHATE
Cyprus
Tigris
SYRIA
Euphrates
Damascus
Baghdad
Alexandria
Jerusalem
Basra
Cairo
FATIMID CALIPHATE
EGYPT
Nile
Red Sea
QARMATIANS

SEA OF THE CALIPHS

INTRODUCTION

The End of the Moorish and Saracen Pirate?

> By He who sent Muhammad with the truth,
> I will never let any Muslim venture out on it [the Mediterranean] . . .
> How could I allow my soldiers to sail on this disloyal and cruel sea?
>
> —*'Umar b. al-Khattab (634–644)*

THIS STATEMENT, attributed to the man seen by Muslims in the Middle Ages as the greatest caliph of Islam and the initiator and organizer of the Arab conquests, has led to a lasting misunderstanding regarding the history of Muslims in the Mediterranean in Islam's first centuries. Indeed, when Fernand Braudel opened his classic study of the Mediterranean by declaring, "I have loved the Mediterranean with passion," he was not thinking of a Christian and Muslim sea but rather of that of the Latin merchants responsible for capitalism's first stirrings.[1] Braudel recognized Islam as one of the great Mediterranean civilizations but saw it as only a minor player in the maritime and economic development of the Middle Ages. In his wake, histories of the medieval Mediterranean have pushed Islam's sailors into the background, generally relegating them to the status of pirates. Beginning with the scholarly works of Henri Pirenne, the Arab conquest (634–732) was held responsible for the crisis of the Roman Mare Nostrum triggered by the plague in the middle of the sixth century. According to Pirenne and those who followed, Muslim expansion resulted in a long economic, demographic, and cultural depression in the Mediterranean basin, sustained by the permanent war between Muslims and Christians.[2] Only the great tenth century stood out as the moment when the Muslim world flourished in the Mediterranean: taking advantage of the effects of economic recovery, the two Mediterranean caliphates of the Umayyads (931–1031) and the Fatimids (909–1171) successfully adapted the power, splendor, and glory of the Abbasid caliphate of Baghdad (749–1258) to the Islamic West, in order to compete for control of maritime space with the Macedonian emperors of Byzantium (867–1059). This ushered in the second period of the Mediterranean Middle Ages, beginning in the eleventh century, an era built on the foundations of Latin capitalism, which now allowed Italian, Provençal, and later Catalan sailors to take over the maritime routes and markets of Byzantium and Islam. The Muslim period in the Mediterranean appeared to be over, at least until the rise of Ottoman power.[3] According to this view of history, conquering Islam's encounter with the maritime space coincides with the period of crisis. As for the Latin period, it is closely tied to the phase of economic expansion.

The accepted version of the sea's medieval history holds that before the tenth century, Muslim expansion on "the Sea of the Romans" (*al-bahr al-Rumi*), as it was referred to by the Arabs, was limited to piracy; that only the Fatimids and the caliphs of Córdoba took the initiative of developing economic and military activity on the sea; and that, with the exception of the Almohad caliphs of Marrakech (1147–1269), Muslim authorities then turned away from a sea now dominated by the great Latin ports.[4] This version of history has generally been elaborated from a chronology imposed by the legacy of historical works on the Latin world, whose tools of evaluation were those of economic measurement, based on figures totally deficient before the eleventh century. Above all else, the first medieval period was one that lacked documentary resources and has largely remained so: the economic situation was not bad, but it was initially impalpable, at least until the active, complex, and varied world that existed before the tenth century was revealed by archeologists ranging from Peter Brown to Chris Wickham, then historians of the medieval Latin world, and more recently those of Byzantium and Islam.[5]

This is how the Muslim pirate came into existence in the annals of Greek and Latin monks, for the victims were the only ones to bear witness to his assaults on Christian coasts. He is present in most histories of the Mediterranean, up to and including those of the present day.[6] Yet, at the same time, a succession of leading works, starting in the period of the remarkable German school in the late nineteenth century and extending to significant texts such as Shlomo Goitein's *A Mediterranean Society* (1967), reinforced new convictions that Islam held an undeniable place in the historical construction of a medieval Mediterranean Sea that was shared, multiple, and complex.[7]

The two half millennia after the fall of Rome and before the discovery of America and the Battle of Lepanto (1571) cannot be separated, for they were both medieval: the rupture that was originally perceived between the High Middle Ages and the time of Latin expansion has been replaced by an infinitely more complex cycle that dismisses any evaluation opposing the two medieval periods. It is equally impossible to partition the medieval Mediterranean into religions, dynasties, naval powers, and especially societies, as defined by Peregrine Horden and Nicholas Purcell, and this despite the political and religious divisions and the effects of a specific environment on the molding of the Mediterranean man dear to Braudel: due to the constant relations between the Byzantine, Latin, and Muslim worlds, the sea remains a central space, both separating and connecting the three imperial areas as of the seventh century.[8] It is also impossible to interpret the medieval Mediterranean without taking into account three continents and two oceans. The Middle Ages saw the opening of the Mediterranean to a larger world—the Sahara, continental Asia, the Indian Ocean, and the areas of the North Sea and the Baltic Sea. Islam contributed significantly to this phenomenon. It was in Baghdad and Iran that the Mediterranean was first described in Arabic, far from the shores of the Sea of Rum, as the Byzantine Mediterranean was known.

The most difficult challenge for those interested in the Mediterranean as seen from the Islamic world is in accessing information on the sea from the initial centuries, ranging from the Hegira in 622 to the middle of the ninth century. Aside from two chronicles by the Andalusian Ibn Habib (d. 854) and the Egyptian Ibn 'Abd al-Hakam (d. 871), both of which have little to say about maritime activity, the first Muslim and Mediterranean accounts of Islamic maritime pursuits come from the capitals of the Fatimid and Umayyad caliphates. To make matters more complicated, like the Iraqi men of letters before them, the Mediterranean chroniclers rewrote the history of the Islamic times that preceded their own at the request of the tenth-century caliphs, specifically concentrating on the areas governed by the two sovereignties, using previous versions that were then eliminated.[9] The chroniclers of both Mediterranean caliphates were very effective in shaping the timing of the Muslim occupation of the Mediterranean for posterity: according to them, the Muslim "pirate," left to himself, prospered in the ninth century and disappeared under the two caliphates, to be replaced by sailors enlisted on the ships of the Commander of the Faithful.

After the twelfth century, the caliph's sailor was once again said to disappear from the history of the Mediterranean, this time due to the Latins. Venice, Pisa, and Genoa gradually chased the "Moorish and Saracen pirates" out of Mediterranean waters and imposed their remarkable naval and commercial organization throughout the entire Mediterranean world. Joined by the Catalans, they developed the practice of international trade with the Byzantines and Muslims and by the thirteenth century had secured a monopoly on maritime trade, at the expense of Islamic and Greek sailors. At this stage, Muslim and Christian piracy no longer appears in Mediterranean sources, as it were, outside of minor pieces of news. A different history of the Mediterranean is imposed, shaped by Latin endeavors and most often relegating Byzantium and Islam's role on the sea to a passive one or that of a victim, particularly in questions of trade.

Since the publication of the works of Braudel and his disciple Maurice Lombard, who returned the Muslim Mediterranean to a central place, the region's history has enjoyed an intense historiographic decompartmentalization, which has modified approaches to a history of the Mediterranean now told in three voices: Latin, Greek, and Arabic. Going beyond the monographs on Italian and Catalonian trading cities and the many scholarly works on their commercial networks, studies of the merchants of Muslim countries and Byzantium have allowed history to reveal an economic and, more specifically, commercial world that is far from limited to the major Italian networks.[10]

Over the last half a century, the study of the lands bordering the sea in the first centuries of the Middle Ages has opened the door to a far different approach to the Mediterranean context.[11] Archeologists are now finding traces of human settlements from every period of the High Middle Ages on a significant proportion of the Mediterranean's shores. There are signs of uninterrupted human activity, including during the worst periods of plague and war. At the same time, the diversity of scenarios revealed by excavations invalidates the idea of the development of an economic situation measured on the scale of the Mediterranean, replacing it with regional, urban, and village contexts. In fact, there can no longer be any question of a lasting economic crisis said to have affected the entire Mediterranean from the sixth to the ninth centuries.[12] While there are numerous references to crises and catastrophes, these have an uneven impact on cities and rural areas across the region and at different times. The fragmented periods and spaces of crisis brought to light by numerous archeological digs dismiss the argument carefully elaborated by Pirenne.

The focus on social changes connected to a state of lasting conflict or the crisis arising from the breakdown of power, particularly in Italy in the ninth to eleventh centuries, has shown that war was no longer the area's sole agent of destruction and crisis. The change in the status of populations and the social reorganization driven by the new forces resulting from the collapse of earlier states, adapted to economic conditions and leading to the disappearance of slavery and serfdom in the countryside, are now considered the principal catalysts of a restructuring of rural societies and landscapes, as seen with the *incastellamento* in Latium. In the tenth century, a new hierarchization of elites benefited local aristocracies born of the former Carolingian and Lombardian structures. Thus the permanence of the Muslim threat to Christian shores no longer appears as the principal reason for regional developments, outside of isolated instances.[13] In addition, accounts showing that commercial navigation was maintained all along Mediterranean shores throughout the High Middle Ages, and, particularly, during and after the Arab conquest from the seventh to the ninth centuries, suggest that activity on the sea was not limited to the misdeeds of Moorish and Saracen piracy. Yet no serious speculation is possible at this stage.

At the same time, the foundations for this regionalized history remain fragile insofar as sources are rare and nearly exclusively come from palace circles or the spheres of the military, merchant, judicial, or ecclesiastical aristocracy. Despite the fact that archeologists have allowed us to penetrate deeper and deeper into the private world of every kind of medieval home, Horden and Purcell argue that this narrow perspective deprives us of direct access to the history of the vast majority of Mediterranean societies, which were incontestably the prime actors of the Mediterranean's development, at least before the tenth century.[14] The two English historians, who seek to break down the barriers of Mediterranean history and get outside the restrictive context of leadership circles, are no different from Braudel in putting aside the part played by the people of the Islamic world in building and developing the medieval Mediterranean, despite the commentary provided by two leading sources on Islam, the letters of Jewish merchants discovered in Cairo and the Arabic geography text by al-Muqaddasi (d. ca. 1000), a native of Jerusalem.[15]

The collection of thousands of letters written by Jewish merchants discovered in the Geniza—the storeroom for writings containing the name of God—in the Ben Ezra Synagogue in Cairo shows that the Muslim world's written sources do not exclusively come from chancelleries and judicial circles. Nonetheless, Goitein's remarkable study emphasizes the exceptional nature of these documents in the context of the written production of medieval Islamic cultures, despite the fact that other stores of letters by merchants have been found on the shores of the Red Sea.[16] Al-Muqaddasi's passages devoted to the Beqaa valley in the mountains of Lebanon detail a land admirably put to use by the low mountainous region's rural communities, though this is not the geographer's aim, other than to associate the region's prosperity with good government by the Fatimids. The geographer traveled the world as a purported Ismailist missionary, but he kept his mind open to any display of Muslim superiority: "The depiction of the world is limited to Islam, even more strictly than with the predecessors."[17] This description fits into the unique framework of the Mamlakat al-Islam, the Islamic empire. Al-Muqaddasi described and hierarchized the different parts of the empire that he visited, particularly those east of the Mediterranean; like his fellow geographers, he provides a report on the state of the Muslim world, which includes the Muslim Mediterranean—in this case, that of the Fatimids. Its stated prosperity is the proof of good government, but it does not yield a picture of the agrarian society's structure or of the connections between communities too conventional to be used by a historian seeking to make an economic and social assessment of the region.[18]

Before we ask Horden and Purcell's question, "What is the Mediterranean?" we should perhaps first ask ourselves which Mediterranean and what history of the Mediterranean writers and geographers of the time wanted to leave to posterity, as well as for whom their descriptions of the territories of Islam were intended. Regarding Islam, the answer is provided by André Miquel: "Arab geography is the daughter of the caliphate of Baghdad," and it "is primarily interested in the role and place, in the world, of the new man created by Islam," specifically as it applies to the political and religious context and above all else to the demonstration of the legitimacy of the universal caliphate, in this case the Fatimid.[19]

The Arab scriptural environment had a major impact on the types of documents and content produced by Islam's men of letters. Our perception of the maritime societies of the Islamic coastline is therefore affected by the knowledge that the fleets presented in Christian sources as belonging to pirates—a term justified on the part of the victims—were, in the minds of Muslims, squadrons under orders from the Muslim sovereign to conquer or weaken Christian infidels. These "pirates" lived off privateering, most often under the control of the state, but also from trade, which was active along Muslim shores and, more often than has been acknowledged, all the way to Christian coasts, where Muslim merchants were heartily welcomed by the Greeks and Latins during periods of truce. These sailors, seen by Muslim authorities as defenders and conquerors for Islam and remunerated for their booty, were recognized as pious and worthy men for having pillaged infidel monasteries and shores that had to be depopulated to stock the palaces with slaves. In the same spirit, the Mediterranean described by al-Muqaddasi appears either as a Roman sea, and consequently as a space to be conquered, or as an Islamic sea, generous and open. The geographer was himself indebted to the way the caliphal chancelleries had imposed a view of the Mediterranean developed "under orders from the Caliph," beginning in the earliest times of the Abbasids.[20]

Whatever scenarios one adheres to regarding the formation and development of a politically divided medieval Mediterranean in a permanent state of war, the populations that appear in the documentation left by the three empires are not ones that were allegedly ruined by the plague and raids of the High Middles Ages until the maritime and merchant Latin powers took over the now-prosperous area. Looked at as a whole, these sources offer another version of the Mediterranean's development: for all the regions, the men of letters more often describe societies increasingly well adapted to mutations, beginning with the crisis of the sixth century and related to permanent confrontation on the vast land and sea frontier. This socioeconomic context, often idealized by administrators and religious men, does not provide an overview of Christian or Muslim society, let alone a comprehensive picture, but it does occasionally allow one to understand how these hardworking populations adapted to constantly changing worlds.

The texts written by the first generation of Muslim men of letters were the fruit of a civilization that was not seeking to turn the Mediterranean Sea into a new Mare Nostrum but rather intended to cross it to impose Islam on the European continent. These writings focused on the description of the state supervision of a coastal and maritime space that was constructed for defense but also to develop profitable activities. War is constantly present but appears as an essential instrument for the organization of border regions, under the control of the Latin, Byzantine, and Muslim states, thus underlining the role played by those in power. As seen in the texts, the sea remained an affair of state throughout the Middle Ages.[21] Perhaps the real medieval rupture, having started with the Italian city-states in the twelfth century, began when the references to a military and imperial environment were replaced by those to the bankers and merchants who were able to impose their "capitalist" ways on the church.[22]

While Arabs produced a tremendous quantity of writing, particularly beginning in the tenth century, across the entire vast Islamic area, very few of these texts concern actual maritime or trading activity on the Mediterranean. As for the archives assembled by the great Italian port cities of Pisa, Genoa, and Venice or kept by the Crown of Aragon, they do not contain the notarized agreements, wills, contracts, or other written documents that would allow us to delve into the closed circle of trade networks, notaries' offices, and dockyards, let alone into the crews—pirates or sailors of the caliph—on ships' decks. Nearly all of the Arabic documents resulting from Muslim naval activities on the Mediterranean are by writers in princely entourages, all perfectly familiar with the ins and outs of Muslim palaces, but rarely with maritime techniques, in which they had no interest. In most cases, only the legal and fiscal perspective or military framework was of interest. With the exception of Sinbad the Sailor on the Indian Ocean and a few heroes who built their reputations by leading Muslim fleets to victory over Greek or Latin ships, Muslim seamen were rarely popular subjects, for the record of the construction of Mediterranean Islam was devoted to men of the caliph, emir, or sultan or to the circles of jurists and Sufi saints, countless figureheads who fill the many biographical volumes written by scholars. As for the Sea of the Romans, often referred to as such in Arabic sources, it remained a boundary first and foremost and thus a space over which was exercised the sovereignty of the Prophet's successors.

Unlike the literature of the Indian Ocean, none of the available literature on the Mediterranean Sea originates from the world of sailors, with the exception of indirect references via jurists or employees of the sultans' administrations. Documents on the sea, the navy, and sailors were indeed written or drawn by and for seafarers, at least since the tenth century on the Mediterranean, but all that survives is the production of Arab geographers and encyclopedists who took this prose and removed technical details considered useless to produce a literary work for a general audience, intended to be read in the lounges of the capital and leading cities of Islam. The sorting of copied texts led these same men of letters to remove from shelves and offices works considered obsolete or unrelated to the definition of the standards of Islam. Muslims archived documents, but then they threw out parchments or used them to make palimpsests, washing the paper and erasing outdated text to use the paper for new text. More generally, a palace's archival documents disappeared as soon as they were no longer useful or when the palace was destroyed or vacated by successors or usurpers who had a new residence built and amassed new archives, which were equally perishable if they did not serve to prove or demonstrate the ruler's legitimacy. Only those documents containing the name of God, like the letters in the Geniza, had to be preserved. Like all the information that would allow us to piece together the organization of Muslim navies, orders regarding dockyards, crews, the requisition of supplies, and the recruiting of oarsmen—discovered "by chance" on Egyptian papyri dating from the beginning of the eighth century—were kept only as long as they were useful.[23]

Does this indicate that Muslim sailors and merchants sailed and traded less than Latin sailors? Not at all. Muslim sailors certainly roamed wider than the Muslim documents suggest. This is clearly demonstrated by the fact that Muslim "pirates" are known to have existed merely because Christian victims spoke of them, while the Muslim authorities did not deem it useful to record every one of the raids actually carried out by crews under orders from the caliph or the emir, which left the sailors and their actions to vanish into oblivion. Did the Muslims engage in less sea trade? Anyone who takes the time to read the Arab geographic and legal sources will see this is far from the case, and the discovery of the Geniza letters has shown that the Muslim world's trade networks could be as structured as those of the great Latin ports.

Most information on the sea is nearly entirely drawn from a chancellery literature devoted to supporting the sovereigns. Even critical, independent minds such as al-Muqaddasi could not avoid thinking and writing like men trained in the circles of scholars and administrators. However, this Arab geographer's description of the Mediterranean reveals how well he knew that world and navigation. While most of his information on the sea, fleets, sailors, and commerce was intended to advance the naval and trading policy of whatever sovereign was in power, it also included references to many aspects of maritime life and revealed the extent of the Muslim occupation and exploitation of the sea and its riches, for sustenance and other uses. It even reveals the sea's Islamic universality and humanity, as praised by the Almohad caliph 'Abd al-Mu'min in a speech to his officers in Marrakech.[24]

This brings us back to the question raised by Horden and Purcell and many other historians before them: What is the medieval Mediterranean? If we take into account the Arabic records of the time, it is not the sea of the Muslim pirate but rather the domain of the sailor, whether military or commercial, in the service of his own fortune and the caliph. The sailor competed for control of the Mediterranean with the Greek and Latin peoples and was honored for it, though not on the same level as the other heroes of Islam.

We must give credit where credit is due: this period in history belongs first and foremost to the caliphs, buttressed by scholars and particularly jurists. According to the precept that it is the time of writing, rather than the time described in the writing, that marks the first historical time period, we must follow the pace set by the texts written for the caliphs.

The first period to yield an Arabic description of the Mediterranean was that of the Abbasid caliphate, beginning in the middle of the ninth century. Recorded accounts come from oral and written traditions that reached the capitals and other cities of the Dar al-Islam, or territory of Islam, through a series of transmitters and were passed down from the conquerors and those who succeeded them: nothing is invented or supposed, subject to discredit, but the texts are shaped by the period during which they were rewritten. The use of these selected versions orients the narrative according to a logic that most often leads back to the Iraqi caliphs' Mediterranean strategies.

Beginning in the tenth century, the written production of the Mediterranean caliphal capitals in Córdoba, Kairouan, and Cairo rivaled that of Baghdad, at a time when the caliphs were losing both actual power and prestige. The texts produced by the Andalusian (756–929) and Aghlabid (800–909) emirates were later adopted by writers working for caliphs in al-Andalus and Ifriqiya, for the same reasons that the writings concerning the sovereigns of Iraq were adopted. This caliphal production suffered the effects of time; only a very limited part of this literature has reached us. Most of the Mediterranean production on the first centuries of Islam is found in the histories that proliferated in the major capitals from the eleventh century onward.

We can therefore assert that it was the Eastern men of letters, from Iran to Egypt, who imposed the forms of so-called classical Arabic literature. To a great extent, the outlines of the Mediterranean as depicted by Eastern men of letters are found in the geographic and historical descriptions of the scholars of the two Western caliphates in the tenth century, as well as in the Arabic descriptions and chronicles of the last centuries of the Middle Ages. However, both the Fatimids and the Umayyads imposed new outlines of their sea's history and geography, geared to the new context and the sea's importance in establishing their own legitimacy. The men of letters in the circles of the Almohad caliphs, the last sovereigns of the Middle Ages to conceive of the sea as a full-fledged Muslim imperial space, produced an even more voluminous literature on the sea.

At the same time, the features of this caliphal literature of the Mediterranean had a profound impact on descriptions of the Sea of Rum, particularly in the Maghreb and Cairo, until the end of the Middle Ages. Though the Ottomans did not deny this past, it fell to them to impose their own view of the sea, as seen from the palace terraces of Istanbul after 1453. All the other Islamic powers that shared the shores of the Mediterranean, particularly the sultanates of Egypt, left traces of their own literary commitment.

The sea holds a significant place throughout the extant texts and appears in every kind of Arabic written expression, as long as it is in the service of "imperial"—and consequently restrictive—promotion.[25]

It is through this construction of a Muslim and Arab world on the Mediterranean, mobilizing every form of expression of the prolific Arabic literature, that one can understand a profile of the Sea of the Romans as written by Arab writers, more rarely by Persian writers, beginning in the ninth century and continuing throughout the medieval period. The chronological framework we find here is primarily the one imposed by successive caliphates. Their representations of the Mediterranean must therefore serve as a fundamental basis for the history of the Muslim Mediterranean: The Arab conquest of the sea and its shores from 634 to 749, led with an iron hand by the Rashidun caliphs of Medina (632–661), followed by the Umayyads, is only known to us through the Abbasid versions of the maritime region's history and subsequent texts. Al-Tabari's history, completed around 915, was considered by his peers to be the greatest Arabic chronicle of all time.[26]

References to the expansion onto the sea and its shores beginning in 750 are limited in the sources produced in Baghdad and Samarra, but they are sufficient to observe the Iraqi caliphs' constant interest in the Syrian coast and, additionally, in the maritime space of the Mediterranean as a whole. Rather than focusing on actual strategy, most references to the Mediterranean area in caliphal and legal literature deal with the caliphs' involvement on the Byzantine frontier in Anatolia from 754 to 945, to a lesser extent with military policy along the coasts of the Near East, and especially with the updating of jihad made necessary by the lasting stabilization of the fronts. Beginning in the ninth century, several dissident powers in the Muslim West took over from the Abbasids, drawing direct inspiration from the model of the caliphs. The Iraqi sovereigns thus imposed the practices of jihad, which were adapted to every Mediterranean frontier until the end of the Middle Ages.

The Mediterranean caliphates of the Fatimids and the Umayyads picked up where their predecessors left off. Their scribes took great care to describe involvement in the war against the Christians, particularly on the sea, in the context of a demonstration of their universal legitimacy on the path to seizing Baghdad. Ibn Khaldun (d. 1406) declared that this period was marked by Islam's near total domination on the sea. However, the impact of the rivalry between the two Mediterranean caliphates on both caliphates' maritime strategies extended far beyond the aspiration to conquer Iraq until al-Muʿizz (953–975) moved his dynasty to Egypt in 971. Once al-Muʿizz settled in Cairo, his policy evolved with the establishment of good relations—primarily commercial—with the Byzantines, then the Latins. Following the crisis that starved the Nile valley from 1065 to 1072 and during the time sailors from Pisa, Venice, and

Genoa were coming to trade in the Egyptian capital and Alexandria, the development of maritime and commercial activities on the Red Sea and the Indian Ocean allowed the Shiite sovereigns to reinforce their control over traffic between these two maritime regions.

Beginning in the eleventh century, Latin offensives forced regional powers, and, in particular, the Almoravids of Marrakech (1072–1147), then the Almohad caliphate in the West and the Egyptian caliphs (971–1171) in the East (until the loss of Ashkelon to the Crusaders in 1154) to maintain their military presence on the Mediterranean to deter attacks from the sea. The Berber caliphate was to be the last Muslim maritime power able to compete with the Latins. After the defeat at Las Navas de Tolosa in 1212, the crises faced by the Almohad state beginning in 1215—and the maritime and commercial ventures of Latin ports—turned the Mediterranean into a Latin sea once and for all. In Egypt and Syria, neither the Ayyubids (1171–1250) nor the Mamluks (1250–1517) presented the navy as an emblem of their power, though they were able to fit out galleys when they needed to.[27] Saladin (1171–1193) acknowledged that only the caliphs of the Maghreb could rival the Latin enemy on the water.[28]

The Marinids (1258–1465) in Fez and the Hafsids (1229–1574) in Tunis paid sufficient attention to their fleets to mostly resist Christian pressure and maintain control of the Strait of Gibraltar, at least until the fourteenth century. Was this the end of the Muslim Mediterranean? Muslim sailors were now only found in a few zones along the African coast and, beginning with the Turkish settlement of Anatolia in the eleventh century, the Asian coasts of the Sea of Marmara and soon the Dardanelles. Until the sixteenth-century exploits of Hayreddin Barbarossa (d. 1546), admiral of the Sublime Porte, and especially the Ottoman domination of the Mediterranean, as of the thirteenth century neither the caliph's sailor nor the Moorish or Saracen pirate could claim to compete for the sea with the Latin world's maritime forces, outside of carrying out a few raids that announced the return of the Muslim pirate.

I

THE ARAB MEDITERRANEAN BETWEEN REPRESENTATION AND APPROPRIATION

1

THE ARAB DISCOVERY OF THE MEDITERRANEAN

THE MEDITERRANEAN SEEMS to have a very limited place in the history recorded by Arab men of letters in the first centuries of the Hegira.[1] The two Mediterranean authors to have left Arabic chronicles before the tenth century, the Andalusian Ibn Habib and the Egyptian Ibn 'Abd al-Hakam, practically make no reference to the inland sea, other than to mention the crossing of the Strait of Gibraltar by Berber and Arab troops to invade Visigothic Spain.[2] Before the prolific geographic production of the tenth century, the chroniclers and geographers of Baghdad seemed to want to cultivate the Mediterranean's marginality, treating the sea and its shores in the same manner. From the earliest Abbasid record of the conquest, a reconstructed text by Sayf b. 'Umar (d. 796), to the "books of conquest" of the late ninth century, little information appears regarding the Umayyads' maritime activity; what traditions these authors did collect are unclear.[3] As for firsthand accounts of the Sea of the Romans, they are virtually limited to the Aphrodite papyri in Egypt.[4] One has to wait until the end of the tenth century for the maritime and mercantile world of Mediterranean Islam to truly become visible, thanks to the letters of Jewish merchants discovered in the Geniza of the synagogue in Fustat.[5] In the same time period, the advent of the Fatimid and Umayyad caliphates in Kairouan and Córdoba apparently broke Western Islam's silence, with the Muslim Mediterranean becoming one of the most fertile centers of Arabic literature. The great Muslim capitals of the region now rivaled Baghdad and the large Asian cities of Islam that had previously monopolized the majority of Arabic production.

Nonetheless, the texts by Muslim authorities offer the richest resources to understand the relationship of the first generations of believers to the Mediterranean: expeditions, treaties, the organization of governments, and coastal defense are among the favorite subjects of the Arab chroniclers who reported the facts of the conquest. The first generation of Arab chroniclers to whose work we have access drew from the primitive Arab histories (*akhbar*), probably produced at the time of the Marwanid caliphs (692–749) and themselves indebted to traditions that could date back to the second generation of Muslims.[6] This work of collecting and writing texts, updated in accordance with caliphal affairs, came to an initial culmination with the historian al-Tabari (d. 923).[7] Having emerged in the ninth century from the offices of the Abbasid caliphate's administration, cartography and descriptions of the world were also devoted to demonstrating the legitimacy of the Islamic religion and its guide, the caliph. Naturally, Baghdad was placed at the center of the ecumene. The capital's prestige proved so durable that this choice would extend to the entire Islamic koine, no matter the period or place of production. This cartography of Islamic universalism led to an impressive series of maps and accompanying descriptions of the earth.[8] Beginning with the first works of geography, the Mediterranean was logically included alongside the Indian Ocean and the Caspian Sea.[9]

The chronicles and geographic studies complement each other in providing a picture of Islam's domination of the world, particularly under the pen of multifaceted authors such as the geographer and historian al-Ya'qubi (d. 897). It is hardly surprising to find that these documents offer a reconstruction of Arab history and the representation of Islam, produced by men of letters in the ninth and tenth centuries after the sorting of previous histories geared to the periods of successive caliphates.[10]

In the Arabic texts describing the beginnings of Islam, the maritime space of the Mediterranean remains in the background, to the point that one might think the caliphs, established in Iraq, had not had any reason to take a particular interest in the distant Sea of the Romans. Having given up on the conquest, the Baghdad caliphate had presumably left the sea to the Christians. In contrast, the Indian Ocean, which was described as a sea of sailors and merchants, would be seen as the Muslim maritime space par excellence, and was all the more familiar given that the Arabs of the Hejaz were in the habit of roaming it long before the Hegira.[11] As early as the ninth century, descriptions of the Indian Ocean could be found in the capital. The beginning of the narrative of Sinbad's exploits in *The Thousand and One Nights* seems to confirm the mercantile atmosphere in major ports of Islam on the Arabian-Persian Gulf such as Basra, at the mouth of the Tigris and Euphrates, in the ninth and tenth centuries:

> I collected the remains of my estate. I sold all the furnishings I had at auction in the market. I then fell in with some merchants who traded at sea. I consulted those who seemed able to give me good advice. Finally, I resolved to make the most of the little money I had left and as soon as I had taken this resolution, I did not take long to execute it. I traveled to Basra, where I embarked with several merchants on a ship, sharing the expenses of fitting it out. We put out to sea and followed the East Indies route through the Persian Gulf.[12]

Descriptions of the Indian Ocean, which began to appear in Iraq in the middle of the ninth century, provide an idea of the role played by the trade networks that drove long-distance maritime commerce beginning in the Abbasid period.[13]

Only the creation in Egypt of a Muslim naval force and a few specific military events such as the expeditions toward Cyprus in 645 and the naval victory over the Byzantines at the Battle of the Masts in 655 drew the attention of the writers in the caliph's circle. Information on Muslim activity in the maritime space was exclusively focused on the legal conditions of relationships with islanders or, after negotiations, on their submission. Another area of special interest was the division of booty and its irregularities, which often led to a summons from the leader mandated by the caliph. Indeed, the conditions of conquest and the status of conquerors and populations subjected to them were of direct interest to the sovereigns, insofar as the foundations of the government of the provinces, particularly in regard to taxation and land statutes, were set or justified by these agreements with the defeated and the conditions for the division of land and booty among the soldiers of the army (*jund*). The sea was a route for fleets; it was neither a space to be shared nor, strictly speaking, one to be governed. Consequently, the use of the maritime route, for instance to go attack Constantinople or enemy islands and shores, could hold the authorities' attention, but most references to the maritime space concern the defense of the Dar al-Islam's coastlines from terra firma. The open sea is most often left aside.

The history of the first believers on the sea and on its shores was therefore not distorted but rather exploited to explain and justify the caliphs' policy, a policy that was legitimate as long as it was in keeping with what the companions of the Prophet, the first conquerors, had accomplished under Muhammad's guidance and then on the authority of the first caliphs, particularly ʿUmar b. al-Khattab.[14] The Abbasid historians' Mediterranean was not a forgotten or rejected sea, but one that had become a specific space for war. The Mediterranean was also confusing compared to the Arabs' sea of reference, the familiar Indian Ocean, which had been free of imperial enemies since the fall of the Sassanids in 652 and was now left to converted merchants.

Curious about this Roman world, Arab geographers and encyclopedists took over the representation of the spaces of the ecumene, naturally doing so in the service of the caliph, at the very time when the Latins and the Greeks were forgetting the sea—the latter beginning in the eighth century—probably to preserve the memory of the Mare Nostrum. The number of Arab descriptions and maps is unrivaled before the thirteenth century, particularly among the Christians.[15] In the Latin world, travel narratives written by pilgrims abandoned any representation or description of the sea after the period of Orosius and Isidore of Seville and until the Crusades. The few accounts of travel to the Holy Land, such as the eighth-century text by Willibald, remain focused on pilgrimage sites.[16] During this period, representations of the world were limited to a cartography that "iconizes space."[17]

Within the actual Dar al-Islam, the appearance as of the tenth century of a geography composed by men of letters native to the Mediterranean, in Córdoba, Kairouan, and Cairo, was a turning point in that the sea now held a preeminent place in descriptions: as a favored space for the expansion of the two Western caliphates, both rivals of the Abbasids, it was now represented as the other central maritime realm of Muslim civilization, including trade activities and travel descriptions. *The Book of Curiosities,* a tenth- or eleventh-century cartographic manuscript, particularly its map of the Mediterranean, embody this readjustment of Arab geography's focus toward the Mediterranean world, now on a par with the Indian Ocean, in the Umayyad and Fatimid periods.[18]

However, the geographers' attention was primarily drawn to the regions bordering the sea, such as the Maghreb, which was described on behalf of the caliphate by the Andalusian geographer al-Warraq in the tenth century. This description has partially reached us through the revised and updated version by the Andalusian geographer al-Bakri (d. 1094). During the same period, the production of geography books, including maps and text, constantly enriched the libraries of Islam. New descriptive forms such as chapters and books devoted to "wonders" (*'aja'ib*), derived from narratives of the Sea of the Arabs, began to appear on the shores of the Muslim Mediterranean. At the end of the twelfth century, personal accounts by traveling men of letters, known as the *rihla,* supplanted caliphal works of geography as Islam lost all control over the maritime space in the face of the Latins' unstoppable domination.[19] However, during the same period, the commission received by geographer al-Idrisi (d. ca. 1172) from Roger II of Sicily (1115–1154) for a world map whose geographic center was not Sicily—though the island does appear excessively enlarged—but Baghdad proves the extent to which the Arab model of cartography and astronomic geography, born in Iraq, had become a universal standard.[20]

The proliferation of these Arab representations and descriptions of the world is not the only reason for an increasingly precise recognition of the Mediterranean space as measured from the Islamic world. Arab encyclopedists and geographers, in both the East and the West, used a descriptive form—*masalik wa l-mamalik,* "roads and kingdoms"—to constantly update the situation of the world; their cartography was first

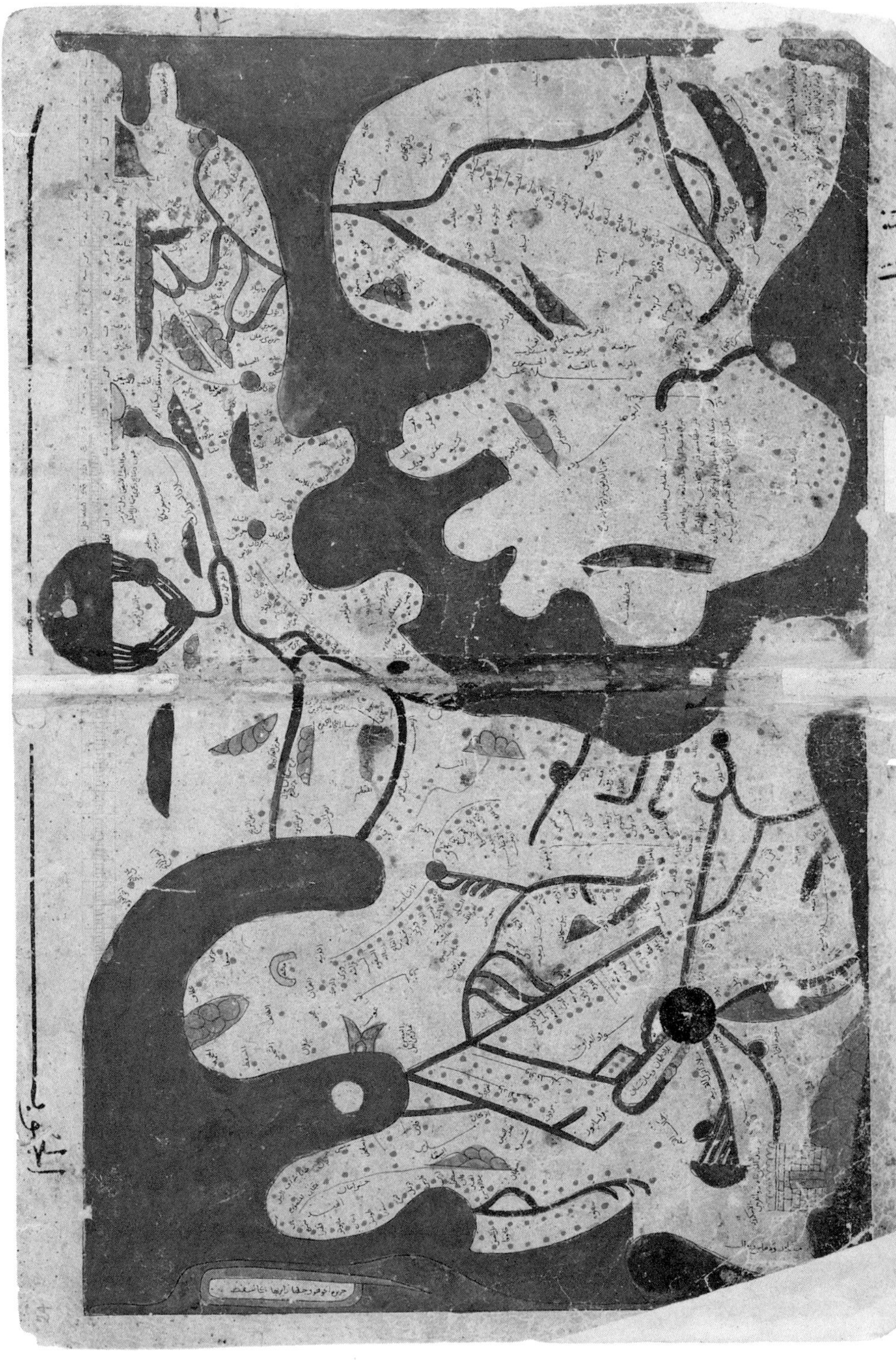

and foremost a hymn inspired by the ancient geography that put Islam at the center of the world and thus above other imperial spaces in the hands of the infidel. By reporting situations witnessed by geographers, who were nearly always also travelers, these accounts reveal constantly updated perceptions of the Mediterranean basin in an Islamic framework that remains connected with infidel spaces.[21]

Portraits of the earth, whether in part or in whole, are not limited to geography or to the Arabic language.[22] They make up countless analytic pictures of the situation of the Islamic Mediterranean in the Middle Ages. Three of the most well-known Arab men of letters will serve as our guides to summarize them. Indeed, the works of al-Mas'udi (d. 956), al-Idrisi, and Ibn Khaldun reveal three Mediterranean seas at different times, while conserving an identity stemming from the authors' shared education, which dated back to history's Iraqi roots.

A GEOGRAPHY OF TRAVEL

Maritime experiences made a deep impression on the Eastern polymath al-Mas'udi, as he reports in *The Meadows of Gold* and *The Book of Notification and Verification,* both written shortly before the middle of the tenth century. A scholar "concerned, as we imagine him today, with completely pure knowledge and truth," he also wanted to be a "popularizer, driven his whole life by the desire to make his work accessible."[23] This precept is particularly applicable to his descriptions of the seas. More than a century after the beginning of the Arabic literary ferment born of the Abbasid environment, al-Mas'udi's vision is certainly one of the most accomplished examples of the spirit of the travelers' geography.

The world in *The Book of Curiosities* (Fatimid area, eleventh or twelfth century)
The map is a representation of all inhabited land areas, including the two seas that separated them, the Sea of the Arabs (Indian Ocean) and the Sea of Rum (Mediterranean). *Kitab Ghara'ib al-funun wa-milah al-'uyun,* MS Arab c. 90, fols. 23b–24a, The Bodleian Libraries, University of Oxford.

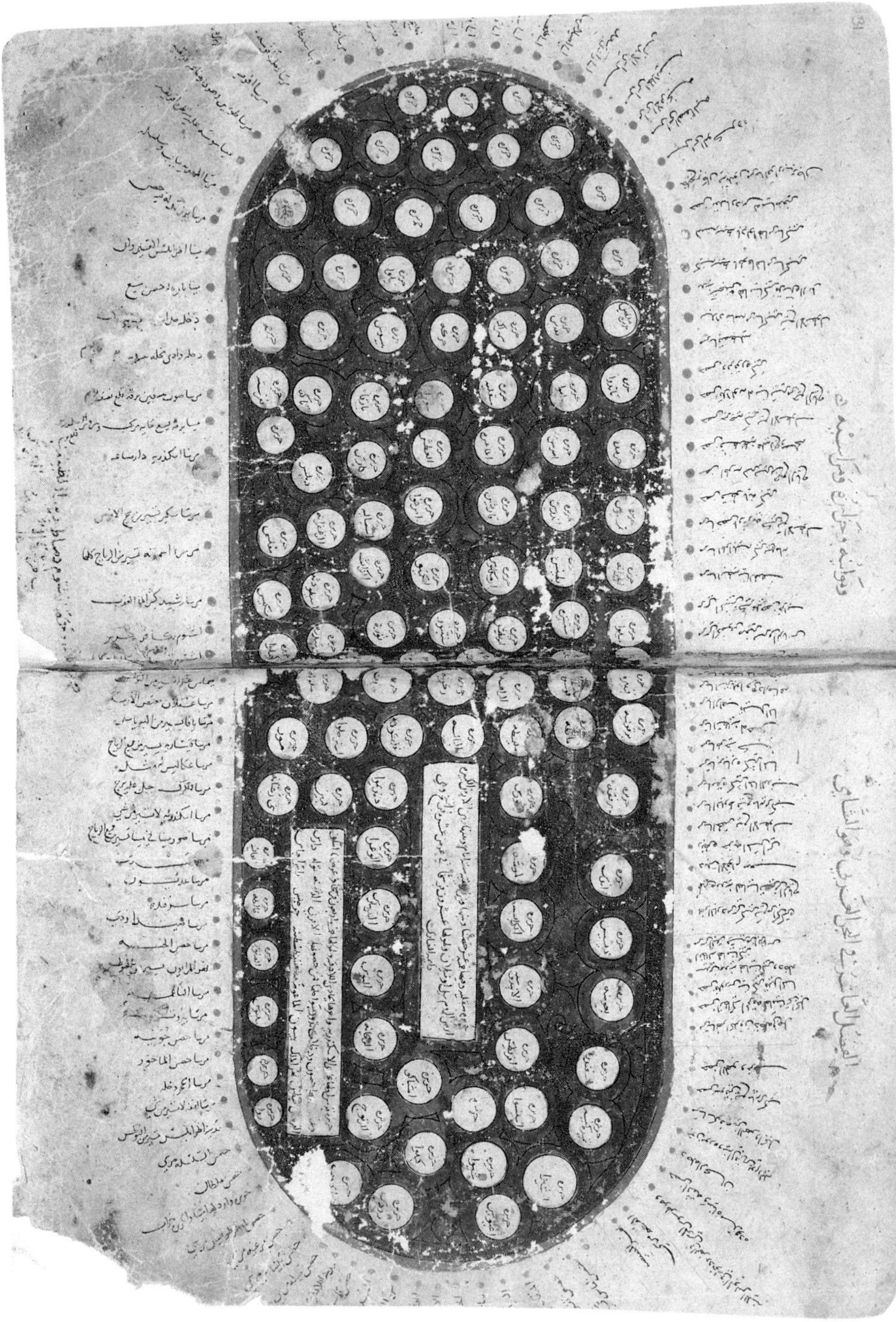

Al-Masʿudi wrote *The Meadows of Gold* around 943. This encyclopedic description of the world is presented as a digest of his lost monumental work, the *Akhbar al-Zaman* (The history of time). The two surviving works by this prolific author were the last he wrote, and they sold very well from the time they were issued, which may explain why they are the only works of his to have survived.[24]

The method al-Masʿudi used to discuss the world and man was one employed since the ninth century by every Baghdad man of letters steeped in the atmosphere of the *adab*, a literary current comparable to the spirit of the encyclopedic culture of the *honnête homme*—the well-educated, nonspecialized man of the French seventeenth century. It relied above all else on quotations from the ancients.[25] The first stage of al-Masʿudi's work as a writer was to consult texts in the libraries of the capitals he visited, initially to gather the ancient wisdom the Arabs had considered worth preserving, in particular that of the Greeks—starting with Ptolemy—who were considered the greatest experts on the sciences of the universe and the earth.[26] At the same time, it had become indispensable for any geographer embarking on descriptive writing in the tenth century to roam the world, which in practice was limited to the Arab world.

Al-Masʿudi's two encyclopedias contain 165 discrete references to the sea. The many references taken from ancient works are reminiscent of the education of everyone of the ulema in the law and science of Muslim tradition (Hadith). These disciplines, fundamental to the believer, had produced a rigorous process (*isnad*) adapted to all fields of knowledge embraced in Baghdad. Citing one's sources served as proof of the accuracy of one's argument, unless one chose to contradict them by comparing them to information from more recent or reputedly more reliable texts. The rhetoric of the *adab* was another methodology to distinguish

---

The Mediterranean in *The Book of Curiosities* (Fatimid area, eleventh or twelfth century)

The map shows the Mediterranean, with the islands (captioned circles) in the maritime space, without regard to their position, and the names of the ports around the shores. *Kitab Ghara'ib al-funun wa-milah al-ʿuyun*, MS Arab c. 90, fols. 30b–31a, The Bodleian Libraries, University of Oxford.

between truth and falsehood. The writer made particular use of personal interpretation and the controversy born of comparing contradictory opinions to draw out what became the "truth."

The other source of knowledge was the fruit of the writer's own observations and the accounts he collected during his travels.[27] These statements were considered reliable because the people the writer questioned were experienced sailors. Some are well known, like Leo of Tripoli, whom al-Masʿudi could not have met in person but who was famous enough that his opinions were passed down and collected by the polymath. Al-Masʿudi knew and deeply appreciated this maritime world; he sailed extensively, particularly on the Indian Ocean, but also on the Caspian Sea and the eastern Mediterranean. It is extremely unlikely, however, that his claim of having reached the China Sea is true. Given that a traveler's direct observation was considered the most reliable source, al-Masʿudi did not hesitate to bolster his writing's recognition by replacing his library research with a probably fictitious journey beyond Sri Lanka.[28] For example, he states, "I have sailed on many seas, the China Sea, the Mediterranean, the Caspian, the Red Sea, and the Sea of Yemen, I have run countless risks on them, but I know of none more dangerous than this Sea of Zanzibar of which we have just spoken."[29]

The polymath borrowed the method used by his precursors, particularly al-Yaʿqubi and Ibn al-Faqih, both of whom died around 900. This was a method essentially characterized as "the very act of seeing."[30] The approach was closely tied to travel, which had become indispensable for the geographer to become personally aware of the realities he discovered on his travels. As an outgrowth of the pilgrimage to Mecca and the ninth-century narratives of merchants on the Indian Ocean, travel had become a necessity to deliver a truth only accessible through investigation. Wandering was instructive and enabled the gathering of direct evidence, lending the description a hint of reality: "[The traveler] no longer proceeds by literary borrowing, but works from memory, based on the observations recorded during the journey."[31] The journey (*rihla*) was a preliminary stage that was practically indispensable for lending credibility to the opinions expressed. As one of the first representatives of this movement, Ibn al-Faqih reminded the reader of the educational virtues of travel and its constraints in a chapter called "In Praise of Traveling

Away from the Native Land": "Ask for your daily bread by traveling far abroad, for while you will not make much money, you will acquire much reason."[32] Al-Mas'udi, who was himself a great traveler, perhaps as an Ismaili missionary and likely as a merchant, made this guideline his own:

> All the sailors who frequent these waters [take advantage of] winds of which they perfectly know the periods. Among them, this science is the fruit of habit and long experience, and they pass it on to each other through oral [teaching] and practice. They guide themselves based on certain indications and particular signs to recognize the period of agitation, the quiet times and those of excitement. What we say here about the Indian Ocean is also [true] of Roman and Muslim sailors who travel the Mediterranean and of the [seafarers] who cross the Caspian Sea [to go] from Khazaria to Gorgan, Tabaristan, and Daylam.[33]

The organization of his work borrows that of the Baghdad chroniclers, which had become classic thanks to al-Tabari's *History* (915), and adapts it to the encyclopedic form. Al-Mas'udi identifies two major periods of Muslim history: the pre-Islamic period and the period initiated by the Hegira. The first section includes a general description of the earth, the ecumene, and the seas. Additionally, one finds an explanation of the ebb and flow of the tides and remarkable facts about the maritime spaces. As set forth here, the time of Creation precedes the time of the prophecies, up to and including the last prophecy, the prophecy of Muhammad—essential stages that had to be included in any encyclopedia. This part of the book covers the Greeks' knowledge of astronomy, which was passed down by Arab translators, and that of the Persians.[34] From libraries, Al-Mas'udi took the Arabic treatises that contained all the learning translated from ancient works. Similarly, he took an interest in the traditional tales of the earliest Arab era, whether moral or secular, and particularly the "wonders," without neglecting the knowledge accumulated by scholars.

Accounts by renowned seafarers also allowed him to call into question certain assertions of the ancients, to which he preferred the experience of Syrian sailors under Abbasid command, considering it more valuable than any book knowledge:

> I have noticed that the seafarers of Siraf and Oman . . . provide information about the Indian Ocean that is for the most part different from what the philosophers and other [scholars] say. . . . I have made the same observation in the Mediterranean, with sailors and captains of war ships and trading ships, with commanders and officers, and finally with those who are appointed to organize the military navy in this vicinity, such as Lawun [Leo] who was the governor of Tripoli in Syria, on the coast of Damascus after the year 912. . . . Additionally, the truth of this has been confirmed to me by ʿAbd Allah b. Wazir, governor of the city of Jableh, on the coast of Homs, in Syria; today [943] this man is the most knowledgeable on the Mediterranean—as well as the eldest—and there is no captain of a war or trading ship sailing on this sea that does not submit to his advice and pay tribute to his intelligence and his skill, as well as to his devotion and [his service to] the jihad.[35]

The subjects al-Masʿudi chooses to discuss in his chapters on the seas in general and the Mediterranean in particular also draw from the shared base of the literature of the *adab,* which marked his era. In referring to the Mediterranean, which then represented the western march, he made use of the "wonders" to mark out the boundaries of the ecumene. Narratives pertaining to Solomon's cities of copper and to statues located on the shores of the western sea, intended to help seafarers navigate, played a pedagogical role, with a moral slant, by making it possible to characterize these regions by "particularities" that personified each zone, like the lighthouse of Alexandria, the symbol of Egyptian antiquity still standing in al-Masʿudi's time. The scholar made his own contribution to the knowledge of the world's boundaries by discovering new sources, which sometimes originated in the regions concerned. For example, he informs the reader that the conquest of al-Andalus gave rise to a series of traditions of which Baghdad had kept a record in the libraries he visited.[36] He writes, "It is to this place [the city of copper] that Musa ibn Nusayr went in the time of ʿAbd al-Malik ibn Marwan and here he saw all the wonders of which he gave a description in a book that is passed from hand to hand. Others say that [this city] was in the deserts bordering al-Andalus and called the *Vast Land.*"[37]

The Okeanos of the Greeks, or the surrounding ocean that encircles the ecumene, was another essential boundary of Islam, particularly along the coasts of Iberia and western Maghreb. To describe it, first of all as a "marvelous" space closed to man, the scholar could draw on traditions from the Iberian Peninsula: "It is quite a common opinion that this sea [the ocean] is the source of all the other seas. Marvelous things are said about it, which we have reported in our *Akhbar al-Zaman*. . . . Thus, an inhabitant of al-Andalus named Khashkhash, who was a youth of Córdoba, gathered a group of young people of the city and sailed with them on the Ocean on boats which they had fitted out. After quite a long absence, he returned loaded with booty. Furthermore, this story is known to all inhabitants of the region."[38]

At first glance, al-Masʿudi's view of the Mediterranean does not seem particularly original; the material and method used, like the objectives of his encyclopedia, are derived from the education related to the *adab,* which André Miquel defines as a "human geography" established in the tenth century, of which the encyclopedist was one of the most notable representatives, along with Ibn Hawqal (d. ca. 988) and al-Muqaddasi. Innovation was not al-Masʿudi's goal. Like al-Tabari in the previous generation, he intended first and foremost to report the opinions of the ancients and compare them with his own experience. The polymath's approach thus appears quite classic, primarily resting on a conception of space that blossomed in Iraq and took advantage of the exceptional collections of the libraries of Baghdad and neighboring cities.[39]

TWO OBSERVERS OF THE MEDITERRANEAN

Al-Idrisi and Ibn Khaldun share a geographic background: both came from the western part of the sea. In that sense, they were both "true" Mediterraneans. Yet they had very different, if complementary, ways of observing this maritime space. Al-Idrisi was probably born in Norman

Sicily to a prestigious family related to the Prophet, which entitled him to use the honorific "Sharif."[40] Working in the service of King Roger II, he became an eminent representative of Islamic culture in Christian lands. His body of work is entirely within the Arabic tradition and his geography is directly descended from the discipline born in the East.

Born in Tunis in the fourteenth century, Ibn Khaldun also came from a prestigious Arab family. His Himyarite ancestors had settled in Seville during the conquest of al-Andalus. While he never traveled beyond Islam's borders, he explored the Islamic regions along the Mediterranean, from Granada to Damascus, in the service of the grandees of his time, even visiting Tamerlane (1336–1405) in the recently conquered Syrian capital. He later lived and worked in the Maghreb before settling in Egypt, where he served as a qadi (judge) and lived out his days. His remarkable knowledge of the Muslim Mediterranean was an insider's view, developed by spending time in nearly all of its chancelleries. He lived in a period of crisis, during which the Muslim Mediterranean region suffered the double blow of plague and the threat of Latin imperialism. The conditions of the period had a significant influence on the way these two thinkers placed the Mediterranean at the heart of their work.[41]

Seen by his peers as the greatest geographer, the Sicilian al-Idrisi was the only scholar to describe all the regions of the Mediterranean, having had access to both the Latin sources and the Arabic and Greek sources in Palermo. He was also set apart from other Arab geographers by his remarkable knowledge of the Latin world beyond the shores of the Mediterranean, reaching all the way to Toulouse and other Frankish cities. He himself visited several regions, notably the Maghreb and al-Andalus, but also Palestine. The rest of his information was brought to him by researchers who had traveled through other areas thanks to the generosity of Roger II. His treatment of Latin and Slavic countries, which had previously been ignored or hastily depicted by Arab geographers based on the notes written by the traveler Ibrahim b. Ya'qub, a Jewish merchant from Tortosa, around 965, was unprecedented. While these countries are hardly given equal treatment or as much detail, the Sicilian geographer was nonetheless the first to attempt to provide a complete picture by putting descriptions of Muslim and Christian regions in the Mediterranean on an equal footing. The treatment of the Latin part of the Mediterranean makes his *Diversion for the Man Longing to Travel to Far-Off Places,* also known as *The Book of Roger* (*Kitab Rujar*), the most humanist, comprehensive medieval description of the Mediterranean world. The section devoted to Norman Sicily and Italy is particularly thorough, which proves that his description of the world was in every respect descended from the Arab geography of Baghdad. Indeed, it is remarkably well adapted to the Sicilian sovereign's ambitions in the Mediterranean and further differentiates the Norman kings' sovereignty from the other Latin dynasties.[42]

The sea has a prominent place in the Mediterranean part of his description—one could say it is at its center. The combination of al-Idrisi's Sharifian background—he was related to the Quraysh of Mecca—and his highly classic Arab education in Palermo and through his travels makes him the archetype of the "medieval Mediterranean man," as Leo Africanus would be, in his own way, at the beginning of the sixteenth century. This aspect of his identity largely explains the quality and specificity of his description of the Mediterranean area in his universal geography and the importance the islander gave to maritime space. For instance, his work reveals an intimate knowledge of fishing activities, especially those of his homeland.[43] He considered the sea to be the heart of a single region divided by his predecessors into the infidel Christian North and the Muslim South. Without denying his Islamic background and beliefs, the geographer describes the remarkable human density of its three shores in the middle of the twelfth century, as well as the vigor and richness of its activities, the epicenter of which was the sea itself, joining the Christian and Muslim worlds into a whole that was the fruit of relationships then primarily forged by Latins with Byzantium and the Islamic regions.

Al-Idrisi had a talent for demonstrating Sicily's centrality based on facts that could at first glance seem insignificant: "To the west [of Palermo] is a very pleasant destination, known by the name of Tribia, where waterways keep many mills turning; there is a plain there and vast fields. They make a kind of vermicelli there that is exported in large quantities to the rest of the world, to Calabria, the Muslim provinces, and the Christian countries."[44]

Along with this picture of the Mediterranean garden, al-Idrisi's work also focuses on maritime itineraries, which were found in all Arab geographies, and a considerable number of facts about the sea. The geographer also consciously exposes the reader to another side of twelfth-century reality, that of unprecedentedly devastating war. He initially touches on the subject when describing activities specific to the frontier, oddly similar on both sides of the border, and focuses on al-Andalus: "[Trujillo] is a large city that looks like a well-defended fortified town, surrounded by solid outer walls, endowed with well-stocked markets. This city's cavalrymen and foot soldiers constantly launch incursions against Christian localities. Most of the time, they engage in armed robbery and resort to ruses."[45]

Al-Idrisi describes the ruinous situation of the coast of Ifriqiya, plagued by incursions of Arab tribes, particularly those of the Banu Hilal, who were sent by the Fatimids of Cyrenaica to what is now Tunisia to punish the Zirids (973–1148) for declaring independence. According to al-Idrisi's account, the Norman conquests launched by his master beginning in the 1030s had exacerbated the desolation of Ifriqiyan ports and their surroundings. He emphasizes the Mediterranean contradictions of which he was a privileged witness and creates a complex picture in which cultural fault lines did not prevent ties between the two enemies.[46] He reveals this other Mediterranean paradox by describing commercial relations between Latins and Muslims. At a time when the clash between Muslims and Christians was at its fiercest, the two sides were bound by their desire for shared benefits. As a whole, his body of work, dedicated to the Norman king Roger II of Sicily, represented "a vast attempt to construct a new scientific object, the world captured as a whole, without exclusion."[47]

Nonetheless, this body of work consisting of two volumes remains the heir to the universal geography born in the Abbasid capital.[48] One first notices this through the unanimous recognition of al-Idrisi's colleagues, particularly Sa'id al-Maghribi (d. 1274) and the Syrian Abu l-Fida' (d. 1331), and all the way to Ibn Khaldun, who proudly copied him.[49] One of the reasons for their esteem was that al-Idrisi had respected geographic tradition, which produced an *imago mundi* based on a division of the seven inhabited regions into seven latitudinal climates, the *iqlim* of Greek geography, and ten longitudinal sections. The seventy maps that formed the basis of his geography more or less respected these divisions and, once stuck together, composed one vast world map representing the earth and its seas, waterways, and mountains, with an accuracy revealing the progress that had been made.[50] Nevertheless, al-Idrisi left Baghdad at the center of the ecumene, contradicting his text and the reality of his time.

Indeed, the richness and profusion of information on the Mediterranean space led the geographer, whether consciously or not, to put the East's place in perspective and to give the Mediterranean increased importance within the Islamic world. This shift appears all the more clearly in his description of the rivers and mountains of the north, particularly of the Alps, and in the number of Latin toponyms used. His descriptions of regions such as southern Italy and Sicily are as detailed as those of the Arab countries. Al-Idrisi shifted fault lines by combining the densely inhabited worlds around the sea, whether Islamic or Christian, and pushing the boundaries of the marginal zones farther toward the north of Europe than his predecessors had. By doing so, he freed himself from the political and religious borders imposed by the Abbasid geographers and embraced a shared Mediterranean polarity. Consequently, he highlighted the networks of economic relations that connected the two shores and did not hesitate to underline examples of syncretism like shared Christian and Muslim pilgrimage sites such as Cape Saint Vincent, at the very time when both religions' authorities were increasingly rejecting such practices.

IBN KHALDUN'S MEDITERRANEAN: "GEOGRAPHY AS THE MEMORY OF HISTORY"

The sweeping geographic description provided by Ibn Khaldun at the beginning of the introduction to his *Book of Lessons* (*Kitab al-'Ibar*) was openly inspired by the geography of al-Idrisi. Ibn Khaldun implicitly admitted that he could not find a better foundation for a subject that was not central to his own book: "All this [description of inhabited zones, seas, and rivers] is indicated in Ptolemy's book and in *The Book of Roger* by al-Sharif al-Idrisi. . . . All the mountains, seas, and rivers of the inhabited world are depicted and dealt with exhaustively."[51]

While geography allows the historian to verify or invalidate "history in the name of the constancy of the possible and the impossible," he later goes beyond the traditional context of Arab geography and includes his history of the Mediterranean and the rest of the world in a spatial context that is no longer that of the traditional seventy sections by which the world was organized in Arab geodesy, but now that imposed by the history of mankind.[52] Here, Ibn Khaldun explains the age-old reasons: the East and West, which had been divided and set against each other from time immemorial and which only the solidarity (*'asabiyya*) of the Arabs had succeeded in uniting at the dawn of Islam, were once again divided, after caliphal unification was lost in the tenth century.[53] Nonetheless, Islam remained the unifying instrument of this space that brought together two extremes and the source of all the forces standing against the infidel. Another constant was the pattern by which arid Bedouin countries gave rise to the impetus that drove hardened tribes to conquer and dominate fertile lands. These areas then witnessed the flourishing of the governments of civilizations established throughout the territory controlled by the *madina,* the capital where wealth converged over the course of three or four generations. The dynasty born of the conquest prospered thanks to revenue from the predominantly rural population, until a new momentum led to the establishment of a power that eliminated the current rulers, now corrupted by the capital's solicitations.[54]

According to Ibn Khaldun, these patterns were also responsible for the changes of the Mediterranean Sea, which is described in the third part, devoted to "universal states, power, caliphate, governmental functions," and particularly in the chapter on "command of the fleet." This choice alone is an indication that the sea, constantly fought over by Christians and Muslims, is in the category of sovereign spaces whose history was shaped by the changes in the balance of power between Christian and Muslim adversaries. Roman in its essence, but mostly Byzantine if one agrees with Ibn Khaldun, the Mediterranean could be dominated by Islam when regional authorities—in this case, the three Mediterranean caliphates—made the necessary effort to harness the extraordinary potential of the sailors living on the coasts of Islam, particularly those of the Iberian Peninsula and the Maghreb. Ibn Khaldun continues by disclosing the reasons for Islam's decline on the Mediterranean, attributing the shift in favor of the Latins not to the energy of the Christian powers, which would have implied acknowledging and thus legitimizing a Christian solidarity stronger than that of Islam, but to the Muslim sovereigns' inability to keep up the necessary commitment to maintain a naval force. Without a proper naval force, they left the entire sea to the Byzantines and Latins.[55] This highly original explanation in the context of Arabic literature could only have taken shape in the mind of someone with intimate knowledge of the crisis of the Muslim Mediterranean unfolding before his eyes.[56]

Ibn Khaldun based his reasoning on the close connection between the power of the sultans and the domination of the seas, thanks to numerous fleets built in the dockyards of the caliphates' major ports and commanded by celebrated admirals such as the Banu Maymun, who embodied the skill of the Andalusians, and, under the Almohads, Ahmad al-Siqilli, who Ibn Khaldun believed was from Djerba. The weakening of the Muslim presence on the Mediterranean was not due to the quality of the sailors but rather to the shameful shortcomings of those in power, who went to pieces after a few successions. The example of the Western caliphate is explicit: from 1147 to 1198, the first three caliphs, up to and including Abu Yusuf Ya'qub al-Mansur (1184–1198) and his triumphant reign, produced the most formidable fleet of Islam, which dominated both the Mediterranean and Atlantic shores of the Muslim West. After the defeat at Las Navas de Tolosa in 1212 and Caliph al-Nasir's premature death in 1214, the caliphate's naval power disappeared amid the upheaval of a long dynastic crisis. Maritime domination, which required the constant investment only a stable state could provide, was by nature the work of governments at the height of their power, just like the strongest land armies, which were composed of Bedouins drawing their energy from tribal cohesion and their strength from the pressures of life in an arid environment. It is conceivable that because Ibn Khaldun had lost his family in a shipwreck, he considered the sea an environment as hostile as the desert. Finally, he offers a lesson in sociology—one forgotten by some contemporary historians—by explaining how the Arabs of the desert were able to build a naval power capable of getting the upper hand over experienced Christians: "Once the Arabs had firmly established their power and demonstrated their might [around the Mediterranean;] . . . once every experienced man came to offer them his services in exchange for their protection; once they had employed foreign navigators for the needs of their navy and that, in this manner, they had acquired skill and experience, they had their own experts and aspired to fight on the sea."[57]

Only learning and experience are relevant, not geographic origin. The desert people attained the ability to teach themselves the art of seafaring through the experience they had acquired from sea people. The same causes producing the same effects, Muslim power is condemned "due to the weakness of the State and the oblivion into which the customs of the sea had fallen." By reasoning this way, Ibn Khaldun seeks to indicate that the Mediterranean Sea, tamed and exploited by man, was the actual space in which the fate of Islam in the West was decided, going back to the period when "Carthage made war on the master of Rome." The sea he describes appears as the ultimate site of the secular confrontation between dynasties ancient and medieval, Christian and Muslim.

As his entire body of work reveals, the Mediterranean Ibn Khaldun contemplated was a mirror reflecting the trends of his era: it had once again become a zone abandoned by Muslim sovereigns, allowing the Latins to dominate it. His sole reason for focusing on the Mediterranean was to use it to find reasons for Islam's decline. Once he settled permanently in Cairo, he turned his attention to the East with the new hope of an Islamic future brought by the Mamluk sultanate and, a little later, Tamerlane.

The works of these three great Arab men of letters do not encompass all the sea-related subjects in the body of Arabic descriptions, but they do provide an idea of the creative richness of Arab geography, particularly regarding an Islamic maritime space that remains marginalized by contemporary historians of the Mediterranean and medieval Islam.[58]

2

ARAB WRITING ON THE CONQUEST OF THE MEDITERRANEAN

In the Islamic era, the earliest Arabic references to the sea are those found in the Koran.[1] Yet neither the Mediterranean nor any other sea is referred to as such. The first generation of Arabs to describe this maritime space was therefore that of the conquerors. However, accounts of the conquest are only accessible in the versions gathered in the chronicles of the third century of the Hegira (816–912), which were the first to be preserved, according to a principle described by Ibn Khaldun: "The great historians of Islam exhaustively collected the accounts of the glorious days."[2] In these stories, the Mediterranean appears as the sea of war.

THE ABBASID CHRONICLES

These stories, which are presented in the form of annals setting forth events year by year, were established from traditions that could date back to the second generation of believers and were preserved and passed down in the same way as the deeds, teachings, and sayings (Hadith) of the Prophet. Most of the historians of the first generations of

Muslims were primarily specialists of the *isnad,* the chain of authorities attesting to the authenticity of the Prophet's sayings, and their transmission by those who had heard him speak. This implies that the historical facts of the beginnings of Islam, as reported by the Arabs, were filtered through several generations of transmitters before being recorded in the form in which they have reached us.[3]

Thus, the Arabic sources cite more than two hundred titles by about ninety-nine authors of traditions, produced before the first preserved text was written.[4] The list of these titles provides an idea of the earliness and strength of the writing movement initiated in Medina. However, the complete disappearance of this body of work continues to raise many questions about the conditions of its production, particularly in the case of the texts relating to the Mediterranean.

The first accounts to have survived date from the middle of the ninth century, at best: the first chronicles available are those by the Andalusian Ibn Habib, the Egyptian chronicle by Ibn 'Abd al-Hakam, and the Iraqi narratives by Khalifa b. Khayyat (d. 854), al-Baladhuri (d. 892), al-Ya'qubi, and al-Tabari. These authors had themselves repeated as their own the narratives of the conquest gathered and recorded by traditionists from written and oral "drafts" dating back to the events described.[5] The chroniclers also drew from the annals of Christian authors, primarily the millenarian tales, which had a particular influence on Ibn Habib and al-Khwarizmi (d. 847), the author of a lost "History Book."[6] Wherever their location in the Islamic world, the chroniclers mostly repeated the traditions and certain narratives, which were composed in the form used to report the battles of the Prophet, the *sira* or *maghazi.* These writings were initially collected in Baghdad and the large cities of the Abbasid realm by men of letters in caliphal circles, particularly Sayf b. 'Umar, al-Waqidi (d. 823), and his secretary Ibn Sa'd (d. 845), the authors most frequently cited in the Iraqi chronicles. The period during which these works were produced corresponds with several phases of turmoil in the history of the caliphate, such as the ousting of the Barmakid viziers by Harun al-Rashid (786–809) in 803 and the war of succession that brought al-Rashid's sons al-Amin (809–813) and al-Ma'mun (813–833) into conflict.[7] These rewritings were intended to give the events a specific significance and provide a basis for caliphal legitimacy. This historiographic cycle ended with "the chronicle of Abu Ja'far Muhammad b. Jarir al-Tabari[, which] shines among all (historical) compositions and is superior to them."[8] Narratives by regional authors, such as those of the Egyptian Ibn 'Abd al-Hakam, were inspired by the same early ninth-century texts, particularly since al-Hakam wrote his chronicle in Baghdad.

The way in which these narratives were written implies that the caliphal authorities and their provincial governors had a very significant influence on this production. Indeed, as early as the death of Muhammad and especially beginning with the succession of 'Umar in 844, the caliphs felt it necessary to strictly control not only the writing of the holy texts of Islam, the Koran and the Sunna, which were the foundation for the development of Sunni Islam, but also the history of Islam's beginnings. The written account of the Community of Believers from its origins was the basis for the caliphs' legitimacy, to the point that, starting with the reign of 'Abd al-Malik (686–705), which began with a civil war, the caliphs insisted on having control over any historical writing on Islam.[9] This task was entrusted to scholars, the ulema, who were specialists in the transmission of the prophetic Hadith, and, increasingly, authorities on jurisprudence, the *fuqaha'*.[10]

Similarly, the emergence of an early scholarly environment in newly conquered provinces with long-established state traditions, such as Egypt, Ifriqiya, and Iberian Baetica, fostered the appearance of a local historiography to rival that of the caliphal capitals. The same kind of ferment was found in the former eastern provinces of the Sassanid Empire beginning in the late ninth century. Provincial governors like 'Abd al-'Aziz b. Marwan (685–705), who was appointed to Egypt by his brother the caliph, were essential players in encouraging the development of productive, autonomous literary centers, particularly in Fustat and Kairouan. As with the caliphal centers, none of this first generation of writing has survived, but a good deal of it was passed down and can be found in the texts—histories, biographical works—written as of the beginning of the ninth century and especially after the advent of the Mediterranean caliphates in the tenth century.[11]

With the exception of Ibn Habib's chronicle, in the Maghreb (including al-Andalus), only a few legal rulings made by Sahnun (d. 854), a chief qadi of Ifriqiya, and his successors, later collected by jurists, have survived the centuries.[12] Despite the existence of prolific centers of production, at least in the two capitals, the writings of the generation of the Aghlabid and Umayyad emirates have not survived the passage of time and the radical filtering of the Kairouan and Córdoba caliphates. These regions' ulema circulated the first doctrinal formulations of the law, but they were also responsible for other forms of writing that brought about a historiography parallel to that produced in the caliphal palaces. Early on, the ulema of the Mediterranean assembled the lives of the pious and worthy men of these regions in biographical collections (*tabaqat*), of which the oldest surviving examples date from the tenth century, thus contributing to reinforcing a regional tradition that could sometimes produce a historiography different from or even contradictory to that left by the men of letters in the sovereign's circle. For instance, the narratives of the conquest of Egypt include contradictory information about the personality and policy of 'Amr b. al-'As (d. ca. 663), which was circulated very early and, despite strict censorship, was not entirely filtered out by the sovereigns' circles.[13]

UNDER THE CONTROL OF THE SULTAN: THE MEDITERRANEAN AS WRITTEN BY THE CHRONICLERS OF BAGHDAD

The various chroniclers of the ninth century generally approached the history of Islam by using the same themes and often by drawing on the same traditions. They imposed the chronological divisions and subjects found from one chronicle to the next, which continue to be included in most histories about the beginnings of Islam. However, there are certain differences in conception and interpretation in the chronicles: though Ibn 'Abd al-Hakam and al-Baladhuri both wrote histories of the conquests (*futuh*) inspired by the traditions devoted to the Prophet's battles, their respective versions diverge. Al-Tabari wrote the first universal chronicle to cover a far more extensive period, from the time of the prophets to that of the Abbasids. From the traditions to the chronicles, the accounts of the times of conquest were updated for each generation of believers, though the events reported are most often derived from the same transmission.[14] At the same time, the events of the conquest were interpreted differently from one region to another: aside from strong Egyptian regionalism, al-Dinawari (d. 889), a historian of Iraq and Iran, bears witness to a "localist" spirit that asserted itself with those regions' Islamization.[15] As a result, al-Tabari was, on several occasions, in a position to provide different versions of the same event, citing the channels through which they had been passed down: "There is a difference of opinion regarding the date of the conquest of Alexandria. Some say it was conquered in 646, two years after the beginning of the caliphate of 'Uthman b. 'Affan, under the command of 'Amr b. al-'As. According to Ibn Humayad, Salama, Ibn Ishaq, al-Qasim b. Quzman, a native of Egypt, Ziyad b. Jaz' al-Zubaydi, who reported that he was one of the soldiers of 'Amr b. al-'As's army when Misr and Alexandria were conquered: 'We conquered Alexandria during the caliphate of 'Umar b. al-Khattab, in 21 / 642 or 22 / 643.' "[16]

The great historian's ambition to be historically rigorous highlights the aim in Baghdad literary circles to unify the historiographic versions of Islam's beginnings in a single, universal current.

The Development of Narrative to Promote Abbasid Universalism

The loss of the original strata of reported accounts of the century of the birth and conquests of Islam complicates the task of studying the first forms of the historical narrative. The biographies of the Prophet and the accounts of his battles, written in Medina as of the beginning of the eighth century, probably made up the first generation of stories whose form would be adapted to the texts accompanying the community's expansion. The impetus provided by the Marwanid sovereigns coincided with the appearance of chronologies of the sovereigns' reigns, with varying amounts of commentary, under the title "history" (*ta'rikh*).

Shihab al-Zuhri (d. 742) may have written the first history of the caliphs, commissioned by Caliph al-Walid I b. Marwan (705–715). It was reportedly presented in the form of a dynastic chronicle going back to the earliest period of Islam. Al-Zuhri is also credited with a history of the Arabs.[17] Caliph 'Abd al-Malik, after having lost control of Mecca, then in the hands of the anti-caliph ʿAbd Allah b. al-Zubayr (d. 692), is said to have asked al-Zuhri to collect the traditions that would make it possible to present Jerusalem as another major pilgrimage site, at the time when he was ordering the Dome of the Rock to be built.[18]

Al-Zuhri's knowledge of the Sunna and his background as a jurist—he was appointed a qadi under ʿUmar II (717–720)—made him the best possible expert on the history of Islam's past and the most apt to write historical treatises commissioned by the Umayyad caliphs. His art of transmission provided him with the necessary command of gathering traditions. This close relationship between the development of the two channels of traditions designated the men of letters, well versed in religious matters, to take on the role of historians. This explains the absence of history as a specialized field in the first centuries of Islam: even al-Tabari was initially recognized as a great jurist by the Arab scholars of the Middle Ages. Al-Zuhri's role as a historian of the Marwanids before the generation of traditionists and chroniclers of the Abbasid caliphs was an essential stage in the development of sultanic historiography and would have a powerful influence on the caliphs' approach. During the same period, the Arab historiography of the second century of the Hegira was enriched by the texts left by traditionists of Persian background and those Christian traditionists who joined the sovereigns and the authorities in the regional capitals, particularly the men of letters of the monasteries of Upper Mesopotamia in the area of Harran.[19]

A Historiography of Conquest in the Service of Abbasid Legitimacy

As of the reign of al-Mansur (754–775), the second Abbasid caliph, the Byzantine frontier became the primary scene of the jihad led by the sovereigns of Baghdad. In the expert hands of the chroniclers, the previous caliphates' policy of expansion consequently became an essential argument for reforming frontier defenses, particularly as encouraged by Harun al-Rashid.[20] This takeover initially concerned the aristocracies and tribes who guarded the Umayyad front, then the Barmakid viziers in charge of the frontier at the beginning of the ninth century. At the same time, the history of the Umayyad conquest in Syria and Anatolia and as far as the Bosporus was presented as the most important area of the war of the caliphs. The construction of the warrior images of Muʿawiya (661–680), founder of the Damascus dynasty and universally recognized as a great strategist both on land and at sea, and Maslama, despite his defeat outside Constantinople in 717–718, was largely due to the necessity of connecting the Abbasid jihad to that of the first conquerors, for as long as the Iraqi caliphs personally led or supervised the campaigns against the Byzantines. Thus, the glorious feats of arms of the caliphs and their representatives could rival the exploits of their predecessors' armies.[21]

The legitimization of jihad had to be based on the government of the previous caliphates, which had led the conquerors all the way to the Atlantic, while the Abbasids had to take responsibility for the effective end of the conquests and find other expressions of the jihad incumbent on the Prophet's successors. Traditions reporting governmental decisions by the Rashidun and Syrian caliphs were judiciously selected with a particular emphasis on jihad and the government of conquered provinces, all with an eye to reinforcing the legitimacy of the sovereigns of Baghdad.

The authority of ʿUmar b. al-Khattab, who was presented as the greatest of the caliphs, was largely called on for anything relating to military operations and the administration of the conquered provinces, starting with Sassanid Iraq; al-Tabari provides a detailed account of the episodes leading to the foundation of Kufa, the first Iraqi capital and one of the bases from which the Abbasid conquest was launched.[22] The Syrian caliphs' displays of force were also potentially powerful reminders that the caliphs' authority extended to all the conquered regions. Thus, the announcement of the nomination of governors in the provinces, by both the Rashidun caliphs and the Umayyads, had a particular resonance at a time when the western territories were slipping out of Baghdad's control in favor of dissidents who had left the East to escape repression: regions inaccessible to the caliph's armies were taken over by the Umayyads in al-Andalus as of 756, the ʿIbadi Rustamids (777–909) of Tahert in the center of the Maghreb as of 777, and the Idrisids (789–984) farther west as of 789. Other weapons were necessary to condemn and reject these groups, in particular the writing of the

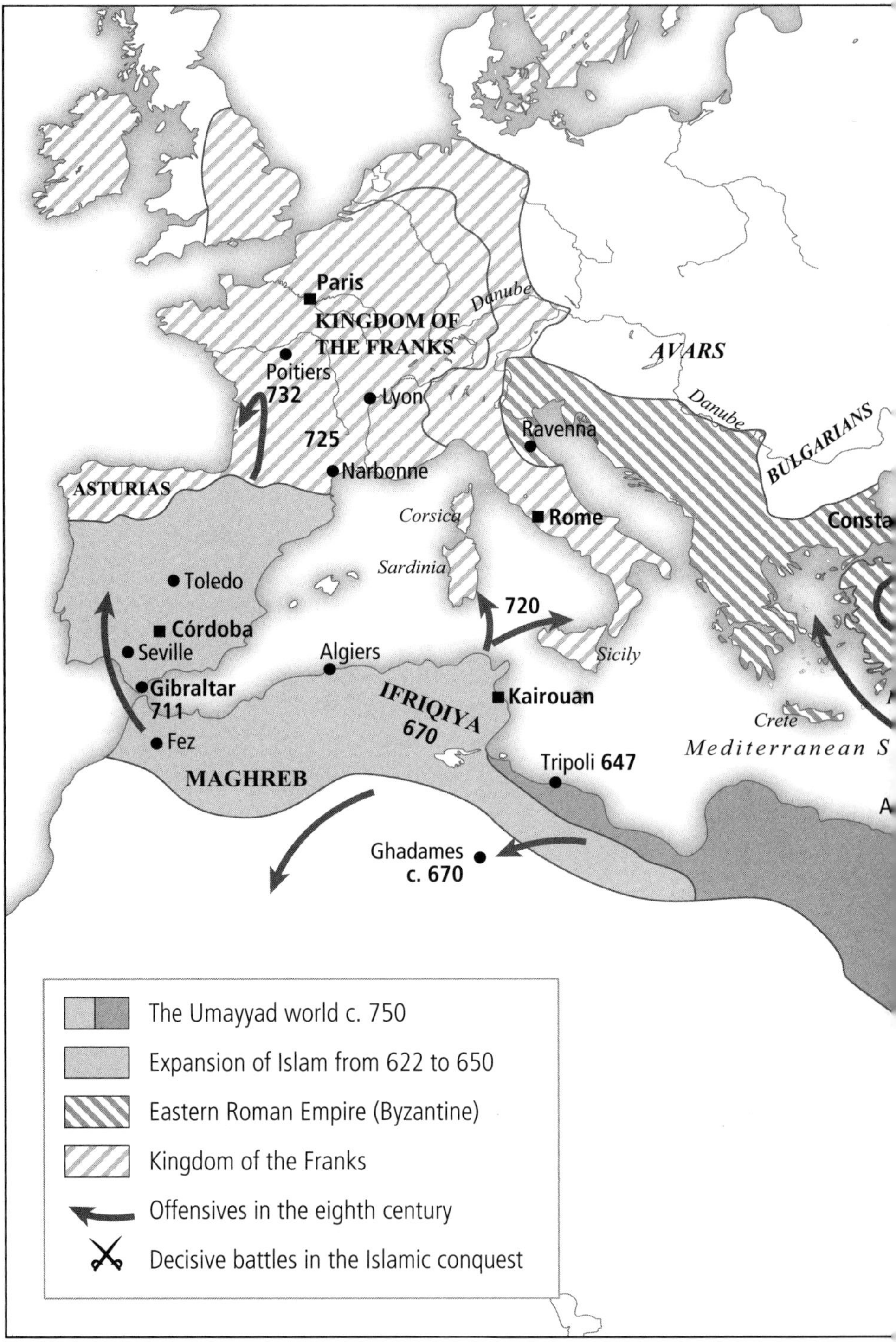

Paris
KINGDOM OF THE FRANKS
Danube
AVARS
Poitiers 732
Lyon
725
Ravenna
Danube
BULGARIANS
Narbonne
ASTURIAS
Corsica
Rome
Consta
Sardinia
Toledo
720
Córdoba
Seville
Algiers
Sicily
Gibraltar 711
IFRIQIYA 670
Kairouan
Fez
Crete
Mediterranean S
Tripoli 647
MAGHREB
Ghadames c. 670
The Umayyad world c. 750
Expansion of Islam from 622 to 650
Eastern Roman Empire (Byzantine)
Kingdom of the Franks
Offensives in the eighth century
Decisive battles in the Islamic conquest

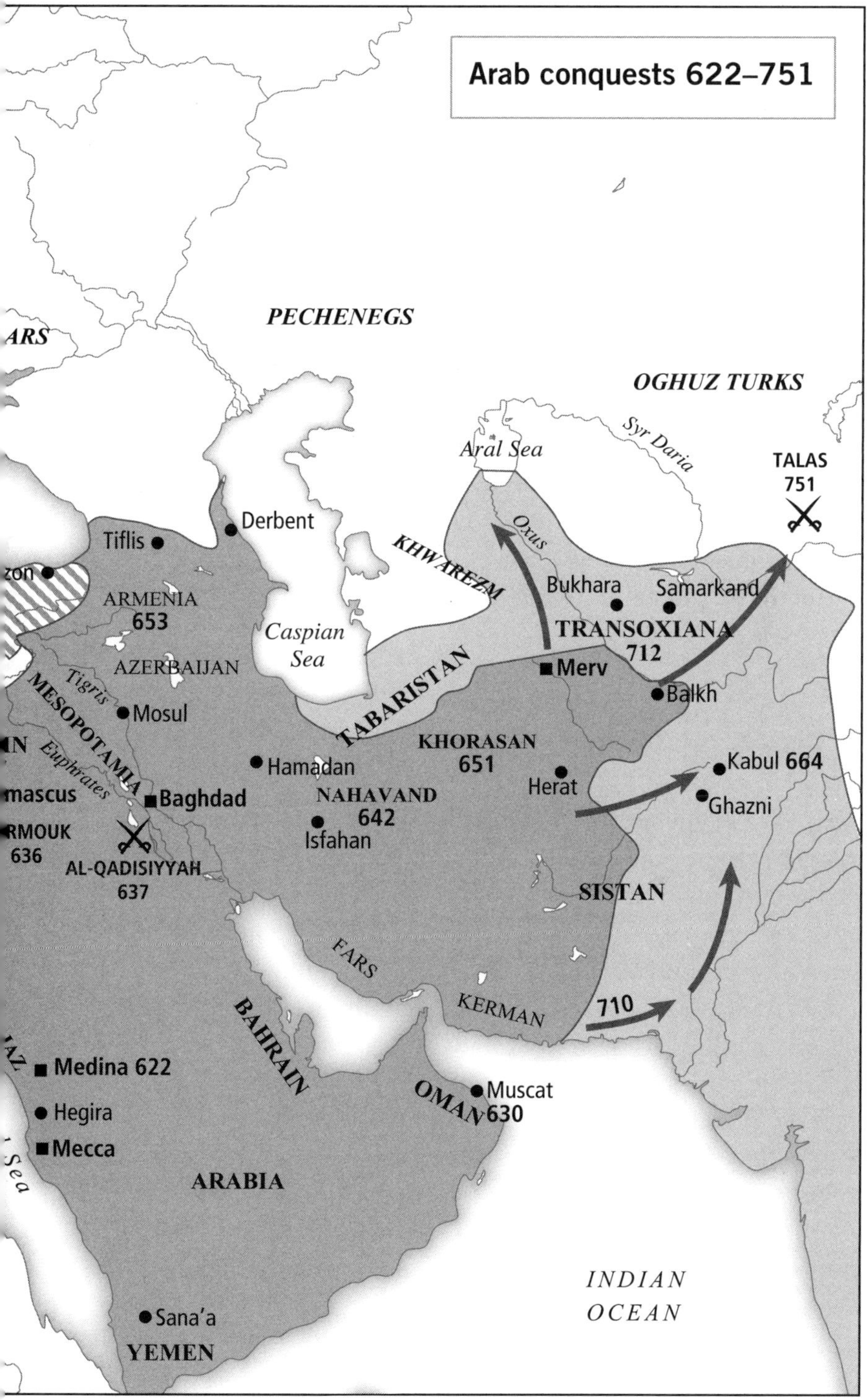

Arab conquests 622–751
PECHENEGS
ARS
OGHUZ TURKS
Aral Sea
Syr Daria
TALAS
751
Derbent
Tiflis
zon
KHWAREZM
Oxus
Bukhara
Samarkand
ARMENIA
653
Caspian
Sea
TRANSOXIANA
712
AZERBAIJAN
Merv
Tigris
MESOPOTAMIA
TABARISTAN
Balkh
Mosul
KHORASAN
651
IN
Euphrates
Hamadan
Kabul 664
Herat
Ghazni
mascus
Baghdad
NAHAVAND
642
RMOUK
636
Isfahan
AL-QADISIYYAH
637
SISTAN
FARS
KERMAN
710
BAHRAIN
Medina 622
OMAN
Muscat
630
Hegira
Mecca
Sea
ARABIA
INDIAN
OCEAN
Sana'a
YEMEN

history of the beginnings of Islam, which served as a reminder that the only legitimate authority was that of the successor to the Prophet.

In the same spirit, traditions reported the numerous convictions of governors and generals accused of misappropriating booty while leading the conquest, including Musa b. Nusayr, despite the fact that he had conquered the kingdom of Toledo. Others were dismissed because they were a potential threat to a sovereign's authority, such as 'Amr b. al-'As, who was appointed by 'Umar, then recalled by 'Uthman (644–656) along with his lieutenant 'Uqba b. Nafi'. Despite his successes, 'Uqba was removed from command in Ifriqiya after his first campaign, then returned to his post and rehabilitated under the following reign.[23] Reports of these indictments served as a reminder that the regional administration was always under the direct authority of the sovereign, even if the caliphate's seat of power was located thousands of miles from the theater of operations.[24]

THE UMAYYADS AND THE CONQUEST OF THE MEDITERRANEAN IN THE ABBASID CHRONICLES

The events of the conquest appear like a continuous movement that brought together the caliphs of Medina and the Umayyads until 749, with the caliph conducting. Only 'Umar II appears as a caliph who broke with the past.[25] Strategic development was dictated by the facts of war, with the principle of global conquest remaining unchanged. Thus, after the collapse of Iraq and the Sassanid Empire following the Muslim victories at al-Qadisiyyah in 636, then in Nahavand in 641, the caliph turned his principal efforts toward the Mediterranean and against the emperor of Byzantium. The end of the Sassanid dynasty in 651 put the heart of the Persian Empire—its men, riches, and culture—in the hands of the caliph. It also made the basileus, whom Muslims saw as the head of Christianity, Islam's only true adversary, since the emperor of China was too far away to be made a direct enemy among the earth's great sovereigns.

On the other front, in Central Asia, the Muslims had remained highly active since the conquest of Mesopotamia, but the ties between the Arab and allied tribes of the region had loosened with the caliphate, in particular under the Marwanids, to the point of crystallizing discontent within the eastern *jund*. The *jund* formed the core of the army of Abu Muslim (d. 755), head of the revolt that won the decisive victory over the Umayyads in the name of the Abbasids in 749 on the banks of the Great Zab, in northern Syria. Conversely, beginning under the reign of Muʿawiya, the Greek border served as the caliphs' principal military buffer, particularly during the period of offensives against Constantinople.

Under the Abbasid caliphate, this vast zone of marches remained the principal front line. More than ever before, relations with Byzantium were the crux of the war. Al-Mansur, the first caliph of the new dynasty who was able to reorganize this frontier, took back control in Syria, where several Abbasid clans were established, in order not only to eradicate the Umayyad presence but also to consolidate the position of Islam's new masters on the frontier, particularly by entrusting its defense to the most powerful clan in the region, the Banu Salih, who supported the new regime and won the Qais tribes over to the caliphate's cause, entrusting them to become the main defenders of the marches of the Taurus Mountains and the Caucasus.[26]

The caliph was faced with an urgent crisis. Taking advantage of the civil war between the Umayyads and the Abbasids, the Byzantine soldier-emperor Constantine V (741–775) had recaptured a considerable amount of territory and was directly threatening Syria. The caliph appointed his uncle Salih b. ʿAli to head Jund Qinnasrin, the strategic border district of the Bilad al-Sham (Syria). The Banu Salih clan's patrimonial and economic power was such that Salih was able to strike coins. He also had significant military resources at his disposal, to the point that he posed a serious threat to the caliphate when internal rivalries over the succession broke out within the caliphal clan. The potential danger the clan posed to the caliphate led to the arrest of its last chief in 803 on orders from Harun al-Rashid and the dismantling of the rule of the Banu Salih lineage, which had become a real "viceroyalty" in the frontier area. Meanwhile, the three sovereigns had been able to rely on their Banu Salih cousins to fortify and organize the defense of the Anatolian front against the powerful army of the Isaurian emperors.

With the pressure from Byzantium remaining intense, the caliphate's intervention on the frontier reached a new level beginning with the reign of al-Mahdi (775–785). The caliph took over the frontier territory to turn it into the scene of caliphal jihad. Unlike their Umayyad predecessors—with the exception of Marwan II (744–750), the only caliph of the Umayyad dynasty to take the helm of the army against the infidel—the Abbasid sovereigns personally took part in the war, first as the heirs to power, then as the heads of Islam until the end of the reign of al-Muʿtasim (833–842).[27] Al-Muʿtasim's move to Samarra in 836 and the relocation of the caliphs' army of Turkish slaves after turmoil in Baghdad coincided with the suspension of the sovereigns' personal engagement against the Byzantines. This lasted until 892, by which point the caliphs had resettled in the former capital and headed back to the frontier. Meanwhile, Caliph al-Mutawakkil (847–861) made plans inspired by the memory of the Umayyads and decided to return to Damascus in 852 to prepare to move the caliphate's seat there. Yet it is worth considering that the decision to restore the Syrian capital might also have been due to the stature of al-Mutawakkil's ancestors, who had led the jihad in Anatolia.[28] After his assassination, the caliphs lost their grip on the Syrian frontier. They began to regain control of frontier affairs as of the reign of al-Muʿtamid (870–892). In 902, Caliph al-Muktafi (902–908) regained full control of the region, and particularly Tarsus in Cilicia, the principal port of the border zone with Tripoli. The frontier then remained under the caliphate's dominion until the crisis of the 930s, shortly before the Buyid emirs (945–1055) seized power and left the frontier under the command of the Hamdanids (905–1004), a Shiite dynasty from Aleppo, to face the Greek emperors.

The depiction of the ghazi-caliph in the chronicles of Baghdad served to underline the personal commitment of the sovereign and members of the dynasty.[29] Thus the Abbasid jihad was viewed as superior to that of the Umayyad caliphs who had remained far from the frontier, with the exception of Marwan II, who sought a new kind of legitimacy and inspired the Iraqi sovereigns. For this reason, the chroniclers gave their full attention to the caliphal frontier's Mediterranean space, but they did not neglect other fronts, in particular those in the east, though these areas were not the scene of caliphal jihad. Harun al-Rashid proclaimed that during one of his campaigns he had reached the Bosporus, like the Umayyad general Maslama before him; consequently, it was necessary to keep alive the memory of the Umayyad campaigns.

Muʿawiya, the Abbasid Historians' First Conqueror of the Mediterranean

Al-Baladhuri and al-Tabari describe the stages of the rise of Muʿawiya, a companion of the Prophet, in Syria, first under the protection of his older brother Yazid b. Abi Sufyan, then, after his brother's premature death, under the protection of ʿUmar. The traditions emphasize his gifts as a tactician and a leader of men—"a man above men," as Caliph ʿUmar reportedly said of him—particularly on the occasion of the conquest of the port of Qaysariyya / Caesarea, which was resisting thanks to supplies and reinforcements brought by the Byzantine fleet. Due to Byzantium's unrivaled domination on the sea, the seaboard was the hardest part of the Bilad al-Sham to conquer.

Muʿawiya pleaded with ʿUmar to raise a naval force to prevent the Byzantines from launching raids and supplying the besieged cities. If the Arabs were unable to counter the Greek naval force, they ran the risk of ultimately compromising the conquest of the Near East and Egypt. The temporary recapture of Alexandria in 644 proved the Umayyad chief right.[30] According to some traditions, he took the risk of personally leading the fleet that brought him to Cyprus in 645, embarking with his wife at ʿUthman's request and putting his own fate and that of his descendants on the line. On the other hand, the chroniclers of Baghdad avoided mentioning the majority of Muslim maritime offensives referred to in the Greek and Latin chronicles, beginning with the Umayyad caliphate and extending to the end of the dynasty. Even the maritime components of the two offensives against the Byzantine capital from 668 to 677 and in 717 are ignored, with the exception of a reference to the sending of reinforcements from the port of Tunis. The historians of the Iraqi caliphate were only interested in heroizing Maslama. The only accounts of the naval battles are found in the work of Theophanes the Confessor (ninth century), representing the winning side.[31]

The Marwanid Umayyad Era (685–750)

With the exception of Khalifa b. Khayyat, chroniclers ranging from the Egyptian Ibn ʿAbd al-Hakam to the Andalusian Ibn Habib did not pay much attention to the Marwanid caliphs' naval policy, despite the fact that these caliphs took advantage of the military navy left by Muʿawiya to resume maritime offensives, including the attack on Constantinople in 717–718. After having reinforced their authority, ʿAbd al-Malik and his successors picked up their predecessors' maritime program and their plan for an attack on the Byzantine capital, beginning no later than the reign of al-Walid I b. Marwan. The other major project implemented by the Marwanid sovereigns was the conquest of the Mediterranean West.

Texts dealing with the conquest of the West—from Tripoli to Narbonne—were basically limited to the deeds of the "heroes" who led the Muslim troops. Yet some maritime operations were recorded, particularly in Andalusian texts: an account of the founding of the dockyard in Tunis, which was ordered by Caliph ʿAbd al-Malik, was included in al-Bakri's geography text. The caliph's son appointed Musa b. Nusayr governor of the western province, which was now independent from the government of Egypt; he was charged with conquering Byzantine territory as far as Tangier and the islands. Though some traditions mention the caliph's skepticism, it was also under his reign that the conquest of al-Andalus began, with the help of Tariq b. Ziyad. This same sovereign is identified as the initiator of the second expedition against the Greek capital, which was eventually launched by his brother Sulayman in 717 and 718. Whatever the outcome of these unfinished conquests, the Arab traditions could not avoid mentioning Islam's extraordinary expansion under the Umayyads, both to the west and, even more so, to the east, in Khorasan and Sindh. The Baghdad chronicles' selective reporting of Umayyad undertakings in the West only confirms that their authors took practically no interest in the conquest of the part of Islam unknown to them: the western Mediterranean.

ʿUmar II and the End of the Conquests: The Premises of the Abbasid Program

After the second failed attack on Constantinople in 717, the jihad against "polytheists" continued to be presented as an indispensable objective in all caliphal programs. In the eleventh century, al-Mawardi (d. 1058) stated in his treatise on caliphal government that, along with the Turks on the eastern border, the Rums of Byzantium were Islam's principal enemies.[32] The description of the acts of war carried out by the caliphs' predecessors on the Syrian front reinforced the legitimacy of the caliphate's waging war on this same frontier. At the same time, the military defeats of 717, as serious as they were costly, were responsible for the first reversal in the policy of conquest, which was initiated by ʿUmar II, the only Umayyad caliph venerated by the Abbasids. The apocalyptic traditions that began to appear during this period justified postponing the conquests to a later era, thereby also putting off the time of eschatological reckoning.[33]

Yet under the reign of ʿUmar II's successor, Yazid II (720–724), offensives to conquer new territories picked up again and would continue until the end of the Umayyad period. The soldiers of the frontier zones continued to lead expeditions on land and at sea. Even after the change of regime and the subsequent establishment of the caliphate, the conquest of Constantinople was always presented as a major objective and both Harun al-Rashid and al-Ma'mun ordered preparations to be made to launch a new assault on the Byzantine capital.

However, ʿUmar II's decision to prioritize the administration of the empire, at the expense of conquests that had become too costly, especially after the disastrous double defeats outside the walls of the Greek capital and on the banks of the Indus, was perfectly in keeping with the future policy of the Iraqi sovereigns. Their military program would consist in establishing a frontier buffer zone, rather than implementing an offensive strategy. The sovereign's larger-than-life personality was certainly an excellent means of legitimating the caliphs' new jihadist policy. As early as the years immediately following his death, the historiography devoted to his sanctification presented him as a model administrator, often associated with ʿUmar b. al-Khattab. In particular,

'Umar II's personal approach, which was closely tied to his piety and scholarly knowledge, and his reforms aimed at boosting the managerial nature of the empire's administration enabled historians of the dynasty to depict him as the caliph who broke with his predecessors' ways.[34] The chroniclers did not lack for traditions about this exceptional figure, which were used to create a hagiography later magnified under the Iraqi caliphate. Indeed, 'Umar II's political decisions, both to give up on a conquest that had become too costly following the defeats of 717–718 and to advocate for sound administration of the empire based on the model of his illustrious homonym, provided an ideal basis, among other programs, for the sovereigns of Baghdad to promote a break in the conquests and the reform of the frontiers on the Taurus front.

Probably as early as the reign of Hisham (724–742), during which the Muslims were experiencing severe setbacks on the frontier, texts with apocalyptic resonance showcased the deeds of 'Umar II and the "hero" Maslama, the successor to Alexander.[35] 'Umar II was praised as the ruler who called for an end to the cycle of conquests and Maslama as the one who implemented the break. The instrumentalization of these two remarkable figures' roles by historiographers of the period led to the appearance, in numerous traditions dating from the dawn of the Abbasid caliphate, of a history of the Hashemite caliphate dedicated to the defense of the Muslim territory from behind now relatively stable borders in order to prevent the gates of Gog and Magog from reopening and letting through a flood of barbarian invaders, an event described as heralding the end of times.[36] The advent of the Abbasids did not bring the end of the jihadist caliphate but rather a new kind of jihad that profoundly transformed the role and place of the Byzantine Empire and the maritime spaces of the Mediterranean in the representation of the space of war and, consequently, of the Muslim zone as a whole.[37]

THE GATHERING OF TRADITIONS BY THE ULEMA: THE EGYPTIAN EXAMPLE

The Iraqi sovereigns' flatterers were not the only ones to make use of the traditions reporting the stages of the conquest of the Mediterranean area. The men referred to as "ulema," a term used for scholars in science and transmitters of traditions, were themselves "historians" who were very active in promoting the legitimization of Islam as a whole by listing companions of the Prophet and "those who followed them" and, in subsequent generations, those Muslims who played a major role in the spread of Islam.

Regionalism's Role in the Development of the Historical Tradition of Islam

Early on, the Nile valley was home to a strong Islamic cultural identity that developed from the local populations' reaction not to a new imperial power but rather to the early and vigorous Arabization and Islamization of zones occupied by Arabs. The initial centers of this diffusion were Fustat and Alexandria. The personality of the governors appointed by the Rashidun and Umayyad caliphs played a role at least as determining as that of the Arab tribes: ʿAmr b. al-ʿAs (641–646, then 649–663), Maslama b. Mukhallad (668–681), and especially ʿAbd al-ʿAziz b. Marwan were responsible for the development of a highly productive Arab cultural center comparable to those in Syria and Iraq.[38] Similarly, the departure of the Byzantines, who were expelled once and for all after the second conquest of Alexandria in 646, hastened Greek and Coptic authorities' adhesion to Arab government in the region, which is notably visible in the papyri and the chronicle of the Patriarchs.[39]

The Role of the Tribes

The discovery of the papyri, which were annotated in Arabic as early as the third decade of the Hegira, and of a large number of administrative documents written at a later date, confirms that Arabic spread in the region early on.[40] One also finds proof of Arabization in a reference to seven recorded local histories written at the beginning of the second century of the Hegira. The authors of these histories were all notables, members of Arab tribes that had settled in Egypt.[41] These tribes had a well-defined role as a military force within the *jund,* initially on the battlefield, then as administrators spread over the territory as far as Middle

Egypt and the Sa'id. The roughly forty thousand individuals counted by Ibn 'Abd al-Hakam were established in the districts of the capital and the delta, in the coastal towns of the Mediterranean as well as the Sa'id.[42]

The large number of Egyptian traditions, written early on, must be connected to the tribes' need to assert their place within the empire, which put them in competition with the Arabs who had settled in Syria and supported the Umayyad caliphs, as well as in Iraq and even Iran, rather than a product of the "parochial" patriotism suggested by André Miquel. These traditions enabled Egypt to become one of the most, if not *the* most, prolific centers of writing in the Muslim Mediterranean until the end of the Middle Ages.[43]

A Regionalist Tradition

The construction of the highly distinctive stature of the personality and policy of 'Amr, a companion of the Prophet, by Egyptian authors such as Ibn 'Abd al-Hakam, who borrowed an Iraqi tradition to do so, is thought to stem from 'Amr's attitude, often interpreted as the result of his desire to implement his own policies without referring to the caliph. The development of 'Amr's singular profile began with the description of his role as a military commander under the caliphate of 'Umar b. al-Khattab, in which he particularly distinguished himself as the first victor of a decisive battle in Palestine, at Ajnadayn in 634, before embarking on the conquest of Egypt and pushing Islam's boundaries back to Tripoli (644). At the same time, the traditions about 'Amr create a contradictory image: a protégé of Abu Sufyan (d. 653) at Mecca, he was an eleventh-hour convert; during the first unrest (*fitna*), he joined Mu'awiya against 'Ali.[44] During the same period, he was presented as one of the favorite advisers to Caliph 'Umar, who is said to have authorized him to conquer Egypt.[45] As a Quraysh, a companion of the Prophet, a conqueror, and an administrator, he was in every way the "hero," liable to singlehandedly embody Islam's legitimacy on Egyptian soil, thus allowing the rich province to rise to the level of its rivals, Syria and Abbasid al-Sawad.

In 'Amr's wake, the governor (*wali*) appears in the texts as "the most important figure in the life of the province [Egypt]."[46] *The History of the*

Patriarchs of Alexandria highlights the role of these figures drawn from the Umayyads' inner circle, who acted at times as benefactors to the Copts, as was the case with 'Abd al-'Aziz b. Marwan, governor of Egypt, and at other times as oppressors. References to a large number of works produced under the government of 'Abd al-'Aziz confirm that it was inconceivable to regional elites that their country not participate in creating a historical memory that placed the region at the very heart of the caliphal realm; accordingly, very close ties had to be maintained with the capital of the sovereign of Islam.

The ulema, and particularly the jurists among them, followed a similar pattern, playing a leading role in the spread of traditions on the history of the Muslim community by making the land of the Nile an essential way station between the eastern centers where major doctrinal currents were taught and the western regions that were home to students who traveled to hear Egyptian masters such as Malik b. Anas (d. 796) of Medina so they could later spread their teachings in their native areas.[47]

The Egyptian Ulema's Major Role in Circulating the Traditions

Egyptian ulema such as 'Abd al-Rahman b. 'Abd al-Hakam, grandfather of Ibn 'Abd al-Hakam, author of the *Conquest of Egypt,* and renowned, like several other members of his family, for being a "man knowledgeable in Hadith and Akhbar," played a major role in the propagation of the law in Egypt.[48] The first of these ulema, 'Abd al-Rahman's own grandfather 'Abd al-Hakam ibn A'yan ibn al-Layth al-Ayli (d. 787 or 788), was a native of Ayla in Jordan. After the Abbasids took control of the region, he fled the city on the shores of the Gulf of Aqaba and settled in Alexandria, where he held the position of qadi.[49] Living under the protection of the Umayyad caliphs, he spent time with Malik b. Anas. He acquired a solid reputation as a jurist, which was passed on to his descendants until the family was disgraced in the inquisition (Mihna) over Mu'tazilism under the reign of al-Wathiq in 842–847. Ibn 'Abd al-Hakam's son 'Abd Allah became known as the author of a *sira* about Caliph 'Umar II ibn 'Abd al-'Aziz.[50] Having inherited his father's position, he himself wrote several judicial treatises. After listening to the teachings of Malik, he became the renowned leader of a current already brought to prominence by his fellow student Ashhab; ʿAbd Allah also trained several eminent jurists, beginning with his own sons, Muhammad (d. 881) and ʿAbd al-Rahman. He also played a prominent role in the spread of the Maliki school in the West by holding discussions with most of the apprentice jurists passing through from the Muslim West, particularly those going to Mecca who would later return to teach in Kairouan and Córdoba. His son Muhammad picked up the torch and ʿAbd Allah's reputation grew steadily: several centuries later, al-Suyuti (d. 1505) would still declare that scholars "made the trip from the Gharb and al-Andalus to [learn his] knowledge and the law."[51] The great Andalusian polymath and poet Ibn Hazm (d. 1063) compared ʿAbd Allah to Sahnun and several major masters from his own country. According to the Western biographers al-Khushani (d. 981) and al-Maqqari (d. 1632), ʿAbd Allah trained several well-known Andalusian qadi and numerous eminent Ifriqiyan and Eastern jurists.[52] At the time, he was far better known than his brother, the author of the chronicle of the conquests. Al-Tabari was probably his most famous disciple.

Though remarkable, the example of the Banu ʿAbd al-Hakam is nonetheless representative of the role of Egyptian jurists in the transmission of Malikism to the West and is a fair representation of the place held by ulema in the process of reception and recirculation of traditions in the western zone. Looking in the opposite direction, these same figures contributed to the Eastern chronicles, particularly those of Baghdad, by making oral and written records of the traditions of the conquests and Islam's first steps in the West.

It is not surprising that these accounts were disseminated in Ifriqiya as elsewhere by those invested in the promotion of Islam in new lands. Kairouan played a role similar to that of Fustat and Alexandria during the first Muslim centuries in the regional transmission of traditions dating back to the conquest.[53] The life of Sahnun b. Saʿid was recounted in a text by his son Muhammad b. Sahnun, who had himself become a renowned jurist and the author of a lost history of the emirate. This account of the career of the qadi recognized as the man who introduced Malikism in the West began with his long stay in Egypt with Ibn al-Qasim (d. 806), a close companion of Malik b. Anas; the Egyptian master's decisive influence can be felt in Sahnun's *Mudawana*, the pillar of Western Malikism. Sahnun made his own contribution to the judicial current, distinct from the teachings of his master. As can be seen, at the dawn of the ninth century, both Fustat and Alexandria had become active centers for the teaching of Islamic law.

The Mediterranean of the Conquest, the Cemetery of "Heroes"

The primary reason for the recording of traditions and biographies (*tabaqat*) was the creation of a memory of Islam going back to the time of the companions of the Prophet (*sahaba*) and their "followers" (*tabi'un*). Ifriqiyan biographers like al-Maliki (d. after 1072) wrote about those who participated in the conquests and were buried in the region.[54] There followed the lives of those Muslims whose merits justified a biography. In the eyes of the ulema, this living chain represented the real memory of Islam and included certain representatives of the caliph. The Aghlabid emirs could benefit from this recognition and, consequently, reinforce their legitimacy. The value of these works was primarily based on the author's stature, which guaranteed the validity of the criteria and the selection of figures chosen.[55]

In consequence, the first generation of Muslims was an essential link in the chain, both as a record of the first believers made in the soil with their martyrs' blood and, in the context of the *isnad*, as a guarantee of the validity of the diffusion of the divine message in new territories.

The Enviable Fate of the Martyr

> Lead me as far as you can into the land of the enemies, for I have heard the Envoy of God say that a holy man would be buried beneath the walls of Constantinople, and I hope I will be that man.[56]

These words in memory of Abu Ayyub al-Ansari, one of the most venerated companions of the Prophet, who died in about 668 on the path to Constantinople during the expedition led by Yazid I (680–684), reveal certain companions' desire to be buried on the site of decisive battles, far from the ancestral homeland. One even finds references to fictional interments of eminent figures, generally companions of the Prophet. For instance, the tomb of Abu ʿUbayda b. al-Jarrah, who had distinguished himself in combat at Muhammad's side, was reported to be located under the battlements of Constantinople, where he was said to have been killed during the siege led by Maslama. Yet it has since been shown that he died of the plague in Syria during the epidemic of Amwas in 639.[57] More generally, the wish for burial on or at the edge of infidel soil was closely connected to the desire to die a martyr (*shahid*).[58] To refer to the site of the 732 battle known as the Battle of Poitiers, the Arab traditions used the single name Balat al-Shuhada', the "path" or, more likely, the "palace" of the martyrs, thereby uniting all the Muslims who died during the clash, saber in hand, but more particularly focusing on their leader, the governor of al-Andalus, ʿAbd al-Rahman al-Ghafiqi, who "threw himself into a new incursion, but perished, a martyr of Islam, with all his companions."[59]

The sites of martyrdom and burial thus marked out the boundaries of Islam, providing another explanation for the provisional end of the expansion. Locating the tombs of the companions of the Prophet in specific places with a strong eschatological aspect, such as the Greek capital, delimited a sacred frontier of Islam, now a territory for jihad, and identified objectives for volunteer combatants of generations to come. It is notable that beginning in the Umayyad period, in a pantheon well stocked with war heroes, specific attention is paid to volunteers who fought at sea. Men such as the first admiral of the Muslim fleet in the Mediterranean were considered particularly valiant: "[In 648, Muʿawiya] appointed to the command of the sea ʿAbd Allah b. Qays al-Jasi, an ally of the Banu Fazara.[60] ʿAbd Allah led fifty maritime campaigns, both in winter and in summer, and no one was drowned or wounded. He appealed to God to bring prosperity to his troops and to protect him and his soldiers against ill fortune. It continued this way until God decided to afflict him alone."[61]

Al-Baladhuri left a list of the companions of the Prophet who accompanied Muʿawiya during the first Arab maritime campaign against the island of Cyprus in 648. These men were all the more worthy given that "this was the first time the Muslims sailed on the Mediterranean."[62] Tradition granted a fighter who had died at sea the death of a martyr with twice the value of that of a fighter who died on solid ground, insofar as the former could not be buried.

The Conqueror-Hero, Flag Bearer of Islam

Alongside the martyr, the figure of the conqueror, as embodied by a few individuals raised to a level above the ordinary, played an essential role in the texts of the Abbasid period in marking the limits of the conquest under the caliph's responsibility. For the same reason, the Iraqi caliphs called on the merits of the Umayyads and those who pushed Islam's boundaries to the ends of the earth. Judging by the contradictory traditions about these extraordinary figures, the memorial stakes were high.

As we have seen, ʿAmr b. al-ʿAs is one of the "founding heroes" to whom the caliph delegated his authority in order to allow him to establish Islam on infidel soil: the foundation of Fustat and the building of the mosque bearing his name served as the first acts to anchor Islam in a new land. It is less often reported that ʿAmr b. al-ʿAs was the first of the Muslims to establish relations with Berbers, the Luwata of Barca. The treaty signed with the inhabitants of the pentapolis reveals the way that an entire people, the Berbers, allied itself with the Muslims, marking the beginning of a distinctive relationship between them:

> ʿAmr b. al-ʿAs progressed at the head of his cavalry until he reached Barca. He made a peace treaty with its inhabitants, in exchange for a tribute of 13,000 dinars, on the condition that they could sell whichever ones of their children they chose in order to pay this contribution. . . . In the clauses of his peace treaty, ʿAmr b. al-ʿAs prescribed [the following convention] to the Luwata Berbers: "You must sell your sons and daughters to pay the tribute." . . . Antabulus [the pentapolis] submitted following a treaty made by ʿAmr b. al-ʿAs. . . .'Abd al-Malik told us . . . : I heard Amr b. al-ʿAs pronounce these words from the dais: "The inhabitants of Antabulus have a peace treaty (*ʿahd*) which we must scrupulously observe."[63]

The treaty infers that the Arabs are superior, but simultaneously announces an alliance, as well as the Berbers' specific place in the world of Islam, at the side of the Arabs. This alliance would be renewed when the Prophetess—the Kahina, the incarnation of the Berber people before Islam—decided on the eve of the decisive battle to entrust her sons' future to Hasan b. al-Nuʿman, the conqueror of Ifriqiya. The attitude of the Kahina and the Arab leader, who would bring about her death and adopt her sons, symbolized the Berber Maghreb's adherence to Islam by giving up a bygone world and adopting the new law.[64]

When presented as a hero, ʿUqba b. Nafiʿ provides a fairly good illustration of the distinctive figure of the man who was considered the real conqueror of Ifriqiya, though he was not the first Muslim to penetrate its territory. This tradition promoting the "national hero" thus eclipsed the deeds of the generals who preceded or succeeded him, particularly those of Hasan b. al-Nuʿman, despite the fact that it was he who permanently established Muslim authority up to Carthage in 698.[65] ʿUqba, who belonged to the prestigious Qays clan of the Banu Fihri, was placed on the same level as ʿAmr b. al-ʿAs. Ibn ʿAbd al-Hakam considers him the first Muslim to have reached the edges of the "Land of the Blacks," by which he made his own contribution to pushing back the boundaries of Islam.[66] He rose to fame by founding Kairouan in 670; the account of the setting up of a new camp, *misr,* on vacant land identified him as the real founder of Islam on Ifriqiyan soil, simultaneously erasing from the collective memory ʿAbd Allah b. Saʿd's victory over the Byzantines in 647 and the setting up of a camp by Muʿawiya ibn Hudayj, an earlier Arab general, probably in 660 or 663. This first Muslim settlement completely vanished from the historical memory. The Arab-Muslim tradition imposed ʿUqba as the real conqueror of the western regions, while, at the instigation of the Aghlabids, the new city became the primordial site of Western Islam. The Aghlabids chose the city as a capital and had the mosque rebuilt, making it the most venerated site in the Maghreb.[67] Ibn ʿAbd al-Hakam writes,

> It was a valley covered in trees and bushes, a real den of fierce beasts, wild animals, and snakes. "Inhabitants of the valley," ʿUqba called out with all his strength, "leave this place—may

> God have mercy on you—for we are going to stop here." Three days in a row, he proclaimed this invitation to depart. Then without exception all the wild animals, all the fierce beasts, all the reptiles cleared out. He had the site cleaned up and it was divided in lots. ʿUqba then had the people of the place where Muʿawiya ibn Hudayj had settled transported to Kairouan's current location.[68]

After having temporarily fallen into disgrace, ʿUqba recovered his command under Yazid I's caliphate or, perhaps, as early as his father's reign. He led a second and final expedition, which brought him to Ceuta, where, according to a tradition recorded by al-Waqidi, he allegedly met the Byzantine emperor Julian. After having conquered Tangier, the westernmost city in the Byzantine Empire, he pushed to the south into the Sous and reached the ocean: "Having thus reached Maliyan [?] on the Atlantic Ocean, he cried out: 'O my God if I were not stopped by this sea, I would continue my conquests by fighting in Your path.' "[69]

The statements attributed to ʿUqba clearly indicate that he believed he had reached the boundaries of the inhabited world, as set by God, thereby legitimating the Arab conquest and the domination of Islam to the outer limits of the West.[70] The producers of historical memory turned him into another hero of the closing of the world, like Maslama in the Caucasus: because ʿUqba had been the first Muslim to reach the Atlantic Ocean and the world's other boundary in the West, his campaign's failure, his defeat at the hands of the Berber chief Kusayla in 683, and his death in combat were turned into the triumphant path of a martyr. In several capacities, he was considered the man who imposed Islam, establishing by his status as a "follower"—certain traditions even refer to him as a companion of the Prophet—the link between the city of the Prophet and the West, as early as the second generation after the companions of Muhammad and as far as the surrounding ocean. The site of his tomb, which is still venerated in Biskra, near where he was defeated, became one of the region's first official "places of visitation" (*ziyara*).[71]

Sometimes the figure of the conqueror-hero is murkier. This is the case with Musa b. Nusayr. As was allegedly reported by Tariq b. Ziyad, whom he met up with in Córdoba, Musa was indeed the designated leader of the expedition that led Visigothic Spain to submit to Islam: "I am nothing but your client, this conquest is yours."[72] Other versions even suggest that he took the initiative to launch the conquest without the caliph's agreement. However, according to Ibn Habib, he was told by a "wise old man" that the Berbers were the true conquerors of Hispania. According to the Eastern historian Ibn al-Athir (d. 1223), who was highly knowledgeable about the traditions from al-Andalus, Musa met Muhammad, who told him he was the chosen one charged with carrying out the conquest.[73] Also, after a dream, the Berber chief himself appeared as the one who would have the honor of "opening" Spanish soil to conquest. On the beach where they landed, Musa told him, " 'There is a statue, an idol of a bull. Destroy that idol and use a tall man, in the prime of his life, with brown eyes, whose hands are struck with paralysis. Put him at the head of your army during your entry into al-Andalus.' When Tariq read the letter, he wrote back to Musa b. Nusayr: I will come where you order me to go and, as for the man you described, I find him in none other than myself."[74]

Another tradition gave a darker image of the conqueror, despite the success of his conquest. The two most serious accusations leveled at the caliph's representative responsible for establishing Islam on the Iberian Peninsula had to do with his attitude toward the Berber chief who defeated the Visigothic king Roderic on the Rio Barbate in 711 and seized Toledo, the capital of the Visigothic kingdom, and, especially, the misappropriation of part of the spoils (namely the table of Solomon). When the Umayyad chroniclers took over the telling of Andalusian history, the image of the conqueror was turned into that of an antihero, ultimately giving the Umayyad caliphs sole credit for the actual Arab conquest of Hispania by the chiefs of the Quraysh tribe.[75] However, other traditions made a case for the chief's merits. In Ibn Habib's chronicle, he appears as the real strategist behind the landing and the organization of the conquest, but he was especially recognized as "being among the people the most well-versed in astrology." The latter quality naturally made him the one on whom it fell to close the Muslim space, marking the end of Arab expansion in Europe: when he reached the edge of the world, possibly at La Coruña, where a statue of Hercules was said to mark one of the ends of the earth, he found the inscription that warned him of the end of the expansion, inviting the sons of Ishmael to turn back. According to other versions, the Muslims discovered this warning after the taking of Narbonne, in a place considered another extremity of the Muslim realm: "Sons of Ishmael, this is your extreme point, and you must turn back."[76] As an Islamic capital on Gallic soil, consecrated as such by the Syrian caliphate, the city was permanently part of the Dar al-Islam, even after it was lost: this may be the reason why Narbonne continued to mark the limit of al-Andalus in most geographic descriptions long after it was conquered by the Carolingians.

THE EMERGENCE OF AN EXCLUSIVELY ISLAMIC MEDITERRANEAN

From the beginning—and despite the mobilization of the prestigious pantheon of legendary heroes—narrators limited the Mediterranean landscape as it appears in the sources on the Arab conquests to an exclusively Islamic space. Only what concerned Islam was deemed worthy of a place in the chronicles recounting the conquest, which basically erased anything representing previous domination, with the exception of the ruins Muslims exhibited like trophies of Islam's victory over the Christians. Only the populations that converted to Islam, such as the Berbers, now the Arabs' allies, were granted the honor of being included in this new world. However, this alliance had to rest on shared origins. The Berbers were considered a people who had been exiled from the East to seek shelter on African soil, now rediscovering their roots thanks to Islam: "These peoples [of the central Maghreb] formerly lived in Palestine—at the time when Jalut ibn Daris ibn Jana reigned—ancestors of the Zenata of the Maghreb, sons of Lawa b. Barr b. Qays b. Ilyas b. Mudar. David—peace be with him—having killed Goliath the Berber, the Berbers passed into the Maghreb and here they spread."[77]

An opaque silence prevailed regarding non-Muslim populations. The objective was for their past to be forgotten: only judicial sources mentioned the presence of the "protected" (*dhimmi*), in order to emphasize the residual trace of the error lodged in them.[78]

Having made a clean sweep of the past, Arab authors described an exclusively Islamic and caliphal Mediterranean space. The chroniclers of Baghdad only referred to the infidel spaces as territories to be conquered in order to finish the task bestowed on believers before the end of times.

3

THE SILENCES OF THE SEA

The Abbasid Jihad

ENOUGH ACCOUNTS HAVE survived to prove that, contrary to what was long asserted, the Abbasid caliphs did not abandon the Mediterranean. In fact, representations of the Mediterranean in medieval Arabic literature owe practically everything to how the Sea of the Romans was described and represented by the Baghdad men of letters. Indeed, once the conquest of Byzantium had become an impossibility, the writings of Iraqi men of letters reflected an evolution in the notion of the frontier (*thaghr*) and the forms of war associated with the areas bordering Christian territories and the Muslim shore of the Mediterranean. The Iraqi writers updated the connection between the caliph and war in accordance with a strategy now based on the balance of forces and the setting of lasting frontier zones. The vocabulary used, taken from the Koran, had been the same since the beginnings of Islam, but the meaning of the terms changed according to combat practices on a stable front.[1]

The caliphs of Baghdad formed diplomatic relations with the Byzantine emperor early on. However, references to these contacts were totally recomposed for the Basileus by Greek scribes and for the caliph by Arab scribes.[2] These literary adjustments to grandiose receptions, which are not limited to the diplomatic sphere, served the dynasty's universal legitimacy. As we shall see, knowledge would be a key issue of Islam's universal domination.[3]

> When 'Umar b. 'Abd al-'Aziz became caliph, he said: "I see in the mosque of Damascus riches inappropriately spent. . . . I will remove this marble and this mosaic." . . . As it happened, Byzantine ambassadors came to introduce themselves to 'Umar; they entered the mosque of Damascus to see it. While they were raising their heads to look at the mosque, one of their leaders lowered his head and grew pale. He was asked why and he answered: "All we people of Byzantium say that the Arabs will not last long. But having seen what they have built, I have recognized that they have before them a period of time that they will fill." Once told of these remarks, 'Umar declared: "I see that mosque irritates the infidel." And so he gave up on what he had planned to do with this edifice.[4]

The Marwanid caliphs had already developed a form of discourse on the superiority of the Islamic Prophecy, which accompanied their military campaigns and relied on the highly publicized Dome of the Rock, built on the order of 'Abd al-Malik after 692 as a sensational tool to affirm the oneness of God and implicitly condemn the Trinity of the Holy Sepulcher.[5] In similar fashion, it is reported that Byzantine workers were sent to participate in the building of the mosque of Damascus, following a request by al-Walid I, as a kind of tribute the basileus was forced to pay by providing mosaicists.[6] The geographer Ibn al-Faqih devotes a long passage to the mosque, taking the opportunity to reveal the controversial nature of the edifice's decoration and some of its inscriptions, addressed to Christians and particularly to Byzantium.[7]

SASSANID UNIVERSALISM IN THE SERVICE OF ISLAM

Al-Saffah (749–754), the first Abbasid sovereign, and particularly his son had found a strong clan to support them in Iran, which had in turn led them to power. Surrounded by Persian men of letters converted to Islam such as Ibn al-Muqaffa (d. 757), known for his many translations into Arabic from Pahlavi (the official language of the shahs and the Zoroastrian liturgy), the caliph encouraged the diffusion of the culture inherited from the Sassanids (224–651). In the Persian Empire's state religion of Zoroastrianism, knowledge was considered a divine emanation, transmitted to man according to the will of Ahura Mazda through the Avesta, the sacred book of Zoroastrianism containing all the knowledge accessible to humans. These ideas had a profound influence on those in power under the first Abbasid caliphs, who wanted to apply them to Islam. Abu Sahl b. Nawbakht, himself a convert, replaced his father as the official astrologer to al-Mansur and al-Mahdi and translated an astronomical history of the Persian emperors into Arabic from Pahlavi, making particular note of the fact that Khosrow I (535–578) had been the last of a long line of sovereigns of the dynasty who collected the Zoroastrian books containing the substance of all knowledge. Persian tradition held that the Greeks had co-opted this universal knowledge after Alexander the Great pillaged and destroyed Persepolis and sent back to Greece all the books containing the scholarship the Greeks would later claim to have discovered themselves.

Presenting the Acquisition of Knowledge to Undermine the Basileus

The description of the ceremony welcoming the Byzantine ambassador to Baghdad under the reign of al-Muqtadir (908–932) is another classic example of the way the Muslims represented the superiority of the caliphate—and thus of Islam—over Christianity and the emperor of Byzantium.[8] Ibn al-Faqih and other Islamic men of letters report protocol similar to that used in Constantinople, but they twist the scene to proclaim Islam's superiority over Christianity.[9] Thus all the information regarding utterly normal, commonplace diplomatic relations was distorted in service of a war of religions fought through messages and descriptions exclusively addressed to subjects of the empire, and particularly to the caliphate's Christian subjects. The rivalry over the acquisition of knowledge was based on the same principles.

In the eleventh century, the Toledo scholar Sa'id al-Andalusi wrote a book identifying "the categories of nations." He used as his reference the relevant populations' degree of knowledge and ranked nations according to those that were learned and those that remained ignorant.[10] Fittingly, al-Ma'mun's achievement was to invigorate universal science by having it studied by the people of Islam, who were alone in being able to identify the fields of knowledge that would allow the nation of believers to approach the truth.

Al-Ma'mun's Achievement: The Stigmatization of the Christian World

The translation movement was apparently initiated by the Umayyads, later to be taken over by the Iraqi caliphs, who gave it a breadth far exceeding that of the Umayyad endeavors. Translation work appears to have begun under the reign of al-Mansur "at the time of [his] adoption of the salient aspects of Sassanid ideology . . . which was also visible in his choice of personnel for the civil service."[11] Persian ascendancy and the influence of Zoroastrianism explain why the first translations were of works in Pahlavi. This phase also corresponded to a transfer of learning, probably from Gundeshapur, the Sassanids' former city of science, to Baghdad.

The translation of Greek works on a large scale is thought to have begun at the instigation of Caliph al-Mahdi, motivated by the need for a method of dialectic like Aristotle's *Topics*. This work coincided with the beginning of the polemics organized by the sovereign in the form of oral debates between Christian clerics and Muslim scholars. The rise of Islamic proselytism, with sovereigns encouraging the growing number of Christians in the alcoves of the caliphal palaces to convert to Islam, provoked or accentuated a defensive reaction on the part of Christians in the region. This led to theological debates for which Christian scholars educated in Aristotelian logic were well prepared.[12] Muslims therefore had to be given access to the treatises on logic that would provide them with the rhetorical abilities to demonstrate Islam's superiority over other religions of the book, as well as Sunni Islam's superiority over dissenting currents within Islam.

For his part, Caliph al-Ma'mun wanted to ensure that only the emir of the believers had the power to dictate Islamic doctrine, at the expense of the ulema. By doing so, he wanted to give knowledge—originally taken from the Greeks—a dominant role as a symbol not only of political but especially of religious authority, embodied by the Prophet's successor. In the spirit bequeathed to the Arabs by the Persian Zoroastrians, this appropriation of knowledge included every discipline. The first step in using these disciplines to promote Islam required the acquisition of texts, many of which could already be found in the Christian monasteries of the Muslim area, from Alexandria to Iraq, and including the region of Harran. However, Constantinople's collections also needed to be included, at least in official discourse, in order to proclaim scholarly Islam's victory over Byzantium, stripped of its most precious books. The works selected were gathered, translated into Arabic, and placed on the shelves of the capital's libraries and, especially, the palace library, which may be the House of Wisdom (Bayt al-Hikma) mentioned by Ibn al-Nadim, who left an invaluable inventory of its holdings.[13]

According to Ibn al-Nadim, the rivalry between the two imperial cities led the caliph, inspired by a dream encounter with Aristotle, to vie with the Byzantines for control of knowledge, the prerogative of civilizations bearing a universal culture. It was the sovereign's obligation to wage this war, in the same way that it was his obligation to wage jihad. Indeed, the Prophecy of Muhammad had given the Arabs, then all Muslims, the responsibility to promote knowledge, to the exclusive benefit of Islam. Even if apocryphal, the Hadith encouraging the people of Islam to go looking for knowledge as far as China if necessary basically authorized the caliphs to try to monopolize the disciplines of which the Greeks claimed to be the guardians: "This dream was one of the most certain reasons for the appearance of [new] books. While al-Ma'mun had achieved a victory over the Emperor of Rum, the two rulers began a correspondence. Al-Ma'mun wrote to the Emperor of Rum to ask him to send him [books] of ancient science selected from those kept in the country of the Rum. He initially refused, then agreed. . . . When the envoys [of the caliph] brought them back to al-Ma'mun, he ordered them to be translated, and this was done."[14]

This account must be considered in the context of the war, with the issue at stake being the victory of Islamic universality over the Christians (as represented by the Byzantine emperor). Since the Muslims—

in this case the Umayyads—had been unable to seize Constantinople, the honor of achieving victory over the Greeks fell to the Abbasids. This they did by forcing the Greeks to yield—or, from the Persian perspective, to return—the knowledge their ancestors had taken from the "Eastern" civilization that now held the true Prophecy. By shifting the crux of the struggle between the two universal religions from the battlefield to the field of knowledge, the sovereigns could claim to replace their predecessors' victories with the one for which al-Ma'mun took credit, with the help of the great Greek philosopher. This victory appeared far more commendable in that knowledge allowed for the revelation of the only prophecy that could trigger the eschaton: the quill prevailed over the sword once and for all, particularly since the latter had failed to destroy the second Rome. The acquisition of the Greek texts was accompanied by growing philhellenism, which was presented as a symbol of the universality of knowledge. This philhellenism was carefully distinguished from Byzantine and Christian culture, which was charged with ignorance both religious and cultural.

THE NEW CONDITIONS OF WAR

The Arab chronicles covering the first centuries of Islam identify two distinct periods of Muslim naval activity in the Mediterranean. For the period up to 752, there are references to several maritime expeditions taking place at a sustained rate, suggesting a relatively heavy maritime commitment. Despite phases of inactivity imposed by internal problems and a few defeats, the number of naval expeditions recorded is impressive, particularly for a nation said to fear the sea: more than fifty major expeditions have been counted in the sources—not exclusively Christian sources—covering the years 643–752.[15] While the objectives had changed, the coherence of the Umayyads' maritime strategy characterizes their naval investment as a carefully considered initiative, effectively supported by logistical organization.

Consequently, the contrast with the Abbasid period, after a last reported foray into western waters in 752, seems all the more striking. During the period that followed, no naval expedition is mentioned until 779, whether in the Arabic sources or those of the opposite side. There were a few reported launches of the fleet from 779 to 838, from the reign of al-Mahdi to that of al-Muʿtasim, during land raids in Anatolia led by the caliph or his sons, with ships following the Anatolian coast to accompany the land expedition headed by the sovereign, but these naval deployments did not have much in common with the Umayyads' naval war effort, particularly since the fleet stayed back to prevent any potential attempt on the part of Byzantine units to attack the Arab column from the rear.

The Mediterranean during the height of the caliphate would thus have been considered a territory located outside the domain under the jurisdiction of Islamic law. Consequently, since the activities of Muslim sailors on Mediterranean waters did not have to be recorded, only the victims—particularly Greek and Latin monks—and the Latin authorities made any reference to naval raids. This line of demarcation between those territories covered by the Arabic annals and those that were not led most historians of the Mediterranean to believe that the sea had become a no-man's-land. Consequently, Muslim attacks could only be the work of "pirates." The sense that the Sea of the Romans had been abandoned was reinforced by the fact that, during the same period, men of letters in Baghdad were describing naval activity on the Indian Ocean, driven by merchants of Muslim ports such as Siraf and Basra. The Indian Ocean was open to sailors and merchants of Muslim shores, who sailed along the coasts of Swahili Africa, India, and as far as Canton (Guangzhou) in the ninth century. Meanwhile, on the shores of the Mediterranean, the great coastal cities of antiquity—Antioch, Alexandria, Carthage—had been destroyed or were on the decline, while all the Muslim capitals were cities founded or captured inland.[16] The Mediterranean naval space, which had been in crisis since the sixth century and neglected by the authorities on every side, with the exception of the Byzantines in a few ports, was becoming an ideal setting for commerce raiding.

This quick reading of Arabic and Christian sources raises questions about the caliphs' policies regarding the Sea of the Romans. At the height of their power following the defeat of the Umayyads, the Abbasids shifted every effort of caliphal jihad to the Byzantine frontier, including the Mediterranean shores of the Near East. Yet is it really conceivable that they had no maritime policy and settled for reinforcing coastal defenses? After all, during this same period, the Abbasids were hiring historians to describe the naval policy of Mu'awiya, the founder of the reviled dynasty they had brought down, asking them to try to justify his engagement on Byzantine waters. These interpretations gleaned from the information drawn from Arabic history's omissions regarding the Muslim powers' maritime policy in the eighth and ninth centuries, thus exclusively considered from the Greek and, especially, Latin victims' perspective, are in total contradiction with the Mediterranean ambitions displayed by the Iraqi caliphs at the time when they were personally leading their troops in Byzantium's Anatolian territory.

Once the caliphal armies seized control of Syria and the Anatolian marches, Caliph al-Saffah and his successors got involved in frontier policy.[17] Between the second half of the eighth century and the middle of the ninth century, a new generation of fighters appeared on the frontier landscape alongside the "aristocratic" armed forces and military men to support the caliph by supervising jihad in the field.[18] These were "armed scholars" competent in legal matters, some of whom were involved in the development of the quickly disseminating major schools of jurisprudence (*madhhab*).[19] Beyond that, the presence on the Anatolian front of the forces of the *jund*, of volunteers, but also of groups close to those in power and even of members of the caliph's own family (*abna'*), while admittedly rivals, is a good indication of the vitality of the commitment of Muslim troops to the frontier under the caliphs' banner.

The chronicles covering the dynasty's first century included accounts of the campaigns led by the caliphs and their sons. The real reason these expeditions were mentioned was the sovereign's presence, even if it meant pushing the achievements of the experienced generals who organized them into the background. The chroniclers were particularly interested in demonstrating the sovereigns' legitimacy in acts of war. Difficult successions and civil wars provided opportunities to emphasize the caliphs' involvement in the field, to the point that "in terms of historiography [these chronicles] mark the birth of a new type of official historical narrative, financed by [caliphal] power, . . . [and retaining] the idea that the principal objective of jihad no longer consisted in conquering the *Dar al-harb* [territory of war], but estab-

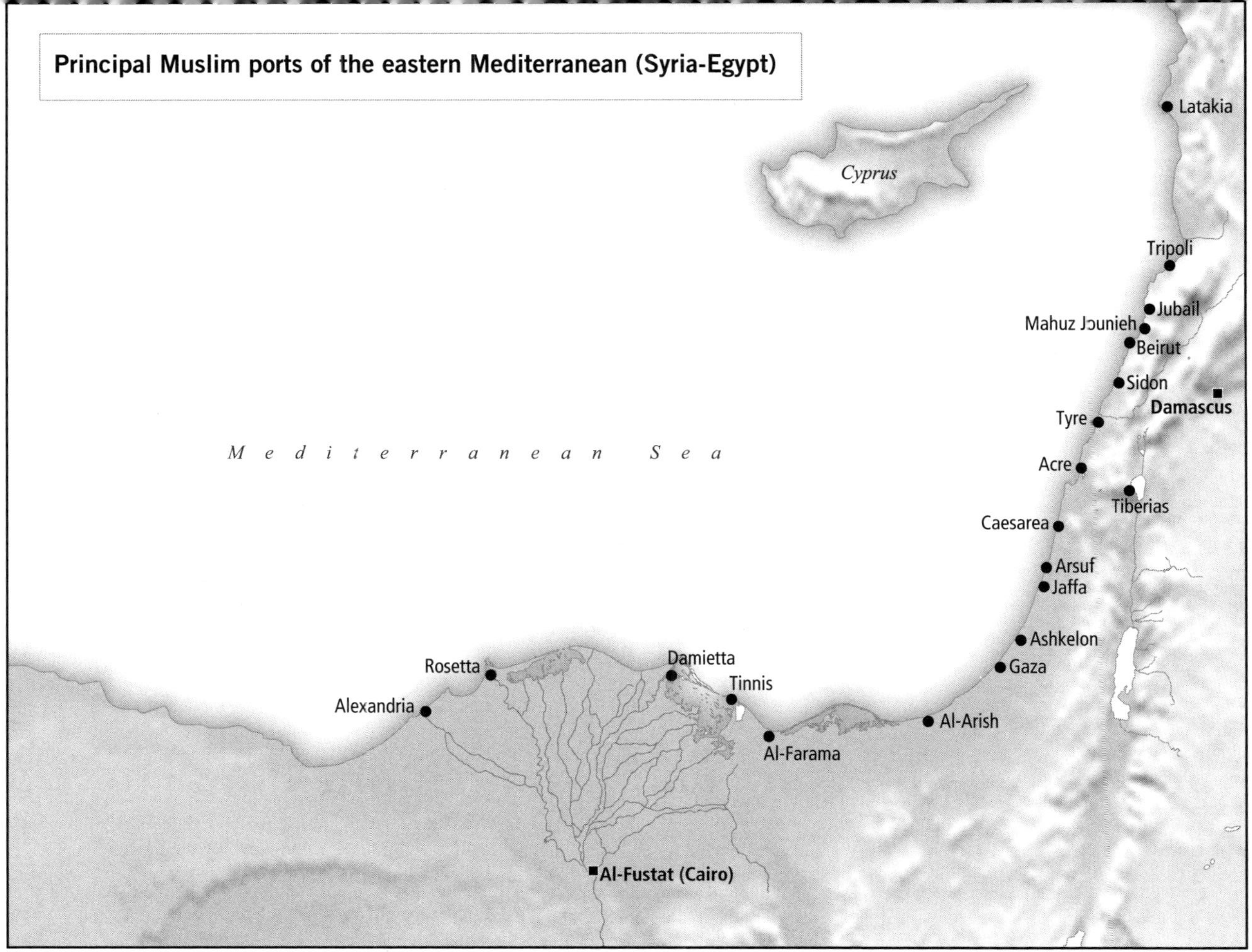
Principal Muslim ports of the eastern Mediterranean (Syria-Egypt)
Cyprus
Mediterranean Sea
Latakia
Tripoli
Jubail
Mahuz Jounieh
Beirut
Sidon
Damascus
Tyre
Acre
Tiberias
Caesarea
Arsuf
Jaffa
Ashkelon
Gaza
Al-Arish
Al-Farama
Tinnis
Damietta
Rosetta
Alexandria
Al-Fustat (Cairo)

lishing the authority and legitimacy of the leader of the Muslim community."[20]

In the official sources, the sea itself never appears as a territory of the war of the caliphs. However, the sovereign remained responsible for the maintenance and fitting out of fleets, the mobilization of crews referred to by al-Baladhuri and the jurist Qudama b. Jaʿfar (d. 948), and the installation of defensive measures on the Egyptian and Syrian coastlines. To do so, the sovereign delegated his authority to the governor of the coasts and ports.[21] The sovereigns' concern with the sea appeared early on, from the moment Caliph al-Mansur ordered the seat of the admiralty to be moved to Tyre from Alexandria, where it had remained throughout the Umayyad period. Well protected by its defenses, the port of Tyre had become the caliphate's maritime capital after Hisham ordered the Umayyad caliphate's dockyard to be moved there from Acre. This probably explains why the Abbasid caliph praised the administration of the Umayyad caliph, who was otherwise heavily criticized by the Baghdad writers. To reinforce the basis of maritime policy, the same chroniclers made a point of repeating that it was the great caliph Muʿawiya who had founded the victorious, conquering Muslim naval force. There is no doubt the Abbasids had adopted and claimed as their own not only what was considered the effective coastal apparatus put in place by the Umayyads but also their policy of maritime investment. The only change the Iraqi dynasty made to the Umayyads' maritime organization was to move the naval command. By doing so, the Abbasids put an end to dual Egyptian and Syrian management and placed the entire chain of maritime command under the direct control of the caliphs.[22]

SPACES OF MEDITERRANEAN JIHAD IN ABBASID DISCOURSE

The first caliphs' military policy, which was applied at least until the reign of al-Mutawakkil, was widely commented on by administrators who had become historians.[23] While the chronicles have taught us the defensive tactics and strategies advocated by successive caliphs for use along the coasts and in the marches, it was the jurists and armed scholars who described the rules of war.[24]

Al-Mahdi, Harun al-Rashid, and, after the civil war, al-Rashid's sons al-Ma'mun and al-Mu'tasim took measures that led to an extensive reorganization of the frontier zone as far as Armenia. Like the Aleppo writer Ibn Shaddad (d. 1285), who described the fortified sites on his region's frontier, when describing the caliphs' accomplishments on the front, Arab men of letters primarily focused on the fortifications they built.[25] Yet there is no doubt that, beginning in the Umayyad period, both the zone of the Taurus Mountains and that of the coast (*sahil*) were provided with defenses: al-Baladhuri and al-Ya'qubi made a list of the measures implemented by Mu'awiya, the region's governor under the caliphate of 'Umar and 'Uthman. This has been confirmed by excavations in the fortresses of the Syro-Palestinian coast.[26] This policy was carried on by Mu'awiya's successors, particularly in the region of Upper Syria, with the redevelopment of Qinnasrin, and along the front in Upper Mesopotamia, around Harran, which had been chosen as Marwan II's capital. The relative stability of the zone separating the two empires fostered a certain continuity in the policy for defending the Dar al-Islam under the Abbasids.

The reorganization of the frontier credited to Harun al-Rashid owed its innovative character to the discourse disseminated by the caliphate, rather than the actual scope of reform. The texts the chroniclers drew on to report changes on the frontier were taken from sources written by the caliph's administrators, such as Abu Yusuf Ya'qub (d. 798), the author of the first known work of its genre, *The Book of Taxation*.[27] Terminology sheds some light on these changes, but the words' meanings remain unclear. From the first years of Islam, the word *thaghr*—often used in the plural, *thughur*—referred to the mountainous "thresholds," a rough equivalent of the Byzantine *kleisourai* and the Latin marches.[28] These frontier zones were now doubled up at the rear by *al-'Awasim*, which referred to Qinnasrin and Antioch, the strongholds in which were stationed troops and their command. Despite the details provided by the Aleppo writers Ibn al-'Adim and Ibn Shaddad and the findings of recent excavations, which have provided increasingly precise knowledge of the region, this organization remains hard to reconstruct.[29]

The Caliph and the Armed Scholars Redefine Jihad

Now that sovereigns were directly involved on the front, the system of government had to be adapted. The caliph made changes either before or on the occasion of the elimination of the Barmakid viziers in 803. These changes coincided with the point when the caliph returned to the head of operations beyond the border. The caliphs replaced the Syrian patrimonial system and the mobility of Umayyad power with personal involvement that connected them to the war zone.[30] This was manifested in the construction of two caliphal residences on the Upper Euphrates—al-Rafiqa under al-Mahdi and al-Raqqa under al-Rashid—which brought the caliphs closer to the front. Following al-Mahdi's accession to the caliphate, the caliphs or their sons—primarily those destined to succeed their fathers—took the leadership of several expeditions, marking a new development and a change from the Umayyad period, before the reign of Marwan II, the last caliph of Syria: the participation of the sovereign, waging jihad against the infidel in a personal capacity, was intended to counteract the effect of the distance between the center of power and the caliphs' principal war front. Al-Ma'mun took this logic to its conclusion by choosing Tarsus as his residence for the last three years of his life. Along with al-Massisa, Tarsus had become the principal stronghold on the Byzantine front, a center for the men of the ribat as well as an active port.

This unprecedented configuration of the relationship between the sovereign and the war required the development of a vocabulary to define the new forms of caliphal jihad and terminology to refer to the new spaces of war. The legal treatises reveal a constant evolution in the interpretation of the legal forms of war. Under pressure from the caliphs, the jurists in the sovereign's entourage defined the outlines of jihad, generating a new definition of caliphal war. The Koran still provided all the terms necessary, but the sense of the terminology had to be redefined based on conditions in the frontier war.[31] Beginning in the Umayyad era, other jurists had come to settle and fight on the frontier and wrote works on the law of war (*kitab al-siyar*), defining its rules based on the Hadith and the accounts of the Prophet's battles, the *maghazi*. The most famous treatise was probably the one by Abu Ishaq al-Fazari, "master of the sunna and the *ghazwa* [raid]," who was inspired by the great Syrian jurist al-Awzaʿi (d. 774).[32] Al-Awzaʿi had himself been appointed a qadi by the last Marwanid sovereigns and retired to the maritime frontier in Beirut after the accession of the Abbasids. His opinions on the role of volunteers in war were in keeping with the tone of the times, proposing that they "perform the campaigns of the Prophet again."[33]

Redefining the Frontiers

The jurists changed the sense of terms such as "jihad," "martyr," and "ribat" by taking into account their meaning in the Koran and adapting it to the strategic and ideological evolution of the conduct of war under the first caliphs.[34] However, this formalization of combat remained closely tied to the practical aspects of war. First of all, there was no conflict between divine reward and the material rewards of booty.[35] The combatant's status and remuneration, and the obligations entailed in voluntary engagement, already occupied an essential place in the *maghazi* and the Umayyad management of the conquests. Using this framework, jurists in the service of the caliphate changed the combatant's material status in a space of war confined to the Taurus border zone. The treatise by Qudama b. Jaʿfar, jurist to the sovereign, emphasizes the obligations brought about by the organization of frontier jihad, describing the conception of war developed by the caliphate over more than a century. Similarly, the influence of Byzantine treatises on strategy can also be felt in these chapters devoted to the organization of frontier war.[36]

A century later, al-Mawardi, both a jurist and a close adviser to a caliph who had lost actual military power to the Buyid emirs (as well as control of the Syrian region), repeated these same rules in his treatise on the "ordinances of government" (*Ahkam al-Sultaniyya*). Though he followed the example of the deeds of Muhammad, his references to war were borrowed from the treatises by the jurists of the dynasty.[37] In the chapter devoted to "command of the jihad," which was carefully kept apart from internal military operations, the enumeration of "methods to be used in war" shows that military movements were limited to the frontier, a space for combat defined as licit or illicit; there followed rules on conduct with regard to polytheists during razzias. Next, al-Mawardi presents articles on war in enemy territory that concern the volunteers who participated in jihad and, more specifically, their duty of obedience to the sovereign and his emir. Al-Mawardi then goes over the emir's duties. The emir commanded the armies in the name of the sovereign and was responsible for the fate of the defeated and the populations who had come under Muslim law according to the rules of capitulation and the *dhimma* (pact of protection), either on the battlefield or after a siege.[38]

The frontier zone marked the boundary between the Dar al-Islam, a peaceful territory inhabited by populations who obeyed Islamic law and where war was normally prohibited, and the war zone, which was pushed back into infidel territory and exclusively accessible to Muslim soldiers and sailors through the marches (*thughur*). In the enumeration of the ten duties incumbent on the caliph, the fifth and sixth articles specify those that fell under Islamic religious authority: "To supply the frontier stations and man them with sufficient garrisons so that the enemy cannot take advantage of some negligence to do harm there or to spill the blood either of a Muslim or an ally; to fight those who refuse to embrace Islam after they have been invited to do so, until they convert or become tributary, to this end, to establish the laws of Allah by giving them superiority over any other religion."[39]

The second article, based on three verses from the Koran (9, 33; 48, 28; 61, 9), dealt more specifically with the conditions under which summer expeditions were to be conducted. Areas were defined not by the faith of their populations but by the religious law in force: the border had to clearly separate the zone of Islamic law from the zone of the infidel. For enemy lands that it was the Muslims' duty to attack, al-Mawardi used a legal tradition dating back to the time of the first Abbasid sovereigns, here too distinguishing areas based on their populations' status in regard to Islam: "In enemy territory, the polytheists are divided into two categories: those who live where the preaching of Islam has been carried out, who have refused to hear it and fought it. To fight them, the emir can . . . harass them day and night by using weapons and fires or declare war on them and attack them in pitched battle. As for the polytheists who have not been reached by the preaching of Islam . . . we are forbidden to attack them by surprise . . . before having called them to Islam."[40]

These distinctions between territories of war, *dar al-harb,* and spaces of the infidel, *dar al-kufr,* reveal gradations distinguishing the different zones beyond the frontier. The era of an undefined space, open to conquest from the base camp (*misr*), was long over: jihad had been redefined based on the military reality of the period.

The Ribat on the Frontiers and the Syrian Coasts

The work of Ibn al-Mubarak (d. 797), one of the great armed scholars and an inhabitant of the region of Cilicia, possibly of Tarsus, moved away from the models of jihad adapted to the martyrdom of the conquest period. Instead, Ibn al-Mubarak was one of the first to define the forms of a jihad adapted to the position of the volunteer on the frontier. As the author of a book on jihad and one biographical text, Ibn al-Mubarak defined voluntary engagement as the fruit of an individual process, based on the Hadith, that combined the two forms of the Muslims' fight, known under the general terms "major jihad" and "minor jihad." He argued that these volunteers should be integrated into the frontier army, either to monitor enemy territory from frontier cities or to participate in razzias on the territory of war.

This close association between relatively strict forms of asceticism and combat or frontier monitoring would blossom with the practice of the ribat. To refer to the practice of the two forms of jihad, texts about war most commonly used the verbal form *rabata,* "to make ribat," rather than a reference to a specific place.[41] The exercise of the ribat could only be performed on the frontier and required believers to remain more or less stationary, in a place where they could theoretically see the enemy and isolate themselves to meditate. It appears that the importance of asceticism, combined with combat and sometimes pushed to excess and criticized, was one of the armed scholars' principal contributions. Now the *murabit* (one making *ribat*) perpetuated the memory of engagement in combat in the spirit of Medina and since the time of Muhammad, but in the context of combat rooted on the frontier in a single location where one could withdraw to pray and practice asceticism, rather than in the context of the conquest, which entailed mobility.

Among the practices of war that appeared on the Anatolian front and the Syrian coast, the ribat was certainly the institution that best symbolized the changes marking the beginnings of the Abbasid period. Antioch was referred to as both a fortress (*maʿqil*) and a ribat, which implies that the city was suitable for the individual practice of jihad. Its reputation drew many. According to a maxim attributed to Abu Saʿid al-Khudri, a companion of the Prophet and traditionist who died between 682–683 and 693–694, "A year of devotion in this city is worth a year [elsewhere]. To those of your community who die here, God promises the day of resurrection as the reward of the *murabitun*."[42] This connection to the earliest period of Islam made it possible to trace the practice of the ribat back to the prophetic period.[43] Descriptions of this practice in coastal cities such as Beirut and border cities such as Antioch and, especially, al-Massisa and Tarsus, where many *murabitun* spent time, are found in numerous literary accounts as of the end of the eighth century, as well as in the first written accounts by volunteer scholars.

In the process of rearranging the frontier, Harun al-Rashid turned the ribat into a caliphal institution and launched its spread on the empire's borders. During the same period of 795–796, two of the sovereign's officers were sent to be governors at the outer limits of the caliphal domain: Harthama b. Hayyan was posted to the border of Ifriqiya and al-Fadl b. Yahya to the border of Khorasan. Both soldiers had garnered experience as commanders on the Taurus frontier. Harthama had been charged with supervising the rebuilding of Tarsus, which became the ultimate city of ribat. In 796, Harthama ordered the construction of the first Ifriqiyan ribat, in Monastir, while al-Fadl built the first ribat on the eastern border, in Paykent.[44]

Both structures were part of a much larger program aiming to protect frontiers attacked by the Byzantines of Sicily on one side and the Turks of the Oxus region on the other. This religious and military institution, developed in Syria in the context of the reorganization of the frontiers, was imposed on all of the caliphate's frontiers, as it were. A parallel can be established between this institutionalization of voluntary service in the context of jihad and the caliphs' desire to channel and, if possible, control the energy of voluntary combatants. In this way, the Abbasids "reinvented" a frontier in the places where they were waging a war, while trying to control the manpower responsible for its defense.[45] The ribats' immediate popularity is revealed by the presence alongside the soldiers, at least as of the Umayyad period, of many pious men, who were now supervised and whose energy was thus channeled.[46] Regional particularities in the institution of ribat and its evolution can be explained by the need to adapt this religious and military practice both to conditions of war that varied from one end of the Mediterranean to the other and to the needs of the states concerned.

An Active Defense

At the beginning of the tenth century, Qudama b. Jaʿfar reported the obligations incumbent on the governor of the maritime regions, then based in Tyre. This text shows that the Sahil—the coastal region of Bilad al-Sham, between Cilicia and the Sinai—was considered a strategic march under the direct control of the caliph, as it had been in the Umayyad period:

> He [the caliph] ordered him [the governor] to continually review his troops to know them and to be aware of their actual state and the maintenance of their ships. He ordered him to supervise the observation posts and look-out posts; to be generous with them [the look-outs] and the soldiers by paying them regularly. He orders him to inspect the ships, [to make sure that] they are solid and well fitted out. . . . When the government decrees an expedition, the governors of Egypt and Syria receive the order to make the necessary preparations. The meeting point for the fleet is Cyprus. Its commander in chief is the governor of the Syrian frontiers.[47]

At the end of the ninth century, the geographer al-Yaʿqubi listed the moorings of the fleets defending the coastline in the name of the caliph. These included Tyre: "Tyre, maritime city, [is] equipped with a dockyard, in which they build naval vessels of the empire, intended for the war against the Rum."[48]

The caliphs of Baghdad personally got involved in the war against the Byzantines. They presented their commitment in such a manner as to impose the image of the caliph fighting in the name of jihad and to outdo the conquering Umayyads. With a program of coastal defense and naval offensives intended to cover the empire's maritime frontier, their exclusive commitment in Anatolia reinforced the identification of the Mediterranean with the frontier and the caliphate's war zone.

THE GHAZI-CALIPH

Chroniclers focused on the sites of jihad, chosen by the caliph or those who headed razzias in his name—his sons, often the heir to the throne, or the generals who represented him—at the expense of other fronts.[49] References to border combat follow in the sovereign's or his representative's footsteps. This distorted view excluded practically any information about most contact zones with the Christians and most of the players in this frontier war, unless it was reported by the Muslims' adversaries.

The emergence of regional powers brought the image of the ghazi sovereign to the other fronts, in the East but also in the western regions. To prove their legitimacy, the Aghlabids presented themselves as the caliph's representatives; far from Baghdad, however, they enjoyed total autonomy. Thus, the decision by Emir Ziyadat Allah (817–838) to entrust the leadership of the conquest of Sicily, which was essentially motivated by sedition in the Ifriqiya *jund,* to Qadi Asad b. al-Furat in 827, marked a change from the Anatolian campaigns led by the caliph, his sons, or the generals: "This episode . . . allows us to observe that within the Abbasid empire, political, judicial, and institutional innovations are in fact constant on the regional level and are the product of extremely varied instruments."[50] Nonetheless, the model created by the caliphs on the Anatolian frontier became the standard for all Muslim powers waging war on the frontiers, at least in regard to their discourse. Even dissidents such as the emirs of Córdoba drew heavily from this caliphal model, the only one recognized to be in compliance with the laws of Islam.

The caliphs' particular interest in the frontier can also be measured by the position of the governors of the marches and the "protector" cities. 'Abd al-Malik b. Salih, the uncle of al-Saffah, the caliph who had eliminated Marwan II in Egypt, was the first governor of the Syrian march under an Abbasid mandate. The clan's power rested on significant assets and its ability to rally Qais tribes formerly in the service of the Umayyads and now placed under the command of the caliph's uncle. This regional base allowed him to develop his autonomy and plant the seeds of a real "local sub-dynasty."[51] The caliph used the governor to stop the destructive raids of the Basileus, thereby ensuring the stability of this sensitive zone, then eliminated the dangerously powerful rival. Al-Mahdi went a step further by appointing his son Harun to the command of the frontier zone in 779. The future caliph headed two expeditions toward Cappadocia. In 780, his father personally took command, leading troops to Dorylaeum for the first time and possibly to the Sea of Marmara, during a second expedition.

Harun al-Rashid became caliph in 786 and left the government of the marches of Syria and Azerbaijan to the Barmakid viziers until 803, in other words for the entire period they were in power. At that point, the sovereign brought his sons closer to exercising power by deciding to involve al-Amin and his eldest, al-Ma'mun, in military activity on the border. Al-Ma'mun was appointed to Khorasan, an appointment long considered compensation for the fact that his younger brother al-Amin, born to an Arab mother, had been chosen as heir to the caliphate. In fact, al-Ma'mun had not inherited the caliph's frontier. On top of the succession to the caliphate, the younger son inherited the government of the entire western region, from Iraq to the Atlantic. Aside from Baghdad, the Bilad al-Sham, Arabia, and the Maghreb, his actual authority now extended to the frontiers of the Taurus and the Sea of Rum, frontiers that had revealed the legitimacy of the ghazi-caliph since the Umayyad period and, even more so, under the following caliphate. The command of the Byzantine frontier fell to Harun al-Rashid once his father designated him as his successor, at the expense of his elder brother al-Hadi (784–785), who had previously been chosen by the caliph. While the details of the difficult succession to al-Amin are unknown, there is no doubt that the frontier of the caliphs, which legitimated the future ghazi-caliph, was not the eastern frontier but the one facing the other emperor's territory. Harun's participation in the expedition of 805–806, now as the caliph, further reinforced the connection between the caliphate and the eastern frontier. After having defeated his brother and reestablished control of the capital in 819, al-Ma'mun also sought to establish his authority as a war caliph by expanding the scope of the battle against the emperor of Byzantium, rather than going to fight the Turkish tribes beyond Khorasan. He entrusted the command of his armies to his brother, the future caliph al-Mu'tasim, and his son Ali, who pushed into Cappadocia on three occasions beginning in 830. That same year, the caliph settled in Tarsus, using it as a base from which to supervise these expeditions. He also prepared to head an expedition in 833, but he died before he could realize his wish. His son and successor, al-Mu'tasim, saw the raid through to Amorium, which would be the last triumph against the Byzantines under the command of a caliph.

4

THE GEOGRAPHERS' MEDITERRANEAN

As we have seen, Baghdad was the cradle of a discipline that came into being in the ninth century, at the same time that the surviving Abbasid chronicles were written. Geographic and chronographic texts are in fact inseparable, for both proceed from the will to prove Islam's universal legitimacy. Contrary to long-standing opinion, the Mediterranean found a singular place in the heart of the Muslim domain, once again as the favored space for caliphal jihad.

THE LEGACY OF BAGHDAD

Arabic tradition established al-Ma'mun as the founder of geographic science: among others, al-Mas'udi reported seeing in libraries a "geography" (*jughrafiya*) that had no text but featured the climates (*iqlim*) in a table of astronomical readings, along with a map bearing al-Ma'mun's name (*surat al-ma'muniyat*). This map represented "the world with its spheres, its stars, the land and the seas, the inhabited regions and those deserted, the habitats and the cities."[1] Arab geography was one of the many disciplines that had pride of place in Baghdad during the blossoming of "encyclopedic" studies that drew on every type of knowledge that could showcase the image of Islam desired by the caliph and the men of letters in his circle.

Before becoming "the study of the earth's physical features, resources, and climates," Arab geography as it has reached us was primarily aimed at representing Islam at the center of the ecumene and including the power and legitimacy of the caliphate on world maps.[2] Translations, particularly of Ptolemy's *Almagest* but also of Marinus of Tyre's *Geography* and many other treatises of Hellenic geography, were at the root of a geography of astronomical figures and calculations, long before geography represented the parts of the earth and described its physical features and human activities.[3] Astrolabes and astronomical spheres were the first objects collected by the capital's sovereigns, a practice then followed by the city's upper classes.[4] During the same period, the maps of Greek antiquity, particularly those by Ptolemy, became the models for the first world maps, which were divided into segments or climates by which the location of specific sites, regions, rivers, seas, or mountainous areas could be identified.

References to Arab geography, both cartographic and descriptive, were a cultural and propaganda tool of Islamic and caliphal sovereignty, unrelated to guides or itineraries used for orientation, which were known through other (primarily oral) vectors of transmission.[5] Yet the same concerns are found in administrative geography, in references to the itineraries and stages leading to Mecca or crisscrossing the empire: this justified the choice of the Abbasid administration's epistolographers to apply the terms "paths" or "itineraries" (*masalik*) to their descriptions of the land and maritime routes to the various cities and other inhabited areas within the space controlled by the sovereign (*mamalik*). However, usage of this practical geography was transformed to meet another requirement: representing the space under the prince's authority in works written for the edifying education of the caliphate's future elite. This brought forth an encyclopedic type of geography that was far from a travel guide but gave the curious enough information to make conversation.

In keeping with the precept that, for Arabs, "science cannot be divided," the "sciences of the earth" were a major source of inspiration for geography, but in the same way as medicine and other disciplines:

through what they could contribute to knowledge of the earth's origins, physics, and climates, and man's adaptation to his environment. The birth of Arab geography is closely connected to the development of the *adab,* embodied by Jahiz (d. 868) and Ibn Qutayba (d. ca. 883–889), whose influence on the writing of geography was decisive. The *adab* is defined as "a literature of technicians, in the sense that it is made by administrators and is also addressed to administrators," but refuses "to let itself be exclusively confined to technical concerns."[6] Geography was not conceived of as a science in and of itself but, unlike history, as a full-fledged discipline that made it possible to set out what was known about physical space and was part of general culture; it was only significant if it was put in the service of Islam, that is to say, of the caliph and those who served him.

In parallel, geography developed into what would become a more specifically descriptive genre used to promote the imperial space.[7] It is during this period that one finds the first appearance of administrative geography, under the title "book of roads and kingdoms" (*kitab al-masalik wa l-mamalik*). Over the following centuries, administrative geography would become established throughout Islam. Initially composed of traditions in which travelers' recollections were recorded in the form of a succession of tales and stories for the pleasure of lettered circles, the inventory of the world became the concern of those in the *diwan* (government), who transformed these descriptions through a more elaborate, less spontaneous approach in which the same types of stories were now arranged to serve the Abbasid cause. The will to make Islam as it was seen from Baghdad appear as the only universalism in the human space pushed geographers to always speak of the entire universe: the cosmos, the earth, the ecumene.

THE MEDITERRANEAN IN THE LIGHT OF THE INDIAN OCEAN

The geographers of Baghdad used the Indian Ocean as the reference by which to measure the Mediterranean.[8] Their oldest sources of maritime descriptions were the oldest descriptions of seas available to us today—*The Account of India and China* (ca. 851); *The Book of Roads and Kingdoms* by Ibn Khurradadhbih (d. ca. 885), which largely borrows from the *Account* to describe the ocean; and *The Wonders of India,* the surviving edition of which dates from the middle of the tenth century. The Baghdad geographer al-Mas'udi used the Indian Ocean as his principal reference to describe the Mediterranean and Caspian Seas. Whatever genre these descriptions combining "wonders" and itineraries fell into, they were addressed to a cultured circle whose principal readers were people of the chancellery like Ibn Khurradadhbih, al-Mas'udi, and al-Muqaddasi. They used the traditions (*akhbar*) drawn from marine and merchant circles to describe the Mediterranean, but, contrary to depictions of the ocean, they presented it as an imperial space dedicated to jihad. For instance, the reference to the Mediterranean and European itinerary followed by Rahdanite Jewish merchants from Iraq in Ibn Khurradadhbih's book of geography does not provide a single example of merchants' maritime activities, though there is some discussion of the traffic in eunuchs between Verdun and Baghdad. Instead, it features the remarkable example of merchant networks that brought to the caliphs' palaces the rarest and most precious "products" from the most distant lands. The subject here is not the merchant but the caliph and his capital, which receives all the products on earth, to be enjoyed by the sovereign and his circle. This was another way of underlining the universality of the caliphate, which could thus claim to control the Sea of the Romans and extend its influence beyond the borders of the Dar al-Islam. For the Mediterranean as seen from Islam to be considered a maritime space for merchants, one has to wait until the eleventh century and the treatise by the merchant al-Dimashqi, which offers the first description of the commercial products circulating on the western sea, and, especially, the letters of the Geniza.[9]

There are two known versions of Ibn Khurradadhbih's book: the first dates from 846, while the second, which is actually the same work with some additional passages, was written before 885, the probable year of its author's death. The book is the work of both a technician and a man of letters, in keeping with the *adab.* Its definitive version is presented as an educational text intended for administrators in the author's circle: it defines what must be known of the empire for which the author is said to have been responsible, outside of al-Sawad, as the vizier of the *barid,* the imperial postal service. The book's influence was therefore decisive, not only on regional geography but also on that of other areas of Islam: "A picture appears: that of the world inventoried, the world of Islam, seen from the inside, with a few glances thrown to the outside, toward the [Byzantine] neighbor, through a more or less legendary tradition."[10] Ibn Khurradadhbih names all of Islam's parts, relying first on his knowledge and the information gleaned through his work in the heart of the *diwan;* the Muslim empire is represented as a whole through its cities, its itineraries, and the assessed tax in al-Sawad, all of which were signs of imperial authority. He also reports the existence of regional dynasties unreachable by the caliphs, such as the Idrisids of Fez: "The son [Muhammad al-Muntasir] of Idris [II] b. Idris b. 'Abd Allah b. Hasan b. Hasan b. 'Ali b. Abi Talib—May God have them all in his Mercy—is master of Tlemcen, 25 days by foot from Tiaret on a territory everywhere cultivated; he also possesses Tangier and Fez, his residence 24 days on foot from Tahert. . . . This prince is not greeted by the title of caliph but only the formula: 'May salvation be upon you, son of Allah's Envoy.' "[11]

He also includes references to the sovereigns and great states outside Islam, such as the Byzantine Empire, and the itineraries of merchants.[12]

The Traveling Geographers' Marginalized Mediterranean

While the geography of Baghdad benefited the caliphs by legitimizing a single Islamic space, it did so by establishing a hierarchy of space within the Mamlaka (the Islamic empire), highlighting its center and both the land and maritime sections of the East, at the expense of the western margins. Persian-inspired maps more or less reproduced this qualitative division by placing al-Sawad at the center of the world map. It was also a Persian tradition to describe the ecumene as an animal, often a bird: "The appearance of the world here below is divided in five: it is like the head of the bird, the two wings, the chest, the tail. The head of the world is China. . . . The right wing is India and, beyond India, the sea after which there is no one; the left wing is al-Khazar;[13] the chest of the world is Mecca, Hejaz, Syria, Iraq, and Egypt; the tail reaches from

Dhat al-Humam to the Maghreb, and the worst part of the bird is the tail."[14]

In the tenth century, the advent of a geography based on "a study of the land of men" coincided with the rise of a generation of particularly gifted writers.[15] The school of Balkhi (d. 934), a scholar whose work has been lost but who is considered the founder of this geography of humanist travelers, produced geographers like al-Istakhri (d. after 951), who endeavored to describe and draw maps of a world in which man had become the principal subject.[16] These descriptions were also intended to express the brilliance of the civilization of Islam by drawing on the legacy of the geography of the previous generation's Abbasid administrators. Following the example of al-Muqaddasi and, even more so, Ibn Hawqal, who preceded him by a few years, these great travelers proved more sensitive to the evolution of the situation in the regions of Islam than their predecessors.

The West Marginalized

Al-Muqaddasi's book is organized in a classic fashion, opening with a general presentation of the earth and its parts. The ecumene appears divided into fourteen climates, with the empire therefore separated into two large wholes by an axial line that follows the pilgrimage route to Mecca, from western Iran to Arabia, through Iraqi, Syrian, and Arabian steppes and deserts.[17] In the chapters devoted to each of Islam's land regions, al-Muqaddasi emphasizes the disparity between the West and the Mashriq, though he notes the latter's decline under Buyid rule: "Be aware that Baghdad, formerly magnificent, is now headed for ruin and lives in discord, its splendor buried. I do not appreciate or admire it, and if I praise it, it is to [conform to] the custom."[18]

The chapter on the seas plays an important part in the general presentation of the world, in particular to give the author's opinion on the varying number of liquid bodies reported in the Quran: two, seven, or possibly even eight. (This figure was obviously the subject of intense debate among exegetes.) It was especially important to reconcile Quranic tradition with the tradition inherited from ancient geography. Al-Muqaddasi paid particular attention to the contrast the Arabs perceived between the two seas bordering Islamic soil. The Sea of the Arabs or Sea of Fars (Persian Sea), which was bordered by the coastal regions of the Arabian-Persian Gulf up to the Indus on one side and the Sea of Yemen, then the Red Sea, on the other, was far more familiar than the Mediterranean, which remained the Sea of the Romans. To better mark this difference, al-Muqaddasi repeats the words of a pious man calling on the judgment of God, the implacable arbiter who separated the two bodies of water here personified:

> God, when he created the Sea of Sham, made the following revelation to it: "I created you and am going to leave you to my servants who, wanting some grace from me, will say: Glory to God! or God is holy! or God is great! or there is no other divinity but God! How will you treat them?"—"Well, Lord, answered the sea, I will drown them!"—"Away from me! In truth, I curse you! I will make you less beautiful and less filled with fish!" Then God made the same revelation to the sea of Iraq, which said: "Lord, I will carry them upon my back . . ."—"Go! I bless you! I will make you more beautiful and more filled with fish!" This proves there are only two seas.[19]

This story invites one to consider the two seas as the symbols of an insurmountable opposition between two civilizations, with the Mediterranean permanently belonging to Christianity. At the same time, al-Muqaddasi provides one of the most complete descriptions of the Mediterranean by an Arab geographer. He displays an excellent knowledge of the Sea of the Romans and its shores as they were in his time, revealing for this sea, on which he had sailed and interviewed sailors, an attraction reminiscent of that felt by al-Mas'udi:

> I have heard many people of the Maghreb say that this sea narrows in the vicinity of Tangier; they were unanimous in saying that, when you pass into Andalus, you can still see this continent as the other one appears before you. . . . This sea contains three living and populous islands: Sicily, across from the Maghreb, Crete, across from Egypt, and Cyprus, across from

> Sham [Syria], as well as famous gulfs; on its shores, many countries, prestigious border-cities [*thughur*], *ribat* of the first order. One of the sides of the sea marks the boundary of the land of the Rum up to the borders of Andalus. Naval supremacy belongs to the Rum, who are greatly feared, and are, along with the Sicilians and the people of Andalus, the most familiar with this sea, its boundaries, and its gulfs, for they roam it to attack those who come within their reach; their routes to Egypt and Sham are across this sea. I sailed long enough with them, asking them constant questions about this sea and everything pertaining to it; I submitted to them everything I had heard about it, and rare were the times when they did not agree.[20]

Al-Muqaddasi insists on the image of a sea dedicated to jihad by recalling that Byzantium competed with two caliphates, the "Sicilian" Fatimids and the Andalusians, for supremacy over the Mediterranean.

IBN HAWQAL: THE MEDITERRANEAN AT THE HEART OF ISLAM

Ibn Hawqal was the first Eastern geographer of the Abbasid generation to truly free himself from the mental borders that separated the East from the Islamic West: he did not reject the geographic works of the past, but was the only one of the Iraqi authors of the *masalik wa l-mamalik* to give the Mediterranean zone a central place in the heart of a prosperous and populous Islam.[21]

A Space No Longer Focused on Baghdad

The geographer traveled a great deal, particularly in the West, claiming he got as far as Sijilmasa, a desert city in the south of present-day Morocco, and reached the European limits of Islam at Santarém, the Gharb al-Andalus's sentry facing the Latins on the Tagus.[22] Ibn Hawqal's account of this part of the Muslim world is his most important contribution to the work of al-Istakhri, his master and model, and contrasts sharply with the way previous Eastern geographers presented the Muslim West. More than anyone, Ibn Hawqal took note of the historical situation of the moment, which was favorable to the Shiite caliphs, whom he, a fellow Shiite, considered the legitimate imams. A native of Nusaybin in Jazira (Upper Mesopotamia), he observed that under Buyid rule the traditional political center of Baghdad and Iraq no longer played the unifying role that had allowed the caliphs' power to extend into the Mediterranean. He made apparent the influence of peripheral areas that had become cradles of Islam's dynamism. The future of Muslims was now decided in these "new" worlds; Iran remained the center of Islam, but Ibn Hawqal already observed or foresaw the role that would be played by the Turkish peoples. As depicted by this traveler, Islam had become a multipolar world.

Ibn Hawqal's Mediterranean: A Rich but Threatened Area

Ibn Hawqal foresaw that a change in Islam's destiny would be decided in the Mediterranean, first because the Muslim world's major players were now based there, and second because he thought the war between the Greeks, Latin, and Muslims would be decisive:

> I have described this sea, the cities and regions located on its shores, from the region of Tangier to the territory of Egypt, from the end of Syria, that is to say of the Marches, to Aulas, which was once in the hands of the Muslims and belonged to them. I represented all that and added to it the frontiers of the Byzantine empire, the countries located on this side of the canal [the strait of the Bosporus] and on the other side of the Bosporus. I have specified most of the regions that are found beyond the canal, such as the territories of Constantinople, the lands of the Peloponnesian, the gulf of Venice, the lands of Calabria, Lombardy, France, Rome, Galicia, and the neighboring Spanish regions.[23]

Ibn Hawqal was the first to deal with the Mediterranean area, both Muslim and Christian, as a singular and coherent whole. A merchant by trade, he discovered a world that was sufficient unto itself. Exchanges around the basin had led to the area's enrichment, which was also stimulated by a population density greater than that in other regions and particularly in Asia. Ibn Hawqal changed practically nothing in the part of al-Istakhri's work that covered the "old world," for he believed that his master's inventory of the East remained relevant. In fact, it was said that al-Istakhri himself had suggested that Ibn Hawqal visit and discuss the part of Islam that he had been unable to study. While Ibn Hawqal updated passages about a few places he visited in northern Syria, then under the control of the Hamdanids, and Transoxiana, another region he thought was full of promise, the major changes he made were to the image of the Mediterranean. He was the only Eastern author of the *masalik wa l-mamalik* generation to represent the Muslim West using the same criteria as for the East.

Emulating al-Istakhri by keeping his "roads and kingdoms" structure as the thread of his progress, Ibn Hawqal followed the itineraries, passing through the cities—representatives of authority—to reach the frontier zones. This allowed him to give his often critical opinion on the state of defenses on Islam's boundaries. The geographer drew from the Eastern tradition of maritime itineraries to enumerate ships' ports of call, getting his information from nautical rutters possibly found in the "archives" of the Fatimid or Umayyad admiralties. In this way, he leads the reader along the African coastline, continuing along the Anatolian and European coasts to end up in al-Andalus. His final remarks show that he did not hesitate to combine this data with accounts of the little-known boundaries of the northern Mediterranean, which he found in Baghdad's libraries: "It [the Mediterranean] goes beyond Almería, the districts of Algeciras and Seville, and meets the ocean at Santarém, the outer limit of the territories of Islam near al-Andalus and the frontier of the European domain."[24]

Ibn Hawqal's choice to give a political reading of the boundaries of the Mediterranean, which significantly spilled over into the Atlantic Ocean, led him to follow several of his predecessors in setting the inner sea's limit not at the Strait of Gibraltar but at Islam's maritime frontiers, which extended from Santarém on the Tagus in the north to the territory of Nul Lamta in the south. Similarly, his choice to identify the three port cities as the capitals of the maritime districts was not happenstance, since they were also the three principal Umayyad dockyards: a political vision of the maritime space was more significant in his eyes than one based on physical criteria.[25]

Having had access to information from the archives of the states he visited, Ibn Hawqal uses administrative language, specifically the language of taxes, as was the practice of all geographers when they named localities: the enumeration of cities (*madina,* pl. *mudun*), fortresses (*hisn,* pl. *husun*), villages (*qarya,* pl. *qura*), and other types of secondary habitats, located on roads converging in the state's capital, reproduced a hierarchy found in administrative and fiscal classifications. As applied to the Fatimid and Umayyad caliphates, the hierarchization of the living environment demonstrated the order and power of Muslim states bordering the Mediterranean. Far from merely enumerating tribes and cities, he applies a critical mind to painting an updated picture of each sovereignty (*mamlaka*). His sources enable him to evaluate the power of the two caliphates based on each state's revenue and military organization and their capitals' wealth: "One of the details most likely to give an idea of this enormous opulence [of Caliph 'Abd al-Rahman III in al-Andalus] is the amount of money collected by the tax office, which in dinars and dirhams, reaches 200,000 dinars a year. . . . Add to that the country's contributions and revenues, property taxes, tithes, leases, tolls, head taxes, customs taxes on the numerous goods that enter and exit aboard ships, and the duties paid for taverns in the urban markets."[26]

His analysis was uncompromising, particularly when he asserted that the prince was poorly managing his principality by choosing non-Muslim viziers: "The productivity [of Egypt] was interrupted with the coming of the Maghrebis, and this must be attributed to the accursed Abu l-Faraj b. Killis, the vizier [of Caliph] al-'Aziz [975–996], for he ruined this industry with harmful measures, with taxation."[27]

Islamic Forces in a Mediterranean Shared with Byzantium

Another highly original aspect of Ibn Hawqal's work was his ability to grasp the importance for the whole of Islam of the role of the Mediterranean Sea.[28] He views the sea as a homogenous and shared space, despite the recurring confrontation between Christians and Muslims. He reveals the existence of networks connecting the Mediterranean's northern and southern shores and observes the tremendous potential of regions richer and more heavily populated than many Muslim countries of the East: "There is no sea whose shores are as intensely populated as this one: inhabited regions stretch on both sides, uninterrupted, easy to access. The other seas are bordered by uncultivated and desert plains."[29]

Taken as a whole, this information allowed him to evaluate the forces on the field. He piles on the superlatives regarding Córdoba, which he depicts as a model of the sumptuous Arab capital at the outer limit of the West. However, it was Fatimid Egypt that he saw as the embodiment of Muslim supremacy, now located on the shores of the Mediterranean and headed by the Ismaili caliphs. Ibn Hawqal's position, while influenced by his support for the Shiite caliphs, is based on their economic track record, of which he details certain aspects using precise data about the Nile delta, particularly in the area of taxes. His description of the coastal cities is accompanied by a relatively systematic list of sources of revenue from production and trade and in connection with the hinterland: here too, the merchant was highly attentive to the management of potential. Though his analysis was critical, he believed that Muslim power was now equally divided between the West and the East.

He devoted an important passage to the Byzantine administration, citing the account of one of his compatriots who had long been held prisoner in Constantinople.[30] This report on the Greek world, his remarks on Italy, and recollections of his stay in the region of Antioch, where he fought as a volunteer, allowed Ibn Hawqal to assess the situation on the frontiers with his own eyes; he was very critical of the Sicilians facing the Christians and more divided on al-Andalus, which was at the height of its power during his stay under the reign of al-Hakam II (961–976). He insists on the importance of maritime relations, from one anchorage to another and between the major ports; he does not lack for opportunities to mention the commercial networks between north and south, or the many reasons for nonviolent encounters between enemies, for example on the occasion of prisoner exchanges on the coast of northern Syria. However, he recognizes the essential role that the confrontation between Muslims and Christians played in the evolution of relations in the region: he notes that while Byzantium was not as powerful as the Muslims seemed to think, the Macedonian emperors had been able to seize the territories of "Islam[, which is] morally disunited in the state of hearts and minds. Disorder, the frequency of revolts and rebellions, the internecine strife to which Muslims devote their time leave the way open to Byzantium."[31]

5

MUSLIM CENTERS OF THE WESTERN MEDITERRANEAN

Islam without the Abbasids

ONE OF THE DISTINCTIVE features of al-Bakri's work of universal geography, *The Book of Roads and Kingdoms,* completed in 1068, is that it was composed without its author leaving his native Andalusia. Aside from what he wrote about al-Andalus, the renowned botanist relied entirely on texts he found during long stays in Córdoba and Almería, taking the opposite approach to his Eastern colleagues who considered it necessary to travel in the regions they wanted to describe before writing about them.[1] His description of the Maghreb, a highlight of his work, provides the first detailed picture of the region in the Middle Ages. Al-Bakri had access to the descriptions of al-Warraq, as well as information provided by Maghrebis, whom he is the only one to cite. His book, the title of which indicates a kinship with Iraqi geography, is one of the most remarkable examples of the cultural change that marked the western Mediterranean to the west of Egypt as of the tenth century. Accompanying a more sweeping movement, the flourishing of an Arabic chronographic literature made this region, once mocked by al-Muqaddasi for its inhabitants' ignorance, one of the most prolific in the field of Arabic literature and science.[2]

AN ABBASID FRONTIER ON THE SHORES OF IFRIQIYA

Ifriqiya's separation from the Eastern caliphate was brought about by three major events. A reassessment of the status of the Berber regions, which had been integrated into the Islamic space after the Arab conquest, was ordered by Caliph Hisham with the aim of providing Berber women for his palaces and led to an uprising of the tribes beginning in 739. This revolt would reach as far as the Iberian Peninsula. The return to calm, which coincided with the Abbasid "revolution" of 749–750, provoked chronic anger in the *jund* by preventing soldiers from continuing to reap profits from raids. At the same time, the Khawarij movement of the Sufris and ʿIbadis—an Islamic movement born in the East that rejected the legitimacy of the Sunni and Fatimid caliphates—began to cause problems for the caliphate's governors.[3] Officers close to the caliph were charged with restoring order until Ibrahim b. al-Aghlab (800–812) was appointed by Harun al-Rashid. While the Aghlabids never officially broke with the caliphs, who guaranteed the emirs' legitimacy by sending a diploma of investiture at each enthronement, the Kairouanian dynasty was de facto independent.[4]

Aside from the caliphate's formal recognition of governors, the maintenance of strong ties with Iraq is borne out by the way the Ifriqiyan emirs conceived their military strategy against the Byzantines. In terms of jihad, both al-Yaʿqubi's quick but explicit enumeration of coastal defenses at the end of the ninth century and the information found in the Ifriqiyan texts unmistakably confirm that the organization of the armed forces and coastal defenses was heavily inspired by the structure put in place by the caliphs in Syria and the valley of the Nile. The governors sent by the caliphs were all career officers who had served and acquired experience in military command on the frontiers of the Abbasid world in Anatolia. They were therefore in a position to bridge the gap between the region where caliphal jihad had begun and the two frontier provinces, particularly Ifriqiya.[5]

It was in these circumstances that the ribat of Monastir was built in 796, during a period when the coasts were under attack from Byzantine "pirates." Soon backed by the Maliki ulema, the authorities promoted jihad to reinforce the maritime front. However, a tradition dated the foundation of the first fortified edifice in Sousse to the period of Yazid

b. Hatim al-Muhallabi's government (772–788), decades before the ribat financed by Ziyadat Allah was built there in 821.[6] Like the volunteers in Syria some time earlier, the Malikis had become increasingly committed to the practice of ribat as of the ninth century and even tried to date the founding of Monastir to the period of the holy caliph 'Umar II.[7]

The prominence of these two ribats underlines the preeminence of jihad in the Ifriqiyan emirate's coastal defense system at the time. These sacred places developed a widespread reputation, drawing a large number of pilgrims every year, to the point that the ulema had to rule on the proper way to receive the visitors.

The diversity of names used for places of ribat and the recent discovery of new sites along the coasts of al-Andalus confirm the varied forms taken by this pious exercise, here and in the East and Ifriqiya. They also reveal the profound influence of the Near Eastern frontier, which was under Abbasid control, on the other Mediterranean fronts. As in Syria, "to make ribat," an expression that recurs frequently in the texts, referred to varied forms of the personal and collective practice of jihad. The only essential aspect was the Muslim believer's position in relation to the marine or land horizon from which the armed infidel could suddenly emerge. The spatial setting referred to by the word "ribat" was clearly defined by the *murabit* Abu l-Ahwas in his remarks to Emir Ibrahim II (875–902). Abu l-Ahwas believed that a place located in a zone facing the enemy became a ribat if people withdrew there to practice the two forms of jihad: "This country [Ifriqiya] is populated, it is a frontier region and it is the destination of the people of Ifriqiya; it is their place of ribat. The people of Kairouan perform ribat there every Friday; the mosque cannot hold them all, I would like you to make it bigger. . . . In the city of Sousse at this time [according to al-Maliki], there was nothing blameworthy. . . . Its inhabitants were busy making war, standing guard for the Muslim men and women, praying at night and fasting during the day."[8] The introduction of the practice of ribat in Ifriqiya, which was contemporary with the erection of the first edifice specifically dedicated to ribat on the caliph's orders in Monastir, closely followed its appearance on the coasts of Abbasid Syria. Sultanate in its essence, the practice of ribat was carried on and developed by the emirs who built the ribat in Sousse some twenty-five years later, as laconically mentioned by al-Ya'qubi: "It takes eight days to walk from Sfax to a locality called Bizerte. At each stopover, there are small forts (*husun*), close together, to which the pious men and *murabitun* would withdraw."[9] Twenty-five ribats built by the Aghlabids, mainly under the reign of Ahmad (856–863), have been identified along the coast between Sousse and Sfax.[10] Most were forts (*qusur*); the word "ribat" was more specifically applied to the edifices in Monastir and Sousse. However, the practice of ribat was not limited to these edifices: watchtowers (*maharis*) and especially small towns—those of the two ribats, but also Sfax, Gabès, and others, which accommodated many volunteers—were themselves places of ribat. Another area of ribat, the Cap Bon peninsula, which was particularly exposed to Christian attacks launched from Sicily, still bears traces of several defensive structures that served as retreats for the *murabitun* along the coastline. These sites were fortified thanks to the generosity of the princes but especially of devout individuals who had become wealthy and financed the construction of defenses to accommodate volunteers. However, the authorities remained constantly in control, as seen in these remarks by Qadi al-Qasibi (d. 1012): "The castles (*husun*) cannot be modified according to individual initiatives but one can make changes intended to increase the number of those who retreat there without spending the pious donations (*habus*) gathered for these institutions. Women cannot live in ribats and coastal fortresses, which are to be distinguished from ordinary fortresses [when ribat is performed there]."[11]

According to a fatwa decreed by Sahnun, the wives of those who performed ribat could accompany their husbands, but only in safe and well-populated places such as the cities of Alexandria and Tunis; their presence was not desired in Sfax and Sousse, and there could be no question of them residing in a fort (*qasr*) where volunteers mixed with soldiers of the *jund*.[12] Also in the Aghlabid period, a notable who wanted to demonstrate his piety followed the advice of the chief qadi and paid for the construction of the Qasr ibn al-Ja'd, better known by the later name of Qasr al-Kabir, in the city of Monastir so that the city could welcome more volunteers during the annual gathering (*mawsim*). During busy periods, the city contained a wide variety of places of ribat, including rooms rented to volunteers in private homes. When the city ran out of room for worshipers, the outskirts also became areas of retreat, with tents occasionally serving as places for isolation. Similarly, during busy periods, both the Friday mosque and those in the neighborhoods became places of retreat for the *murabitun*.

The practice of ribat evolved throughout the Middle Ages. For instance, Dunas de Guardamar, located on Spain's Levantine coast in an isolated area near the mouth of the Rio Segura, was devoted to ribat from its foundation: the first structure, which has been dated to the end of the ninth century, consists of long cells with a mihrab placed in the middle of the oblong wall, facing Mecca. Neither the site nor the built structure has fortress-like characteristics like those of the two Tunisian edifices.[13] In fact, the places where the people of ribat withdrew could be very different according to their locations, as al-Idrisi confirms in his discussion of a ribat in the eastern part of al-Andalus: "From there (Mojacar) to Rabita, one day. It is neither a village nor a fortified town, but a castle in which the guards are charged with ensuring that the road is safe."[14]

The Aghlabid Emirs' Jihad, a Continuation of the Abbasid Model

The Aghlabids carried on the military policy of the governors who had preceded them, initially out of necessity. Attacks launched from Byzantine Sicily were probably one reason for the expedition to Mazara in 827, which would mark the beginning of the island's conquest, against a backdrop of political crisis and rivalries between Byzantine leaders, but also of internal problems in Ziyadat Allah's emirate.[15] The installation of coastal defenses and expeditions into Sicilian and Italian territory quickly became useful tools for promoting the emirs' legitimacy. The publicity orchestrated by the emir, particularly regarding his ambitious religious and military architectural program, demonstrated this desire to be seen as following on from the Abbasids in every respect. The emir, occupied with subduing the *jund*, did not make any secret of the reasons for this display: "I do not have to worry about what I will find on the day of resurrection, for on my sheet of paper four good works will be written: the construction of the great mosque in Kairouan, of the Abu Rabi bridge,[16] of the fort (*qasr*) of the city of Sousse, and my appointment of Ahmad ibn Abu Muhriz as qadi of Ifriqiya."[17]

Aside from courting the *fuqaha*'s support, the achievements with which the emir credited himself in his funeral oration for the qadi made up a program for claiming legitimacy: there were reminders of Abbasid policy in the extension of the sacred mosque of Kairouan; the maintenance of the capital's defenses and improvements to the city itself, as symbolized by the large Aghlabid basins; the construction of fortifications in Sousse overlooking the sea; and the exercise of sovereignty, which gave the emir authority to appoint jurists to rule on the law and even to innovate by appointing a jurist to head the expedition to Mazara. Jihad figured prominently among the emirs' merits; once Palermo was taken in 831, the invasion of Sicily could be seen as a continuation of the glorious period of conquests.

The fortification work on the port during Ziyadat Allah's emirate and especially under Ahmad, if one is to believe the men of letters' praise for his work as a builder, turned the coastal city into the capital's principal military and commercial port. Kairouan now overtook the port founded in 702 in Tunis, where the *jund* so often clashed with the government that control of the city was uncertain. The construction of the great tower of Khalaf at the corner of the citadel (*qasaba*), which probably took place under Ahmad's reign, reinforced defenses on the seaside. Muhammad I (841–856) built the port's dock, which was protected by a surrounding wall and two towers flanking its entrance. His successor was particularly attentive to reinforcing coastal defenses: "Abu Ibrahim Ahmad [I] built 10,000 forts, in stone and mortar and reinforced with iron doors."[18] This figure indicates the sovereign's commitment to defending the Ifriqiyan Sahel. Ahmad had a reputation as a very pious man and was considered the best of the princes. He was even compared to 'Umar II, and not only for the brevity of their two reigns or because of his reforms. Even Ibrahim II, whose long-serving government weathered profound crises, was credited with great piety, largely for his contribution to jihad and in particular for having reinforced coastal defenses: "He had forts and guard posts built on the maritime coastline, so that it only took one night to get news from Ceuta to Alexandria, by using fires lighted from one place to the next; he surrounded Sousse with walls."[19]

The war waged against the Christians not only remained under the control of the Ifriqiyan authorities but was constantly presented as one of their major actions, under the control of the sultans, throughout the entire Aghlabid period. The sovereigns of the dynasty coordinated the emirate's defense and encouraged naval operations in Southern Italy in order to be recognized as "ghazi emirs." However, the most significant act of jihad was the entire Sicilian conquest, carried out under nine of the dynasty's eleven sovereigns. Among these rulers, the disturbing figure of Ibrahim II, who distinguished himself from his predecessors by personally leading the jihad in Sicily and southern Italy, where he died of disease, produced a historiography composed of two opposing currents. One current, which was primarily spread by the ulema, praised the piety of this sovereign presented as a martyr, while the other, which may have been circulated by the Fatimids' supporters, emphasized the signs of the apparent insanity that marked the end of his reign. It is also conceivable that the periods of his reign led to a synthesis of contradictory traditions.[20]

The fleet was an indispensable instrument of war, if only to defend access to the coastline. The maintenance and construction of ports and dockyards, particularly in Tunis and Sousse and primarily as of 827, supported the conquest until the end of the reign of the Aghlabids. Based in Palermo, the fleet played an essential role as of 831, sending reinforcements or backing the siege of coastal cities such as Syracuse, the Byzantine capital of Sicily, which was impregnable without naval support. While nonquantifiable, the scale of the Aghlabid maritime investment was sufficient to sustain nearly constant offensives on the island and the seasonal launch of razzias on Italian coasts and islands. The Latin sources confirm the scope of the maritime raids regularly launched against the Italian coasts.

Other signs reveal that the Ifriqiyans made a maritime commitment to commerce, which had nothing to do with demonstrating the emir's legitimacy. Trade activity had continued on the sea, particularly during the first two decades of the Aghlabid ninth century, and despite the breaking of the truce with the Byzantines. As of the ninth century, the Ifriqiyan jurists began producing maritime jurisprudence inspired by Byzantine law—the *lex Rhodia*—and adapted to the Islamic context.[21] Sahnun was the first Maliki jurist to adapt the rules of maritime commerce to Islamic law, taking into account the existence of both piracy and trade with the Christians. He wrote on the subject in his seminal work, the *Mudawwana:* "As for Christian ships captured at sea, either close to our ports or far off, it is necessary to distinguish two cases: if they are merchant ships which are known to trade with Muslims, it is illicit to capture them, unless it takes place in the [waters] of their own country, as they are traveling to other shores than those of Islam. If they are ships not commonly known to specialize in trade with Muslims, their capture is licit."[22]

The clues left by contemporary geographers such as al-Ya'qubi and Ibn Khurradadhbih and, one century later, Ibn Hawqal and al-Bakri regarding seasonal shipping between Ifriqya and al-Andalus via Ténès confirm that merchant activity survived and developed, specifically on the western coast of the Mediterranean, at a time when the regional governments were able to supervise these exchanges. During the same period, in al-Andalus, 'Abd al-Rahman II (822–852) sent a fleet to bring the Balearic sailors to their senses and stop them from disrupting maritime commerce in the area. However, whether commercial or military, naval activities did not yet warrant being mentioned in the literature dedicated to the emirs' most remarkable deeds: despite the qualities for which he takes credit, Ziyadat Allah mentions neither the sea nor the fleet as a prop or symbol of his sovereignty.

The sovereigns strove to leave a trace of their piety, particularly as emirs of the jihad. Nominally faithful to the Abbasids, they adopted the same modes of representing the war sovereign, the only ones then held to be a source of legitimacy in Islam. The sea occupied an important place here, but it was not yet a setting for the representation of caliphal legitimacy.

Malikism, Another Zealous Agent of the Spread of Jihad in Ifriqiya

The Fatimids continued the Aghlabids' work by maintaining and building forts to defend the coast.[23] Despite this continuity, the Maliki opposition in the tenth century transformed the practice of ribat into a form of passive resistance to Shiite power, which was spread by al-Maliki and other Ifriqiyan biographers. More broadly, the edifying depiction of venerated figures practicing the two forms of jihad in the context of ribat made it possible to turn one of the symbols of jihad against the infidel Fatimids, who were considered illegitimate sovereigns by the Malikis. The author of the *Garden of Souls* quotes Jabala b. Hammud al-Sadafi (d. 909), one of the renowned ascetics of the Ifriqiyan Sahel, saying that "we used to be in garrison facing an enemy from whom we were separated by the sea [but] today we have abandoned him to be in garrison facing an enemy now in our midst."[24] Probably the most famous anecdote concerns a highly respected ascetic, Abu Ja'far al-Gammudi, who had retreated with other *murabitun* to the Qasr Ziyad: "['Ubayd Allah] chased away the *murabitun* settled there and turned the place into a warehouse for naval equipment. He drove out all those who lived in the fort, with the exception of Abu Ja'far al-Gammudi, whom no one dared to chase away. [Having noticed that the fort was empty], he took his goatskin and a woolskin and went to settle in Qasr al-Tub, near the city of Sousse."[25]

The Shiite imam did the same thing at the ribats in Lemta and Jimma, which he emptied of occupants to resettle them in Mahdia. Ibn Hawqal, a supporter of the Fatimids, gives a similar reason to explain the decline of the institution of ribat in Sicily: "[Those who lived in them] caused uprisings and revolted against those in power."[26]

These accounts attest to a rivalry over collective memory, pitting a tradition that strove to emphasize the role of the Aghlabids and was passed down by Arab historians against the tradition the Malakis spread by recording those deeds of pious men worthy of being immortalized.[27] This production of memory coincided with the period when the Malikis of Kairouan regained their position of power after the departure of the caliphs, taking advantage of the situation to launch a series of proselytizing missions. The most famous of these missions was undertaken by Ibn Yasin at the beginning of the eleventh century and led to the founding of the Almoravid emirate in the Western Sahara.[28]

Additionally, both the formation of small Muslim principalities on the Italian coasts, particularly in Bari and as far as Fraxinetum in Provence, and the conquest of Crete by Andalusian sailors revealed that a spirit of "private" enterprise survived, making the Mediterranean, then poorly defended by the Christians, an environment still conducive to razzias, which could lead to martyrdom and, if fortune smiled, lasting conquest. The ulema therefore saw no discrepancy, let alone conflict, between a tradition of jihad tied to the war of conquest as it had been waged by the first caliphs and a tradition of jihad on the coasts, adapted to the defense of Islam's territory. This now-universal model traveled well, including into the territories that rejected Abbasid legitimacy.

ABBASID JIHAD IN AL-ANDALUS, THE MARITIME FRONTIER

After defeats in Gaul, at Poitiers in 732 and at the river Berre in 737, followed by the Berber Revolt that erupted in 739, any hope of conquest was eradicated, all the more so given that, until the accession of ʿAbd al-Rahman I (756–785), the government of Córdoba was wholly absorbed in the struggles between Arab clans and parties.[29] After the Carolingian offensives and the stabilization of the front against the Asturians, the emirs organized the defense of the frontier march but encountered strong opposition from the military aristocracies, which were emboldened by their relative autonomy and ad hoc alliances with the Latin sovereignties. Despite these difficulties, the front was more or less stable to the south of the Pyrenees until the eleventh century, facing the Asturians—whose kingdom aligned itself with the Visigothic tradition—Navarre, and Catalonia, a march organized by the Carolingians, after the fall of Barcelona in 801.[30]

A long phase of border clashes began in the ninth century, some of which would extend into the maritime realm beginning under the rule of al-Hakam I (796–822). During the same period, the emirs used the principles and terms of the treatises written on the Anatolian frontier to spread propaganda about their commitment in the name of jihad.[31] In the tenth century, these same references were borrowed by Ahmad al-Razi, a self-described faithful disciple of al-Tabari and official chronicler of Caliph ʿAbd al-Rahman III (912–961) who imposed the only known version of the history of al-Andalus "dictated by the caliph." In fact, this work of history is only partially known to us, through the version transcribed by the eleventh-century Andalusian scholar Ibn Hayyan, which has itself reached us in an incomplete state.[32] Other "histories" of al-Andalus appear in later chronicles, notably that by Ibn ʿIdhari of Marrakesh (d. after 1312), which is the only universal chronicle—covering all the periods of Islam—to have survived in its entirety in the Islamic West, and that by Ibn al-Athir, a historian from Mosul.[33]

The western Mediterranean stood out as a sea on which the Andalusians had no enemies, beginning with the conquest of the Iberian Peninsula and ending with the arrival of the Vikings in 844. Indeed, with a few rare exceptions, the range of the Byzantine fleet, the only enduring Christian naval force until the end of the tenth century, did not reach beyond Sicily, the Ifriqiyan coasts, and Sardinia. Despite a few naval operations backed by Charlemagne and Louis the Pious and carried out in Corsica and Sardinia early in the ninth century to repel Muslim raids, the Latin coasts under the rule of the Carolingian empire were most often left defenseless, prey to the razzias of Islamic sailors as far as Italy. The situation for the Latins only got worse as the Carolingian empire gradually fell apart.[34]

The jihad on the frontier marches was described using terminology similar to that found in the other regions of the Mediterranean frontier, the origins of which extend back to the Syrian march of the Abbasid period.[35] As in the East, the recording of combat practices here had become a specialty of jurists.[36] Their accounts are as economical as those by the Iraqi historians: references to border expeditions are limited to *sayfas* (summer expeditions) led or directly backed by the emir of Córdoba, to the exclusion of seasonal razzias by frontier soldiers (outside of extraordinary events). In reality, until the reign of al-Hakam I, campaigns were primarily directed against internal dissident movements; most took place in the regions of the marches and were often followed by incursions onto Christian soil.[37] Ultimately, it was the Asturians and Carolingians who succeeded in pushing the border to the Douro in the west and to Barcelona in the east. Once ʿAbd al-Rahman II came to power and put an end to the major period of revolts in frontier cities, the image of the ghazi sovereign began to spread, heralding the policy that ʿAbd al-Rahman's illustrious homonym would uphold beginning in 912.[38]

During the same period, the Arabic sources never mention naval expeditions carried out by communities of autonomous sailors, which theoretically implies that these sailors enjoyed total autonomy. In short, the situation here is the same as the one described on the land frontiers, in that nongovernmental expeditions are only referred to when Christian victims had cause to report them, in general due to issues of internal policy. Since the Umayyad emirs never set foot on a seagoing ship, only the Latin and Greek sources about the eastern Mediterranean provide any information about naval operations that set off from Andalusian and Maghrebi coastlines: the presentation of the emirs' naval commitment is practically identical to the record left by the Abbasid historians.[39]

As the first Andalusian sovereign to be confronted with an enemy from the sea (the Vikings), 'Abd al-Rahman II decided in 844 to make use of a fleet. Like his ancestors in Syria, he put in place infrastructures necessary to realize this new initiative: after the sack of Seville, he had a dockyard built to cover the Atlantic maritime front, as well as a Friday mosque, an emirate souk (*qaysariyya*), and fortifications to defend the city.[40]

The report by Ibn al-Qutiyya, a tenth-century Andalusian man of letters, on the founding of the Seville dockyard repeats the comments made by al-Bakri, another Andalusian man of letters, in an account of the founding of the Tunis dockyard in 702:

> Then, to guard against all eventualities, 'Abd al-Rahman [II] ordered the construction of a dockyard (*dar al-sina'a*) in Seville and the building of boats. To this end, men of the seas were recruited on the coasts of al-Andalus and were given good salaries, and tools and machines for spitting naphta were obtained. This way, when the Vikings (*Majus*) made their second incursion in the year 858–859, under the reign of Emir Muhammad (852–886), men went out to meet them at the mouth of the river in Seville and drove them away; a few ships were burned and they left.[41]

Defensive measures taken on Andalusian shores were very similar to those on other Muslim coastlines of the Mediterranean, leading in particular to the founding of ribats. The sovereign also took advantage of this structure to attempt to put the Balearics under Umayyad control: "He sent troops charged with fighting them [the Majorcans] to punish them and subdue their pride, since they lacked any respect for the treaties and interfered with the Muslim ships that passed in their vicinity. 300 vessels attacked them and God, heavily favoring our side, gave our troops victory, so that they conquered the greater part of these islands."[42] Simultaneously, Andalusian and probably Maghrebi sailors followed the sovereigns' orders to hammer away at the coasts of Provence, a campaign that peaked with the sack of the Saint-Césaire monastery in 850. However, neither these campaigns nor any of the razzias against Christian coasts were mentioned in the Arabic sources, while the scope of the attacks coordinated by the Muslim sovereigns suggests that the same crews participated in the razzias on Provence and in subduing the archipelago, and that their moorings were in ports on the eastern rim.[43] The chronicles also credit 'Abd al-Rahman II with spreading the institution of ribat on the Iberian Peninsula.[44] One states, "Once the Normans had advanced all the way to Almería and had gone around the coasts of al-Andalus, the Arabs used Almería as an observation point and built watchtowers there. The Muslims performed ribat there."[45]

To be legitimate, the description of the coastal defenses had to connect these measures with the principles on jihad stated by the caliphs of Baghdad. However, the implementation of defensive measures also allowed the dissident prince to assert his autonomy by taking responsibility for defending the territory he controlled.

THE SILENCES OF THE COASTAL MAGHREB

Due to the absence of emirate chronicles, we do not have enough information about the area west of Ifiriqya to complete the already tenuous picture of Islam's Mediterranean policies in the ninth century. However, thanks to al-Bakri, we know that the appearance of ribats along the Mediterranean and Atlantic coasts of western Africa was a consequence of the first two Viking invasions, in 844 and at the end of the following decade. The ribats to the south of Tangier in Asilah and on the coast of the Rif in Nekor, the capital of the Salihid emirate, were founded after the Norsemen's attack in 844, which was the first assault on this region beyond the reach of Byzantine ships since the Arab conquest. However, al-Bakri's slightly more detailed account of the development of the ribat of Asilah suggests that the appropriation of the port, which had been abandoned since or perhaps even before the Arab conquest, was not undertaken by the Idrisid emirs but rather by the Lawata tribe.[46] One of the emirs, then in control of the area of the strait, seized the ribat long after these events. This type of operation was frequent throughout the Muslim regions of the western Mediterranean and indicates the limits of the sovereigns' actual power.

6

THE MEDITERRANEAN OF THE WESTERN CALIPHS

"In the time of the Islamic Empire, the Muslims controlled the borderlands of the entire Byzantine sea. . . . But later, when the ʿUbaydi [Fatimid] and Umayyad states were overcome by apathy and impotence and entered into a phase of decline, the Christians set out to conquer the islands."[1] This assessment from the introduction (al-Muqaddima) to Ibn Khaldun's masterwork *The Book of Examples* establishes Muslim naval supremacy in the Mediterranean in the tenth century. Contemporary historians frequently quote Ibn Khaldun's words, for the tenth century is often presented as the only period during which the Muslim states gained the upper hand at sea, at the expense of the Christians. The tenth century is also considered the period when the Islamic Mediterranean was at its most prosperous. The historian associated Muslim superiority with the advent in the region of caliphates far more powerful than the emirates they replaced. Owing to their greater wealth, the caliphs were able to conduct a naval policy that gave them the means to control the maritime space for which they competed with the Latins and the Greeks. This shows the extent to which the fourteenth-century Arab scholar believed that control of the Mediterranean was a crucial issue in the clash between Islamic and Christian countries, at a time when the sea had practically fallen under the exclusive control of the Latins. Ibn Khaldun attributed Arab decline to the sovereigns, rather than to the communities of sailors that populated the shores under Muslim domination.

The contrast between the century of the Mediterranean caliphates and earlier periods seems all the more pronounced given that the advent of the two sovereignties marked a historiographic leap that shifted the Mediterranean out of a long period of silence into a production that would constantly increase from that point: as of the tenth century, chronicles, works of geography, legal texts, and also documents from commercial activity—in particular the letters of the Cairo Geniza—provided a far more imposing body of data on naval activities. Amid the general development of seafaring and trade, this production fed on the rivalry between the two caliphates and their ambitions on the scale of the Mediterranean and Islam as a whole. This media war broke the silence of the Muslim regions' maritime world. Now competing with Latin and Greek versions, Arab texts revealed the relationship between the Muslim sovereigns and the sea in a new light.

THE AGE OF THE UMAYYAD CALIPHS

The advent of the Umayyad caliphate in 929 also marked the advent of geography in al-Andalus, a geography "[imitative] of, certainly, but not a slave to the Iraqi tradition."[2] This geography would reach its peak with *The Book of Roger,* written by al-Idrisi toward the middle of the twelfth century. The Umayyad caliphate generated the production of a geography alternative to Eastern geography, dedicated to the Umayyads' domain and neighboring regions, in particular the Maghreb, the major objective of caliphal expansionism. Having spent most of his time in the region, al-Warraq wrote a *Book of Roads and Kingdoms* in which he clearly affirmed his attachment to the Baghdad tradition but devoted himself to the description of western North Africa; his analysis of the region was reportedly completed by several "reports" sent to Córdoba.[3] While his entire body of work has been lost, a significant part of it was reproduced by the Andalusian geographer al-Bakri.

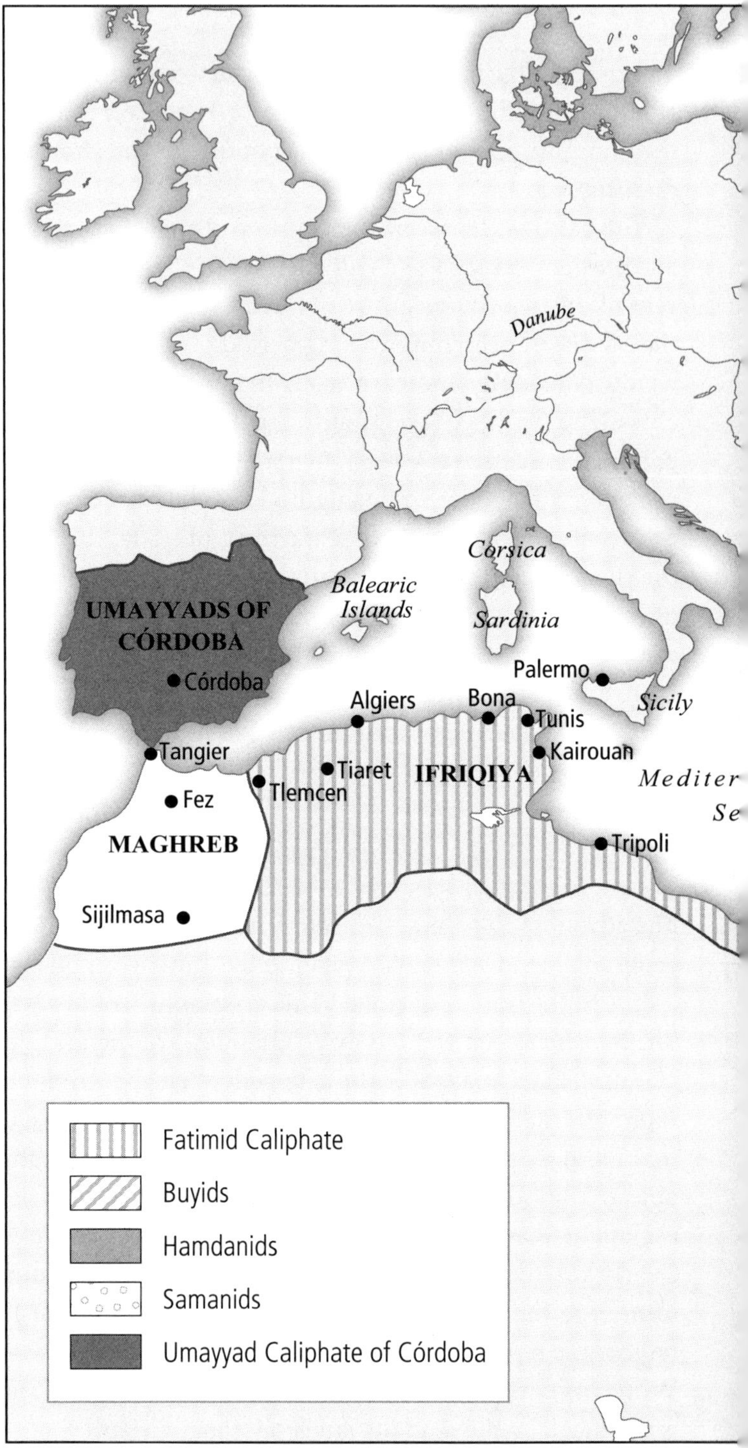

Danube
Corsica
Balearic Islands
Sardinia
UMAYYADS OF CÓRDOBA
Córdoba
Palermo
Sicily
Algiers
Bona
Tunis
Kairouan
Tangier
Tiaret
IFRIQIYA
Tlemcen
Fez
MAGHREB
Tripoli
Sijilmasa
Fatimid Caliphate
Buyids
Hamdanids
Samanids
Umayyad Caliphate of Córdoba

hates and the Mediterranean in the tenth and eleventh centuries

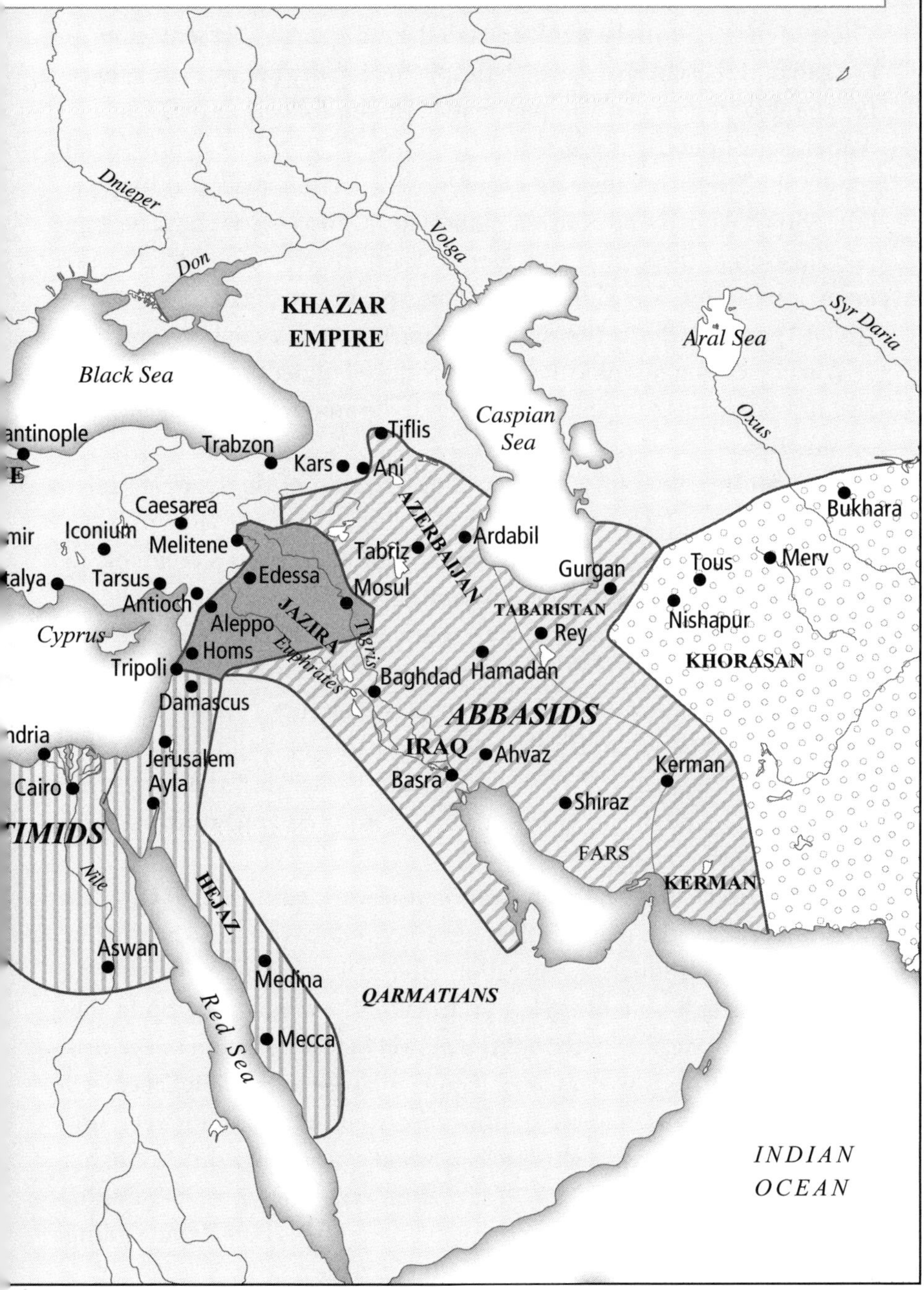

Ahmad al-Razi and ʿIsa al-Razi wrote the official chronicle of the reign of the Umayyad caliphs ʿAbd al-Rahman III and his son al-Hakam II. These dynastic annals were preceded by a general presentation of the Muslim Iberian space, which despite its brevity became a reference for the geographers of the peninsula. In the following periods, the Andalusians' descriptive literature remained faithful to a "provincial geography," thus creating a new center of the Islamic space, in competition with Baghdad and Kairouan and later Cairo.[4] As we have seen, a reevaluation of the spatial balances of Islam in favor of the Mediterranean was under way during the same period in Eastern scholarly circles, particularly in the hands of Ibn Hawqal, a contemporary of al-Warraq. Chronographic literature produced under the Umayyad and Fatimid caliphates considerably increased the amount of Mediterranean production.

By devoting some fifty pages to a description of the regions under Umayyad control, Ahmad al-Razi isolated the caliphal space from the rest of the Dar al-Islam. His geographic study served as a preamble to the chronicle, which was itself devoted to the history of the space governed from Córdoba, from the Arab conquest to the caliphate: "The love of history and historical investigation prevailed in his case: it was not then a discipline to which Andalusians devoted themselves. . . . He was therefore the first to codify the rules of historical composition in al-Andalus. . . . Between the two of them [the father and the son], they provided the Andalusians with a science not previously successfully practiced by that people."[5]

In this tribute to the father by his son, the work's innovative character does not exclude the major influence of Baghdad: Ahmad, who died in 959, wrote his chronicle a generation after al-Tabari, whom he considered his master, wrote his.[6] He too drew on the *akhbar,* the traditions he quotes to cover the history of the period before the reign of the Andalusian caliphate. This version of history adapted to the caliphal era led to the disappearance of earlier, now obsolete traditions. However, unlike his model's universal chronicle, Ahmad's history was limited to his masters' territory. In this way, Ahmad al-Razi, known as al-Ta'rikhi, "the Chronicler," imposed the annalistic genre in his homeland, adding a personal touch adapted to his sovereign's wishes.

By beginning with the Peninsula's geography, Ahmad could first present the state of the territory reigned over by the caliph, succinctly enumerating the Andalusian realm's riches, cities, and administrative framework. Nonetheless, the few lines devoted to each district are sufficient to appreciate the order and wealth that reigned under the caliphs' iron rule, and they set up the short geographic introduction as a preamble to the chronicle of the reign of the two caliphs. The chronicle first describes the age of the emirs (756–912), following the conquest—the description of which has been lost—and until the accession of 'Abd al-Rahman III, whose reign opens the second part (912–976), devoted to the reign of the two caliphs and written in a style very different from that used to recount the earlier period of the emirate. The history of the reign of al-Hakam III, written by Ahmad's son 'Isa, is presented as the continuation of the father's work. Here, al-Andalus is shown as the perfect model of caliphal government, to be reproduced throughout the Dar al-Islam. Consequently, it appears as the center of the world, sufficient unto itself. This picture, presented in the form of a final assessment, was completed by a history of Córdoba, also written by the younger al-Razi and now lost. Though there is a significant imbalance between geography and history here, these two parts should be seen as a single whole.[7]

The Assertion of Umayyad Sovereignty on the Mediterranean

This objective is clearly expressed in the chronicle through the reproduction of letters and panegyrics addressed to the sovereign, particularly those by the representatives of the communities of the Maghreb al-Aqsa (Morocco), who rushed to Medina Azahara to make official their peoples' support for the Umayyad cause. Among them was Muhammad al-Jazar, "the emir of the Zanatas," whose tribute to the caliph was read before the sovereign: "Obedience [due to the caliph] against disobedience, until God has opened to the caliph the east of the earth and its western part, its plains, its steep regions, its deserts and its seas, by our favor and our hand, and extended his power, if God wills it, to the end of Iraq, thus reclaiming the legacy of the caliphate [of his ancestors], pious and noble fathers."[8]

Vital control of the maritime space became one of the major means of demonstrating the universality of the Umayyad sovereignty. The struggle with the Umayyads' Fatimid rivals for control of the maritime territory and especially the Maghreb considerably enhanced the strategic importance of the Mediterranean. The Strait of Gibraltar was the first objective on an itinerary that was set to end in Baghdad and that the caliph's ancestor 'Abd al-Rahman I had followed in the other direction to Córdoba after the fall of the eastern Umayyads. The Muslim West thus became the principal battlefield of two rival caliphates. And now that the Mediterranean had the potential to become the fastest route to the East, naval supremacy was decided in the western basin.

Direct maritime clashes were rare, though the sack of Almería in 954 illustrates how violent the struggle could be. Consequently, the Latin coasts were what was crucially at stake for the two naval powers of Islam as long as the Shiite sovereigns remained in Ifriqiya. In the zone running along the Peninsula's land border, the sea was the principal theater of operations for the razzias launched by the Umayyads in the name of jihad, to the point that the commander of the fleet was considered equal to the commander of the caliph's armies on the land frontier. Muhammad b. al-Rumahis, then 'Abd al-Rahman b. al-Rumahis, both admirals of the caliphate, acquired a position and a level of prestige that put them on equal footing with Ghalib, the caliph's general-in-chief:

> The most important business that the Umayyad caliphs had to deal with was only settled after they consulted three people: the general of the army of Saragossa, administrative center of the Upper March . . . , the qadi of Córdoba, capital of the caliphate and gathering place for scholars . . . , finally the head of the fleet at Almería, because that city contained the naval shipyard for al-Andalus and because it was in the central part of the empire; to a certain extent, under the Umayyads the command of the fleet shared sultanate power with the caliph: one commanded on land, the other [in the name of the caliph] on sea.[9]

Defending the coasts remained another major obligation. This required the maintenance of a fleet, particularly to face the Vikings, who were a threat until 975. Naval operations against Christians or Norsemen were now exclusively decided on by the caliphate, while such enterprises on the part of the emirs in the ninth century were obscured. Only their engagement against the Norsemen, who had attacked the coasts of Islam, was not to sink into oblivion. In the context of a media competition with the Fatimids, several formats praising the Umayyads' naval mastery were mobilized to present the fleet and the sovereignty of the seas as prestigious emblems of the caliphate's universality.

'Abd al-Rahman III could also rely on a long-standing and effective naval infrastructure, thanks to the extensive experience of the many sailors' establishments dotting the coasts of the western Mediterranean that had rallied behind Córdoba. Formed in the second half of the ninth century on the site of the future caliphal city, the community of Pechina had prospered beginning in the 880s, during the unrest of the late ninth century.[10] This city of sailors grew wealthy thanks to the sea, both through acts of piracy carried out on Christian coastlines and through commerce—particularly the slave trade—which had lucrative outlets, notably on the capital's markets. According to the opinion expressed in the caliphal sources and largely taken up by modern historiography, these Andalusian sailors occasionally worked on behalf of the emirs: in 902, 'Abd Allah (888–912) succeeded in getting their help to subdue the Balearic Islands, which had previously escaped Umayyad authority.[11] Nonetheless, this venture, which mobilized no fewer than three hundred ships—a large number, according to the standards of the Arabic chronicles—is presented as a "private" venture.

As soon as he reestablished the sultanate's authority over Seville and the zone of the strait in 914, the caliph took control of al-Andalus's rich naval potential. The first opportunity to express his authority arose through the fight against the Umayyads' worst enemy, the rebel Ibn Hafsun (d. 917), who was then solidly established in his capital of Barbastro in the south of the Peninsula.[12] According to one chronicle, "Al-Nasir entered Algeciras on June 1, 914. . . . During his stay in Algeciras, he made arrangements to establish his authority over the sea and protect access to it for the people of both shores. He ordered that all the seafaring vessels based in Malaga, Seville, and the other centers in his power bring their equipment along with their reliable crews . . . and go to the entrance of Algeciras. . . . Since that time, he governed the sea."[13]

The revelation that the caliphs had regained control over the Peninsula from the very beginning of their reign through reorganization of the fleet and assertion of their claim to govern territorial waters was not happenstance. The primary objective here was to quash the power of the rebel solidly established in the south of the Peninsula. Ibn Hafsun had created ties with the Idrisid Maghreb, which provided him with supplies. Aside from serving to cut off his supplies, the control of both shores through naval policy is presented as the first maritime investment in Umayyad history. However, ʻAbd al-Rahman II had earlier taken similar measures, aimed at controlling maritime circulation when traffic was growing on the Alboran Sea.[14]

The Caliphal Rupture, a Writers' Invention

Among the many mediums that helped to demonstrate the dawn of a new era—for want of a new strategy—the monumental and administrative program for coastal cities and fortifications is evidence of the process by which the caliph appropriated the coasts.[15] His forbears, at least as of the reign of ʻAbd al-Rahman II, had already sponsored an ambitious program to protect the coastlines by fortifying coastal cities; erecting fortifications and, in particular, ribats; and stationing fleets in Seville and Tortosa, both cities with shipyards. However, the caliph now choreographed several spectacular projects, while the scribes remained very quiet about earlier undertakings.[16]

The practice of ribat in al-Andalus, which dated back to the emirate of ʻAbd al-Rahman II, became the exclusive domain of the caliphate. Dunas de Guardamar, which was founded by volunteers to perform ribat toward the end of the ninth century, was appropriated on behalf of the caliph, as indicated by the inscription on the foundations of the ribat's mosque, built between 933 and 941.[17] The redevelopment of the ribat, which primarily consisted of the construction of a "great" mosque, allowed it to be presented as an Umayyad edifice, despite the fact that it had been founded by volunteers for jihad, without any known participation on the sovereign's part. Other places of ribat, such as the Setúbal Peninsula to the south of the Portuguese capital, were also claimed by the caliphs, in this case within the framework of the administrative reorganization of the coastline at the beginning of ʿAbd al-Rahman III's reign. The populating of the area's mountainous southern part, known to this day as Arrábida (al-Rabita), was described by Ahmad al-Razi in a Castilian version: "At the edge of the regions of Beja and Lisbon are mountains which we call the Benamocer [Banu Matar] mountains and which the inhabitants call Arrabida [al-Rabita]."[18] Located between the mouths of the Tagus and Sado Rivers, the peninsula occupies a major strategic position from which one can monitor land and especially maritime routes.[19] The Banu Matar Berbers justified this appropriation of the area by performing ribat, including surveillance and military protection, but now did so in the name of the caliph. Other Berbers, the Banu Danis, settled a little farther south, on the river Sado, close to the coast, by "founding" what would become the city of Qasr Abu Danis (present-day Alcácer do Sal) on a site already inhabited. The caliphate chose this city to be the capital of the region (*kura* of al-Qasr). When the caliph personally took the reins in the Gharb al-Andalus toward the end of the 920s, the region was reorganized and given new administrative boundaries, as in other areas of the Peninsula: "[In 344 / 945] vizier Isa b. Futays [was charged with] monitoring the letters [sent by] the inhabitants of the marches (*thughur*), the seaboards (*sawahil*), the capes (*atraf*), and other places of that kind."[20]

Presented as a complete overhaul of the administration attested to by lists of gubernatorial appointments (governors were regularly replaced), the organization of coastal defenses as an extension of the land marches created the impression that for the first time the coast was defended from one end of the territory to the other—despite the fact that ʿAbd al-Rahman II and Muhammad (852–886) had both taken similar measures. Likewise, it was no longer possible for communities of sailors to be autonomous, now that any naval operation had to be decided on by the caliph and passed down by the admiralty.

The status of the Tortosa fortress located on the left bank of the Ebro, just upriver from its mouth, initially changed under the reign of al-Hakam I, when it was made the regional capital and a military and naval base. It was from here that the general (*qaid*) appointed by the emir organized razzias on Catalan territory. It was also here that the "pirates" described in the Latin sources embarked in the service of Córdoba, leaving to pillage monasteries and islands or, in 830, to lend their support to the Ifriqiyan Muslims in Sicily in the name of emirate jihad.[21] Tortosa had been a leading military and naval base since the ninth century, yet it was a program of major building works, including the construction of a dockyard, that allegedly turned it into a true military capital under the Umayyad caliphate.

The city's growth in the tenth and eleventh centuries is indisputable and can notably be measured by the number of scholars who were born or lived there and whose memory has been preserved by the authors of Andalusian biographies. Al-Turtushi (d. 1126) stands out among these local scholars.[22] While naval activity had been intense during the emirate period, it seems to have faded in the face of the large-scale urban planning projects launched by the caliph himself after he visited Tortosa in 924, as well as the city's rapid expansion in every field. An inscription on the dockyard's foundations is a fine epigraphic record of the sovereign's urban policy, though sadly it is all that remains: "Ordered the creation of this building, to be used as a yard for maritime equipment and ships, Allah's servant 'Abd al-Rahman, emir of the believers, may Allah assist him!"[23]

The city's ramparts, made of cut stone and including four gates, were erected under the direction of the governor who had coordinated work on the dockyard. The Friday mosque was built in 955–956, with five naves, four baths, and a market. The enumeration closes with a reference to the frenzy of commercial and military activity in the port.[24] Thus it is made to appear that the city's principal structures and axes were exclusively built during the caliphal period, to replace what the texts present as a mere citadel built to face the infidel and provide an anchorage.

Though the Andalusian authors all agree that Almería was founded in 954–955, the date of the creation of the city is problematic in that this site was already the location of the dockyard for the caliphate's fleet, which had been redeveloped in 931, more than twenty years before the new city was built, on the port installations of the city of Pechina twelve kilometers (7.5 miles) upriver. In fact, the new city was located on the site of two earlier establishments: Pechina's harbor area and a ribat consisting of towers (*mariyya*) built and occupied by a group of Yemenites at the request of 'Abd al-Rahman II after the Viking attack of 844. The sovereign had already asserted his hold over this city of sailors and its naval establishments before the founding of the caliphal port. In 933, he dispatched a new governor to officially take possession of the naval installations in his name and turn them into the seat of the admiralty of the caliphate of Córdoba. After being pillaged and destroyed by the Fatimid squadron, these installations were replaced by a fortified city containing new naval installations in 954 or 955. The Andalusian geographer Abu l-'Abbas al-'Udhri (d. 1085), an inhabitant of the city, summed up the magnitude of the construction project as follows: "Description of the city: Almería is not a city of old structures, with the exception that the Arabs used it as a ribat after erecting defenses to that effect. The people found shelter and practiced the life of ribat there, though there were no buildings and no homes. It was surrounded by an unassailable rampart, which was built on the order of al-Nasir, emir of the believers, 'Abd al-Rahman III, in the year 343 / 954–955."[25]

Some writers, like al-Rushati, a native of the area, focused on the local founding of Pechina, which prospered as of the 880s, during the period of unrest that weakened the Umayyad dynasty (875–912). It was located upriver from the Andarax valley in a good agricultural zone but derived most of its wealth from the sea. The settlement of Almería in 1011 or 1012, the year al-Rushati chose as the date for the birth of the new regional capital, coincided with the period when the inhabitants of Pechina left their town to move to the new city, which diminishes the caliph's achievement.[26]

However, it was the caliphal appropriation of the dockyard that was to be remembered as the event that turned the city into the caliphate's port, before the attack of the Mahdi's fleet and the building of the new city:

> At the beginning of *muharram* 322 [January 933] of this year, al-Nasir dismissed Abd al-Malik b. Sa'id, known as Ibn Abi Hamama of Pechina, and chose Ahmad b. 'Isa b. Ahmad b. Abi 'Adba, governor of the *kura* of Elvira, to manage it [the fleet and the dockyard]; he entrusted him with repairing the fleet that was established in the Almería dockyard; he repaired, enlarged, and fitted it out with all that was necessary, all things he promptly took care of in Almería, to perfection. When this was

> done, al-Nasir sent him mercenaries from Córdoba, [under the command of] the generals Saʿid b. Yunus and ʿAmr b. Maslama al-Baji, so they would lead the expedition he had ordered. Ibn Yunus . . . headed for the Frankish country. . . . To his general Saʿid b. Yunus he gave the order to reinforce [the defenses] in Ceuta.[27]

This choice was justified by the fact that the port had become the most active one on the Peninsula. The presence of a ribat had also given it a certain symbolic power, as indicated by the name chosen for the new city: al-Mariyya, which refers to the towers that had been erected to house the *murabitun* and established the city as a direct rival of Mahdiyya.[28] In a second phase, the city founded on the site of the former town's shipyards was given every consideration owed to caliphal establishments: the most notable structures of the major construction project were the *madina*'s formidable rampart, which protected the shore and anchorage (defenseless at the time of the Fatimid attack in 954); the dockyard, which was fortified and protected by a tower that would house a garrison in the next century; structures for commerce and skilled trade, including two *qaysariyya,* closed markets dependent on the power of the sultan, one of which was inside the dockyard and the other adjoining the Friday mosque; the baths; and the citadel, which was then only a shelter, without a princely edifice.[29] These served as reminders of the invisible presence of a caliph who never once visited the city, while the squadron embodied caliphal sovereignty.

Whether in Almería, Tortosa, Seville, Algeciras, or Ceuta, the caliphate's ports were designed to offer astounded visitors the sight of the power of al-Andalus and its fleet, built in the caliphate's dockyards.

The Dar al-Sinaʿa and the Fleet, Symbols of the Umayyad Caliphate's Universal Ambitions

Pechina became the seat of the admiralty, a choice al-ʿUdhri justified by stating that "the city contained the naval shipyards because it was in the central part of the empire," the place from which the caliph had decided to launch ships to conquer the Mediterranean. Due to the men of letters' limited interest in technical details, the descriptions of the dockyard's functions are perfunctory: "Its dockyard is the oldest [of this type] known and was divided in two parts. In the first were the warships with the equipment; in the second part [was] the *qaysariyya*. Everything to do with the dockyard is organized in such a manner to avoid any problem and the merchants store their goods there in safety and people come there from all over."[30]

Other Andalusian authors made a connection between earlier establishments founded by the emirate and those built by the Umayyad caliph. Indeed, a few brief references, all in Andalusian texts, describe the foundation of dockyards before the advent of the caliphate. The first reference is by al-Bakri and deals with the dockyard in Tunis, built on Caliph 'Abd al-Malik's order in 698. Since the new Ifriqiyan dockyard was built by Coptic workmen from Egypt, a filiation is established with the dockyard of Alexandria "founded" on Caliph 'Umar's order. The second reference is by Ibn al-Qutiyya, who inspired or wrote a tenth-century Andalusian chronicle that reports 'Abd al-Rahman II's decision in 844 to fit out the Seville dockyard to prevent further Viking attacks. This information is also found in Ibn Hayyan's chronicle. The organization described is the same and includes the hiring of skilled laborers, soldiers, and sailors considered the best in their areas of expertise and paid a fortune for their labor: Egyptians in Acre, then Tunis; Persians in Syria; Berbers at the mouth of the Ebro; sailors from the east coast of al-Andalus; and Greek fire launchers sent to the admiral port from Córdoba for each new expedition. This practice was reminiscent of an old royal custom, whose origin dates back at least to Achaemenid Persia, on which the caliphs heavily relied from the beginning of the conquests. However, it was not considered useful to describe the operation of these shipyards, which bustled with laborers and sailors poorly regarded by those in power, where all these trades considered at the very least worthless, if not vile, were mobilized to build and maintain ships.

The Andalusian authors did focus their attention on the dockyards' architecture, but only for its defensive aspects, which had nothing to do with the operation of a shipyard. They were particularly interested when the edifice was also used as a barracks or selected to be the site of a palace, as seen in this description of the building of the Algeciras dockyard, also erected during the caliphal period and later used as a palace for the Hammudids (1035–1059): "There was a dockyard (*dar al-sinaʿa*) in Algeciras that the emir of the believers ʿAbd Al-Rahman III b. Muhammad built for his fleets; he had it built solidly and surrounded it by tall walls; later, during the period of the *fitna* [early eleventh century], the independent princes of Algeciras turned this dockyard into a palace."[31]

However imprecise, these few references to the architecture of dockyards built on the caliph's orders from Tortosa to the capital of Andalusia and the African coast only interested the Arab authors because of the architecture's sultanate character, as was the case with the *qaysariyya,* or sultanate markets. In this way, the Umayyad dockyard perpetuated the caliphate's universal authority in the port cities and, by extension, on the sea, and had done so since the time of Muʿawiya.[32]

While the association between the dockyard and the fleet is inherent, the sovereigns were proudest of the fleet. Once he was made caliph, ʿAbd al-Rahman never saw his beloved ships again, but poets' verses kept alive the memory of the siege of Seville and the measures he had taken in Algeciras to create his own naval force. Similarly, al-Hakam II never visited the coasts after he had become the caliph, yet this did not stop him from following in his father's footsteps, without ever leaving his palace. As for Ibn Abi ʿAmir al-Mansur (978–1002), officially a servant of the caliph, he employed the fleet as backup for campaigns against areas close to the sea, but it was no longer used to support his legitimacy.

To launch his campaigns in the Maghreb, the *hajib,* as the Andalusian sovereign was officially referred to, had to look after his squadrons: already under the Umayyads and even more so during the African expeditions, the military leader had supervised the extensive fortification work on Ceuta, the Andalusians' African bridgehead.[33] Al-Andalus's two seaboards were also restructured on the occasion of two of the reign's most prestigious naval expeditions (*sayfa*). Restructuring of the ports and fleets on the Andalusian territory's eastern rim may have motivated Ibn Abi ʿAmir al-Mansur's decision to have his army take a detour through the area of Murcia—an unusual choice for a campaign headed for Catalonia—before following the coast and laying siege to

Barcelona in 985.[34] The expedition targeting Santiago de Compostela in 997 required the assistance of the fleet for logistical reasons and led the *hajib* to build naval infrastructures, notably a dockyard in the harbor of the estuary of the Sado River, at the foot of Alcácer do Sal.[35]

The Caliph's Fleet, Emblem of the Universal Investment of the Umayyad Caliphs of Córdoba

Never present on the battlefield, whether on land (as of 939) or at sea, the caliph of Medina Azahara remained "immobile" in his palace but was at the center of an extraordinary choreography of departures of land and sea expeditions.[36] Those that took place from 912 to 942 and 971 to 975 were described by Ahmad and 'Isa al-Razi (and copied by Ibn Hayyan).[37] The importance ascribed to maritime affairs here is exceptional in the Arabic historiographic landscape of the Middle Ages. The first novelty, compared to the emirate period, is in the appearance of paragraphs specifically devoted to the fleet's movements year by year, presented under the title *khabar al-ustul* (report on the fleet) or simply *al-ustut* (the squadron); when war operations in the Maghreb were discussed, the account of naval operations on the African coast was sometimes preceded by the title *al-'idwa* (the shore). It can reasonably be assumed that Ahmad al-Razi had had access to "archives" of the caliphal administration, perhaps even of the admiralty and African affairs. The *Muqtabis* features more than twenty references to the fleet's movements between 912 and 941. The new maritime district of the Strait of Gibraltar, which was named the region of the "two shores" (*'idwatayn*), was placed under the authority of the Almería admiralty. Under the reign of al-Hakam II, nine fleet movements were reported from 970 to 974, most notably those in response to the Viking incursions of 966 and 972:

> On Saturday 21 of Ramadan of that year [July 6, 972], Caliph al-Mustansir bi-llah received Qaysar, Sa'd al-Jadari and Rashiq (his father al-Nasir li-Din Allah's principal *mawlas*), as well as Isma'il b. al-Shaykh, 'Abd al-Rahman b. Yusuf b. Armatil, and 'Abd al-Rahman b. Abi Yawshan [among the principal high-

> born / free men] and ordered them to prepare to launch a campaign with the squadrons at their disposal: those of Seville and Almería. All were given ceremonial garb; they went away with decorated swords and received many gifts. They left for their destination from Medina Azahara, on the way to Seville, preceded by expeditions of supplies, on the 23rd of the month of Ramadan.[38]

These accounts are structured to systematically emphasize the essential role played by the caliph through descriptions of the formalities that accompanied mobilization, as was also the case with land expeditions. The scene always takes place in the reception room of the caliph's palace. Though sitting still on his divan, the sovereign is the focus of attention: through his silent presence, he controlled every stage of the ceremony, from the presentation of the staff of authority to the reading of the bulletins announcing that the mission was accomplished.[39] As of 933, the descriptions of the fleet's sorties were entirely kept to the throne room, which constantly remained at the heart of the account, rather than the sea or the squadron's anchorage. While the fleet was prepared in the Andalusian dockyards, then gathered in Ceuta, it could not raise anchor until the arrival of the admiral (*qaid al-bahr*) who had traveled to the caliph's residence to receive the command insignia and gifts. Similarly, supplies and special armament such as Greek fire were stored in Córdoba, which was also home to the elite troops, until the departure of the procession that paraded to the fleet's anchorages in Seville for operations on the Atlantic and in Almería for operations on the Mediterranean.

Once the caliphate imposed its direct authority over all the ports and their fleets, every naval operation had to be included in the annals, for it participated in demonstrating Umayyad sovereignty in the context of the jihad orchestrated by the caliph. The sailing of the squadron was an opportunity to praise the qualities of the proud armada: "That year [931], al-Nasir sent the entire squadron, perfectly equipped, toward the African coast, the biggest [fleet] that any sovereign ever fitted out . . . by the number of its very well-equipped units and its many crews, of which the people of the coast widely spread news, though they also feared it. . . . ‘Ubayd Allah b. Yahya b. Idris mentioned this famous squadron in excellent verses, in a panegyric in honor of al-Nasir, describing its composition for the year’s land and sea campaigns.”[40]

The extension of the territory of war to the sea made it possible to significantly expand the imperial space as far as Sicily—where Umayyad vessels attacked a ship belonging to the Ismaili caliph, provoking a violent reaction that led to the sack of Almería—and the Christian coastline, which had apparently previously been left to private enterprises. Though al-Istakhri never left the Muslim East, he was the first Arabic author to mention the existence of Jabal Qilal, also known as the Fraxinetum of Moors, located near Saint-Tropez and shown on the map as an island between the “Island of Slavs” (Sicily) and the coast of Rum. His disciple Ibn Hawqal gave a slightly more detailed account of this Muslim enclave in the South of France:

> [Jalal Qilal is] located in the region of the Franks, in the hands of the fighters for faith. . . . It was Muslims who made this place livable as soon as they settled there. They became a threat to the Franks, but it was impossible to reach them because they were posted on the slope of a mountain, in a den accessible from a single side, by a single road where their precautions were effective. . . . Mallorca is an important island governed by [the caliph] of al-Andalus. Jabal al-Qibal also belongs to that State.[41]

According to Ibn Hawqal, who was faithful to Ahmad al-Razi, Hugh of Arles, Count of Provence (d. 947), sent a delegation to Córdoba in 941, led by a representative of Sunyer, Count of Barcelona, to ask the caliph to put an end to Muslim attacks. The sovereign’s favorable response to this request includes the name of the stronghold’s “military governor” (*qai’d*), Nasr b. Ahmad, to whom he sent orders to decree a ceasefire, as he did to his representative in the Balearics.[42] The fact that the caliph was willing to negotiate with the Catalonian count and Hugh of Arles reveals that he considered them clients. This theoretical reconfiguration of the political map of the western Mediterranean under the control of the caliph included all the Latin states of the Peninsula, the islands, and

Fraxinetum. Four references to maritime attacks against Christian coasts between 933 and 942, as well as the political map of the Umayyad caliph's direct and indirect possessions drawn by Eastern geographers, gave the impression of a considerable expansion of imperial "territory." The Latin coasts were now accessible at all times and the entire Tyrrhenian Sea was considered a full-fledged space of sovereignty, extending the territory of Andalusia and the western Maghreb, since it was controlled by the Umayyad sovereign.[43] The Umayyad squadron served as the link between all these parts of the caliphal domain, making it possible to consider expanding this maritime territory to the coasts of Syria. It was now feasible for the Umayyad sovereign to once again plant the white flag of the descendants of Quraysh in Syria, by taking the opposite path to the one the "exile" 'Abd al-Rahman al-Dakhil had had to follow from 750 to 756.

THE FATIMID CALIPHATE, A POWER FOCUSED ON THE SEA

After the army had eliminated the last Aghlabid emir, 'Ubayd Allah al-Mahdi (909–934) inherited the significant maritime force left by his predecessors: port infrastructures, fleets, and seasoned crews. With his power now bolstered, the caliph hastened to claim the impressive remains of this structure, benefiting from naval activity tied to the ports and dockyards of Sousse, Tunis, Tripoli, and Palermo. Founded in 912, Mahdia was added to this list of maritime centers, but it stood out by briefly becoming the caliph's place of residence in 919. The need to control traffic between Ifriqiya and Sicily, from the Tyrrhenian Sea to Tripolitania, justified carrying maritime policy over from one period to the next, particularly since the reinforcement of the Byzantine presence in southern Italy and at sea, instigated by the Macedonian emperors beginning in the last quarter of the ninth century, which had revived the struggle between Christians and Muslims from the south of the Italian peninsula to the African continent. The move of the caliphal capital to Egypt in 971 did not affect the sovereigns' will to dominate the sea, at least according to what they said.

The wealth of accounts of the Fatimids' maritime commitment serves as an initial clue to the dynasty's particular relationship to the maritime space.[44] Not only do state sources provide a record of the government's sustained ties to the sea, but the preservation of the first "archival" resources—primarily the Geniza letters originating in the "private" sphere of Jewish merchants, written between the tenth and twelfth centuries, and found in a storeroom in the Ben Ezra Synagogue in Fustat—reveals a fundamental change in the role of Egypt, which under the rule of the Shiite caliphs reclaimed its place as the principal Muslim, naval, and commercial center of the eastern Mediterranean.[45] The rich selection of documents found in Ayyubid and Mamluk administrative literature confirms the importance of the sea in the eyes of the Ismaili government. The copying of letters and administrative treatises from the caliphal period in works used to train future managers in the administration of the two Egyptian sultanates bears witness to the admiration of the Egyptian men of letters and Ayyubid sultans, particularly for the structure of the maritime and commercial administration of the dockyards that housed customs and were dependent on a single *diwan*. Some of their administrators were employed by Saladin and devoted part of their texts to preserving treatises of the *sinaʿa,* which was a combined dockyard, customs house, and warehouse for products coming in and going out by sea.[46] The customs organization in Alexandria, Cairo, and other ports of the delta even had a very good reputation among Latins.

In their descriptions of Cairo, men of letters like al-Maqrizi (d. 1442) and Ibn Duqmaq (d. 1406), both historians of the Egyptian capital, highlight the dockyards' important position in the capital at a time when, outside of Barsbay's reign (1422–1437), the Egyptian sultans were no longer active on the Mediterranean.[47] Instead, the period of the Mamluk historians was devoted to putting together a memorial register, the primary purpose of which was the description of the capital. The Fatimids' maritime legacy figured prominently in this endeavor, for it gave a flattering image of the city's maritime past.[48] Cairo's dockyards had been part of the city landscape since 971 and would continue to symbolize the capital's ties to the Mediterranean and the Red Sea until the fifteenth century. In fact, the period is presented as the peak of Egyptian activity on the Mediterranean.[49] According to al-Maqrizi, "In his history, Ibn Abi Tayy' wrote that al-Mu'izz li-Din Allah had had the dockyard (*dar al-sina'a*) of al-Maqs built. He had 600 ships (*marakib*) built there. Such a dockyard had never been seen on a stretch of water bordering a city. As for Al-Musabbihi, he said that it was the son of al-Mu'izz, the caliph of al-'Aziz, who had had the dockyard at al-Maqs built."[50]

The Sea, the Domain of the Caliph

The Egyptian al-Muhallabi (d. 990) was the author of a book of geography entitled *Kitab al-'Azizi,* after the sovereign to whom this universal description that became famous in the author's own time was dedicated. Al-Muhallabi's book seemed to so thoroughly exhaust the resources of the kind of geography associated with the *masalik wa l-mamalik* that he did not have any imitators in Fatimid Egypt.[51] Though the loss of his geography book was not compensated for by the many later references borrowed from his description of the world, a few surviving fragments provide a basic idea of the importance he gave to the maritime space, particularly by drawing up an itinerary of Mediterranean ports, which can be found in the *Book of Curiosities* written in the tenth or eleventh century. Al-Muhallabi also reveals a few aspects of the installations in Cairo.[52] His description, which expresses the imperial ambitions of the caliph now embodied in these installations, should be considered in the context of the reigns of al-Mu'izz and his son al-'Aziz (975–996), as suggested by al-Mu'izz's commission in 964 of a map drawn on blue silk, which was intended to represent the world and accompanied the caliph to the banks of the Nile: "High quality workmanship, woven with gold and all sorts of [silk] thread . . . on which were represented the provinces (*aqalim*) of the earth, its mountains, its seas, its cities, its rivers, and its roads, similar to a geography [map]. It featured representations of Mecca and Medina, which attract the eye, and the names of each of the cities, mountains, countries (*balad*), river, sea, and of each road in gold, silver, or silk [thread]."[53]

The city's rapid development and the numerous references to the places where power was represented, in direct competition with Baghdad, could only boost Egyptian pride and, in particular, that of Cairo's inhabitants. This explains the Mamluk authors' interest in aligning themselves with the prestigious legacy that had allowed the country to become another one of Islam's caliphal hubs. Egypt also had major strategic importance on the Mediterranean chessboard due to its position as an isthmus between the Mediterranean and the Red Sea and its control over Ifriqiya and Sicily, commanding the passage between the two principal basins of the interior sea. The Fatimids were threatening Mesopotamia's previously unrivaled commercial position by capturing a dominant share of trade between the Indian Ocean and the Mediterranean.[54] Ibn Hawqal and al-Muqaddasi—a contemporary of al-Muhallabi—both present the Nile valley as the nodal point of the Mediterranean world. Writing in Persian, the Iranian traveler Nasir Khusraw (d. 1060), who had become a dedicated proponent of Ismailism after his stay at the court, offered an original point of view on this recentering of the Islamic space.[55]

A native of the Oxus region, Nasir Khusraw spent about seven years in Egypt, from 1045 to 1052, before heading for Hejaz, his initial destination, and returning to his homeland to settle in Balkh. He even sought to put himself in the service of Caliph al-Mustansir (1036–1094). His geography book stands out from those of his predecessors, heralding the literary genre of the *rihla,* or travel journal.[56] The Persian traveler reevaluated the evolution of the balance between the regions of Islam, accounting for what was then a palpable rise in power of the Fatimid-controlled eastern Mediterranean.

His description of the Ismaili world is distinctive, tracing two principal axes. The land axis follows the different stages of the conquest, beginning at Sijilmassa. The other axis is maritime and connects the Shiite empire's various Mediterranean territories, then continues via Egypt to Mecca and via Qulzum to the Red Sea and the ocean:

> The Sea of Alexandria stretches to the [land] of Kairouan which is at a distance of 150 parasangs from Egypt. . . . Not far from Sijilmassa is Mahdia, which was founded by al-Mahid, one of the descendants of the prince of believers, Husayn, son of 'Ali, after he achieved the conquest of the Maghreb and al-Andalus.

> When I was in Egypt, the province of Kairouan was under the authority of that country's sovereign. . . . Sicily is one of the islands of the Mediterranean Sea. A vessel leaving from Egypt takes 20 days to reach it. There are also many other islands. Sicily covers 80 square parasangs; it is under the authority of the sultan of Egypt. Ships travel there every year to bring its products back to Egypt. . . . When one leaves Mirs [Fustat] in the direction of the East, one reaches Qulzum [on the Red Sea]. . . . To go from Misr to Mecca, one must walk in the direction of the East. . . . Sultan Mu'izz li-Din Allah took the sea route to go to Egypt. His ships traveled up the Nile nearly as far as Cairo.[57]

The first itinerary was the route taken by 'Ubayd Allah and al-Mu'izz, founders of the two successive imperial spaces. The former had answered the call of his representative (*da'i*) Abu 'Abd Allah, who had seized Ifriqiya in his name, and followed the path to Sijilmassa, where he took refuge to escape the caliph's henchmen. The next stage was Mahdia, the first capital founded by the Shiite caliphate. The region of Kairouan—particularly the caliph's residence of Sabra-Mansuriya—and Sicily, a place of jihad, completed the first caliphs' Maghrebi domain. In a second phase, General Jawhar (d. 992) took control of the delta and set up camp in Cairo in 971. The description of this axis continues to the holy city, which had passed under the control of the Shiite sovereigns and was thus returned to its position as the natural center of Islam, and therefore of the world, at the expense of Baghdad. This central axis of the Fatimid world could ignore Iraq and Iran, still in the hands of the Abbasids, to stop at southern and coastal Syria and recenter the heart of Islam, now dominated by the Ismaili imam, on the valley of the Nile and the holy cities of Arabia. The other axis—the maritime axis—connected the caliphal port to Sicily and from there led to Alexandria, also by sea.

Nasir Khusraw emphasized the importance of the maritime territory within the empire, particularly as a space connecting its different parts, above all in the Mediterranean. This territory then extended over the isthmus separating Misr from the Red Sea port, "a branch of the Ocean that breaks away from it at Aden and stretches back up to the north." The crossing times reported reveal profitable naval and commercial activity, but also the importance of the control of maritime routes for caliphal power. The choice to mention that, once the country was conquered, Caliph al-Muʿizz had taken the maritime route, contradicting every other source, seemed motivated by the major role the sovereign attributed to the sea submitted to the imam's sailors. The description of the Syrian ports, veritable maritime fortresses protecting the frontier against Greek attacks, confirms the function of the fleet and coastal fortifications, now in Ismaili hands, against the Byzantines:

> [Tripoli] is built so that the sea washes against three of its sides, reaching the top of the ramparts when the water is rough. The land side of the city is protected by a defensive wall and a large ditch. An extremely solid iron gate opens in the direction of the East. Both the walls and the crenelations are made of cut stone; war machines are arranged on top of the walls. Tripoli's inhabitants fear the ventures of the Greeks, who might attempt an attack with their vessels. . . . Tripoli is a dependency of the sultan of Egypt; I am told this has been the case since the period when the infidel of Byzantium attempted an attack against this fortified city and were repelled by the Egyptian Muslims, who subjected them to harsh defeat. The sultan of Egypt has abolished taxes in this city, and he constantly maintains a garrison here commanded by a general whose mission is to defend the city against any enemy initiative.[58]

Referring to the role of the stronghold and its fleet on the Syrian frontier served to emphasize that the Shiite imams had taken over the caliphal jihad against Byzantium. According to the Persian traveler, the central and eastern Mediterranean had clearly become an essential area of the Ismaili empire. Its new center was now in Cairo, pushing the Abbasid "old world" back to the margins, which were now in the east. Nasir Khusraw thus established a new polarity between the sea of jihad on the one side, under control as far as Sicily, and, on the other, the Red Sea and Arabia, which opened the road to the Islamic East, with Cairo now the principal haven for the merchants and men of letters of the Muslim world.

Many Fatimid chronicles were written, though nearly all were later lost.[59] These basically covered the period of the caliphate, but here too all the information on the sea is found in later works. Particular events such as the Fustat dockyard fire and the massacre of several Italian merchants in 996, committed by a population infuriated by fiscal advantages granted to Latin merchants, more specifically drew historians' attention to the importance of maritime and commercial policy, which was tied to the sustained growth of business relations with the Greeks and Latins.[60] More significantly, references to decisions regarding the fitting out of ships or certain symbolic acts—such as the sovereign's attendance at the parade of ships leaving for war from the *dar al-bahr,* the "house of the sea," located in the al-Maqs or Fustat dockyards—are all evidence of the caliphs' intention to reveal their highly specific ties to the fleet and, beyond that, to the sea.[61] One chronicle states, "No ship in the fleet was built elsewhere than the dockyard (*sina'a*) which is on the island [Rawda]. But Vizier al-Ma'mun was not satisfied with this situation. He ordered that the [ships] and the other ships of the diwan, intended for sailing the Nile, be built in the construction yard at Fustat, to which he added the raisin warehouse, on which he had a belvedere built. . . . The caliph came down here on the day of the presentation of the fleet or of its launch."[62]

The administration of the dockyard, dependent on the Exchequer, is primarily known to us through texts of the Ayyubid period.[63] As the last vizier of the last Shiite caliph, Saladin had governed the country in the tradition of the Ismaili government, waiting for the death of the last imam to reestablish the *khutba* (the direction of prayer) in favor of the Abbasids. Studies of the laws in effect during the Fatimid period show that these did not truly differ from the Sunni, Maliki, and Hanafi schools and allowed for the former regime's rules to be adapted within a Sunni administration.[64]

Several eminent members of the maritime services wrote descriptions of the operation of the dockyards under the imams' administration. Claude Cahen defines the *Minhaj,* a treatise by al-Makhzumi (d. 1189) found in fragmentary form, as a book on taxes in the ports of Alexandria, Tinnis, and Damietta.[65] The surviving version, which dates from 1185–1186, reveals the changes implemented in the Abbayid era while providing a description of taxation in the late period, when taxes were collected at the *sinaʿa,* the dockyard. Ibn Mammati (d. 1220), who wrote a treatise between 1182 and 1193, held a high position in "the administration for (naval) construction," which the sultan renamed "the administration of ships." Other administrators also wrote treatises.

The Fatimids appear as innovators in the organization of commercial activity. They mobilized all means of expression related to the sea as instruments to demonstrate Ismaili legitimacy: urban planning; architecture; administrative, chronographic, and legal literature; and also poetry were put to use to promote a caliphate that sought to dominate and administer the sea, now an imperial space rather than a frontier. While competition with the Umayyads was a powerful stimulant to this promotion, one must look to Islam as a whole for the reasons the Shiite imams instrumentalized the Mediterranean.

The Maritime Emblems of Fatimid Universality

Two descriptions of the construction of the capital city Mahdia present different but complementary ways of defining the imam's relationship to the sea. In the chronicle of the conquest of power in Ifriqiya by al-Qadi al-Nuʿman (d. 971), completed in 958, a brief presentation of the founding of the city establishes a close connection between spatial planning and the prophetic nature of the accession of the dynasty:

> The Mahdi founded Mahdia, which the prophetic books had heralded and nicknamed "the White One," and it was said that the *dajjal* [Abu Yazid, "the Imposter"] would never be able to reach or penetrate it. It was one of the most marvelous achievements: indeed he had it built in cut stone and provided it with solid iron gates. He emigrated there in 308 / 919–920 and established his residence there. Then one could contemplate the miracles of which Allah allowed the accomplishment. The Mahdi had the construction moved forward into the sea, the rock dug

> to create an artificial port that penetrates into the city and communicates with the sea by a channel with a chain to close it.[66]

Two major structures stood as symbols of dynastic power: the defensive wall closing off the isthmus, which would indeed prevent the Kharijite leader from taking control of the city in 945, and the port installations, which were spread over two sites and consisted of the basin, possibly dug into the rock by the Phoenicians and restored and fortified by the Fatimids, and the anchorage located along the artificial esplanade built to house the great mosque.[67] Both structures symbolized an opening to the rest of the world through the sea. With its prophetic atmosphere, reminiscent of that conveyed by the texts describing the foundation of Baghdad, ʿUbayd Allah's city combined the two fundamental qualities of a capital worthy of the Prophet's successor: invulnerability, tested during the Kharijite rebellion, and a universal character, which made it the center of a world that remained to be conquered and united under a single power.

From the beginning of the caliphate, the fleet appeared as a major instrument for the universal expansion of Ismailism. Thanks to the fleet's presence in the port during the Kharijite siege, al-Mansur (946–953) had been able to resupply Sousse, also blockaded, and to transport troops there to attack the Kharijite army from the rear, leading to the first decisive victory over "the man with the donkey."[68] The qadi therefore did not take the trouble to enumerate each edifice, choosing instead those that represented the Ismaili universalism put to the test by the revolt led by the Kharijite leader, and that were more important than the palaces. The victory over the Kharijites outside the city's walls signaled a rebirth of the Ismaili caliphate. The founding of the capital was thus doubly associated with divine favor.

The other, more detailed description was written by al-Bakri and fits neatly with the Baghdad tradition of geography: according to the Andalusian author, the construction of the port was directly in line with the architecture of Ifriqiya's ports, of which the oldest known example in the region was Tunis's port, built in 698 and taken over by the Aghlabid emir Ziyadat Allah to prepare for the conquest of Sicily. These ports were characterized by a surrounding wall flanking a basin (such as the one dug into the rock in Mahdia), the entrance to which was guarded by two towers and an arch that could be closed off with a chain. The dockyard area was behind the basin and consisted of an open space encircled by a wall, dedicated to the construction, fitting out, and repair of ships. Buildings housed the ship's equipment: sails, apparel, masts, and other equipment sensitive to the weather and insects. The port's architecture had itself been inspired by the Byzantine architecture of ports of the Bilad al-Sham such as Tyre and Acre, which were restored and used after the conquest of the region.[69]

Al-Bakri borrowed the description written by al-Warraq in the 970s and intended for the Umayyad caliphs, but he found other arguments to note the remarkable characteristics of this stronghold that was also used as the caliphs' residence: he refers to the urban area's duality, with Mahdia, an area reserved for the prince and his entourage, on the peninsula, while the outlying Zawila housed those who worked for the imam but were not in his inner circle. Following the official version, he credits the Fatimids with digging the port's basin and building the esplanade reclaimed from the sea and the defensive structures that surrounded the peninsula and were the pride and joy of the founders. The urban design of Cairo was prefigured here not only in the main mosque and the court of accounts but also in the layout of the two palaces, which were separated by an esplanade or a garden—the first belonged to 'Ubayd Allah, the second to al-Qa'im (934–946). The largest dockyard structure on the esplanade—and the only one mentioned by al-Bakri—was an edifice consisting of two long galleries in which sailing equipment was stored. The part of the dockyard for naval construction was normally open-air.[70] As the son of the emir of Huelva and Saltes, an important port of the Ta'ifa period equipped with a naval shipyard in the eleventh century, the geographer had a solid understanding of the layout and organization of a port and its dockyard.[71] Nonetheless, technical details did not have a place in a work like his. Like Qadi Nu'man but in a very different narrative context, he described those aspects of Mahdia he found singular and remarkable.

The Ismaili rulers gave many other signs of their ambition to integrate the Mediterranean space into the sphere of caliphal sovereignty. One of the clearest examples of this endeavor is the narrative framing of the administration of the ports, including the dockyard. This is attested to by a diverse range of sources. Among these, the biography (*sira*) of Jawdhar is an exceptional record of the administration and especially the dockyard at Mahdia. The *Life of the Ustadh Jawdhar* [a title he gave himself, along with that of a eunuch] is a compilation of letters collected by his secretary, including correspondence sent to him by the caliphs al-Qa'im, al-Mansur, and al-Mu'izz; his replies; and requests addressed to his masters. It shows that the administration of the admiralty and the navy was the exclusive domain of the sovereign. Having managed the dockyards and, more generally, matters relating to Mahdia, the eunuch was in a particularly good position to make sense of the city's complex inner workings: his primary role was to keep the three successive sovereigns informed. Initially in office in Mahdia, he was brought to Sabra-Mansuriyya by al-Mansur in 948. The eunuch's proximity to power, in particular to al-Qa'im, is verified by the fact that he was entrusted with the name of al-Qa'im's successor, which according to protocol was only known to the caliph. He was also appointed to head the treasury.

A series of letters denouncing the negligence of a few somewhat apathetic "civil servants" at the dockyard reveals the sovereign's concern with the efficient functioning of the port administration, which cast a good light on the prince's government. Mistakes could not be forgiven, for to do so would be to risk calling into question the credibility of sultanate power: "The *ustadh* wrote a note to Our Master in which he said that he had not neglected to shake up the civil servants charged with presiding over the purchase of the necessary provisions for the ships. This was in response to the impatience expressed by Our Master due to the late delivery of these provisions and the laziness of those who were in charge of managing purchases and their negligence in this matter."[72]

This is another clear example of the display of power, as orchestrated by the sovereigns. Proper management of the fleet was one of the preferred areas for demonstrating the caliph's infallibility, which according to Ismaili doctrine was inspired by his ancestors through a spiritual bond reaching back to the Prophet through Fatima. The desire to control the entire chain of command is clearly apparent in a letter relaying the caliph's order for the fleet to cast off, a command he could delegate to his principal war chief Ahmad b. Hasan b. al-Kalbi:

> Order has been given by Our Master to hold back the ships and prevent them from leaving for Sicily because he wanted to have equipment, weapons, and supplies carried onto them to support the troops after Ahmad b. al-Hasan returned from Sicily and the island's government was entrusted to his brother Abu l-Qasim b. ʿAli b. al-Hasan al-Kalbi. However, some ships disregarded his order, their captains diverted them from the [set] route and made them leave from [another] port. The imam was intensely irritated by this and sent Abu l-Qasim the order to burn these ships and put their captains to death.[73]

This concern with the fleet is also found in the relatively many references to the Shiite sovereigns' policy. Al-Muʿizz laid claim to the statement "A dockyard cannot be separated from its master," originally made by Muhammad b. Tughj al-Ikhshid, a representative of the Abbasid caliphate in Egypt (935–946) who had had to order the rebuilding of a dockyard on the right bank after the burning of the installations on Rhoda Island during the attempted conquest by al-Qa'im in 935.[74] Having brought the fleet from Ifriqiya to Cairo two years after it was conquered, the caliph had the admiralty established in his new capital. In all likelihood, the old dockyards in Fustat and on the island, the latter of which had been refurbished since the Fatimid attack in 935, continued to operate, enabling the construction of warships. The al-Maqs dockyard built close to the palace in Cairo, on the eastern bank of the Nile, was the work of al-Muʿizz or his son, al-ʿAziz. According to the authors of the Mamluk era, it was here that ceremonial ships for sailing on the river were built, particularly those used at the ceremony of the measuring of the water levels, during which the caliph traveled by boat to the Nilometer as crowds looked on from the banks of the river. The dockyard's warehouse held military equipment for ships leaving on expeditions, such as mangonels (catapults) and Greek fire. When the squadron was fitted out before its departure, the caliph came to al-Maqs from the palace on foot and presided over a large ceremony.

Another ritual that connected the sovereign to his squadron was the ceremonial review of the construction of ships in the dockyard at

Fustat. The caliph was also present at the launch of new ships. The leisure pavilion (*manzar*) specially built to welcome him on this occasion was reminiscent of the *dar al-bahr* at the palace in the Fatimid capital, itself inspired by those erected in Mahdia and Sabra-Mansuriyya. In both capitals, the "house of the sea" in the heart of the dockyards clearly involved the caliph in the work as the sovereign of maritime spaces. Thus, the ship-outfitting establishment addressed the Ismailis' needs, and the layout of the sites allowed the caliph and his descendants to display ceremonial protocol that emphasized the close tie between the caliph's sovereignty and the maritime territory of the Mediterranean. By "blessing" the fleet from the dockyard's pavilion while armaments were being loaded and soldiers embarked, the imam renewed this tie at each new campaign, and the spectacle of the squadron in battle formation served as a reminder that the imam could strike the enemy anywhere in the Mediterranean, without requiring the sovereign to be on the coast or at sea.[75]

The Sea and Beyond, Legitimating Spaces of Ismaili Islam

What was actually said in the triumphalist speeches that accompanied the fleet's parades? Ibn Hani' (d. ca. 973), official poet to the court, gave an eminent place to the caliph's relationship to the maritime space.[76] In a pronounced eschatological tone, the verses declaimed by this panegyrist for the conqueror of Egypt dwell at length on the role played by the fleet, weapon and symbol of Fatimid control in the maritime space, as far as the outer limits of the marine horizon. His lyrical sweep probably recalls that of the narratives on the period of the Arab conquest when they describe the attacks on Constantinople, but the Shiite imams were now aiming for control of the Mediterranean rather than the Byzantine capital, at least in an initial phase. In the logic of the construction of Ismaili legitimacy, the description of the fleet was combined with declamations of its universality: "They lower their eyes before a caliph who knows, without having been taught them, the secrets of God, / Who is the straight path itself, in a body of light, light provided him by rays from the sublime, incorporeal world."[77]

This was followed by a passage reporting the caliph's control over the maritime space and describing squadrons crossing the sea. The verses denounce the Abbasids' negligence and their inability to carry out jihad. After the loss of the frontier regions of Armenia up to Antioch, these sovereigns had abandoned the Mediterranean to the Byzantines as soon as they had taken control of Crete and Cyprus, the islands that controlled access to the Aegean Sea: "It is surprising that the Rums impale the Muslims with their spears, cross the seas, and pass over the mountains while sleep closes the eyelids of the Abbasids and they bring no assistance to Islam other than women singers and goblets of wine."[78]

The same diatribe took issue with the Umayyads, accused of murdering Husayn (d. 786), the second Shiite imam; of usurping the title of caliph in al-Andalus; and of being equally incapable of securing a victory over the Christians. A connection must be drawn between the criticisms of the Andalusian army facing the Latins by Ibn Hawqal, a supporter of the Fatimid cause, and the ungracious denunciation of the shameful behavior of the leaders who kept their distance from the battlefield by Ibn Hani, himself of Andalusian background.

These positions, primarily expressed in relation to the fleet, were above all an excuse to emphasize the caliphs' virtues, their combative zeal, and their ability to coordinate the armed forces, in particular, the naval forces; in a word, everything that distinguished them from the illegitimate pretenders to the caliphate. The Mediterranean remained a space of confrontation, but the Ismaili caliphs were now the only ones who could embody the spirit of jihad on the seas and allow Islam to achieve control over it:

> Our empire leaves far behind the time when the Rums had preeminence; one could even think that this time was never a known period.
> All the firm resolutions they had made collapsed, like all the stratagems that their experience had suggested to them.
> For two thousand years they had completely dominated the sea, as knights of the black tarred ships.
> Today every trace of their great maritime routes that crisscrossed the sphere have disappeared.
> And if they were to be asked about the sea, they would no longer be able to distinguish between the black ships and the tombs the color of earth.[79]

The poet then evokes the formidable nature of the now-invincible Muslim fleets, likening the Greek fire to hellfire coming down on the Christians in an unoriginal but suggestive image:

> To you the ships that dash and tower above the sea, that loudly cut through the water; they sail on your order with docile winds.
> Nothing frightened the king of the Rums like the arrival of these vessels on which floated flags and banners.
> Over them rose a thick and heavy cloud that spit countless lightning bolts and made thunder claps.
> These ships cut through the swelling waves; one would think they were loaded with all the vigor of your resolution and all the generosity of your hands . . .
> When they sigh with anger, they throw a fire that burns without smoke the way the fuel of the fire of hell burns.
> Their burning blasts are the fires of thunder, and their howling mouths are of iron. Their flames burn for the people of the Catholicos . . .
> Your ships on the sea dominate any other ship like the master dominates the slave.
> The kings of the Rums appealed to God against him, at the head of a numerous army, but the judgment of God is without recourse . . .
> You fulfilled the spears' wishes by serving the patricians up to them, and for the Domestics it was a true day of Last Judgment . . .
> The Barbarians must know without any doubt that the cross is weak while you are powerful,
> Let them adore another than Christ, for after this there is nothing to hope from the religion of monarchism.[80]

The sea had taken Constantinople's place and become the space for true faith. Domination of the sea was to usher in eschaton. The squadron had become the instrument of God against the Christian enemy, and the sea had become the scene of the triumph of the Fatimids and the imperial space par excellence.

Echoing the panegyrist's verses, the great maritime victories provided another opportunity to emphasize the caliphate's naval superiority, against both the Christians and the Umayyads. One of the caliphate's great exploits was the attack and sack of Genoa in 934, an account of which has been preserved in a book by the Ismaili Idris ʿImad al-Din (d. 1468), who had access to several now-lost Shiite texts:

> The Emir of the Believers al-Qa'im bi-Amr Allah sent Yaʿqub b. Ishaq al-Tamini to lead an expedition against the Rums. [In June 934] Yaʿqub left Mahdia with twenty ships. . . . On the way, he encountered Rumi ships loaded with merchandise; he captured them and took prisoner those who were on board. Then he continued his journey toward the land of the Rumi, targeting that country's well-fortified city, Genoa. . . . Allah gave him victory thanks to the imam's blessing. [Back in Mahdia] the prisoners were exhibited and the fleet was decorated. He entered the city wearing his most beautiful clothes. . . . The Emir of the Believers al-Qa'im was sitting in the *dar al-bahr* [sea pavilion]. Yaʿqub entered and al-Qa'im saluted him, invited him to come closer, praised his exploits, and ordered that whatever sum of money he requested, it be distributed to the fighters and he honored this.[81]

Here too, it was important that the caliph appear as the organizer of the expedition and the head of the fleet, whose every movement he controlled. The account of the return ceremony underlines the sovereign's virtues as he rewards his officer for demonstrating great competence as a sailor and war leader. These remarks reveal the Fatimids as the only heirs to the generations of sailors and soldiers who had carried out razzias on enemy waters and soil. However, the victory most important to the caliph was the one achieved by the fleet that pillaged Almería, the seat of the Umayyad admiralty, in 954; Qadi Nuʿman personally reported it. The framework of the narrative is quite similar to that of the preceding text, with the sovereign ultimately being credited with the essential role, as the only one able to create the conditions for domination of the maritime space and victory on the sea.[82]

Ismaili Influence on Christian Horizons: Recasting the Fatimid Mediterranean

Under the Cairo Fatimids (971–1171), documents referring to relations with the Christian sovereignties around the Mediterranean reveal the dynasty's attachment to Sicily, despite the fact that the island became autonomous under the government of the Kalbids (971–1050), and again when the Normans conquered it as of 1063. Varied Arabic documentation shows that this loss was never officially accepted, to the point that up to the twelfth century the Cairo caliphs' propaganda continued to show the island as being under Fatimid influence, particularly through the description of the ceremonial protocol of the most powerful king of the dynasty, Roger II.

A letter from Caliph al-Hafiz (1130–1149) to Roger II in 1137 reveals the complex nature of the Fatimids' ties with the Christian world. This was a reply to the king's criticism of the caliph for deposing his Armenian and Christian vizier Bahram. After inviting the king not to interfere with Egypt's internal affairs, the caliph sent him his compliments and thanked him for releasing one of his ships, which had been detained by the Norman authorities; this expression of gratitude was in keeping with customary commercial and diplomatic relations in the cold war atmosphere between the two Mediterranean powers. Playing the role of intermediary is the rather unusual figure of George of Antioch, who acted as a bridge between the two capitals at the time when the Normans were in a position of strength: "It [the friendship between the two states] is evidence of your desire to make this friendship appear in broad daylight in dazzling new clothes every time it starts to get old."[83]

While the letter was intended for the king, its contents echoed internal political issues, at least as they related to the caliph. Thanks to the exceptional architectural and decorative heritage left by the Norman kings in Palermo, enhanced by objects such as Roger II's coronation cloak, and written documentation that is relatively abundant in the medieval Mediterranean context, numerous studies have provided a better understanding of what was at stake in Norman ceremonial.[84] On the other hand, due to the total disappearance of princely edifices and the scarcity of accounts, limited to a few written fragments, Ismaili ceremonial has not revealed its secrets, particularly those concerning relations with enemies of Islam.[85] Consequently, the Shiite sovereigns' ties with the Norman crown remain ambiguous. The content of these messages aimed at Muslim "public opinion" and more specifically that of the caliph's subjects is not original; it is even likely that it was modeled after the Abbasids' approach with the Byzantines, the other diplomatic partners whose presence was heavily felt in Cairo.[86] In this case, it seems conceivable that the objective of these remarks was to leave a glimmer of hope of reconquest or, at the very least, to create the impression of strong Fatimid influence on the island until it was the right time to reconquer the former Muslim territory.

The Muslims' lasting attachment to Sicily, which they continued to consider a Muslim land to be reconquered, partially explains the Ismaili imams' desire to emphasize relations with infidel kings and to present the situation in terms of an Ismaili influence on the infidel. Other sources, such as treatises by Muslim jurists, have also left many accounts of the ties between the people of Islam and the island's Islamic populations until the end of the twelfth century.[87]

The most well-known account is by Ibn Jubayr (d. 1217). On the return journey from his trip to the East in 1185, Ibn Jubayr was forced to stop on the Norman island for a time due to a storm. In his diary (*rihla*), he wrote about his fascination with the insular monarchic system, particularly the large number of Muslims in the entourage of King William II (1166–1189): viziers, chamberlains, and eunuchs. At the same time, while crossing each city still inhabited by Muslims, he became aware of the Islamic communities' distress, assuming they were disintegrating due to their isolation. As for the Crusader states, he hoped for a reconquest of the island, with the help of the Almohads rather than the Ayyubids. In the vicinity of Trapani, home to many Muslims, he said, "The Christians think that it is here that the conquest of this island will take place, if it please God."[88]

The island's Muslim past and Arab-Muslim presence, still strong though on the decline, continued to fuel the dream of a return to the caliphs' authority. The dream even saw a certain empathy for Islam in various aspects of the king's behavior. This hope, which would become increasingly hypothetical and fanciful with every step of Latin expansion, explains some of the content of al-Hafiz's letter on Norman ceremonial. Ibn Jubayr thought no differently: "In the enjoyment of power in which he is plunged, in the fine disposition of his decrees, in the solid foundations of his power, in the fair remuneration of his men, in the brilliance of his royal pomp, in the display of his finery, he [William II] resembles the Muslim kings."[89]

The Arab men of letters' account of the caliphs' relations with the Normans slightly alters the significance of these relationships, characterizing them not through traditional military confrontation, given that any hope of a reconquest had vanished by the twelfth century, but through the interpretation of the Norman kings' ceremonial, which they saw as an imitation of the ceremonial of the Cairo sovereigns. The same idea is found in al-Maqrizi's report on the royal ceremonial of the Normans, the description of which he borrowed from Fatimid documentation.[90] The light he sheds on the Palermitan royalty reveals the extent to which the Normans were apparently inspired by the caliphs of Egypt and foregrounds what al-Maqrizi considered to be George of Antioch's central role as an intercessor: "He [George] veiled [the presence] of Roger [II] from his subjects and made him wear clothes similar to Muslims', he did not ride horseback, and only appeared before his subjects on holidays. Before him [one would then see] horses with gold and silver saddles, blankets inlaid with stones, and chairs covered with cupolas; gilded flags, the parasol, and [the king] wore the crown [*taj*] on his head."[91]

The use of objects such as the veil concealing the sovereign, the *taj* or "crown"—whose appearance remains hard to determine—and especially the parasol, a gift from al-Hafiz, revealed the Norman sovereign's Islamic nature to Muslim eyes. The cloak, the throne, and the veil were presented by the caliphs as attributes of Muhammad, later used by the imams: the first recalled the Prophet's attire; the second, the Prophet's nocturnal journey; and the third, the concealment of his face. The Egyptian man of letters, or the writer from whom he borrowed these descriptions, thus highlighted this ceremonial's Islamic references, inviting the conclusion that it borrowed from the Shiite sovereigns' ceremonial and that by this the Christian kings implicitly recognized a kind of Fatimid preeminence.

The Cairo man of letters points to George, an intimate of the Norman king, as the principal person responsible for the establishment of these privileged ties between the two sovereignties and, consequently, the caliphs' supposed influence on the Norman royalty. George was born to a Christian family from Syria that was captured at sea by pirates while on the way to Constantinople. The man who would become vizier and admiral of the Sicilian sovereign had washed up in Ifriqiya with his brother after being intercepted by an "official" Ifriqiyan expedition. Here, George climbed the ladder of the Zirid hierarchy before having to flee to Sicily, where he became the number two of the Norman monarchy. The exaggerated influence over Roger II with which al-Maqrizi credits him can be explained by this extraordinary life, which had positioned him between two worlds, and his renown as admiral of the fleet and intimate of the king. George particularly distinguished himself during the conquest of the ports of the African coast in 1140.[92] Due to his Syrian, Greek, and Christian background and experience of both worlds, this remarkable character was predestined to establish privileged ties between the Mediterranean's two great sovereignties. He traveled to Cairo several times as the king's envoy. He appears as the ideal mediator, a powerful figure who used his influence with the Norman king to organize the royal ceremonial, thus recognizing the Fatimids' lasting influence in Sicily.[93]

The Egyptian poet Ibn Qalaqis's panegyric in honor of the Sicilian king William II, written as the poet was setting off to put himself in the king's service around 1168, shows the persistence of this fiction of spiritual relations between the two ceremonials. The qualities of the Norman royalty as depicted by the poet are reminiscent of Ibn Hani's verses addressed to al-Muʿizzi, written more than two centuries earlier, particularly in the close association between the sovereign's personal merit and the Normans' maritime successes:

> There is no victory but that of his army, wherever it passes, on
> the front lines on land as on the vast surface of the sea. . . .
> He has thoroughbreds that the mind can barely conceive
> like he has ships that go beyond what can be imagined.

His two armies[94] are like moving clouds always tempestuous in times of war and always carrying [beneficial] rain in times of peace.
He leads against his enemies all that moves quickly, dark swarms of thoroughbreds or dark swarms of small boats. . . .
And the darkness of the ships makes their bodies similar to venomous snakes that can vomit their poison for us.[95]

Many studies of Norman ceremonial have shown that it had a complex nature, due to the multiple sources that inspired representations of the sovereign's image, borrowed from the three great imperial areas of the Mediterranean and put in service of the emblematic display of the Norman royalty's universality. The elements drawn from Arab-Islamic culture, themselves associated with several iconographic and architectural models from different parts of the Muslim world, reinforced the imperial and universal dimension of the representation of Norman royal power and underlined its expansionist ambition, notably at the expense of Islam.[96] As distorted from its original meaning by the Arab men of letters, this syncretic display allowed the caliphate to overcome the fact that it was then less powerful than the Normans and to send another message to the Muslims, foregrounding Ismaili domination over the Mediterranean and, beyond that, demonstrating the imams' influence over the Christian kings of Sicily, manifested by these borrowings from Fatimid ceremonial.

This fanciful projection of domination over Christian lands also appears implicitly in the context of relations between Cairo and Byzantium. Outside of references to a few commercial agreements, the circulation of documentation in the Mediterranean, from the Greek capital to the Egyptian one, remains one of the rare indications of the ties between the two empires. We do not know enough about the undeniable influence of the *Taktika* of the Macedonian emperors—specifically the *Taktika* of Leo VI (886–910)—about Arabic literature on good princely government and, in the legal realm, of the *Nomos Rhodion Nautikos* on Muslim maritime legislation, now a specialty of the Ifriqiyan qadis, to understand the Cairo sovereigns' projections on the Greek empire, which was primarily referred to as the most dangerous Christian adversary.[97] However, this fictitious reconstruction of a Fatimid Mediterranean, including the Christian lands of the Mediterranean borderlands, transformed the Abbasids' Sea of the Romans into an Islamic imperial space under the control of the Shiite imams.

7

THE WESTERN MEDITERRANEAN

Last Bastion of Islam's Maritime Ambitions

IN THE WEST, the Umayyad collapse that began in 1009 did not lead to the abandonment of the maritime space.[1] Among the emirates that rose to power on Andalusian soil, several had fleets serving their maritime ambitions.[2] The emirs of Denia and the Balearics, particularly the founder Mujahid al-'Amiri (1010–1045), distinguished themselves by taking over the jihad at sea and attacking Sardinia in 1015. Other emirates with a seaboard and one or several dockyards, like the Abbadids of Seville (1023–1091) and the Barghawata Berbers, who ruled in Ceuta as of 1056, took advantage of the dockyard installations and crews that had served the Umayyad caliphate.[3] In fact, the naval strength of Andalusia and the western ports enabled Emir Yusuf b. Tashfin (1073–1106) to answer the call of the Andalusian emirs and land on European soil in 1086, using the emirates' naval resources to repel the Castilian kings. Later, the Almoravid dynasty particularly benefited from the skill of the admirals of Almería, the Banu Maymun.

After having seized Marrakech and put an end to the Almoravid dynasty in 1147, the Almohads undertook to conquer all of the former dynasty's territories. Seville, then Córdoba fell to them in 1152, but the entire eastern region resisted until 1172 and the Balearics until 1181.

During this period, the Christians' naval power had become stronger, particularly in Genoa and Pisa, which respectively controlled the shores of Sardinia and Corsica. The two ports, which would join forces to carry out major raids, took advantage of the Almoravid collapse to attack the principal Muslim maritime strongholds in the West: Tortosa (1092, 1146), Mallorca (1113–1114), and Almería (1147), which was taken by the Genoese and left, in ruins, to the king of Castile. The two Tyrrhenian ports repeated the attacks in Ifriqiya, whose Zirid rulers were weakened by the incursions of Arab tribes that had been settling in the Maghreb since 1050, in particular the Banu Hilal. After the pillaging of the port of Bône on the northern coast, Mahdia met the same fate in 1087. While the western Mediterranean routes leading to the Muslim coasts were now under the control of the two Tyrrhenian ports, the Almohads nonetheless inherited a vast seaboard stretching from the Atlantic Ocean to the Mediterranean coast as far as Tripoli of Libya, which came under Almohad control in 1161. The pivotal point of this Almohad seaboard was the Strait of Gibraltar.

It fell to 'Abd al-Mu'min (1130–1163), the first Almohad caliph and himself a native of the coastal region of Hunayn, to build the naval power needed to connect Africa and al-Andalus, as well as to conquer Ifriqiya and conduct jihad against the infidel, using the naval administration of the Umayyad, then Almoravid caliphates as models. The organization of what was potentially the most powerful navy of the Muslim Middle Ages in the Mediterranean allowed the first three caliphs to use the fleet to attack Christian positions, first in Ifriqiya, then in the Iberian Peninsula, until this fine war machine began to go awry after the death of Caliph al-Nasir.[4] At the same time, Arabic descriptions of the sea reveal the extent to which it had become a space familiar to Muslim civilization, as significant in Islam as it was for Latin societies.[5]

THE NAVIES OF THE *TA'IFA* EMIRS IN THE WAKE OF THE UMAYYADS

The sovereignty of the *ta'ifas*—independent Muslim-ruled principalities—is characterized by the fact that "there [was] no particular innovation in that area, for the kings of the *ta'ifas* settled for adapting the Umayyad model to their scale."[6] Likewise, one must reject the false impression that the kings of the *ta'ifas* merely inherited a centralized Umayyad state, insofar as the presence of the administration in district (*kura*) capitals allowed the *ta'ifa* emirs to rely on local supporters to manage the emirate to their new master's benefit. However, the clientelistic Umayyad and Amirid supporters who established themselves in regional cities endeavored to spread the emblems of legitimacy, borrowed from the Umayyad and Abbasid caliphates. Some had their own naval forces and were able to perpetuate the image of Andalusian sovereignty dominating the sea.

This was particularly true of the Amirid Saqaliba (slave) Mujahid, who was appointed governor of Tortosa by his master, Ibn Abi ʿAmir al-Mansur, and Mujahid's son Ali al-ʿAmiri. Beginning in 1010, Mujahid found in the modest port town of Denia the means to build a capital and an emirate largely open to the sea.[7] Having inherited the command of seasoned squadrons and sailors, the Abbadids of Seville borrowed the maritime themes of the representation of caliphal legitimacy, as updated by the Umayyads. The same was true of the Hammudids, who controlled several ports on the Strait of Gibraltar, and the Banu Sumadih of Almería (1041–1091).[8]

At the same time, the legal treatment of questions relating to the sea held a singular place in the corpus of the period's Andalusian jurisprudence, developing with the prosperity of maritime commerce.[9] Among the treatises on market regulation, the one by the Sevillan Ibn ʿAbdun, written about 1100, contains an article on the use of the banks of the Guadalquivir River, which bordered the Andalusian city and served as a port for seagoing ships. Because the port was considered part of the sultanate, it could only be administered by the Almoravid authorities: "There is cause to protect the bank of the river that serves as the port of the city [Seville] for [seagoing] ships, and to avoid that the slightest parcel of it be given up or that any structure be built on it: indeed, this place is the city's vital point, the site from which useful merchandise is exported by the merchants sending it abroad, the refuge of foreigners, the yard for repairing ships; the entire complex must belong exclusively to the state."[10]

The Legacy of a Legitimating Sea: The Maritime Destiny of the Amirids of Denia

The maritime dimension of the *ta'ifa* was a priority of the expansion policy of the sovereigns al-Mujahid and his son Ali b. al-Mujahid Iqbal al-Dawla (1045–1076). It was exceptional due not only to the two sovereigns' commitment on the sea in the name of jihad but to also the maritime and commercial exploitation of their domain and the adjacent maritime regions.[11] Al-Mujahid, a slave (Saqaliba) in the service of the Amirids (978–1009), was the governor of Tortosa when the caliphate disintegrated. He took power and turned the modest town of Denia, previously a dependency of Valencia, into one of the most active Muslim ports of the Sharq al-Andalus seaboard. He also took control of the Balearics, the hub of traffic in the western Mediterranean. Having provided the port city with a dockyard, the emir developed maritime commerce in the region of the Levante to the point that it competed with Almería. Maritime activity undoubtedly made the Amirid emirs' fortune.

Al-Mujahid was probably the only Andalusian emir to borrow the central theme of maritime expansion and jihad from the caliphs to turn it into the essential underpinning of his legitimacy.[12] He capitalized on the razzias against Sardinia, even after the fiasco of 1015, and launched a raid on the coast of Luni: memories of maritime jihad in the caliphal period helped to spread the legitimating image of the "mujahid" sovereign. Thus, the laudatory verses that the Denia poet Ibn al-Labbana (d. 1113) addressed late in the eleventh century to the sovereign of Mallorca, Nasir al-Dawla, a descendant of the emir, are reminiscent of those of the panegyrists who sang the praises of the fleet to the Fatimid and Umayyad sovereigns:

> On this day, some sirens fly with wings that make them look
> like crows, while the others are like gyrfalcons.
> On the gulf we see an army as mobile as the gulf water, for
> both flow [with the same facility].
> The sons of war boarded rapid ships [*jawari*] which run as fast
> as the steeds who win the race . . .

O wonder! Never before I saw them would I have imagined
that boats could carry fierce lions!
They grow restless to go toward you, oars that are like the
lashes of an eye watching the jealous spy.[13]

That being said, al-Mujahid's decision to invade Sardinia raises several questions. Since the 940s, the policy of ʿAbd al-Rahman III had transformed the route to the western islands, particularly that connecting Italy and Sardinia, which continued to the Balearics and the continental ports of al-Andalus, into a trade route open to Latin merchants. Was the trade route cut off under the rule of Ibn Abi ʿAmir al-Mansur, a partisan of unilateral jihad that would put an end to commercial traffic via Sardinia? Did the emir want to take control of traffic at the expense of rival Andalusian ports such as Almería? Was he pushed to wage war by the Pisans settling on the island or by an intense attraction to jihad? What we know with certainty is that both sides entered a new phase of maritime history, dominated by the confrontation between Italians and Andalusians. However, this did not mean that trade in the islands was interrupted. The clash quickly turned to the advantage of the Tyrrhenian ports, in a prelude to the offensives that directly targeted Andalusian coasts as of the beginning of the twelfth century.[14]

Sardinia had been the emir's major military objective. While he suffered military defeat against Genoa, Pisa, and the Sardinians, Arab and Latin documents show that the island remained a port of call accessible to ships from Denia and Mallorca long after the defeat of 1015–1016.[15] Ultimately, his principal success rested in the diplomatic and commercial relations he formed with the Latins in Catalonia and with the ports of the Tyrrhenian Sea, while protecting his reputation among Muslims through jihad, which was presented as the primary objective of his maritime commitment. His son Ali distinguished himself by forming commercial relations with the Fatimids and maintaining regular commercial ties. Several letters from the Cairo Geniza, written during the second half of the eleventh century, bear witness to this. Al-Mujahid and his son were the only *ta'ifa* rulers who created a maritime territory of economic expansion.

Following in his father's footsteps, Ali was able to spread an image of himself that promoted his status as a Muslim emir: in 1056, he generously sent a convoy of ships carrying wheat to destitute Egyptians dying in a famine. The propagation of this other form of jihad, both charitable and personal, was fully successful: 'Ali's initiative was long remembered.

Almoravid Sea Power in the Maghreb and al-Andalus: Disrupting the Western Mediterranean's Islamic Polarity

> At the time of the Almoravids, Almería was a metropolis of Islam. . . . This city's port was frequented by merchant ships from Alexandria and Syria. Throughout the entire Peninsula, there was no other population with such large fortunes, more devoted to industry and various trades, and with better knowledge of how to benefit from the fluctuations in prices and stock.[16]

The wealth of the largest Muslim port of the Mediterranean West in the Almoravid era held a particular place in Andalusian memories because the city was brutally ruined by the Genoese attack of 1147 and the decade of Castilian occupation that followed; Almería would only make a partial recovery, in the Almohad and Nasrid era (1237–1492). The many accounts of the city's earlier prosperity are typical of the impression left by Arab geographers' and historians' descriptions, particularly of al-Andalus during the first half of the twelfth century, when it was reputed to be prosperous, in part due to maritime activity. Similarly, the ownership of a powerful fleet gave the sailors of the caliphate's ports, led by the Banu Maymun, the possibility to conduct commerce raids in the name of jihad, reaching as far as the coasts of Galicia with ships more modern than those in the ports of Santiago de Compostela (until the arrival there of a Genoese naval architect).[17] The extent of Yusuf b. Tashfin's conquests provided the emirate with a vast seaboard, covering the coasts of Andalusia and the Maghreb and stretching to the edge of the Canary Islands in the Atlantic and to Algiers on the Mediterranean. The contemporary geographers al-Zuhri (d. ca. 1161) and al-Idrisi left the most precise accounts of the state of the sea under his control.

Their texts are complemented by the Arabic annals covering the period, most importantly those of the Maghrebis Ibn ʻIdhari and Ibn Khaldun, themselves indebted to chroniclers who were contemporary to the dynasty but whose works have not survived, in particular Ibn al-Sayrafi (d. 1162).

While the Almoravids did not seem to conceive of a ship, however beautiful, as a representation of Islamic legitimacy, they were able to adapt the administrative and military organization of their huge emirate to the configuration of their vast domain, which included an essential maritime area—particularly the zone of the Strait of Gibraltar. Al-Bakri was the first to attempt to explain the new situation that made the Berber region the power base of the Muslim West. This can be seen in the exceptional attention his universal geography devotes to the western limits of the Islamic domain, which had previously been marginalized by every Eastern geographer except Ibn Hawqal.

The Maghreb, a New Power in Western Islam

The real originality of the Andalusian geographer al-Bakri's work is in the attention he devoted to the Berber region, compared to the brief treatment of his own homeland.[18] It is as if he foresaw the Berber region's future. Given that his geography has reached us in its entirety, it is clear that its imbalances are a result of the author's choice rather than happenstance.[19] Al-Bakri gave a relatively detailed analysis of power relations between the tribes. In individually describing the regions held by a tribe or a tribal federation, centered on a capital, often a fortress, and their villages, he succinctly enumerates the tribes' riches or military capacities. This accumulation of "ecological" data according to criteria from Baghdad geography allowed him to show that the Muslim West's true power rested not only on its group cohesion but also on the intensely close bond between each of the tribes and the territory it controlled and exploited.[20] Growing crops and breeding livestock, like Saharan and maritime trade and fishing and coral mining, were the base of tribal societies' power.[21] In irrigated zones, the owners of cultivated land were most often identified by the well and irrigation system, which provides an indication of the group's priorities in terms of identity.[22]

The sultanate rulers' authority was based on the tributary system, defined by Pierre Guichard as the relationship between the sovereign and his representatives on the one hand and the tribal group on the other.[23] These ties were most often determined by the tax base the community agreed or refused to pay the emir or the sultan, the amount of which normally depended on a happy medium between the quantity and value of the riches produced and the needs of the administrative authorities. Tax was often paid in kind: the number of riders the Andalusian geographer reported in several tribes of the northern Maghreb al-Aqsa—the north of modern Morocco—is equivalent to the contingent some tribes agreed to provide, which consisted of riders renowned in al-Andalus and feared by the Christians.[24] This is why all the Arab geographers briefly inventoried the sources of revenue of tribal entities (not only those in the West) and village districts (*qura*), without providing an evaluation in figures but by giving an idea of a group's strength. The source of revenue was relatively unimportant—whether it was cultivation, raising livestock, fishing, trade evaluated by the number of dromedaries, or raids—but naming it made it possible to identify and personalize the tribal group and to size up its potential, which was evaluated based on the number of riders available or other characteristics of this type: "[Tétouan] is the seat of the territory belonging to the Banu Sikkin. . . . The Banu Sikkin can put 100 riders in the field. . . . Majaz Fakkan is the home of the [Banu] Milwatha, who can ride 500 horses."[25]

According to the geographer, the other factor in the region's power was the progress of Arabization and especially Islamization, which reinforced the tribes' cohesion.[26] The geographer was careful to note the situation of Islamization in each of the areas composing North Africa, from Barca to Tangier and from there to the desert. Here, he did not fail to remember the role played by the Arab conquerors, whether companions of the Prophet or those of the generation of "followers," such as 'Uqba b. Nafi'. The adoption of Islam and the cohesion of the Berber tribes were the essential vehicles of the society's in-depth transformation and the fuel for the Berbers' rise in power. Movements judged heretical by the Malikis, such as the Barghawata confederation or, in a different category, Ibadism, had been fought and were on the verge of being repressed after tribal groups like the one put together by the Ifranid emirs, a branch of the Zenata, organized the jihad from the city of Salé, which had been turned into a ribat.[27]

The al-Murabitun or Almoravid movement, born in the Western Sahara, appeared to bring these developments to fruition. Mandated by the Maliki jurists of Kairouan under the leadership of Abu Imran b. Musa b. Abi l-Hajjaj, then in the midst of a proselytizing campaign in western Africa, Ibn Yasin left to reform the still-fragile Islamic faith practiced by the Western Sahara tribes.[28] Their "conversion" was the starting point for the creation of a major military power that could only elicit the admiration of al-Bakri and all his contemporaries:

> They fight on horseback or riding thoroughbred camels; but the greatest part of their army consists of foot soldiers, who line up in several rows. Those in the front row carry long pikes, which are used to push back and impale their enemies; those in the other rows are armed with javelins; each soldier holds several of them, which he skillfully throws, nearly always hitting the person targeted and putting him out of commission. . . . They usually have a man stand before the front line holding a flag; so long as the flag remains raised, they are unwavering; if he lowers it, they all sit on the ground where they remain as motionless as mountains; they never chase after an enemy who flees before them.[29]

As these fighters paraded outside his window, al-Bakri, the son of the emir of Huelva, identified the Almoravid emirate as the principal power in the region, the only one able to save al-Andalus, which was divided and incapable of resisting the Castilians. A few years later, al-Turtushi, an Andalusian scholar who had gone into exile in Egypt, reminded Emir 'Ali b. Yusuf (1106–1143) that it was his duty to conduct jihad against the Christians of the Peninsula because he was the only sovereign who had the means to successfully combat the Latins: "The jihad against the unbelievers is an obligation for you on the frontiers of al-Andalus, for you are the Muslim sovereign closest to it and you have horses, weapons, war machines, Muslim armies, soldiers under your orders."[30]

The momentum of the Almoravid jihad had revived the hope of stopping the Latin advance and reclaiming Toledo. It was the only force capable of allowing tribal federations to form outside of local particularism and of regenerating Andalusian Islam. The geographer also pointed to the Berber world's commercial maritime activities as an example of its vigor. In fact, thanks to the Berbers and the sailors of the European shore, the Alboran Sea between the Iberian Peninsula's southern and eastern coasts and the coasts of the western and central Maghreb had become one of the maritime spaces most heavily frequented by merchants since the ninth century.

The Birth of a Maritime Space in the Maghreb

As of the early years of the ninth century, the Berbers were indeed the main agents of maritime activity, both in the east of the Maghrebi bloc—Aghlabid and Fatimid Ifriqiya—and along the coastal zones under the control of the Rustamids of Tiaret, the Salihids in the Rif, and the Idrisids, up to the Strait of Gibraltar.

The principal indications of the Maghrebis' ties with the Mediterranean and Atlantic are lists of itineraries and anchorages, descriptions of ports and naval infrastructures, and inventories of the systems of coastal defense, including a record of the locations of ribats, all of which the geographer used to illustrate the Berbers' maritime dynamism. Primarily owing to the information left by al-Warraq and at least one Maghrebi, Mu'min b. Yumar al-Hawwari, the Andalusian geographer was able to establish the maritime routes connecting Andalusian shores to those of North and West Africa. These routes were used every year by sailors who had settled on the Spanish coasts under the reign of al-Hakam I. This traffic is also mentioned, albeit episodically, by Ibn Hayyan and in a few rare but precious Christian documents, such Pope Leo III's letter to Charlemagne informing him of the negotiations between the Maghrebis and the Byzantines of Sicily in 813.[31]

Entitled "itineraries of the ships" (*suluk al-sufun*), the maritime stages list the names of all the anchorages of the Muslim-controlled seaboard, connecting the south of oceanic Morocco, at Nul Lamta, to Antalya on Anatolia's Aegean coast, which was the admiral port of the forces of the

Cibyrrhaeot Theme in the ninth century and was accessible to Muslim merchants during periods of truce.[32]

The references to the Muslim West's maritime activity touch on the state of the coast in the tenth and eleventh centuries and largely overlap with the information Ibn Hawqal provided about the same itineraries. Later descriptions, such as those by the anonymous author of the *Kitab al-Istibsar* (twelfth century), update al-Bakri's itineraries, showing the densification of coastal navigation and maritime journeys in the Almohad period: skirting all of the western coasts from the shores bordering the Sahara, maritime activity fits into the long span of coastal navigation and seasonal sailing identifiable as of the ninth century. The maritime route was often preferred for moving people and goods, particularly in regions difficult to access by land, such as the Rif. Thanks to their years of experience, sailors enjoyed great respect throughout the Muslim countries—this was still true in Egypt under Saladin, for example.[33] They were equally renowned on the coasts of Christian Europe—as formidable sailors and pirates.

The geographer established the sequence of the lists of maritime itineraries based on the political context of the ninth century. The description of ports, the selection of sites, and the monuments mentioned generally serve as reminders of the reality of the framework of sultanate power, as in all Arab geographic descriptions.[34] Borrowing ancient systems of measurement for maritime routes from the Fortune (Canary) Islands that were based on astronomical calculations, he designated the ocean coast as the starting point for any maritime measurement, taken from west to east. The Maghrebi origin of the charting of maritime routes is confirmed by the reference to itineraries on the Alboran Sea connecting Maghrebi and Iberian ports, staggered along the coasts from the far Mediterranean to Denia on the north shore, to the center of the Maghreb. The length of the journey was calculated in days.[35] However, the author does recognize that the communities of sailors in Andalusian ports initiated these commercial journeys, stating that they traveled each winter from their Iberian haven to the ports of the Maghreb. This led to the founding or redevelopment of ports such as Ténès, in 875, and Oran, in 902.

The route was charted north from the threshold of the Atlantic Sahara, across the strait and along the shores of the Maghreb, then Libya, to reach the area of the Nile delta. The last stretch described follows the shore of the Bilad al-Sham to the Anatolian coast. Inspired by al-Hawwari, the geographer reproduced a north–south itinerary of the "ports located between the Maghreb el-Aqsa—Massa on the banks of the Sous, then the Banc d'Arguin in Mauritania—and Asilah." This route for transporting Saharan goods would remain unchanged until the Portuguese took advantage of the trade winds to set sail directly from the Banc d'Arguin or ports farther south and reach Madeira before continuing to the Moroccan or Portuguese coast.[36] Once the ocean was reached, the journey was broken into several stages, from Cape Spartel to Aslan, from Aslan to Mahdia, from Mahdia to Alexandria, and from there to Antalya.

The sailors from al-Andalus are presented as descendants of the Berbers who had settled along eastern coasts up to Tortosa. This migration had begun early in the ninth century with the revolt of the two uncles of Umayyad emir al-Hakam I, Sulayman and 'Abd Allah, who took refuge in Tahert. They were supported by the Berber crews in Rustamid ports, particularly those of Ténès. Some remained where they were and entered the service of the Umayyad emir to fight the Carolingians at sea. Berber colonization started again during the reign of 'Abd al-Rahman II and at the beginning of the reign of Emir Muhammad. It was these sailors who would set sail each winter from their base on the European shore to trade with their cousins on the coasts of Africa.[37]

The Berbers, Experienced Sailors

From his field of observation on the western Mediterranean, between the Strait of Gibraltar and the Tyrrhenian Sea, al-Bakri bore witness to a global rise in sea traffic. The principal agents of this development were the Berber communities on both continents. The western African seaboard became one of the major hubs of this trade in the West, as shown by the increase in traffic in certain ports, such as Ceuta, Oran, and Hunayn, during the geographer's lifetime. After the first Viking attacks, al-Andalus initiated regular commercial relations with towns on the Atlantic and Mediterranean coasts of both continents. This dynamism is evidenced by the annual presence of sailors from the Iberian Peninsula at the market in Asilah, close to Tangier, at the foot of the ribat founded by the Luwata Berbers shortly after the Norsemen's attack in 844, as well as the founding of Ténès Lahdar in 875 by Andalusian sailors who were presented as descendants of the earlier city's inhabitants, now returned to the land of their ancestors:

> They [the sailors from Escombreras] were in the habit, when they left [the shores of] al-Andalus, of spending the winter in the port of Ténès. The Berbers of the surrounding area having come to join them, they invited them to settle in the castle [old Ténès, which had thus been repopulated] and to hold a market there. . . . Soon they saw a great deal of people arrive, among whom were all their old [Berber] friends [who had settled in al-Andalus]. At the beginning of spring, they all got sick, and the Andalusians, judging the town unhealthy, got back on their ships [to return to al-Andalus]. The colonists who remained in Ténès saw their numbers increase, their wealth grow, and some time later they welcomed four hundred families from Suq Ibrahim, who were accustomed to sleeping under a tent, and shared their accommodations and goods with them. They all helped each other in the construction work and in Ténès they erected the fortified town (*hisn*) that still stands there.[38]

This fine example of economic dynamism coincided with 'Abd al-Rahman II's opening of the emirate's ports to maritime activity, an initiative taken to enjoy the tax benefits of the development of regular trade by levying a toll at the end of the maritime routes on the Alboran Sea.[39] The records associate the implementation of a defense program, illustrated by the spate of ribats, with the rise in maritime commerce. This correlation would attribute the location of several ribats on coastlines unthreatened by enemies, such as Massa on the Atlantic Coast, to a decision informed by commercial strategy.[40] The designation of the site as a ribat suggests that the primary reason for its founding was related to a religious and commercial function of the coasts. The two causes were perfectly compatible.

Al-Bakri had at his disposal a great deal of information from the maritime environment. As noted earlier, the Eastern geographers and encyclopedists also had access to local sources and reports kept by the Abbasid chancelleries; consequently, while al-Bakri's method was not new, the depiction of the Maghreb as the cradle of the western Mediterranean's commercial dynamism in the ninth century was the product of an uncommon approach. He made use of maritime rutters featuring daymarks, the coastal points of reference by which sailors traveling along the coast could determine their position, to reveal a maritime route established from the open sea rather than dry land. These rutters also included possible anchorages in bays, like the one in Tangier, which was exclusively accessible to shallow-draft boats, as well as the direction of the winds to which anchorages were exposed. However, as with all *adab* texts, the commentary omitted technical details. There is no sign of original rutters again until the Portuguese and Arabic rutters of the fifteenth century, the latter of which are only found on the Indian side of the Muslim maritime domain. In the meantime, the naval itineraries in the geographic sources were heavily simplified.[41] Al-Bakri wrote,

> We will indicate a series of ports here, in the order in which they present themselves to the traveler leaving from Aslan headed for the East. The first they encounter is Marsa l-ma' al-mafdun. There are a few habitations nearby and some springs whose waters flow into the sea. This port is 13 miles from Aslan; it is separated from Marsa l-Rahib, which is located across from it on the coast of al-Andalus, by a crossing of two days and one third. The harbor of Oran, which comes next, is very big and is good for wintering, protected from all the winds.[42]

There were 151 anchorages, ranging from the smallest havens to major ports, available to coasters following Muslim shores from Nul Lamta in the south of Morocco to Antalya in Anatolia.

It is not surprising that the geographer, who was long based in Almería, had access to documents intended for navigation, just as al-Idrisi would a century later, thanks to the admiralty of Palermo.[43] This data seems to indicate that the century of the Fatimid and Umayyad caliphates was marked by a renewal of nautical documentation, coinciding with Muslim efforts to expand their presence on the sea and jurists' endeavors to make sailing legal according to the criteria of Islam. This specialized literature is only mentioned in passing in the medieval Arabic sources, despite the fact that it represented the experience of several generations of sailors, gathered since at least the ninth century and largely memorized and passed on orally before being recorded in writing. Consequently, the accumulation of rutters and oral and written information that al-Bakri drew from was vast, collected at different periods, which prevents us from accurately dating the point at which these documents were composed, with a few exceptions, such as the founding of Ténès (875). Indeed, there is no indication that all of these itineraries were active at the same time, nor any suggestion of the scope of this potential traffic. All that is certain is that the geographer intended to demonstrate the vigor of the maritime activity initiated by Maghreb inhabitants.

Regarding this question, al-Bakri did not fail to mention that maritime activities and coastal ports were also under the control of tribes that exploited maritime resources. This enabled the tribes to pay their tax to the emirs—the Idrisids of Fez, the Salihids of Nekor, and the Rustamids of Tahert—or to provide them with boats and equipment, but the system also guaranteed a great deal of autonomy. Aslan, the first port cited from the Mediterranean rutter, was run by "inhabitants [who] belong to the [Banu] Maghila"; further along, al-Bakri refers to "Marsa Maghila, a port named after the Maghila, a part of the tribe of Hashim." The geographer is even more explicit in the section on the emirate of Nekor, in which he specifies that several ports of the Moroccan Rif were in the hands of the Berbers: "Among the other ports of the same territory [Nekor] one distinguishes Badia, Buquya, and Balish, the port of the Sanhaja."[44] In discussing the Idrisid zone, al-Bakri refers to the "Masmuda [tribal confederacy] on the coast that is part of the dependencies of Tangier."[45] At the same time, as had happened in Ténès and the Andalusian ports revitalized since the beginning of the ninth century, these communities merged into mixed populations of Arab, Berber, and Andalusian background, converted or Mozarab: rather than a specifically Berber phenomenon, what is at issue here is Islamization and Arabization, but also the expansion of maritime trade.[46]

Ibn Khaldun's *Muqqadima* often returns to this social and political rearrangement of Maghrebi society, which pits the short-lived power of a sultanate against the tribal structure that is the inexhaustible base of that society. Ibn Khaldun was apparently heavily inspired by al-Bakri's overview, particularly when he explains the Muslims' maritime development by the sultanates' ability to mobilize the experience of the region's sailors against the Latins.[47]

By considerably expanding the description of the Maghrebi area compared to that of the other regions—and particularly at the expense of his own homeland—al-Bakri revealed a new polycentrism in Western Islam: al-Andalus was relegated to the position of a peripheral frontier, while the East seemed to be running out of steam.[48] The maritime space, which the two Western caliphates had fought over in the tenth century, had largely benefited from the Berber initiatives long responsible for a significant part of its exploitation in the western zone. However, it was the regional emirates, before the caliphs, who were able to put this manpower to work on their behalf, particularly on the sea. The Rustamids had followed the same approach with the ʿIbadi Berbers in the Sahara.

THE ALMOHADS AND THE SEA, MEDIEVAL ISLAM'S LAST IMPERIALIST PUSH ON THE MEDITERRANEAN

Paradoxically, it was Saladin who uttered one of the finest compliments about the Almohad fleet, via the pen of his secretary al-Fadl. Admittedly, this letter his representative Ibn Munqid delivered to Caliph al-Mansur in 1190 requested that the "Muslim West help the Muslims even more than the infidel East helps the infidel." However, the sultan unambiguously recognized that there was only a single naval force in Islam that could measure up to the Latin fleets—that of the Maghrebi caliphate. The large number of ships mentioned in the letter is confirmed by the figures provided by Ibn Abi Zarʿ, a fourteenth-century historian from Fez, who states that in 1162 "ʿAbd al-Mu'min had four hundred ships built."[49] Though its reliability remains questionable, this assessment by a historian of the Marinid period provides an idea of the extraordinary mobilization the Almohad sovereign orchestrated to ensure he had at his command the naval force essential to allow him to conquer all of Islam and honor his title of caliph.

In 1150, ʿAbd al-Mu'min had completed the annexation of Almoravid territory and could now consider pursuing the conquest to the east. He put great care into preparing the campaign against the capital of the Hammadids (1015–1152), the scope of which signaled a change in the scale of military campaigns, with a significant mobilization of human and material resources, both on land and at sea. After the victory at Sétif in 1152, the campaign allowed him to annex the domains of the Hammadids, then the Zirids. In 1160, a new campaign, which had required an equally formidable land and sea mobilization, brought victory over the Norman squadron in Sicily and ended with the conquest of Mahdia and the coastal towns of Ifriqiya up to Tripoli.[50] The sovereigns of Marrakech now claimed a caliphal title, which gave the sultan of Cairo cause to fear that their significant naval and ground resources might be used to conquer Egypt.

However, after the successes in the Maghreb, the situation in al-Andalus completely monopolized the Almohads' military resources against the Christians: in 1162, the caliphate mobilized the army and the fleet for a campaign in the Iberian Peninsula, which was fought on several fronts and therefore justified the construction of the four hundred ships. ʿAbd al-Mu'min would die before they were completed. His successors, Abu Yaʿqub Yusuf (1163–1184) and his son Abu Yusuf Yaʿqub (1184–1198), waged war in the Peninsula while the dissident Ibn Ghaniya, a member of a family formerly in the service of the Almoravids, succeeded in taking control of the Balearics and refused to recognize the caliphs' authority.[51] He seized Béjaïa in 1185, then opened a new front in Ifriqiya, threatening and weakening the Almohads from within their own empire.[52] Consequently, the potential ambition to expand to the east was no longer an option as of 1160.

This universalist ambition rested on a strategy of comprehensive mobilization of ground and naval forces when the objective was located close to the sea. In 1195, after the defeat of Alfonso VIII (1158–1214) at Alarcos, Abu Yusuf Yaʿqub al-Mansur ordered the founding of Rabat, transforming a military camp set up in 1150 on orders from ʿAbd al-

Mu'min into a caliphal city. This camp, which surrounded a palace on the south side of the Bou Regreg river, across from Salé, had become the gathering place for troops on all the campaigns planned by the first sovereign. The Moroccan capital's position had numerous advantages over Marrakech, the capital of the dynasty. Among its undeniable assets was the proximity of the fertile Atlantic plains, which made it easier to provide food for thousands of men and animals; a significantly shorter distance between the base camp and the front, whether Andalusian or Maghrebi; and the accessibility of the sea and the squadron. As indicated by Ibn Abi Zar' 's text, the port of al-Ma'mura, which was built at the mouth of the Sebou, north of Salé, close to the forests that provided some of the lumber for shipbuilding, became the empire's principal dockyard, where 120 ships were constructed for the first naval campaign against the port of Béjaïa.[53]

Building on the Legacies

The organization of the fleet is often presented as a mere result of the takeover of the Almoravid fleet by the Almohads, the new masters of the western Maghreb, with all its weapons, equipment, crews, and admirals included. There is no doubt that the Almohads wanted to take advantage of the infrastructure and fleets available thanks to the efficient maritime organization in place from the Umayyad era through the Almoravid period; for instance, the rallying of the admirals who commanded the Almoravid squadrons, all members of the Banu Maymun family, made it possible to organize the blockade of Ceuta and Oran, without which these coastal cities could not be seized.[54]

The Almohads had control over a significant stretch of the seaboard, ranging from the ocean coastlines to Tripoli of Libya. However, they were not able to take control of all the ports of the Almoravid period. The most serious loss was of two strategic estuaries: the mouths of the Ebro at Tortosa, which was destroyed by Genoa and Pisa in 1146, and the Tagus, which had been seized by the young Portuguese kingdom along with Lisbon in 1147. The Portuguese capital and the ports of the northern coast provided the necessary human and material resources for Afonso Henriques (1128–1185) to form the first Christian naval force to fight Islam on the ocean. On the other side of the Iberian Peninsula, it took an exceptional mobilization and nearly ten-year blockade to recapture Almería. Defeat in the Balearics, which remained out of reach until 1205, was equally damaging. On the other hand, the Almohad seaboard expanded considerably to the east, at the expense of the Hammadids and their capital, then of the Normans in Ifriqiya.[55] Through control of Tunis, Mahdia, and Tripoli, Western Muslims once again had access to the eastern Mediterranean. However, their ground army and fleet were totally occupied by the war in al-Andalus.[56] The rise in power of the Tyrrhenian ports on one side of the Peninsula and of the Portuguese fleet on the other (until its defeat at Cabo Espichel, south of the Portuguese capital, in 1181), followed by the intervention in the south of Portugal in 1189 of largely English crusaders on their way to the Third Crusade, demanded not only terrestrial campaigns but the presence of the caliphal fleet in Iberian waters, ready to intervene on both sides of the Peninsula at once if necessary.

The protection of trade routes was equally important. Maritime traffic benefited from this investment, particularly on the Atlantic rim. The written documents provide convincing evidence that the ports were thriving as the outlets of a now-unified inland region after the elimination of Barghawata resistance. Along with the construction of the dockyard at al-Maʿmura, port infrastructures were reinforced all along the Maghreb's ocean seaboard up to the threshold of the Sahara. Azemmour and Safi, the two cities that served as ports for Marrakech, experienced rapid growth.[57]

The importance of the sea in the Almohad dynasty's plans was therefore not simply a matter of ʿAbd al-Mu'min's being a native of the maritime region of Hunayn. The conquest of strategic coastal towns, particularly Ceuta and Oran, would have been impossible without a fleet; similarly, the major mobilizations of the squadron ensured the success of the campaigns against Almería in 1158, Béjaïa in 1151 and 1184, and Tunis and Mahdia in 1159–1160. The surviving letters of the Almohad chancellery, which reflect the caliphs' positions, provide remarkable insight into the strategic data that put the maritime space at the center of the empire.[58]

The Exceptional Promotion of the Maritime Administration and Naval Campaigns in the Context of the Almohad Jihad

While the available caliphal documentation has not yet yielded all of its secrets, the relative abundance of information about the sea is a telltale sign. The number of chronicles preserved is admittedly higher than under previous dynasties, but the sea plays a relatively important part in all of them. The Maghrebi and Andalusian historians were officials of the chancelleries who were aware of the sea's importance.[59] Al-Baydhaq, who belonged to the small circle of the first companions of Ibn Tumart (1130) and ʿAbd al-Mu'min, left a valuable account of the beginnings of the movement. Ibn Sahib al-Salat (d. after 1173), a native of the Beja area in the Portuguese region of Alentejo, a member of the *makhzin* (royal court / administration), and the head of caliphal finances, wrote a chronicle covering the years 1159–1173, featuring remarkably precise information about the caliphal administration in al-Andalus. ʿAbd al-Wahid al-Marrakushi (d. after 1224) produced a compilation about the dynasty covering the entire period up to 1224.[60] As for Ibn al-Qattan (d. 1231), a native of Fez, the detailed and original nature of the information he provided, in particular about the navy, shows that he must have been highly familiar with the palace and administrative circles.[61]

This nonexhaustive list must be rounded out by the great later chronicles by Ibn ʿIdhari, Ibn Khaldun, and Ibn al-Athir, which I mentioned previously for earlier periods. The number of references to the engagement of the caliph's squadrons, as well as the details provided, show that Ibn ʿIdhari, the author of a history of the Maghreb, had access to precise information about everything relating to the sea, and particularly to naval battles, which are exceptionally described in the Arabic chronicles but are missing for previous periods.[62]

The chancellery letters, many of which have survived, show the caliphs' personal interest in the organization of the fleet. These messages disseminated a variety of news reports that reveal the essential role played by the squadron, the preferred weapon of the Almohad caliphate's "strategy of universalization."[63]

In terms of maritime policy, ʿAbd al-Mu'min's primary concern was to control traffic between the two continents. After capturing Ceuta in 1146, he made the port city the gathering place for the fleet, which used it as a base from which to traverse all of the empire's naval spaces. In one of his letters to the *talaba*—officials who held a high rank in the caliphate's hierarchy, immediately below the *sayyids* (members of the Almohad family), and were taught to spread Almohad doctrine and head the administration of the provinces—serving in the port on the strait, he asked for strict control of sea traffic in this important strategic zone, in order to block off traffic with ports like Málaga and Almuñécar, which did not always submit to caliphal authority. At the same time, he appointed Abu Muhammad 'Abd Allah b. Sulayman to serve as both head of the squadron and governor of the city; he was intentionally creating a precedent by entrusting two positions to the same person, a close friend of the caliph who had originally gained recognition as an admiral. In a letter written to the port city's inhabitants from Rabat in May 1156, the caliph pledged bay'a—which amounted to proclaiming the name of the heir to the throne, in this case his son Abu 'Abd Allah b. 'Abd al-Mu'min—then provided a series of specifications regarding the administration of maritime traffic:

> The *talaba* of Ceuta and its regions—may God assist them—consulted together regarding the sea and the means of crossing it. They debated about the question of the security of ports and the surrounding areas, because it [the sea] is the connection between the two shores. . . . It is necessary to unite the entire Ghomara country and the tribes settled as far as Ceuta and Tangier, the "two islands" [Algeciras and Tarifa], Malága and its dependencies. All these areas need to be brought together and administered by a single governor. This would facilitate the task on an administrative level; this way we could build a war fleet for the great expedition [planned against the infidel] under one leader.[64]

The province of the "two shores" and its ports were under the orders of a single governor headquartered in the naval base.[65] In keeping with a practice expanded to all of the empire's provinces, admiral and governor 'Abd Allah b. Sulayman's immediate superior was one of the caliph's sons, *sayyid* Abu Sa'id 'Uthman. In referring to the two principal African ports, Ibn Khaldun himself drew attention to the strait's strategic importance within the naval apparatus: "Since 'Abd al-Mu'min's accession to the throne, Ceuta and Tangier had always been considered the two most important governments of the Almohad empire, since they were at once maritime fortresses, sea ports, shipbuilding dockyards, and embarkation points for volunteers for the jihad. Therefore, the command of these cities was always entrusted to *sayyids*."[66]

The sovereign also wanted to express the importance he granted to the administration of maritime spaces. By imposing a chain of command headed by the Commander of the Faithful himself, the caliph was reviving a tradition established by the Fatimid and Umayyad caliphs. The choice of the Atlantic coast as the site for the dynastic ribat (Rabat), both terrestrial and maritime, can only be understood by connecting the founding of Rabat and al-Ma'mura to the dynasty's original spaces: Igiliz, the Almohad movement's first ribat, in the Sous valley; Tinmal, the initial base for the doctrine and conquest, founded by Ibn Tumart in the Atlas Mountains;[67] Marrakech, the dynasty's first capital; and Rabat, the departure point for the campaigns aiming to achieve the conquest of Islam by land and sea.

The caliph asked for the regime's dignitaries to be sent a report of the major campaigns, in which the navy often played a determining role. Of the thirty-seven chancellery letters published by Évariste Lévi-Provençal, six concern expeditions that required the squadron's support. Along with the creation of the maritime province of the strait and the circumstances of the founding of Gibraltar, these reports, which were widely distributed in the chancelleries, covered at least five major campaigns during which the navy distinguished itself. These accounts reveal the extent to which the fleet had become a source of pride for the caliphate.[68] The squadrons' interventions showed that the caliphs could strike wherever they wanted and that no land was inaccessible to them. An indispensable tool in an empire with the sea at its heart, the fleet also became one of the essential weapons of the jihad, made a mainstay of caliphal universality by Ibn Tumart and 'Abd al-Mu'min. After the victorious campaign of 1203–1205 in the Balearics, which had required extensive human and material resources, al-Nasir expressed the place that control of the sea held in the sovereign's strategy by presenting the expedition as "a victory against the Christians and their principalities on the Mediterranean coastline. Indeed, the taking of Mallorca is a real catastrophe for the king of Aragon and Barcelona."[69]

With this statement, the Almohad leader also showed that the period during which the Almohads had been unable to control the Balearics had been an even greater catastrophe for them. In fact, the archipelago was lost to Islam by 1229.

The Sovereign's Personal Relationship to the Maritime World

If we exclude crossings of the Strait of Gibraltar, the caliph's presence on a ship in 1160 to inspect the defenses of Mahdia, then under siege by his fleet, was a rare occurrence.[70] However, the texts frequently refer to the sovereigns' fondness for the sea and, especially, their personal interest in the fleet and sailors. Histories about the Almohad sovereigns report a few speeches in which these rulers revealed their constant concern with maritime space, a concern shared with the Umayyads of Córdoba and the Fatimids, and for the same reasons. Several authors of the period even describe practices completely unparalleled in previous periods, emphasizing the navy's place in the representation of Almohad sovereignty. For instance, figures in the highest leadership positions, particularly in the military, had to know how to command a ship and a squadron.[71] Ibn al-Qattan and Ibn Simak (d. after 1383) both described this form of schooling:

> There were nearly three thousand *huffaz* [the "guardians" of the faith, or "those who know the Koran by heart"], all the same age, from good families, and, it was said, born on the same night; they were taught the works of the Almohad Mahdi, such as the *tawhid*,[72] over a period of six months. The caliph personally took responsibility for testing their knowledge and giving them advice. On other days, he trained them and introduced them to all the techniques of combat, fencing, archery, dueling with spears, and throwing javelins; he had them take riding and swimming

> lessons and do physical exercises; the caliph also presided over maritime maneuvers in an artificial body of water close to his palace [in Marrakech] and built for this purpose. Large and small crafts (*qata'i*) participated in these maneuvers and the novice sailors had to learn to row, to fight, to board enemy ships, and to command their units. This teaching was sometimes brutally conveyed, other times more civilly. The expense for these students' education was entirely covered by the *makhzin*.[73]

Next, training courses were held at sea, along with launches of the fleet at Ceuta, both to provide an opportunity to admire the caliphs' formidable black galleys and to teach students the complex piloting of a squadron. The *huffaz* were distinguished members of the Berber tribes, recruited to become "officers" of the caliphate, trained both to be in the administration and to command the army and navy. The *tullab*, the elite that composed the government entourage, were recruited from their ranks. This "school" represented the caliph's close tie to the sea. By building an artificial body of water big enough to simulate a naval battle in his capital, located deep inland, the sovereign created the impression of bringing the sea to himself; more than a real "naval academy," this adornment to the palace, like its fountains and even more so its naval exercises verging on performances, expressed the caliphate's universalist ambitions. The indoctrination of the *huffaz* was achieved by teaching them the doctrine of Ibn Tumart, along with lessons in ethics sometimes taught by the philosopher caliph Abu Ya'qub Yusuf himself. This schooling had an impact beyond mere training for naval warfare, while the symbolic presence of the sea in the caliphal palace was also far from groundless. This is confirmed by a letter, probably dictated by 'Abd al-Mu'min during the reorganization of the navy, in which the importance of the maritime space in the representation of caliphal universality comes into focus:

> You have demonstrated great loyalty to us. You have shown all your ability to work for the common good, on land as on sea. The sea is an unknown that demands great vigilance. Behind this

> sea there are so many nations and countries that reap enormous benefits from maritime activities. . . . There is so much at stake in this area that the sea is vital for your region and that is why we have decided, with Allah's help, to remedy past shortfalls in the interest of all, the traveler like the tradesman. . . . Be aware that the sea is an asset for you. It is a source of life, it provides you daily sustenance and maritime commerce generates great profits.[74] . . . We know that when we are absent from the city you are the guarantors that its institutions function properly. . . . The new admiral allows every hope for we only know him to have qualities and he succeeds at everything he undertakes. He is the best of all the Almohad *tullab*.[75]

The Mother Sea, the defense of the Dar al-Islam, and the protection of the merchant and traveler were themes of sovereignty, referencing the Koran, and were fundamental responsibilities of the caliph's government, delegated to the admiral, a leading figure ruling at the caliph's side. Far from our contemporary notion of "territorial waters," the maritime zone controlled by the fleet was theoretically unlimited, like the caliph's sovereignty, which was supposed to extend to the entire world. However, the caliph's authority on the sea had never previously been theorized in such a clear, precise manner. Coinciding with this idyll between the sultan and maritime space, Arabic literary production about the sea had never been as prolific in the West as in the twelfth and thirteenth centuries.

A Familiar Sea

The earliest preserved letters and maritime travel diaries in which the experience of the maritime journey figures prominently date from the twelfth century, despite the fact that embarking for a crossing—for instance, to make the pilgrimage to Mecca—had by then long been commonplace.[76] Should this be interpreted as a sign of a change in perception of travel by water? The most famous travel diary (*rihla*) is by Ibn Jubayr, who boarded a Genoese ship in Ceuta in February 1183 and reached Alexandria in less than one month, proving that galleys also sailed during the off season.[77] The crossing to and from Alexandria—the return journey was interrupted by the Genoese boat's shipwreck on the coast of Sicily—has an essential place in the pilgrim's narrative. The reason the Andalusian man of letters left one of the most precise accounts of seafaring we have is that he felt he was being put to the test every time he embarked, a feeling that went beyond the usual accounts of a sea crossing's potential risks. The legacy of a long-established practice, the sea crossing was less risky aboard a Christian ship and less expensive and quicker than traveling by land. Like the exploitation of the sea by those who lived on its shores, particularly in the Maghreb, the sea crossing bears witness to the maritime world's essential place in the collective memory of Muslims living close to the Mediterranean. There are numerous traces of the crossing in Arabic literature of the period. Among the writers who passed down their memories of maritime experiences, Ibn 'Amira, a member of the entourage of Caliph al-Rashid (1232–1242), left a long account of his trying journey aboard a Hafsid ship that was to take him from Ceuta to Tunis.[78]

Travel narratives devoted an increasing amount of attention to maritime transport. The hagiographies inform us that with favorable winds a sailboat could reach Salé from the Strait of Gibraltar in under three days. Biographies of Sufis, who were heavily involved in the sea trades and traveled frequently, confirm that travel by sea, whether for professional or other reasons, was commonplace.[79] The caliphal administration set the example. Ibn 'Idhari passes down the travel account of Almohad dignitaries traveling directly between the Guadalquivir and Mazagan; Ibn Sahib al-Salat reports that 'Abd al-Mu'min significantly improved the caliphate's maritime postal service, compared to the Almoravid period, and that it played a significant part in communications between the empire's regions. We also have a description of an inspection tour conducted by 'Abd al-Salam al-Kumi, a representative of the caliph who was able to carry out his mission in fifteen days, including the round-trip crossings between Salé and Seville, with a stop in Córdoba.[80]

Al-Bakri had already reported on progress in the description of the seas and the increasingly accurate knowledge of various areas thanks to far more comprehensive mapping of coastal zones. This evolution of geography reached a peak in the twelfth century with *The Book of Roger,* in particular because its author was able to be equally meticulous in describing the Muslim and Christian areas of the Mediterranean borderlands. He regularly provided details about the sea and its resources, as did al-Zuhri, a probable native of Almería who explained the migration and fishing of bluefin tuna and its treatment in the eponymous business in Tarifa, close to the fishing zones; it is no secret how much tuna fishing in Sicily owes to the Muslim period. The Sicilian geographer al-Idrisi also liked to mention marine fauna, for instance by listing the twelve known species of fish caught in the area of Bizerte. As for the author of the *Kitab al-Istibsar,* he shared al-Zuhri's curiosity about mullet fishing and the inevitable legends that went along with this kind of story.[81] The curiosity of geographers starting with al-Idrisi was also aroused by coral mining, an equally lucrative activity, albeit a difficult one.[82] This rapid overview simply suggests that knowledge of the maritime space and its riches went hand in hand with a more intense occupation of a now-familiar maritime environment.[83]

While the Sicilian's geographic work remained "largely indebted to the classics of Arab geography," in his treatment of both the Islamic world and more distant worlds, it completed and considerably enriched the available facts.[84] Al-Idrisi quite systematically distinguishes the routes "by land" (*tariq al-barr*) from the routes "by sea" (*tariq al-bahr*), both in his book of geography and in a work attributed to him and specifically devoted to itineraries.[85] He had access to information precise enough to allow him to differentiate between those sea itineraries on the Atlantic Ocean that were direct—*rusiyya* (like a taut rope)—and those that ran along the coast—*taqwiran* (in a curve).[86] For Latin Europe, he had access to reports by a variety of sources. Those provided by a Portuguese navigator and a Gascon from Bayonne, transcribed by an Arabic speaker, allowed him to inventory the maritime itineraries to Santiago de Compostela from Bordeaux on one side and Coimbra on the other. He is the only author, including among the Latins, to have passed down knowledge of these pilgrimage routes by sea.[87] As we have seen, the circulation of information on the sea touched on many subjects, including those in the technical realm, and easily crossed the borders between Christianity and Islam.

The Sea of the Jurists and Saints, a Space of Law and Sacredness

A work written toward the middle of the ninth century, the *Treatise Concerning the Leasing of Ships and the Claims between Passengers* (*Kitab akriyat al-sufun wa l-naza bayna ahliha*), marked an acceleration in the region's production of jurisprudence about the sea, which at this date was exclusively Malaki.[88] This jurisprudence would reach an apex in the Almoravid and Almohad period (twelfth to thirteenth centuries). Of the jurists who produced fatwas related to maritime space, three figures of the twelfth century stand out, all of whose opinions are well represented in the fifteenth-century anthology by al-Wansharisi: the Andalusian Abu l-Walid b. Rushd (d. 1126), the Sicilian-born Ifriqiyan al-Mazari (d. 1141), and the Qadi 'Iyad from Ceuta (d. 1179):

> Question: al-Mazari was consulted regarding a partnership contract stipulating that three people were forming a partnership, with one supplying ten *qafiz* of sumac and the other two supplying two donkeys. The deal was made based on a loan from the former to the other two. The negotiation then established that it [would be of] five dinars, of which they would have to pay two thirds in taxes. [They also established] that the owners of the two donkeys would take everything to Sicily. But once both of them were on the ship, an adverse wind picked up and they had to go back to a village near Mahdia. One of them unloaded his donkey and gave up on the trip after having made this agreement for a partnership.[89]

Like all jurists, these three legal experts largely used predecessors' fatwas directly or indirectly relating to the maritime domain, often to update them, as was the accepted jurisprudential practice. At the same time, certain questions led them to deal with contemporary events: thus, in twelve fatwas, al-Mazari more specifically addressed the problems that could arise due to ties maintained by the people of Ifriqiya with Muslims who lived in Sicily, now under Christian domination.[90] In al-Andalus, the "victory of the great Andalusian qadis" under the

Almoravid regime spurred the production of several fatwas up to the Almohad period, all of which related to the development of maritime exchanges and the frequency of crossings between Europe and Africa.[91] One of these qadis was Ibn Rushd, grandfather of the philosopher Averroes, who focused on issues relating to pilgrims' travel to Mecca. Qadi 'Iyad, a native of Ceuta, often expressed himself on legal questions relating to the sea.[92]

These jurists' attention to maritime issues highlights a major societal development that had begun in the tenth century. As of the twelfth century, the rapid expansion of commerce in Muslim ports, the practice of sea travel, and naval war and its effects created a demand for a more precise, updated legislative framework on chartering, the consequences of shipwrecks, and the status of sailors, as well as new social phenomena like the status of wives left alone by seafaring husbands or the conditions for travel in infidel lands, which was theoretically forbidden and required a legislator's intervention.

The importance of mystic "saints" in the society of the Muslim West can be measured by the production of *tasawwuf* literature, new biographical works about Sufi saints, as of the end of the twelfth century. These lives of saints contain a great deal of information about the sea, particularly in works by mystics living on the shores of the Mediterranean, such as al-Badisi (d. 1322), a fourteenth-century biographer who spent his entire life in his native city of Badis on the craggy coastline of the Rif.[93] The attraction to marine horizons in religious circles was not a new phenomenon, as al-Maliki showed in the eleventh century. With the rise of Sufism, retreating to a ribat or a high elevation facing the sea became a favored ascetic practice to follow the mystic path (*tariqa*). This ascetic virtue developed in the ribats in increasingly varied forms, ranging from retreat to a hermitage on the frontier, sometimes built by the saint himself, to the large initiatory fellowships where masters taught disciples. The graves of the most famous masters attracted numerous followers, prefiguring the appearance of lodges (*zawiyas*) in the Maghreb and Iberian Peninsula in the twelfth century.

The rise of Sufism stimulated other forms of mysticism, in both urban societies and rural communities, where many of these respected figures played an important social role.[94] Unlike the Almoravids, the Almohad caliphs found their cohabitation with mystical circles eased by their frequent alliances with the Malikis. This proximity to the power and success of the mystical movements led to the production of biographies devoted to the most famous masters, starting in the late twelfth century and including the treatise by Muhammad al-Tamimi (d. 1208) and, early in the thirteenth century, a major text by al-Tadili. However, the best way to comprehend the Sufi school remains the "classic" biographical dictionaries, which particularly provide a better sense of the movement's size in a city like Ceuta, a major center of Maghrebi Sufism.[95]

This is the context in which the marine world enters the hagiographic literature, insofar as the professions of the sea, but also travel and participation in naval activities, encouraged many vocations to holiness. Al-Badisi's approach is characteristic of this particular tie, formed with the people of his seaside city in the Rif. His fourteenth-century book about the lives of several saints of the Rif describes many acts of piety related to the sea. Throughout these biographies, a great deal of information is provided about maritime life and its trades, as well as the dangers posed by Christian piracy. Before al-Badisi, Muhammad al-Tamimi left many accounts of maritime practices, particularly on fishing and the life of people of the sea. Miracles, these narratives' main subject, often took place on or by the sea. Al-'Afazi, the author of a biography of the saints of the thirteenth century, highlighted several of the saints' baraka (beneficent force): during crossings, they were able to save crews from a raging sea or to deliver prisoners from the hands of Christian pirates without entering into combat. The sea had become one of the preferred settings for theatricalizing miracles, directly or through the intercession of a saint appealed to by another mystic: "Abu Jami' said: 'I arrived in Alexandria. I found a boat there bound for Quz. The sea started to rage, people began to bid each other goodbye.' I said: 'O Sidi Abu Zayd, my thought is with you.' The sea calmed down as soon as I appealed to the shaykh."[96]

Even once the last Mediterranean caliphate had died out, the ties formed between the people of Islam and the maritime space did not disappear. Nonetheless, the Almohad decline brought about an attitude of defiance toward a now Latin sea, a defiance that had already reached the Mediterranean East by the time of the Mamluk sultans. Like the historians of his era, Ibn Khaldun considered the Mediterranean lost to the Muslims. However, the societies of Maghrebi ports such as Béjaïa continued to live off the sea and to perpetuate the tradition of highly skilled sailors who made the region's reputation.[97]

II

MEDITERRANEAN STRATEGIES OF THE CALIPHS

Most of the information provided by the Arabic texts tends to create a picture of a Mediterranean space seized and dominated by the caliphs and the authorities, particularly those in the legal sphere. The Christian perception of the Arab occupation and development of the Sea of the Romans in the first centuries of the Middle Ages reinforces this impression of a maritime space reduced to a field of confrontations, wiping out any other initiative. The discovery of the Geniza letters and Shlomo Goitein's interpretation of this treasure have dispelled the idea of a caliphal monopoly on activity on the sea and brought to light the existence of another Muslim Mediterranean, one of merchants accompanied by pious travelers headed to Mecca and of scholars roaming the Islamic world at the very moment when the Latins were taking over.

However, despite the precariousness of accounts from the "dark" centuries, the sum of information provided by Arab geographers and, sometimes, external documents—in particular Latin sources—reveals a far greater diversity of activity related to the sea. It also shows human development—considerable on the scale of the period—of the shores of the inner sea, at least as of the ninth century in Islam, at the time and in the regions where Islam's authority was reinforced. In fact, the situation of the Muslim Mediterranean mirrors that of the Latin shores in that it must be understood in continuity with the medieval occupation and development of the sea and measured with instruments other than purely "economic" gauges, which are ineffective for a period without available statistics.

The same sultanate sources, supplemented by the tremendous production of the ulema, yield another idea of the Muslims' relationship to the Sea of the Romans. Yes, confrontation was one of the matrices of the Muslim Mediterranean's development. But as the caliphates' commercial strategies show, Islam's impact on developments of the medieval Mediterranean, as well as the diversity of domains opened on the sea and revealed by the Muslims, can be grasped through a group of far more complex factors, supplied by varied records, though most come from the chancelleries of the caliphates and sultanates and the writings of those in the circles of power.

8

THE MEDITERRANEAN OF THE TWO EMPIRES

BEGINNING WITH THE TAKING of Gaza in 634, two years after the death of Muhammad, the Arab conquerors prioritized conquering the Mediterranean Sea and the bordering Christian lands. Muʿawiya declared that it was necessary to use the naval resources left by the Byzantines in Egypt and Syria to attack the Greeks on the water, in order to block supplies from reaching strongholds on the coast of the Bilad al-Sham that were resisting the Arabs. Neither ʿUmar nor any of the men in his entourage could have been surprised or troubled by this suggestion, but only the caliph could decide on the time and mode of maritime commitment.[1]

For the period from 643 to 655, Muslim and Christian historians highlighted three major events marking the beginnings of the Arab engagement on the sea: the Byzantine fleet's counterattacks on the Syrian and Egyptian coasts; the naval Battle of the Masts; and the Muslim landings in Arwad and the island of Cyprus.

Beginning in 634, armed believers set off to follow the itineraries they had routinely taken as merchants before the Hegira. Gaza had long been an essential stop on the trade route from the Hejaz to the Mediterranean basin. Traditions about the Arab conquest gave Palestine a particular place, first in respect to what Jerusalem represented for Islam, and second because the country was one of the principal routes Meccans followed to the Bilad al-Sham. The Arabs' collective memory had kept a record of Muhammad's visit to Hebron before the beginning of the Prophecy, as well as of 'Umar b. al-Khattab's stay in Palestine.[2] Coming from the opposite direction, the merchants of the Near East had begun regularly visiting the area of the Hejaz and beyond several decades before the birth of the Prophet. The presence of several inscriptions on Arabic itineraries confirms the importance of relations between populations of the Near East and Byzantium's influence on the region.[3] However, the Arab traditionists paid more specific attention to the principal Arab armies' progression inland, where they encountered and defeated the imperial armies of the Sassanids in al-Qadisiyya, Mesopotamia, in 634, then in Nahavand, Iran, in 642, and the Byzantine armies in Ajnadayn, Palestine, in 634 and farther north, on the Yarmuk, in 636. These victories opened the path to the two capitals: Ctesiphon, the imperial city of the shahs, located in the center of Iraq and already destroyed by the Greeks in 618, and Damascus, the Byzantine capital.[4] On the other hand, their advance was more difficult along the Palestinian and Syrian coastline, due to the resistance of the port cities, which were resupplied by the Greeks. While touring the Near East, 'Umar appointed 'Abd al-Qays governor of the coastlines (*sawahil*) and 'Amr b. 'Abassa supervisor of granaries (*al-ahra*). He made M'uawiya the governor of Syria.[5]

The siege of Caesarẹa, the longest in the history of the conquests, marked the beginning of Mu'awiya's military glory, though the taking of the city was not presented as a decisive success. According to Theophanes, the venture had lasted seven years, ending in 640, and earned the Umayyad leader a reputation as an efficient and stubborn soldier.[6] It was the presence of the Greek fleet that significantly hampered the progress of the Arab conquest, despite the fact that the number of available Greek units was low, at a time when the Christians remained alone on the water without any serious adversary. The Basileus considered the fleet a potential threat to his power, insofar as it gave the emperor's rivals a direct path to Constantinople; Heraclius (610–641) was keenly aware of this danger, given that he himself had taken power thanks to the squadron that had carried him unopposed from Carthage to the capital.[7] However, there were enough units to resupply and bring reinforcements to the besieged coastal cities, even before Constans II (641–668) bolstered his naval resources to thwart the Arabs' attempt at conquest. With the sea closed to the attackers, the Arabs would have needed exceptional circumstances to take control of the maritime strongholds from dry land. When such circumstances arose in Tripoli of Libya in 642–643, Ibn 'Abd al-Hakam attributed them to divine favor:

> The siege had lasted for a month without any results, when one day a man from the Banu Mudjil left the camp to go hunting with seven of his brothers in arms. . . . The sea reached to both ends of the city ramparts and the city was not separated from the water by any wall, so that the ships (*sufun*) of the Rums could get to their houses via the port. The Mudjili and his companions noticed that the water level had dropped, leaving a passage open by which they could enter. They stepped into it and when they arrived near the Church, they shouted "Allah Akbar." The Greeks could only take refuge aboard their ships. 'Amr and his companions, seeing that sabers had been drawn in the middle of the city, advanced at the head of the troops and penetrated their homes. The Greeks could only escape on the lightest vessels, and 'Amr seized everything in the city.[8]

The taking of the city certainly reveals the limits of its naval support, but it also highlights that the Greeks, once driven back by the Arabs on land, could find safe refuge on board their ships and remain inaccessible. From here, they could threaten the conquests at any moment. The Greeks' return to Alexandria in 645 spectacularly illustrated the Arabs' recurrent weakness due to their lack of a policy to have a presence on the sea. As governor of the region of Jordan, a district that included Palestine's coastal strip, Mu'awiya directed the caliph's attention to the need to provide the army of believers with a permanent naval force in the Mediterranean, taking as an example the attacks launched by Greek sailors from the island of Arwad, visible from the Syrian coast: "O Amir al-Mu'minin, there is a village in Syria whose inhabitants hear the barking of the Byzantines' dogs and the crow of their cock, because the

Byzantines are established directly across the water at a certain distance from the coast of the province of Homs."[9]

Not only could the Greeks threaten Muslim coastlines from any anchorage in the Mediterranean, suddenly coming into view without leaving the Arab forces enough time to react, but the reinforcement of their fleet under Constans II could at any moment compromise the Arab presence in Syria and Egypt. The temporary loss of Alexandria confirmed this prognosis. The conquest of the eastern seaboard had lasted ten years, provisionally coming to an end with the taking of Tripoli of Libya, after the evacuation of the population by the Greek fleet in 644–645 had left the city empty.[10] Following the Egyptian capital's first capitulation in 642, 'Amr b. al-'As had to mobilize considerable forces to recapture it from the Greeks in 645–646. These efforts revealed an obvious strategic flaw that the Arab generals could no longer ignore: from a military point of view, the sea and the coast formed an inseparable whole, and the coastline could not be protected without control of the maritime space.

It was as clear for the Arabs as it was for the Greeks that superiority on the sea went to those who controlled the maritime routes, which required the conquest of the principal islands. On the Aegean Sea, currents and winds limited traffic from the north to the zone south of the Dodecanese and the Cyclades; since it was still difficult for ships to sail against the headwind at this time, the crossing was only possible in certain seasons.[11] In a single decade, the Muslims attacked Arwad, Cyprus, Crete, and probably Rhodes in order to push back the port installations from which Greek expeditions were launched and cut off the route for attacks launched from the coasts of Anatolia.[12]

'Umar could therefore not deny that it was necessary for the Arabs to have a maritime presence if Byzantium and, specifically, Constantinople were to be the Muslims' primary objectives. The caliph sought the opinion of 'Amr, then governor of Egypt, the only country that could supply boats and crews, in order to evaluate the Muslims' naval strength and particularly their naval experience, which was insufficient to face the seasoned Byzantines: "The Sea of Syria surpasses everything on earth in terms of length. . . . Given that, how do we transport troops on this difficult and treacherous creature?"[13] Lengthiness entailed danger, because inexperienced Arab officers did not yet grasp logistics and navigation; the Arabs' sailors were all enlisted Copts, sometimes recruited by force, now up against veteran sailors. At the time, considerations regarding the military balance prevailed, and they would serve as an argument to postpone Mu'awiya's plan: the undertaking was too risky at that point, for the Arabs were not ready to put out to sea—at least not on this sea.

However, 'Umar encouraged Mu'awiya and 'Amr to create the conditions to make such a venture possible, as is confirmed by the chroniclers of Baghdad, notably al-Baladhuri and al-Ya'qubi, who laconically enumerate repairs made to ports, particularly in Acre and Tyre, and efforts to repopulate coastal cities such as Tripoli:

> When Mu'awiya decided to sail from Acre to Cyprus, he had repairs carried out in Acre and Tyre. . . . Hisham b. al-Layth [reports], according to the authorities [the authors of traditions]: "When we settled in Tyre and on the coastline, there were Arab troops and many Greek [tradesmen] already settled there. Later, populations from other regions came to settle with us, all along the coast of the Bilad al-Sham. . . . In 49 / 669–670, the Greek [tradesmen] came to settle on the coast. At that time, [naval] construction was confined to Egypt. Following the orders of Mu'awiya b. Abi Sufyan, several tradesmen and carpenters were established together along the [Syrian] coast. All of the installations in Palestine were concentrated in Acre.[14]

The first preparations were both defensive—rebuilding Syrian ports damaged by sieges during the Arab conquest—and offensive—getting ready the squadron that would attack Cyprus and Arwad in 644–645 and, in the case of the larger of the two islands, again in 648. In the meantime, the reasonably good state of the maritime infrastructures and administration left by the Greeks in the valley of the Nile made it possible to launch a naval expedition as early as 643. Led by Wahb b. 'Umar, the expedition cast off to support the offensive against Amorium, initiated by the Umayyad leader and under the command of General Abu l-A'war al-Sulami.[15] The 648 expedition against Cyprus, one of the bases from which the Greek squadron had left to attack Alexandria in 644–645, was the first to be mentioned in the Arabic and Greek sources. The Umayyad chroniclers gave Amr credit for the conquest of Egypt and the repair of the dockyards, Mu'awiya for the conquest of the Near Eastern ports and the naval initiatives that served as preludes to a lasting Muslim presence on the Mare Nostrum and the attacks on Constantinople. As for the wise 'Umar, who was to be followed by 'Uthman, he set the schedule for the preparations that would lead the Arabs to victory on the Christians' own playing field, thus showing that the Commander of the Faithful remained solely responsible for the strategy of the conquest.[16]

At the time of 'Umar's death in 644, the Arab presence on the shores of the Mediterranean was still fragile, as had been shown by the Greeks' return to their former Egyptian capital. It only became possible to deploy a Muslim squadron once the Arab administration was able to organize an expedition with the participation of former Greek and Egyptian executives: the squadron in question was based in Qulzum (Clysma, Suez), a former Byzantine port and dockyard on the Red Sea, and was sent to resupply Mecca and Medina with wheat. Nonetheless, the rehabilitation of material and administrative structures and the mobilization of local expertise in the service of the new empire allowed the Muslims to move securely into the Aegean Sea.[17]

APPLYING A MARITIME STRATEGY

With the agreement of his relative 'Uthman, the governor of Syria, Mu'awiya was able to put into practice a strategy intended to ward off the Byzantine threat from the sea and to cordon off the routes separating the two empires' maritime frontiers: the Mediterranean was controlled from the islands. Cyprus was attacked in 648, and again in 652–653. The naval victory at the Battle of the Masts off the coast of Lycia in 655 enabled the Muslim fleets to get close to the coasts of Anatolia, to back first the attacks in Cappadocia, then those aimed at Constantinople.

Momentum through Victory: The Battle of the Masts

The wars against the Sassanids and the rivalries between pretenders to the Basileus's throne had weakened the Greeks' defenses in Anatolia; transforming the navy was not on the agenda. Arab offensives in Armenia and Asia went unchecked until 653, when a young emperor returned to the front heading an army once again operational.[18] On the other hand, Byzantine Africa was starting to collapse from Egypt, lost once and for all in 645–646 after Alexandria was forced into submission, to Ifriqiya, where the defeat of Exarch Gregory outside Sbeitla in 649 forced the Christians to pay an enormous ransom and to abandon Tripolitania and the south of Roman Africa. After 'Uqba b. Nafi''s victorious campaign and the founding of Kairouan in 670, the Byzantines could only rely on the north of Tunisia and Carthage to control access to the central Mediterranean. In Italy, the Lombards were proving a threat up to the south of the peninsula; only Sicily seemed safe.[19]

The Basileus was therefore losing critical support from his African provinces. Africa and southern Italy, both continental and insular, had long supplied not only wheat through their grain fleet (probably until 618) but also essential naval resources, as proved by the way Heraclius seized power in 610.[20] Thanks to the Arabs' territorial gains along the African coastline, in particular the important port of call Barca, the Egyptian fleet could now attack Sicily. As early as 668–669, an assault was launched against Syracuse, the island's capital.

At the same time, the Muslims now had the infrastructure, ships, and crews to compete with the Greeks on the Aegean Sea. In 655, the naval victory at the Battle of the Masts—known as the Battle of Phoenix to the Greeks—was significant in that for perhaps the first time since the Battle of Actium, the Romans were faced with an imperial power that had the means to mobilize fleets comparable to those of the Christians, over a long period of time, and crews able to gain the upper hand at sea. Arab and Byzantine references to the naval battle roughly situate the encounter somewhere off the coast of Lycia, while the Egyptian fleet was headed for its shores.[21] No matter how this battle on the open sea actually unfolded—the Egyptians apparently won by boarding Greek ships—and the actual scope of the victory, this success served as recognition of the Muslims' ability to compete with the Greeks for maritime supremacy.

Though more experienced, the Greeks were weakened by the loss of seaboards vital to their power: at that time, neither Anatolia, nor the Balkans, nor Italy, and even less so the Black Sea, could compensate for the loss of the African and Asian coasts, which provided a significant share of naval armament until Constantinople became the imperial fleet's primary dockyard.[22]

The naval victory at the Battle of Phoenix allowed the Arabs to take the initiative and launch repeated operations at sea before Emperor Constans II and his successors could react. Under the government of Maslama b. Mukhallad al-Ansari, the Nile valley's place as the Islamic navy's principal base was reinforced by the construction of a new dockyard on the island of Rhoda, across from the capital, Fustat.[23] An exceptional document consisting of a complete "list" of Egyptian admirals—*ashab bahr Misr,* or "lords of the sea of Egypt"—from 644 to 749, found in Egyptian texts of the ninth and tenth centuries, reveals Egypt's position as a leading player on the Mediterranean in the period up to the fall of the Umayyads, despite the fact that it had no timber.[24] The first appointment in 644 of a "lord of the sea," a title that referred to both the head of the admiralty and the admiral commanding the squadron, coincided with the first expeditions on the Mediterranean. The papyri of Governor Qurra b. Sharik (709–714), written half a century later and found in Aphrodite, confirm that the Marwanids' shipyards and maritime administration functioned effectively, despite possible resistance from the populations solicited.[25] Under the Marwanids' rule, the first naval expeditions to strike in the central and western Mediterranean left from the coast of the Nile delta, reaching as far as the coast of Narbonne around 720.

During the same period, the Byzantine naval force was reorganized: Constantine IV (668–685) and Justinian II (685–695, 705–711) pursued reforms that led to a Byzantine maritime renewal.[26] The fleet's organization was adapted to the new situation created by the Arab conquests and was intended both to guard Constantinople and to provide the Aegean islands and the Anatolian coast with effective means to prevent the Arabs from getting to the Bosporus route. Moreover, the Byzantines took advantage of the unrest that broke out in 684, interrupting the dynamism inspired by the caliph, to regain the advantage on the water.[27] The Dar al-Islam's seafronts had already been exposed to new naval attacks from the Greeks following Yazid I's order to abandon anchorages in the islands that led to the Sea of Marmara, such as Rhodes: al-Burullus, a port on the delta, was attacked in 672, and Damietta in 708, leading to the capture of the governor of the sea Khalid b. Kaysan. Damietta was again attacked under Hisham's rule.[28]

Cyprus, Testing Ground for an Island Strategy

The 648 naval expedition targeting Cyprus was the first act in the Muslims' move onto the Mediterranean. According to al-Waqidi, the expedition was led by Muʿawiya, who may have been accompanied by his wife and family, on Caliph ʿUthman's orders. The island was the key to the maritime routes between Syria, Anatolia, and the Aegean Sea. The first expedition resembled the razzias the Arabs launched on land before they began a conquest. It resulted in an agreement by which the Cypriots consented to pay an annual tribute equivalent to what they were already paying the Basileus. Their religious status remained unchanged, as was specifically recognized by the right of Greeks and Cypriots to marry without prior authorization from the Muslims. This agreement, original for the particular status it granted the islanders, turned the island into a kind of neutral zone. In 652–653, the Cypriots called in the Byzantines, leading to a second expedition, which the Arab chroniclers claimed was due to a breach of the agreement. This time the Muslims decided to conquer the island, once again following an approach similar to continental ventures:

> Muʿawiya invaded them in the year 33 [653–654] with 500 ships. He took Cyprus by force, slaughtering and taking prisoners. He then confirmed them in the terms of the treaty that were previously made, and sent to the island 12,000 men of those whose names were recorded in the register [*diwan*] and erected mosques in it. Moreover, Muʿawiya transplanted from Baalbek a group of men, and erected a city on the island, whose inhabitants were

> assigned special stipends until the death of Mu'awiya. His son Yazid, who succeeded him, sent the troops back and ordered the city destroyed. According to other reports, the second invasion of Cyprus by Mu'awiya was carried out in the year 35 [655–656].[29]

The treatment of the island remained in Muslim memory, insofar as Cyprus was the objective of the first Arab naval expedition recognized by official historiography. To a certain extent, the agreements made with the islanders set a legal precedent. Here, al-Baladhuri cites the most well-known jurists of the earliest period of Islam, who gave an opinion on the way the Umayyad leader proceeded.

The fleet had to try twice to destroy the installations on Arwad Island, in 648 and 650, leaving the small island deserted, following a modus operandi that would later be used several times when the Muslims could not or would not stay on an island. This would be the fate of Malta, which long remained unpopulated, and, in a different era, Pantelleria.[30]

OBJECTIVE CONSTANTINOPLE

Combined with repeated raids in Anatolia, the first insular expeditions mentioned clearly indicate that once the *fitna* opposing the Alids to the Umayyad leader's partisans was resolved in 661, the Arabs' primary objective was Constantinople. By delegating the conquest of the African territories to the governors of Egypt and charging the governors of Iraq, Mughira b. Shu'ba, Ziyad b. Abi Sufyan, and his son 'Ubayd Allah, with overseeing the eastern regions and the war in Khorasan from the two Iraqi capitals of Basra and Kufa, from 661 to 684, the caliph could personally focus on commanding operations against Byzantium, thereby identifying the Basileus and the marches of the Taurus Mountains, Anatolia, and the Syrian *sahil* as the primary objectives of the conquest of the ecumene. This arrangement also prefigured the map of commands under the Marwanids, beginning under the reign of 'Abd al-Malik and later adopted by the first Abbasid caliphs.[31]

To begin with, the Arabs had to take control of the maritime routes, for the Byzantine capital's defenses could not be overcome without support from the fleet. The sea would also provide both the Arabs and Byzantine dissidents easier access to the capital than by land. During the *fitna* opposing the Umayyads to the Alids from 656 to 661, Byzantine counteroffensives pushed the border back to the east. Accounts of the two offensives against the Byzantine capital—the first took place from 674 to 677, the second in 717 and 718—are extremely vague. Arab chroniclers say practically nothing about the military stages of these two consecutive failures and devote most of their account of the second attempt to heroizing Maslama.[32] Theophanes's chronicle remains the most complete source.

The first attack is thought to have been jointly conducted by land and by sea in 672. The army barely got past Pergamon.[33] At the same time, the fleet sailed to Chalcedon, where it spent the winter.[34] Reinforcements were then transported by land, under the command of Yazid b. Muʿawiya, and by sea.[35] According to Theophanes, the Arabs carried out individual attacks over seven years, rather than actually laying siege. The squadron was under the command of Busr b. Abi Artaʾa, who began by invading Rhodes, then anchored close to the European coast on the Sea of Marmara. According to the Arab sources, Constantinople was "besieged" for two years, between 674 and 677. Theophanes reports an attack launched by the Arab fleet to force its way through the Golden Horn. His account became famous for including the first reference to Greek fire, the naval incendiary weapon with which the Byzantines set fire to the Muslim ships.[36] Defeated, the Arabs withdrew and spent the entire winter lying at anchor at a rear base in Cyzicus or Rhodes, according to Arab sources lacking in detail.[37] Around 677, maritime attacks were interrupted, marking the end of the first "siege."

The second attempt mobilized significant forces under the command of Maslama. The actual siege lasted for one year, from the summer of 717 to the summer of 718, after the Arab armies crossed the Bosporus again under orders from ʿUmar II, who had recently become caliph. Supported by a squadron from Tunis, the Egyptian fleet took advantage of the defection of the imperial squadron to approach the walls of the capital, but was finally scattered by a sortie of Byzantine ships from the Golden Horn. According to the Greek chronicler, the Byzantine operation led to the sinking of several troop transport ships, once again with Greek fire. Bad weather, the chain stretched across the Golden Horn that made it impregnable, and the desertion of Coptic sailors from Arab supply ships, followed by another maritime setback resulting from this defection, were the principal military reasons put forward by the Byzantines to explain the subsequent final victory of Basileus Leo III (717–741). This defeat made a particularly strong impression given that the Greek and Arab authors emphasized the magnitude of resources applied by Maslama both on land and on water, with several squadrons launched from Alexandria and Cyprus to support the besiegers.[38]

The Greeks had already reacted to the new naval power facing them after their defeat at the Battle of Phoenix in 655. The emperors had been convinced to reorganize their maritime force by the loss of Syria and especially of Egypt, then of the Maghreb, and the ineffectiveness of their fleet, known as the Carabisians. The Carabisians were hostile to the Byzantine Isaurians and had failed to prevent the Arab squadrons from reaching the Bosporus. The reorganization led to the establishment of a maritime project known as the Cibyrrhaeots, which covered the southern coastline up to Lycia and the islands of the Aegean Sea. Commanded by the strategos based in Antalya, the capital of the theme, these fleets were intended to block the path to Constantinople.[39] This naval reform was only one measure in an extensive overhaul: the Byzantines had to adapt their army and fleet to new forms of war. Soon the Arabs would have to follow suit.

THE ARAB EXPANSION ON THE WESTERN MEDITERRANEAN

Though there have been significant studies on the subject, the role of the sea in the scenario of the conquests of the Mediterranean West remains unclear and is generally considered negligible.[40] Indeed, the Arab sources do not report any intervention of fleets in support of Musa b. Nusayr during the conquest of the central and western Maghreb's maritime regions, nor when the Muslims attacked the kingdom of

Toledo. The use of ships was only mentioned in the context of crossing the Strait of Gibraltar.

After the founding of the dockyard and construction of the port in Tunis, the governor of Ifriqiya and the western regions made good use of a fleet that scoured the western basin of the Mediterranean and particularly the large islands (Sicily, Sardinia, Corsica, and the Balearics) from 702 to 714. These expeditions seem to have been interrupted from 714 to 718, during the conquest of al-Andalus: the Carolingian Fredegar's chronicle (often referred to as Pseudo-Fredegar) mentions the Muslim fleet's intervention when Arab troops first reached the Peninsula's coastal zone—with the exception of the strait—in the regions of Catalonia and Septimania. According to an Andalusian source, the fleet was commanded by Admiral Sharahil al-Himyari and had sailed from Tunis or Egypt (via Tunis). It is known to have reached the Andalusian coast in 718–719 at Narbonne, which corroborates the statements of the anonymous author of the Carolingian chronicle. Raids began again in the following years and continued steadily until 752, most often aimed at the islands.[41]

The native of Medina al-Waqidi provided Baghdad chroniclers such as al-Ya'qubi and al-Tabari, as well as the Iraqi Ibn al-Athir and the Egyptian Ibn 'Abd al-Hakam, most of the information about the operations launched by the conqueror. However, the oldest and in many cases the most accurate reports come from the Iraqi Khalifa b. Khayyat's chronicle about the raids launched after 718.[42]

Generally speaking, all operations for the conquest of the western Mediterranean, on land and at sea, were launched on orders from the caliphs of Damascus or their representatives, for the Umayyad sovereigns intended to keep control over the Arab governors and armed forces operating in the West, on land and at sea. The Maghrebi and Andalusian traditions have passed down the record of this centralization of military command during both the Sufyanid period (661–692) and the Marwanid period (692–749). As on other fronts, the generals appointed were in charge of military operations and the government of conquered regions but were accountable to the sovereign, particularly regarding spoils of war (*ghanima, fay'*). The chain of command was identical on land and at sea, with the governor or admiral supervising the entirety of operations on behalf of the caliph. The caliphate's dockyard was the caliph's responsibility; if he did not personally head the fleet, he appointed an admiral to do so. Beginning in this period, the dockyard was designated as the symbol of the caliph's authority on the sea, as confirmed by a letter from Caliph ʿAbd al-Malik ordering the construction of the Tunis dockyard in 702:

> ʿAbd al-Malik b. Marwan then wrote to his brother, ʿAbd al-ʿAziz, governor of Egypt, ordering him to send to the camp established in Tunis one thousand Copts with their families, to whom he would have to provide mounts once they were ready to leave Egypt, and all the assistance they might need until their arrival in . . . Tunis. He wrote to [Hasan] Ibn [al-]Nuʿman, ordering him to build a dockyard (*dar sinaʿa*), in which these people would be settled and which would be turned into a place for Muslims to assemble troops and get supplies. He ordered him to impose on the Berbers the perpetual duty of having to bring to the dockyard by the strength of their arms the wood necessary to build ships, given that he would have to have a fleet equipped there, in order to fight the *Rumi* on land and at sea and carry out raids on the coastline of their country. In this way, we would prevent the enemy from attempting anything against Kairouan and we would protect the Muslims from any danger. Hasan was still in Tunis when the Copts arrived there. At his order, the waters of the sea were brought from Lake Radès to the dockyard; the Berbers brought wood; ships were built there in great quantities and the Copts took care of fitting them out. . . . By the arrangement adopted, the Tunis dockyard adjoined the port, and the port, the lake, which communicates with the sea.[43]

Caliph ʿAbd al-Malik's decision to launch a new expedition to complete the conquest of Byzantine Africa, which was effectively supported by his brother, the governor of Egypt, also concerned the central and western maritime domain, now accessible from the Ifriqiyan port. The regularity of maritime expeditions undoubtedly implies that domina-

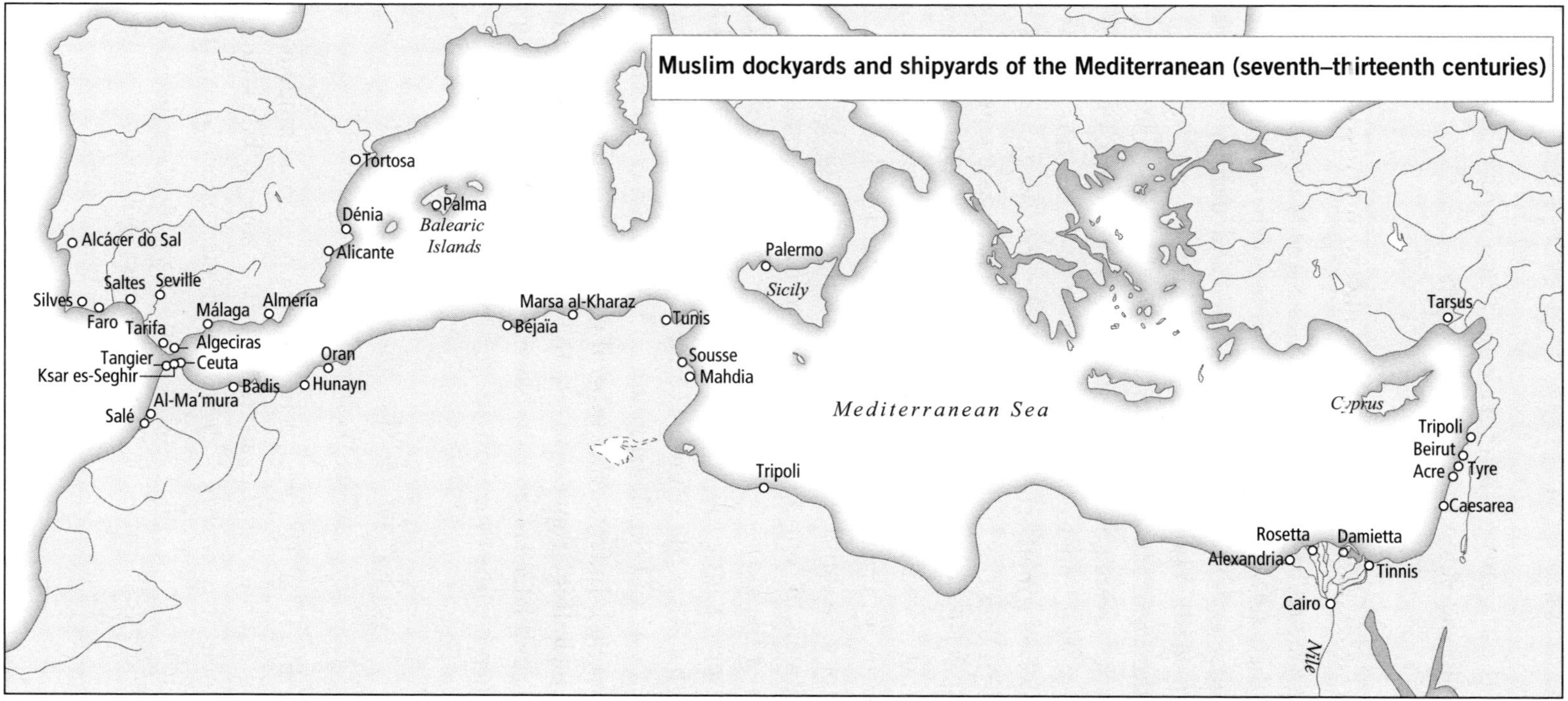

Muslim dockyards and shipyards of the Mediterranean (seventh–thirteenth centuries)

tion of the islands was the other long-term objective, following a series of raids intended to weaken their defenses.

Naval Operations in the West under Umayyad Control?

During the first half of the eighth century, the Marwanid caliphs maintained their authority over the western region by keeping an eye on the governors' activities. Thus, Caliph al-Walid decided to remove the western Mediterranean from Fustat's supervision and put it under the authority of Musa b. Nusayr, who was himself exclusively accountable to the sovereign. While glorified for the lightning-quick conquest of the central and western Maghreb in 709 and 710, regions whose coasts were formerly controlled by Rome and Byzantium, and his victory in 711 over the kings of Toledo, Musa b. Nusayr was not spared by the record left by the chroniclers of the caliph.[44] While on a campaign in the northwest of Spain in 713–714, he was summoned to return to Damascus, where he was tried and sentenced to death by Sulayman, successor to his brother al-Walid, in a clear display of the Syrian caliphs' commitment to controlling these new territories. The caliph succeeded in having the glorious conqueror put to death—probably because he had become a little too powerful in the eyes of the Umayyads—by arguing that since the reign of ʿUmar b. al-Khattab the division of the spoils of war and the distribution and collection of tax fell directly to the sovereign. In fact, every general who led the caliphal armies in Ifriqiya, including, from 647 to 665, Ibn Abi Sahr, Ibn Hudayj, and ʿUqba b. Nafiʿ, and later Hasan b. al-Nuʿman, was accused of misappropriation when it came time to divide the spoils.[45]

Razzias and the Conquest of the Islands of the Western Mediterranean

The term "razzia" (*ghazwa*) refers to the operational mode of Muslims who crossed the march to attack in the war zone. While ideally the declared objective remained territorial conquest aimed at expanding the Dar al-Islam, the results could only be assessed after the fact. The chronicles report the armies of Islam's victories over enemy nonbelievers, either by announcing a territory forced into submission and recording the clauses of the treaty or by referring to the spoils gathered during the incursion. The spoils were divided between the fighters once the share owed the state was set aside according to rules established since the time of the Prophet. These accounts combine the two phases of the razzia, spoils and conquest, but do not describe the incidents of battle, outside of occasional tribute to the martyrs. In discussing attacks on the Mediterranean islands, Arab chroniclers such as Khalifa b. Khayyat and Ibn A'tham al-Kufi only mention successful expeditions, that is, those that led to surrender, or more rarely a treaty, with the amount of booty serving as proof.

This was the case with the 705–706 expedition against the Balearics, which is either presented as a razzia from which the attackers brought back generous spoils or as the beginning of the island's conquest. The second version is closely tied to the ambitions attributed to Musa b. Nusayr, who reported that his son 'Abd Allah had captured the island's kings on his orders.[46] This situation seems very similar to when Mu'awiya ordered the attack on Cyprus: the island was first turned into a land of razzias, following a tactic tried and tested on the continent. Yet the intention to conquer is unmistakable in the reference to relentless attacks launched from Egypt on orders from 'Abd al-'Aziz b. Marwan as of 703–704, then from Tunis on orders from 'Abd Allah b. Musa b. Nusayr. These attacks were aimed against Sicily and up to the walls of its capital, Syracuse, as of 705–706, against the Sardinians every year until 710, and again against the Balearics in 707–708, at which point the islands were forced to surrender. Similarly, the Arab and Greek sources are in agreement that the naval attacks launched against Crete during the same period were the first stage of a strategy of conquest.

The will to conquer these island territories appears clearly in a statement reported to have been made by the conqueror of the Visigothic kingdom when he appeared before the caliph accused of embezzling part of the spoils. After having led offensives in all three directions—the western Maghreb, Spain, and the islands—he states that he has left his legacy to his three sons, like a ruler leaving the shares of his kingdom to his children: "When Musa arrived before Sulayman in 714–715, the latter asked him questions regarding his sons and the confidence Musa had displayed by letting 'Abd al-'Aziz govern al-Andalus and 'Abd Allah govern Ifriqiya and the Maghreb. Musa answered: 'Do you have anyone in your domains who can boast of having sons as perfect as mine? My son 'Abd al-'Aziz imprisoned Roderic, king of al-Andalus; my son 'Abd Allah imprisoned the kings of Mallorca, Minorca, Sicily, and Sardinia, and my son Marwan imprisoned the king of Sous; everywhere they went they took countless prisoners.' "[47]

The capture of prisoners and the deposition of "kings" served as proof of the conquest's success and of the submission of the three "kingdoms" to Islam. With Sardinia referred to as a conquered land several times as of 708, Musa b. Nusayr was thus presented as the leader who had completed the conquest of the western part of the world: "During the year 87 [March–September 706], Musa b. Nusayr sent his son 'Abd Allah on an expedition to Sardinia, which is one of the countries of the Maghreb. It is said that he conquered it. . . . When it was the year 89 [March–September 708], Musa b. Nusayr sent his son 'Abd al-'Aziz on an expedition to Mallorca and Minorca, both islands located between Sicily and al-Andalus, and he conquered them."[48]

With previous attempts against Sardinia having failed, other raids were launched against the island in the following years. The occupation of Sardinia is thought to have lasted only a few years, but to have included the area of Cagliari until at least 732. Indeed, records of the papacy report that in 732, Liutprand, king of the Lombards, negotiated with the Muslims to buy the bones of Saint Augustine, thought to be in what is now the capital of Sardinia.[49] At the same time, the presence of a Greek squadron in Syracuse had prevented the Muslims from settling in Sicily. The Byzantines likely took advantage of the interruption in attacks during the conquest of al-Andalus and the siege of Constantinople in 717, which were mobilizing all Muslim naval forces, to regain control. In 732, they secured control of the access routes to Sardinia. As a result, the Greeks took back or kept control over traffic between the two Mediterranean basins and their island ports of call. However, the Arab conquest of the Balearics blocked all access to the Iberian Peninsula. As of 728, Muslims once again regularly carried out offensives in Sicily, weakened by a victory of the Egyptian fleet in 735, while the Byzantine capital Syracuse was again besieged in 737. In 752, a period of calm in the Maghreb following Berber revolts enabled the launch of a final expedition aimed at the two islands from Tunis.

References to naval expeditions launched under the Umayyad government, selected by the caliphs' chroniclers, and particularly the temporary or lasting failure of the occupation of the major islands could thus show that the Iraqi caliphs had intended to pick up the policy of Mediterranean conquests where the Umayyads had left off.

Before the advent of the Marwanid caliphs, the companions of the Prophet, in particular Muʿawiya—who had served the caliphs of Medina before himself becoming a caliph—and ʿAmr b. al-ʿAs, allowed the Muslims to rival the Byzantines for control of the Roman sea as of 655. To do so, they made effective use of naval structures left by the Greeks in Egypt and Syria and turned their fleet into a real instrument of conquest. This maritime dimension of the Arab conquest was considered prestigious enough that, beginning in the ninth century, the Abbasid and dissident powers that established their authority in the conquered regions of the Mediterranean relayed accounts of the Umayyads' maritime expeditions, so long as these expeditions were presented as the first step of an appropriation of the sea and the islands, the conquest of which the caliphs of Baghdad intended to continue and complete.

9

CONTROLLING THE MEDITERRANEAN

The Abbasid Model

IBN KHALDUN does not say a word about Muslim naval activity in the ninth century in the chapter of his *Muqaddima* on maritime command, most likely because he is following the historical framework imposed by the Western caliphs. His silence can be explained by the earlier silence of the Abbasid, Fatimid, and Córdoba Umayyad caliphal chronicles, which censored any references to Muslim naval activities of the period. Consequently, one does not find a single mention of maritime raids from Muslim shores after the end of the conquests.

THE ABBASID "RUPTURE" ON THE MEDITERRANEAN: A HISTORIOGRAPHIC ILLUSION

As soon as they defeated the Umayyads, simultaneously taking control of Syria and its borders, the new masters of Islam displayed intentions for jihad directly in keeping with the policy of their predecessors, as indicated by the resumption of offensives on the Anatolian front beginning under the reign of al-Saffah. Caliphal involvement would continue uninterrupted until the 930s, outside of periods of crisis such as the conflict between Harun al-Rashid's two sons from 809 to 813. The scope of the land and maritime offensive of 779 signaled major expeditions that would once again allow the Arabs to get closer to Constantinople. This hope was kept alive until the taking of Amorium in 838. In 782, while gazing at the Sea of Marmara after crossing Byzantine Anatolia, Harun al-Rashid allegedly even expressed the wish to pick up where Maslama had left off in 718.

On the other hand, the military balance between Muslims and Christians was deeply and lastingly changed by Baghdad's loss of control over the regions of the Maghreb and al-Andalus, along with the Christians' reinforcement in the east at the instigation of the Byzantine Isaurian emperors, particularly Constantine V, and in the west with the expansion of the Carolingian empire to the Mediterranean's Latin shores. Islam was no longer in a dominant position. Despite declarations to the contrary by caliphs and emirs in the West, it could no longer hope for major expeditions into infidel territory. This balance of forces more or less persisted until the 960s, a decade marked by the Byzantines' decisive advances on land and at sea, with the conquest of Crete (961) and Cyprus (965).

The End of the Conquests: The Abbasids' False Exit from the Mediterranean Stage

After the Marwanid offensives, the caliphal fleets' attacks stopped until 752. According to Muslim and Christian annals, Greek and Latin coast dwellers from one end of the sea to the other slept untroubled by naval expedition until 770. This long naval pause, considered a general halt to the conquest, was attributed to the effects of the "Abbasid revolution" and was sometimes even presented as the result of a long-considered decision on the part of the caliphs.

With the conquest halted and the fronts stabilized, the symbols of the caliphate's military commitment had to change. The sovereigns were increasingly surrounded by Eastern soldiers, whether Arabs from Khorasan who were formerly part of the contingents commanded by Abu Muslim, who had defeated the Umayyads and conquered Iraq; Iranians like the Tahirids (821–873), who had played a decisive part in the fratricidal battle of Baghdad between al-Amin and al-Ma'mun from 809 to 813; or even the Turks, who became the spearhead of the caliphal army under the reign of al-Mu'tasim.[1] As shown by the décor in the palace of Samarra, the caliphal army's orientalization shifted the field of representations of jihad toward values dear to the soldiers of the steppes, which were quite close to those of the Arab tribes, with the lone horseman replacing ships and sailors in representations of combat. A few centuries later, the Ayyubids and the Mamluks would follow a similar course in Egypt.

At the same time, the strengthening of the Byzantine naval force under the Isaurian emperors made it more indispensable than ever to maintain a navy, particularly in the vicinity of Syria and up to Cilicia.[2] There is plenty of evidence pointing to the caliphs' concern with preserving the integrity of the Muslim coast. The sovereigns resumed the strategy developed by Mu'awiya and his successors, which consisted of conquering or neutralizing islands that allowed Christian squadrons to approach Muslim shores. References to maritime attacks launched against Byzantine soil coincided with moments when the Greek emperor's authority was weak, such as the crisis of Iconoclasm, the period following the challenge to the emperor's legitimacy by Thomas the Slav in the 820s, or when the Bulgarian khan Simeon (893–927) came to the walls of Constantinople to demand the imperial crown at the beginning of the tenth century.[3] During the same period, the proliferation of land and naval attacks by the Byzantines prompted a change in war priorities: the caliphs' primary commitment in the war was now the defense of the Dar al-Islam, at least according to the written sources.

The Defense of the Dar al-Islam, Caliphal Jihad's New Priority

While the "Abbasid revolution" claimed to mark a radical break with the Umayyad caliphate, the options for jihad were in direct continuity with the period of the conquest. The new dynasty never decreed an end to jihad, but it was forced to take into account the strengthening of Byzantium, the appearance of the Carolingian state, and the situation on the eastern frontiers against the Turks. In fact, any new advance seemed impossible until the eleventh century—except at sea.

Much of the Eastern army that had won the Battle of the Zab remained in Iraq, leading to a stabilization of the Khorasan front and an end to offensives. The expedition against Talas / Taraz in 751, often presented in the historical atlases as the last attempt to conquer territory beyond the Syr Darya river, is described in Arabic sources as a preventive operation aimed at stopping an attempt on the part of the Oghuz Turks in the service of the Tang dynasty (618–907) to establish an outpost of the Chinese empire in this place frequented by Buddhist pilgrims. Nowhere is there any reference to conquest, nor to a halt to the conquests.[4] In the West, defeats at Poitiers in 732 and the river Berre in 737, followed by the 751 loss of Narbonne, the Muslim capital in Gaul since 719, revealed the rising strength of the Frankish Pippinids in the south of present-day France. During the same period, the crisis unleashed by the Berber Revolt and the rivalries between Arab clans in al-Andalus had worked in favor of the reconstitution of a Christian kingdom in the Peninsula, protected by the mountains of the Asturias.[5]

Within the empire, the Umayyad defeat on the Great Zab had spelled the end of the Umayyad caliphate. Very quickly, the frontier troops resumed razzias against Byzantium, under the reign of al-Saffah. Military command was initially entrusted to al-Mansur's uncle, ʿAbd Allah b. ʿAli (d. 764–765), who had defeated the Umayyad caliph but was to pay for his rivalry with the new caliph with his life. The caliph was later able to rely on an alliance with the Banu Salih, descendants of another of his uncles, simultaneously rallying the Qais tribes to the Iraqi cause. The tribes protected the region of Harran in Upper Mesopotamia, the former capital of Marwan II. Soon amnestied, they joined the Khorasan troops in northern Syria under the orders of Salih b. ʿAli, consolidating the border and resuming operations in Anatolia.[6] Over the course of a reign constantly contested by his own clan, al-Mansur's authority had allowed the Muslims to maintain their manpower against the Greeks and gave the dynasty the opportunity to carry out attacks in Cappadocia until the 830s.

The Syrian-Palestinian coastline, another Umayyad legacy, was put under direct control of the caliph, forming an extension of the Byzantine frontier. The caliph took the initiative by ordering the restoration of the ports and sea defenses and the transfer of the admiralty from Alexandria to Tyre. The Abbasid caliphate's western battlefront abutted a vast zone stretching from Jazira to the Sinai, via the coasts of Syria and Palestine.[7] Soon after the conquest of Iraq, the Abbasid caliphs thus turned to reinforcing their administration in the zones along the front, which were threatened by the Isaurian emperors both on land and at sea.

At the end of the eighth century, the second crisis of Iconoclasm gave the caliphs the opportunity to resume great cavalry charges across Anatolia, with backing from the squadrons, and even to briefly revive the plan to conquer Constantinople, the major objective the Umayyads had had to relinquish. Until 838, several expeditions broke through Byzantine defenses, making the peninsula highly porous. Yet the Byzantines' military reinforcement prevented both Christians and Muslims from gaining a decisive advantage. The Muslim frontiers were themselves subjected to Christian attacks. As a result, the need to defend the empire took precedence over quickly dampened hopes for a new assault on the Byzantine capital. Taking into account the strategic facts, the sovereigns seeking legitimacy in war turned the enormous effort of securing the borders into the foundation of a new caliphal jihad.

On the ground, priority was given to initiatives to prevent enemy forces from penetrating the borders of Islam. However, this did not exclude continuing attacks on enemy territory, on land and at sea. Both before and after 750, there was no contradiction, or even distinction made, between "defensive jihad" and "offensive jihad"—this terminology simply was not used in the context of the war in the Mediterranean. Razzias in Anatolia and at sea continued uninterrupted and sometimes led to conquests, notably of the Aegean islands. Beginning in 827, the Muslim occupation of Crete and Sicily, after Cyprus and the Balearics, reinforced Muslim hold on the sea.[8] However, the rebalancing of forces imposed changes, forcing Islamic powers in the region to prevent attacks from the Byzantine fleet, once again a threat with the establishment of land and maritime plans.[9] The effects of this reorganization were felt throughout the entire eastern Mediterranean, but also in the western basin, with Syracuse and Sicily having been turned into a fortress and naval base from which the Byzantines could reach all the coasts up to Sardinia and Provence.[10]

The significant number of defensive structures on the caliphal frontier suggest that the installation of defensive measures along the coasts was one of the most ambitious programs of the period. At the same time, jihad was updated to fit new combat norms, those considered the most status enhancing and confined to the frontier. Through their support and propaganda, armed scholars played an essential part in the promotion of jihad: Sahnun, who introduced Malikism to the Maghreb and had himself waged jihad in the ribat-city of Sfax, believed that the *murabit* defending Ifriqiya in the coastal strongholds was more worthy than the combatant who crossed the water to Sicily and participated in the island's conquest.

In works describing the virtues of the *murabitun,* whether legal texts about the war (*siyar*) written in the area of the Taurus Mountains beginning in the last years of the eighth century or biographies of the ulema who frequented the coastal ribats, the merits of the conqueror were replaced with those of the defender of Islam. At the same time, the Abbasids, followed half a century later by the emirs of the western Mediterranean, adapted tactical measures that allowed them both to defend Islamic territory and to strike in enemy territory according to realities in the continental and maritime field and to the resources available.

ABBASID SOVEREIGNTY IN THE MEDITERRANEAN

After the formation of western emirates independent of the caliphate—the Umayyads in al-Andalus as of 756, the Idrisids and the Rustamids in central and western Africa at the end of the eighth century—several accounts of the caliphs' interventionism in dissident territories in the West, however short-lived, prove the extent to which the sovereigns considered the entire Islamic Mediterranean part of the caliphate. For instance, Ibn al-Athir reports, "In 146 / 762–764, al-ʿAla Mughith al-Yahsubi crossed from Ifriqiya to the city of Beja [Portugal] in al-Andalus, where he wore the black of the Abbasids and had the *khutba* preached in the name of al-Mansur."[11]

No matter their origin, the different accounts of this uprising, headed by a Yemeni clan from the *jund* of Beja in revolt against ʿAbd al-Rahman I, all mention the interference of the caliphate, which intended to take advantage of the sedition to regain control of al-Andalus.[12] Similarly, the poisoning of Idris I, a descendant of Ali, in 791 after he had taken refuge in Fez shows that Harun al-Rashid could strike his enemies anywhere in the empire—particularly if they were members of the tribe of the Prophet who might lay claim to the caliphate. However, these actions did not have the expected effect.

Baghdad's intellectual and cultural influence on the entire Islamic domain, affecting all the nations of Islam up to the shores of the Atlantic, proved a far more effective weapon. Though written in the tenth century, when the Umayyad caliphate aimed to overthrow the usurper, the Andalusian chronicles confirm how closely Emir 'Abd al-Rahman II had paid attention to the brilliance of great minds of the East such as the musician Ziryab, recruited for an astronomical sum of money to turn Córdoba into a new Baghdad, an indispensable stage in the promotion of the Andalusian sovereigns before the hypothetical reconquest of the seat of the caliphs.[13]

Through several reports about their region, Egyptian men of letters confirmed the Abbasid caliphs' disengagement from the coastal cities of Egypt, starting with Alexandria, as soon as they came to power, much to the dismay of the author of the *History of the Patriarchs*.[14] Al-Mutawakkil's intervention after the Byzantine fleet sacked Damietta in 853 showed the consequences of the caliphal administration's withdrawal from the Nile delta's maritime cities.[15] Beyond the delta, starting in Tripolitania, was the domain of the Aghlabid emirs, who governed the region of Ifriqiya in complete independence while officially recognizing their affiliation with the caliphal domain.

Farther west, in the Maghrebi territories, defensive measures were described in terms of the Iraqi men of letters: the spread of their vocabulary and the description of the fortifications show that the Ifriqiyan and Andalusian jihad had been inspired by the jihad on the frontier of the Taurus and the Syrian Sahel. One has to rely on archeology, which gradually reveals the diversity in the defense systems, to identify regional specificities adapted to each zone's particular conditions, while the Arabic texts attempt to persuade that Muslim defenses along the coasts of the Mediterranean were entirely uniform.

The caliphs aimed to retain total sovereignty over the maritime territory, as attested to by the book of geography by Ibn Khurradadhbih, who, as director of the caliphal postal service (*barid*), was responsible for monitoring the peripheral regions. Ibn Khurradadhbih describes the itineraries followed by the Rahdanite Jewish merchants who brought precious goods to Baghdad from all over the world, including the Carolingian empire (particularly slaves and eunuchs), India (rare spices and essential oils), and China (silks, ceramics, and other refined products). He also mentions Russian merchants who arrived from the steppes of Central Asia with furs and other northern products much appreciated by the capital's affluent population. The author's intention was not to make an economic assessment or an overview of international commerce but rather to reveal a network of land and maritime trade routes stretching from the Far East to the Baltic Sea, in order to show that the caliphate's influence extended to the borders of the ecumene, far beyond the outer limits of the Dar al-Islam, and that all the riches in the world could reach Baghdad. The Mediterranean appears here as a major route, second only to the Indian Ocean.

Abbasid Diplomacy

Embassies, the circulation of letters, and references to visits by emissaries provide a good indication of the density of diplomatic relations between the states along the Mediterranean littoral.[16] Several references to the circulation of representatives of the imperial and caliphal courts, the Roman curia, the principalities, and the emirates attest to ongoing relationships between Christian and Muslim sovereignties around the Mediterranean, confirmed as early as the Rashidun period. Similarly, exchanges between capital cities were part of a long tradition. Byzantium bore traces of a real diplomatic culture around the Sea of the Romans, involving the Latins, naturally, but also the Sassanids and pre-Islamic Arabia.

There is therefore nothing surprising about the relations formed very early on with Medina—according to the tradition, as early as the era of Muhammad.[17] Since that time, written correspondence between the Umayyads and the Greek emperors had continued steadily and was carried between the two capitals by ambassadors. While the campaign of 806 was being prepared, Harun al-Rashid sent a delegation to

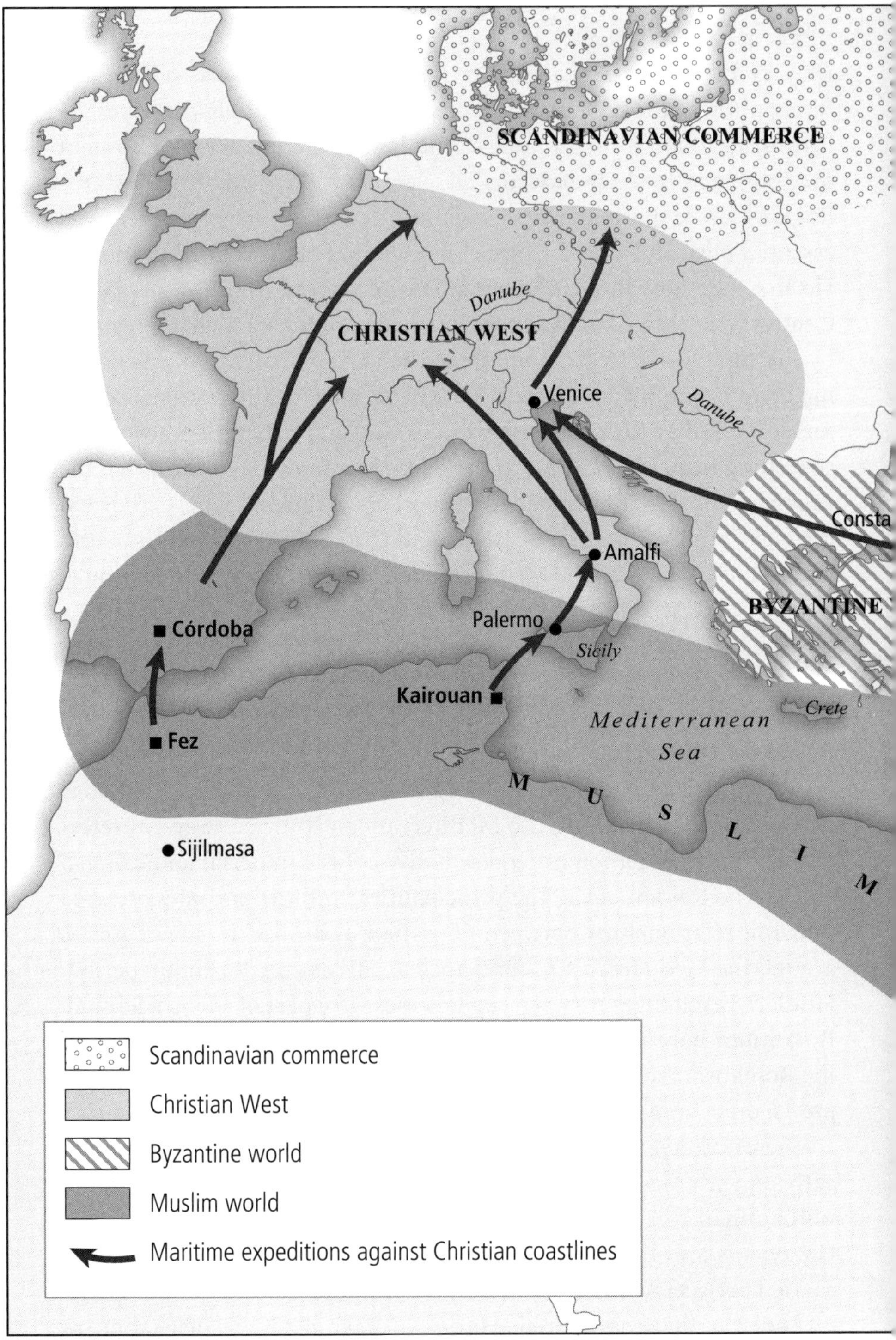
SCANDINAVIAN COMMERCE
CHRISTIAN WEST
Danube
Danube
Venice
Amalfi
Consta
BYZANTINE
Palermo
Sicily
Córdoba
Kairouan
Fez
Crete
Mediterranean Sea
M U S L I M
Sijilmasa
Scandinavian commerce
Christian West
Byzantine world
Muslim world
Maritime expeditions against Christian coastlines

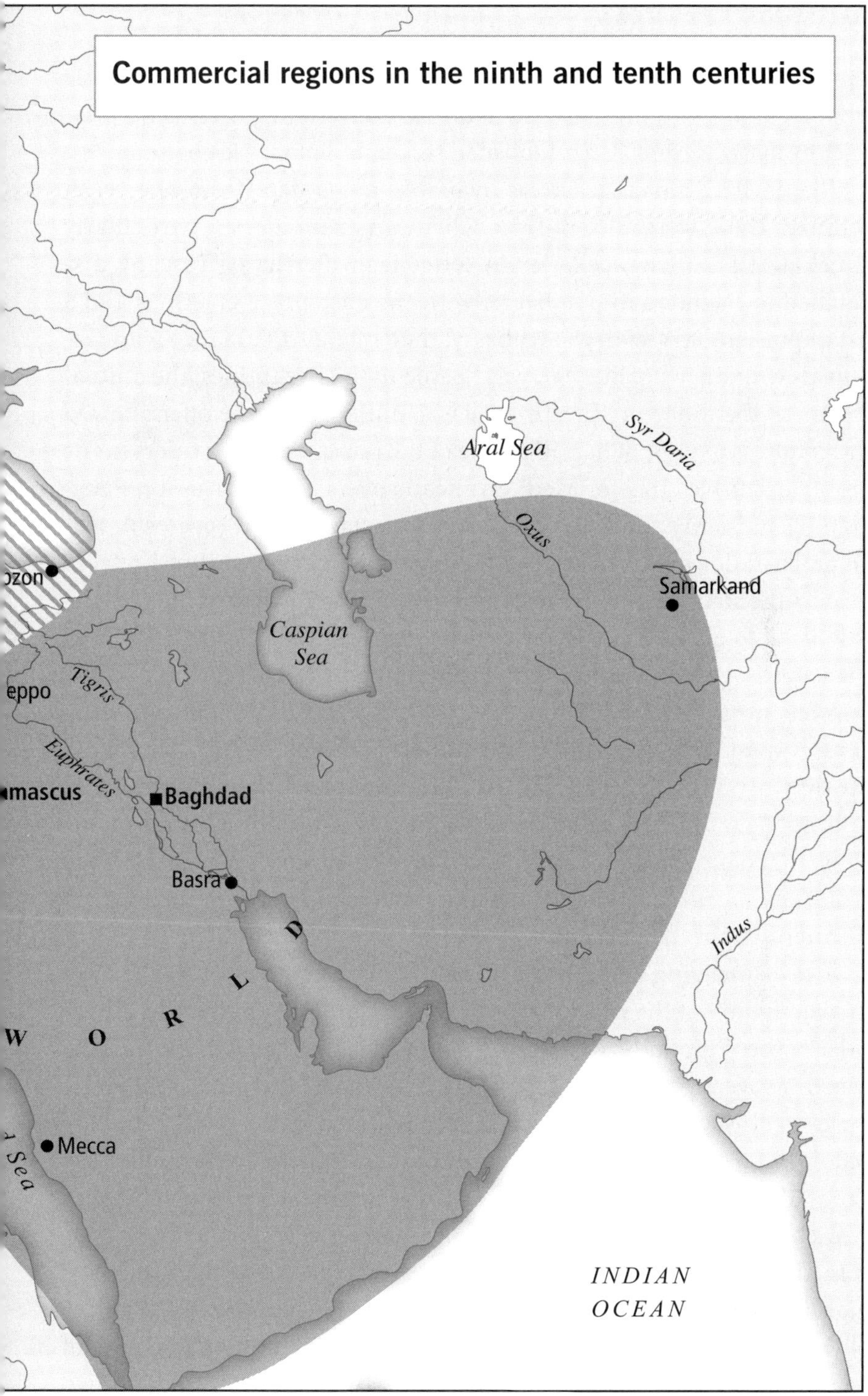
Commercial regions in the ninth and tenth centuries
Aral Sea
Syr Daria
Oxus
Samarkand
ozon
Caspian Sea
Tigris
eppo
Euphrates
mascus
Baghdad
Basra
Indus
W O R L D
Mecca
a Sea
INDIAN OCEAN

Constantinople to present the Basileus with a request for a truce on the frontier, along with the usual invitation to convert. Regulations for prisoner exchanges were also established through diplomatic channels.[18]

The earliest embassy letters available to us date from the tenth century. These were all sent from Christian chancelleries, particularly Greek and Latin chancelleries. A letter from Bertha of Tuscany dispatched to Baghdad in 906 began with the customary greetings and a list of presents sent with the embassy, then offered an alliance with Caliph al-Muktafi, who, like her, was hostile to the Byzantines, the mutual enemy of the moment. The alliance was unlikely, but the offer allowed the countess to present herself as one of the power-wielding rulers in the highly exclusive circle of Mediterranean sovereigns. In 913–914, Patriarch Nicholas Mystikos, then regent of Constantine VII (913–959), sent an ambassador to give a letter to Photios, governor of Muslim Crete, to discuss the status of the Cypriots and negotiate a prisoner exchange. The title used to address the letter clearly indicates that its addressee was the island's governor and that he represented the caliph who had appointed him. Both sides repeatedly formed ties with the opposing camp's dissidents. In 823–824, the Maliki patriarch of Antioch, then a Muslim city, crowned Thomas the Slav emperor at the request of Caliph al-Ma'mun. The caliph was backing this former admiral of the Cibyrrhaeot fleet, a pretender to the imperial throne of Michael II, "the Amorian" (820–829), who was able to establish himself on the Muslim frontier to fight the Basileus.[19]

A few surviving texts in the annals of the emperors of Aachen are instructive about the relations between the Carolingians and the Abbasids.[20] The Pippinids were the first to establish relations with the Muslim sovereigns. In 765, Pippin III, "the Short" (751–768), sent emissaries to al-Mansur. They returned accompanied by the caliph's ambassadors, who embarked on the Syrian coast and landed in Marseille. The caliphal delegation remained in the Latin Empire approximately three years before returning home. As is customary, the content of their conversations is not specified; instead, the importance of the process is highlighted by the list of presents, which provides an idea of the power of the solicitor thus seeking to impress his interlocutor.[21] Exchanges of embassies between Charlemagne and the caliph began in 797. The two

Carolingian representatives were lost at sea on the return trip, but in 801 other emissaries of the caliph were announced in Pisa, escorted by an Aghlabid ambassador. Having earned its name by surviving the crossing, the elephant Abu l-'Abbas (the father of strength) arrived in the capital in 802 with a large delegation. The same year, legates of the emperor traveled to Baghdad with the Muslim ambassadors. On the return journey in 806, the ship carrying Muslim emissaries and two monks of the Church of the East, representatives of the patriarch of Jerusalem, had to circumvent a Greek maritime blockade. Lastly, in 831 the caliph took the initiative to make ties with Emperor Louis the Pious and propose a peace treaty, which was signed in Thionville at the very moment he was ordering his forces into battle in Anatolia.

In the absence of shared borders between the Carolingian empire and the caliphate, the reason most frequently given for these missions is the forming of ad hoc alliances against common enemies of the moment: the Carolingians targeted the Andalusians, particularly in 797, but also the Byzantines, who had become enemies to both empires since Pippin the Short had decided to intervene in Italy. In 806, after the crowning of the Pippinid sovereign in Rome and its consequences on relations with Constantinople, then weakened by the crisis of Iconoclasm, the Peninsula was once again the object of discussions with the Muslims, while Venetia and Dalmatia were under attack by the Frankish army and vigorously defended by Nicetas the Patrician; for his part, the caliph intensified the pressure on Cappadocia, possibly reaching Bithynia the same year.

Aside from the exceptional personalities of the sovereigns, particularly in the case of Charlemagne and Harun al-Rashid, the emphasis on certain gifts that enchanted Einhard and other admirers of pachyderms, highly valued because such animals were not found in Europe, seems to indicate that both sovereigns sought to signal their intention to have a decisive influence on Mediterranean politics. The most important thing to the caliphs was that they were recognized as the only Muslim sovereigns of the Mediterranean, thus marginalizing the dissident emirates' position in the eyes of the courts of Europe. For their part, the Carolingians were at war with the Umayyads on the Catalan front, and they also aimed to take control of the shores of Italy up to the boundaries of the Papal States. Once Charlemagne was crowned emperor, the Carolingian empire was to appear as one of the great powers of the Mediterranean. Receiving and sending ambassadors also allowed the Baghdad caliphate to reclaim a place in the heart of Mediterranean affairs, as a direct interlocutor with the Christian adversaries, while reminding Muslim subjects that both war and peace fell under the exclusive authority of the caliph: though the eastern Mediterranean was no longer governed by the caliph, it remained the sovereign space of the Commander of the Faithful, a fact specifically symbolized by his ambassadors' presence in the imperial courts of the Christian world.

The Maritime Administration against Byzantium

Following the disastrous defeat at the gates of Constantinople in 717, Muslim ships were no longer reported on the Aegean Sea, while the Byzantines went back on the offensive on the water.[22] However, a reference to Caliph Hisham having the dockyard moved from Acre to Tyre due to commercial conflicts of interest suggests that the lack of Muslim maritime activity was short-lived.

The caliphal order to inspect and, if necessary, repair maritime installations on the seaboard of the Bilad al-Sham coincided with the transfer of the admiralty's command from Alexandria to Tyre, around 754. It was also at this time that al-Mansur took in hand the Taurus frontier. As on the terrestrial front, the caliph ordered inspections of the maritime organization, ships, and crews left by the excellent Umayyad administration and entrusted the command of the squadrons to his clients. When the caliphal armies' major raids in Anatolia were resumed, al-Mahdi and his successors were able to rely on the naval forces his father had mobilized to serve as protection from the Greek fleet and to support the troops on land.

The caliphs' intervention in maritime affairs was in keeping with the practices of Medina and the Umayyads. 'Umar b. al-Khattab had been the first caliph to travel to the Syrian-Palestinian coast to organize its defense, in 638–639. Al-Tabari credits him with the first appointment of a "governor of the sea," which distinguished a specific administration and jurisdiction for the coastal zones of Palestine and Syria. The governor was assisted by an inspector of granaries, who ensured that the necessary reserves were available in the ports where the fleets assembled. At the same time, the coast remained a dependency of the capitals of the inland districts. Ibn Khurradadhbih counted five ports then dependent on Damascus: Sidon, Beirut, Tripoli, Acre, and Tyre.[23] At the beginning of the tenth century, Qudama b. Ja'far distinguished the ports located in a specific zone, the "maritime frontiers," still under the jurisdiction of the inland capitals: "The maritime frontiers are Antartus, Bulunyas, Latakia, Jableh, and al-Hiryadha, seaports of the *jund* of Homs; Arqa, Tripoli, Jubail, Beirut, Sidon, the fortress of al-Sarafand, and Adnun, seaports of the *jund* of Damascus; Tyre, where the naval dockyard is located, and Acre, seaports of the *jund* of Jordan; Caesarea, Arsuf, Jaffa, Ashqelon, and Gaza, seaports of the *jund* of Palestine."[24]

There are several signs that the new Abbasid apparatus marginalized the Egyptian seaboard, beginning with the absence of any reference to possible naval expeditions, while at the end of the ninth century al-Ya'qubi barely mentions trade activities. Several significant events in the history of Alexandria, given precedence in the chronicle of the Patriarchs of the city, confirm this downgrading. The landing of the Andalusian sailors expelled by the Umayyad emir al-Hakam I in 818 and their subsequent activity in the city confirm that Alexandria no longer had a naval force or an administration capable of standing up to even a modest squadron.

While the stages of this change in status are not clearly stated, they can be deduced from a few episodes in the area's maritime history, starting with the siege of Constantinople in 717–718. The first cause for alarm had been the desertion of the Copts, who made up the core of the crews sent to resupply the besiegers at the gates of the Byzantine capital. According to the Greeks, fewer than ten Muslim ships survived this incident. The lack of references to maritime raids launched from Egypt following this serious defeat, then the Byzantine report of a naval defeat off Cyprus in 747, confirms that Egypt no longer had a navy capable of imposing itself on the Aegean Sea. The disordered state of the naval organization the Umayyads had put in place at Mu'awiya's instigation is underlined by another defeat, also off Cyprus, against the Cibyrrhaeots' squadron in 755.[25] The Egyptian ports remained operational, particularly after the taking of Crete, but the ancient capital was no longer the seat of the admiralty.

The Byzantine navy's attacks on the ports of the Egyptian coast, particularly against Damietta in 853, forced al-Mutawakkil to attend to the coastal defense of the delta. He had the city rebuilt elsewhere and ordered ports such as Barca restored in order to provide Egypt with the means to protect itself from Greek maritime attacks. The caliph's reaction, motivated by Christian aggression, marked a return to direct caliphal control over the coast. Two of the best-informed Egyptian authors, al-Kindi and Ibn Duqmaq, report that Governor 'Anbasa b. Ishaq al-Dabbi was ordered to rebuild a naval force and recruit sailors, a sure sign the maritime organization had been put in abeyance.[26] We know that the Tulunids (868–905) continued in the same direction, but nothing else. Finally, beginning in 919, the Ikhshidids (935–969), officers sent by Baghdad to restore caliphal authority, decided to contend with the Fatimid threat by having a dockyard built or repaired in Fustat, which involved establishing a maritime administration in the capital. The second Fatimid expedition, launched in 935 on Imam al-Qa'im's order, failed to overcome the Ikhshidids' resistance, though the Fatimid army did succeed in reaching and destroying the capital's dockyard, the existence of which is known to us through this incident. While the country had lost the naval preeminence it had enjoyed under the Umayyads, the reaction of the Iraqi caliphs, particularly under the reign of al-Mu'tamid, proves conclusively that the caliphate of Samarra still intended to control its maritime destiny.

The redeployment of naval forces in the Syrian-Palestinian ports of Ashkelon on the Greek frontier takes on its full significance in the context of the reorganization of the jihad on the Anatolian frontier. While there is no record of any list of admirals of the city of Tyre at the time of the caliphate of Baghdad—probably because the position had lost its luster in a military hierarchy dominated by the Turks—those whose names appear occasionally, in relation to specific maritime events, were under the orders of the caliphate and its governor along the Syrian coast and, to a lesser degree, on the shores of Egypt. Squadrons and sailors of the time enjoyed a great deal of autonomy, particularly in port cities equipped with dockyards, which provided them with autonomy on the sea; the caliphate's most important naval bases were Tyre, Tarsus, Tripoli, and Chandax / Heraklion. Al-Mas'udi provides only a succinct overview of the various ranks and occupations related to the navy (sailors, captains of warships and trading ships, dockyard personnel), but in other parts of his encyclopedia, he mentions the names of several admirals of the Mediterranean fleet, notably Leo, "governor of Tripoli" as of 912, and 'Abd Allah b. Wazir, the governor of Jableh, a port of the *jund* of Homs. Al-Mas'udi had met Wazir and considered him the most experienced sailor, a man who had proved himself by leading the jihad in the name of the caliph. Both admirals were included on the lists of the *diwan* of the Abbasid caliphate's maritime administration.

Tripoli and Jableh were the most active ports, due to their proximity to the combat zone against Byzantium. In Palestine during this period, maintenance of port defenses left a lot to be desired. This was certainly the case in Ashkelon, which the Byzantines targeted around 900, taking advantage of the port's condition to capture a large number of Muslims, notably the man known for having left a long account of Constantinople under the name of Harun b. Yahya.[27] After seizing power in the valley of the Nile and taking control of the coastal regions of Syria-Palestine, Emir Ibn Tulun (868–884) had to carry out repairs in the port of Acre, which were entrusted to the geographer al-Muqaddasi's grandfather. The need for these repairs proves that infrastructures had indeed been damaged.[28] Ibn Tulun's objective was to take control of the ports of the Syrian coast and Cilicia, which would allow him to reap significant profits from razzias and trade in Byzantine territory and on the open sea. As a former officer of the caliph stationed in Tarsus, Ibn Tulun understood the economic significance of ports close to the frontier and the potential profits he could expect them to make. Once the two ports were taken back from the Tulunids, the caliphs al-Mu'tadid (890–902) and especially al-Muktafi followed a similar logic in recruiting Greek sailors who would sail in the direction of the Byzantine coasts on their behalf. Encouraged by Baghdad, the new admirals intermittently regained the advantage for the Muslims in the Aegean Sea until the beginning of the crisis of the caliphate in the 930s. However, Muslim raids were reported until the early 950s.

The Aegean Sea in the Ninth and Early Tenth Centuries: A Pirate Sea or an Abbasid Sea?

While the military decline of the Egyptian ports, and particularly of Alexandria, can partially be attributed to Abbasid reforms, the caliphs nonetheless continued their predecessors' policies on the coasts of Egypt. For instance, 'Abd Allah b. Tahir, the governor of Egypt, intervened to restore order in the 820s, particularly by employing Andalusian crews who had arrived in Alexandria around 821 and contributed to the city's turmoil. This led directly to "Crete [being] invaded by Abu Hafs 'Umar b. 'Isa al-Andalusi, known as al-Iqritishi."[29] Greek and Arabic sources vary in dating the taking of Chandax / Heraklion, ranging from 821 to 827, which seems to indicate that these sailors had already launched several raids against the island before conquering the Cretan capital, a prelude to the conquest of the entire island.[30] The route to the island was well known to Muslims; it had been targeted by several expeditions as of 656, then in 673–674, and again under the reigns of al-Walid and his successors. *The History of the Patriarchs of Alexandria* mentions several landings on the island, particularly under the reign of Harun al-Rashid. These have been confirmed by Byzantine hagiographies. The hagiography of the Cretan Saint Anthony, who had been an admiral of the Cibyrrhaeots in an earlier phase, describes the defense of the island against the Muslims. Al-Tabari repeated the tradition according to which the Andalusian chief had been hired to carry out the conquest by authorities convinced of his unruly sailors' abilities.[31] Once the island had been subdued, it was necessary to maintain ties with Egyptian ports to maintain the fleet: one of the principal reasons for the Byzantine attack on Damietta in 853, according to the Byzantines, was that the Egyptian port served as a rear base for the Cretan Muslims, providing them with weapons and even timber for shipbuilding.[32]

The caliphate's role as a coordinator appears essential to understand the Muslims' maritime movements. Described in the Christian texts as destructive pillage, the razzias launched by independent sailors both for their own financial gain and to weaken the enemy could also be part of a caliphal or emirate strategy still aimed at conquering the major islands like Crete if the opportunity presented itself. At the same time, the intrusion of these "Andalusians" in the Mediterranean's maritime history, though they were answerable to the Egyptian governors, indicates the importance of crews sought for their skills. With the authorization of the tutelary government, these sailors, who were merchants or warriors depending on the circumstances, could take advantage of the caliphate's strategy to lead a private war in which they did not have to answer to authorities and had the possibility to enrich themselves, provided that they only targeted the caliph's enemies.

The caliphs would take advantage of the naval resources at their disposal as long as they were present on the Anatolian front, until 838. In 777, during the second expedition under his reign, al-Mahdi used the fleet to land troops in Cappadocia to attack the Christian armies from the rear. Under the reign of Harun al-Rashid, the fleet won an important victory in the bay of Antalya. During two major expeditions in Anatolia, in 802 and 806, the squadron protected the caliph's army by preventing the fleets from landing troops to attack from the rear. The squadron was involved in nearly every campaign, as confirmed by the broad references made by ulema accompanying the caliphs on these operations: "In diligence for warfare (*ghazw*) and perspicuity in jihad, we saw a magnificent thing in the Commander of the Faithful Harun. He used more skill (*sina'a*) than had ever been used before, he divided up property (*al-amwal*) in the frontier posts, both inland and on the coast, and he caused anxiety to the enemy and subdued him."[33]

During the same period, sailors from Muslim ports preyed on Byzantine coasts and islands from Crete to north of the Aegean Sea. According to the Greek texts, especially the chronicles and hagiographies, periods of pillage generally corresponded with the caliphs' most intense phases of military engagement on the frontier. For instance, maritime offensives peaked during the revolt of Thomas the Slav, which hindered Michael II's ability to react, and were not limited to the conquest of the island. Raids continued until 842, with one fleet even reaching the Sea of Marmara. Beginning in 891 and until the dawn of the 920s, the "renegade" admirals Damian and Leo, respectively based in Tarsus and Tripoli, left an indelible impression on the collective memory, particularly during the dramatic sack of Thessaloniki in 904. These attacks coincided with the Abbasids regaining control of the frontiers of Anatolia and Syria at the end of the ninth century. Himieros, admiral of the Cibyrrhaeot fleet, won several battles against the two ports' Muslim squadrons in 906 and again in 909. He laid siege to Heraklion for six months in 911 but was unable to take the city. The same year, the Byzantine fleet was lured into a trap set by the two admirals and sank with all hands near Chios, which was immediately pillaged. Following this victory, Damian was able to restore Cyprus's neutral status, which would endure until 965. Taking advantage of the imperial ambitions of the Bulgarian khan Simeon I, who traveled to the gates of Constantinople several times to assert his right to the imperial crown, the fleets of Tarsus, Tripoli, and Chandax / Heraklion were able to roam the sea in every direction for a quarter of a century. The caliph was even able to order Thamal al-Dulafi, Damian's successor, to lend Simeon a hand in 924 by organizing a maritime blockade of the Bosporus while the Bulgarian khan besieged the city on land.

However, the communities of sailors in these ports also frequently acted autonomously. The fleet used for razzias and trade was an important source of revenue; by controlling the fleet, local leaders could conduct a private war that provided them with the necessary resources to emancipate themselves from the government's tutelage. This was enough of an issue for the caliphs to react and seek to regain control of a city, when possible. In the 880s, for instance, during a phase when the Abbasids had turned away from affairs on the frontier and Ibn Tulun, Egypt's independent emir, was trying to control the entire Syrian coastline, the eunuch Yazman, who was governor of Tarsus and presented as an independent emir, was credited with several victories against the Christians, both on land and at sea. Yazman initially fought on behalf of the caliph, hoping to prevent the Tulunids from seizing the frontier city. However, once the Tulunids were at the gates of the city, Yazman accepted their tutelage and saved his position by giving the city's tax revenue to the Egyptian emirs. Tarsus was then reconquered by his predecessor and al-Muktafi ordered the fleet to be burned, destroying the city's prime instrument of wealth. Al-Muktafi rapidly rebuilt the fleet and entrusted its command to Greek admirals, who allowed him to find new crews.[34]

The maintenance of ships, recruitment of sailors, seasonal naval operations, and administration of ports were the sole responsibility of the admirals and crews who decided on operations. This autonomy explains why modern historians thought that Leo and other heads of expeditions had been left to their own devices. However, these historians did not take into account the works of Arab chroniclers, starting with al-Tabari, who mentions that troops were sent to put an end to local leaders' actions when they went against the caliphate's interests. Often, the threat of intervention was all that was needed. The leadership crisis that began developing in the 920s under the reign of al-Muqtadir put an end to Baghdad's interventionism. Rule by a young caliph, a financial crisis, and, more extensively, the "disintegration of the Empire" came to an end when the Buyids took power in Baghdad in 945.[35] Having claimed the title of chief emir, these Iranian warlords stripped the caliphs of their military authority, though in fact Iraq had lost its influence on Mediterranean affairs years before.

The Greeks took advantage of the situation: after having opened the way to the Taurus by razing Melitene (Malatya) in 934, they destroyed Tarsus in 955, attacked Antioch in 969, and besieged Aleppo in the 970s. The Syrian frontier had been erased or pushed back. At sea, the Cretan fleet continued its attack on the Greek islands until 950. By seizing Crete in 961 and Cyprus in 965, the Byzantine emperors Romanos II (959–963) and Nikephoros II Phokas (963–969) transformed the Aegean Sea into a Byzantine lake. With Cilicia having been turned into a Byzantine forward base, Tripoli of Lebanon was now the frontier port most exposed to the Byzantines.

For 170 years, government of the Muslim part of the eastern Mediterranean had been in the hands of the Iraqi sovereigns, though their intentions had on several occasions been stymied by autonomous actions. More than naval commitment, the most significant development was coastal defense. This was the initiative that would be remembered.

ABBASID COMMITMENT ON THE MEDITERRANEAN: MARITIME CONTROL AND COASTAL DEFENSES

Toward the end of the eighth century and until its reintroduction by al-Mutawakkil in 853, the temporary interruption of maritime conscription in the Nile delta, a Byzantine legacy that had endured since the time of ʿUmar b. al-Khattab, made it necessary to reorganize the enrollment of seafarers.[36] There is no surviving information about these measures, with the exception of a reference to several dockyards (*dar al-sinaʿa*), where ships under maintenance were docked and the administration for crews was headquartered.[37]

Al-Mansur and his successors tended to use crews drawn from communities of seafaring people, qualified to serve on a fleet for transporting troops or carrying out raids. Like the Andalusians who attacked Crete, sailors from the Syrian ports could rely on a significant number of experienced crews. Maysur, a sailor well known for his victories over the Greeks on the Aegean Sea in the 870s, made the most of crews based on the Syrian and Cilician coasts. He recruited crews experienced in commerce raiding and maritime commerce to trade and pillage, but only according to a schedule set by the caliphal administration, based on relations and agreements with Byzantium. Similarly, there is every indication that the "renegades" Damian and Leo of Tripoli, both natives of the coastal regions of Cilicia and Cappadocia, arrived with hardened crews, many of them probably their compatriots, who spread terror on the archipelagos and the Byzantine coasts.

The fleet that seized Heraklion in 827 is identified as "Andalusian," transporting sailors who had fled or been exiled for having defied the authority of Emir al-Hakam I and refused to respect the truce signed with the Carolingian emperor in 815.[38] These sailors had distinguished themselves by attacking several Ionian islands and Crete, then landing in Alexandria.[39] However, there is little doubt that many of the soldiers who participated in the siege and assault on the Cretan capital in 827, estimated by some Arab and Greek authors to have numbered seven thousand, were Egyptian soldiers provided by the governor. Along with a few other indications, the island's constant ties with Egypt, particularly with Damietta, suggest it was under the command of a governor, the admiral (*sahib al-bahr*), though we do not know exactly what responsibilities the position entailed. What is clear without a doubt is that the admiral was answerable to the Egyptian authorities. The names of admirals such as Photios indicate that Greek natives of the island made up all or part of the fleet at Chandax, at least during certain periods. However, the victorious assault in 827 had been the work of sailors from the Iberian Peninsula, who were renowned for their sailing and fighting abilities and were under the command of a skilled leader, Abu Hafs. The decisive role they played justifies their distinction as the island's conquerors; more specifically, their leader was elevated to the prestigious rank of the man who "opened" Crete to Islam. For this feat of arms, he was called "Abu Hafs the Cretan."

Maritime raids were therefore the work not of "pirates" but of sailors in the service of the caliph or the emir, sailing as often on their own behalf as on the sovereign's orders. From the victims' perspective, they engaged in piracy, but in the eyes of the Muslim authorities, it was commerce raiding. They were mindful of the caliph's interests and participated in operations ordered by the sovereign or his general, just like soldiers on the frontier. Aside from the fact that they had a common enemy, this understanding between crews and the sovereign was solidly anchored in financial interest, not to mention the threat of sanctions as long as the caliph could intervene in the coastal zone. However, the installation of defensive measures along the Muslim coasts, to which the chroniclers and biographers paid more specific attention, appears to have been the most status-enhancing investment in the eyes of the sovereigns of Baghdad.

Volunteers for Jihad and Armed Pious Scholars: A Closely Supervised Enlistment

The Abbasid sovereigns' defense of the coasts followed on from the measures taken by their predecessors and was in no way original. From the beginning of the conquests, the Arabs, having encountered strong resistance from Syrian-Palestinian ports protected and supplied by the Byzantine fleets, found it necessary to defend coastal towns from a possible return of their enemies. They found a dense network of cities and forts, probably consolidated by the Byzantines after the Sassanid offensives.[40] Epigraphic and archeological traces of this investment in several fortresses on the Palestinian coast show that after the difficult conquest of the Syrian coastline, the Umayyads had fortified coastal towns, which were maintained by the local population and guarded by largely "Persian" garrisons.[41]

Any rupture between the Umayyad and Abbasid periods was not due to the necessity to protect the coast and expand onto the sea, which is obvious in every period, but was a result of a development in the discourse of jihad, adapted to new military priorities. Threatened by the Basileus's fleet, which had become much stronger since the reforms of the Isaurian sovereigns after 717, the coastline, like the marches, now seemed the ideal place to carry out jihad, as symbolized by the practice of ribat. At the same time, with the conquest running out of steam, the volunteers who watched the sea and defended the coasts, like those who guarded the eastern frontiers against Turkish incursions, were given the same level of respect as the first conquerors. As a result, the practice of retreating to fortified cities on the Taurus frontier, such as al-Massisa and Tarsus, but also to Beirut and Tripoli on the Mediterranean coast, in the area where the practice of ribat had originated, experienced increasing popularity throughout the bordering countries, particularly in those regions where Muslim political and religious authorities devoted resources to coastal defense.

However, despite this promotion and some effort on the part of the chroniclers, geographers, and biographers to highlight coastal defense programs, we remain poorly informed about the military presence, the administration of fortified towns and garrisons, and, more generally, the financing of this vast frontier. This can partially be attributed to the use of formulaic terminology that highlighted not the defense system per se but the merits of caliphal and emirate jihad and of the scholars who frequented the places of ribat. The accounts of the situation farther west clearly date from after the events described; in Syria, Ifriqiya, and, to a lesser extent, al-Andalus, archeology often provides more detailed information about the technical aspects of defense and military architecture.[42]

Outside of the Near East, there are primarily three regions that have retained written or material traces of the implementation of coastal defenses, which was always carried out with the self-serving support of the authorities. The Abbasids or their representatives reinforced the defenses of Cilicia in the Sinai and, to a lesser extent, those of the Nile delta's maritime shores. Similar programs were imposed in the coastal areas governed by the Aghlabids in Africa and Sicily and, after the first

Viking incursion in 844, by the Umayyads in Iberia. Other regions along the Moroccan Rif under the rule of the Salihids of Nekor and farther west on the Idrisid coasts were also forced to defend themselves against Viking raids.[43]

It would be inaccurate to conceive of these defense systems as a limes that produced a ring of fortresses and towers protecting Mediterranean Islam from seaborne attacks by the Byzantines and Nordic sailors, given that such an "Atlantic Wall" never existed.[44] Arab men of letters give all the credit to the prince said to be responsible for building an innumerable quantity of defensive points and to the individual commitment of religious men. The Baghdad jurists and those who practiced ribat in the land and maritime frontier cities of Syria had a decisive influence, imposing the vocabulary and model of piety of the *mujahid* (one who practices jihad), later borrowed by the emirates and Malikis in the West. However, financial and material interests loomed behind this pious image of jihad.

The *Murabit*'s Reward and Profits on the Border, Affairs of State

Up to now, interpretations of texts produced by victims of the recurrent and institutional violence caused by the permanent conflict between Muslims and Christians have always created a vision of a unilateral crisis that affected every country bordering the Mediterranean. Yet war was not only a source of impoverishment. On the contrary, it was the basis of a high-risk economy that was profitable to certain categories of frontier populations. As for the Arabic texts describing Muslim sovereigns' strategies, they avoid any reference to financing, except to mention the generosity of a few ulema and pious sovereigns, earmarked for building ribats. Here, it should be mentioned that though he reigned less than ten years, Emir Ahmad was given credit for building ten thousand military structures covering the emirate's borders; the Arab writers referred to these investments generally in terms of the obviously exaggerated number of defensive structures built, repaired, or maintained, not in order to calculate their cost but to praise the prince's commitment as a *mujahid*. One has to wait until the fourteenth century to find more reliable financial data both in Ifriqiya and in Egypt, thanks to the institutionalization of pious donations (*habus*), particularly those intended for the ribats of the Hafsid period.[45] Nonetheless, beginning in the ninth century, various types of investment are in evidence, including the commitment of troops, structures located by archeologists or mentioned in Arabic texts, construction work in port cities, the commitment of fleets, and the concession of land to men with ties to those in power. Taken as a whole, these considerable investments raise the question of the resources then available to the governments and populations concerned: war is expensive but, in the ninth century, it produced a human and economic movement that had a profound impact on the medieval Mediterranean, recalling similar but far better documented developments on Latin shores. Latin records, which sometimes include figures, call into question the systematic and unilateral relationship between permanent threat and war on the one hand and an allegedly catastrophic economic situation and demographic toll on the other.[46] Though we are lacking pertinent figures, a similar analysis can be applied to the Muslim coastlines on which the authorities took action.

The Roots of Institutional Jihad

According to al-Kindi, Umayyad Alexandria enjoyed financing from pious donations that made it possible to support poor soldiers and volunteers, who could also be housed in private homes, for each sailing season individuals were required to provide accommodations as a form of tax.[47] The system changed under the Abbasids, with the move of the managing administration to Fustat before the end of the eighth century. Following this reform, volunteers were no longer paid on the spot, but they could continue to be housed and fed by pious Alexandrians. The jurist and chronicler Ibn ʿAbd al-Hakam believed that the port city had become a "rabita" as early as Muʿawiya's era. Using the language of his era, he sought to emphasize the early presence in Alexandria of volunteers who fought the enemy for the glory of God, by defending the Islamic territory's integrity. According to Ibn Lahiʿa, a highly renowned Alexandrian jurist, the joint practice of asceticism and watching the sea for approaching Christians was already common in the Marwanid era.[48] He even recalls a scholar who died in 719 but whom he already considered a *murabit,* though the number of *murabits* primarily began to grow at the end of the Umayyad period, when the Byzantines became more threatening and the advance of the believers was losing steam. ʿAbd al-Rahman b. Hurmuz al-Aʿraj (d. 736), a revered interpreter of the Koran and native of Medina, settled in Alexandria late in life to practice asceticism while keeping watch on the marine horizon. His Egyptian colleagues considered him the great port city's first real *murabit* and turned him into a highly venerated patron saint of Alexandria. This was the kind of practice the Abbasids could use to further their cause, creating a synergy between the individual commitment of scholars and the jihad of the ghazi caliph not in the Egyptian port but on the frontiers of caliphal jihad in the Anatolian marches and along the Syrian coastline.

The first texts codifying the practice of war and asceticism were written by armed scholars of the frontier in the late eighth century. They were encouraged by their sovereigns at a time when they were putting in appearances on the border, particularly under the reign of Harun al-Rashid. Thanks to the self-serving support of the authorities, Syrian pious scholars opened the way to the practice of ribat on all the frontiers. Their works were being circulated in al-Andalus within a decade and were still being published there shortly before the fall of Granada in 1492. In Egypt as in the other provinces, the authorities followed the same measures implemented on the Taurus frontier. During the same period, the pious scholars of Alexandria brought about change by attracting ulema passing through, notably reputed Maghrebi and Andalusian jurists and traditionists on their way to teach law in the East. The delta city remained a busy place of ribat, but its reputation came first and foremost from the rise of legal studies, thanks to the renown of local legal scholars such as al-Maʿafiri (d. 783) and al-Mahri (d. 785), whose scholarly wisdom attracted Western ulema traveling to the East and Mecca.[49]

In terms of defense, the policy of deploying soldiers in fortified edifices along the coasts of Ifriqiya followed the clear necessity of protecting the most exposed sites, which were also the most populated: the Gulf of Carthage, the coasts of Cap Bon, the populated shores of the Sahel, and, particularly, the region of Kairouan. However, there were not enough soldiers. It was desirable to attract ascetics, armed scholars, and, more generally, volunteers, brought by the great annual festivals such as the *mawsim* to ribat cities like Sousse, Monastir, Tunis or Radès, Tripoli, and, to a lesser extent, Gabès and Sfax.[50] In the most dangerous periods, these individuals volunteered to supplement troops monitoring the coasts.[51]

The practice of ribat under the supervision of the authorities, the presence in the same fortified sites of both cavalrymen assigned to the ribat and pious volunteers, and the entire military apparatus on the sea are reminiscent of the measures taken on the shores of the caliphate, from Alexandria to Tarsus, where armies paid by the caliph rubbed shoulders with volunteers. A similar system is duly attested to in al-Andalus, particularly in Tortosa, which was guarded by 150 cavalrymen and the sailors and, later, *murabitun* of Sant Carles de la Ràpita, located farther downstream on the Ebro, beginning under the emirate of al-Hakam I and, as of 844, whenever the coast was threatened by the Vikings.[52]

Waging War on the Frontier: Good Business?

The frontier space of the Mediterranean basin, particularly along coastlines, became a favored area for state interventions and, consequently, a zone of heavy investments.[53] This commitment was crucial in that the sites and edifices sheltering soldiers and volunteers required large sums of money to build defenses and remunerate military men who had settled there with their families. Consequently, the commitment motivated by the military situation simultaneously contributed to populating coastal regions and to making lasting investments that turned these maritime regions into highly active zones. A real economic system was created, adapted to the conditions of permanent cross-border clashes and exchanges, particularly on the sea. As of the ninth century in Islam, the coasts of Ifriqiya, al-Andalus, and Syria up to Cilicia were populated and subjected to significant military and commercial development; Byzantium followed a relatively similar evolution after the Muslims retreated in Anatolia. The Byzantine Isaurian emperors introduced a military policy, known by the term "themes," that was adapted to the stabilization of fronts and led to fundamental changes in social and economic organization.[54] In the Latin regions, feudalism played an essential role after the Carolingian collapse and before the city-states, counts of Catalonia and Provence, and kings and emperors elsewhere took responsibility for the best part of defenses in order to counter Muslim offensives. Thus, along with recurrent war, all of the Mediterranean's shores experienced an evolution in the organization of society and the economy.[55]

Al-Baladhuri and al-Ya'qubi, then al-Tabari and other Arab chroniclers and geographers, had access to information from the Umayyad chancellery on the establishment of exogenous populations in the regions of the Taurus and along Syrian coastlines. The principal groups moved on caliphal or emirate orders were contingents of soldiers, particularly the "Persians," but also skilled laborers such as carpenters and other workers at shipyards set up in Syrian ports to maintain and build ships. These populations were generally identified according to their geographic or ethnic background: they included "Arabs" from tribes of the Arabian peninsula, as well as the "Atrak," who were Turks by language and culture, brought from Iran and Iraq under the command of the *abna'*, members of the reigning family identified by this term referring to the sons of the Abbasid princes. This practice of settling soldiers and their families along the Syrian coasts had begun in the earliest phase of the conquests; most of those who were referred to as Persians (al-Furs) and sent to swell the ranks of soldiers in the coastal districts around 662–663 did not come from Fars but rather from the cities of the region—Baalbek, Homs, and Antioch—where their forebears had been called by Mu'awiya after the conquest of the coastal cities.[56] Similarly, in 648, with Tripoli of Lebanon freshly conquered and deserted by its inhabitants, the city was repopulated by Jews, also on orders from the caliph. The largest groups among these settlers appear to have been the Iranians, called al-Hamra' (Reds), perhaps due to their red hair, and the Persians, reported by al-Baladhuri to have settled on "the coasts of Syria."

The Abbasids borrowed this practice, but focused their efforts on the frontier marches. In Tarsus, aside from the volunteers for ribat, sailors of highly diverse backgrounds formed excellent crews. The regular employment of "renegades" such as Leo, Damian, and Photios, governor of Crete, indicate that Greeks from the Aegean Sea and the Anatolian coasts were highly appreciated for their nautical and military skills. The written records suggest that, like the Andalusians, the crews who had followed the Greek chiefs demanded high fees for their skills, which ensured their reliability.

This practice had already been common in the caliphs' land army since 836, with the massive incorporation of Turkish slaves to replace Arab and Persian contingents.[57] There is little doubt that Greek prisoners were on naval crews, in both Crete and the Near East, though there are no references to allow us to specify the background of the sailors recruited. Many of them were captives able to buy their freedom by working on Muslim ships. Indeed, capturing crews was an excellent business opportunity and could lead to the enlistment of captives in the Muslim ranks. It is therefore difficult to establish a connection between place of origin and sailing ability, despite the system of denomination chosen by the Arab authors; what is clear is that one had to spend a lot of money to have skilled sailors, either by paying high premiums or, more often, by granting resources drawn from revenue generated by the war and taxation of local populations.

While the texts do not explicitly mention the conditions for recruiting and profit sharing with crews in commerce raiding, they do provide a few leads regarding those for fighters in frontier towns in the Taurus. Harun al-Rashid's reform led to the creation of a zone of protection (*al-ʿAwasim*), commanded from the rear in cities like Qinnasrin, but also had the advantage of expanding the exclusive zone in terms of taxation, providing soldiers and volunteers with attractive financial conditions. The same was true on the shore (*sahil*). We basically know nothing about the details of these financial advantages, given that Arab men of letters generally limited their references to an enumeration of fortified towns on the Anatolian border and in Upper Mesopotamia, giving little information about financial support.[58]

In 756, a number of houses were built in six months in Melitene to accommodate four thousand soldiers sent to the front when the caliphs resumed campaigns in Anatolia. Farther south, significant investments were made to turn the fortified town of al-Massisa into an essential strategic point of the frontier military presence. The caliphs had it reinforced and settled two thousand soldiers there. Al-Baladhuri reports that these soldiers received a regular salary, as well as revenue from land in the region, in the form of concessions (*iqta'*), as was also the practice in Ifriqiya at the time. They also received their share of the booty after each razzia. In Tarsus, settlers were exempted from taxes and given plots of land. In this way, the authorities encouraged soldiers' families to settle in fortified towns on the frontier for the long term. The number of Muslim fighters who settled in the region with advantageous fiscal conditions is estimated at forty thousand. Ibn Hawqal refers to a relatively similar system on the Umayyad borders of al-Andalus in the tenth century, but he does not provide the same level of detail.

There is every reason to believe that similar measures were in effect in coastal regions, where razzias and maritime commerce could generate good revenue in periods of continual warfare: already in the Umayyad period, Arab soldiers took advantage of the summer months to raid Byzantine coasts and returned to the hinterland in the winter months. Similarly, when al-Ma'mun took over a plan to attack Constantinople, beginning in 830, he ordered his brother, the future al-Mu'tasim, then governor of Syria, to send troops from the districts of Homs, the Jordan River, and Palestine to join the maritime expedition under the command of one of his sons in 831–832. The coastal districts were reorganized on orders from al-Mansur and al-Mahdi, who had the port cities repaired or reinforced.

Though we do not have access to figures, it is safe to say that this revenue represented a significant financial commitment, with positive repercussions on populations working for the Muslims on the frontiers, at least so long as Islam prevailed over Byzantium. During the Islamic empire's weak phases, these positive effects were unreliable, even unlikely. Long-lasting borders have always stimulated trade, benefiting both sides. Under al-Ma'mun's reign, the Byzantines tried to focus turbulent Muslim soldiers' energy on commercial exchanges by proposing a treaty designed to increase the trade brought in by the former "silk roads," the principal market for which remained the capital city. As of 842, "lobbies" were developed to control the sources of frontier income from taxes, razzias, and trade, until Ibn Tulun attempted to misappropriate the profits.

Like Anatolian frontier cities, ports on the Syrian coast had always offered economic opportunities that made them the focus of the attention of the region's chiefs, leading families, and groups of soldiers. For instance, Umayyad caliph Hisham's decision to move the Acre dockyard to Tyre stemmed from commercial disagreements with the Arab family that had obtained the exclusive right to operate maritime traffic through the dockyard and adjoining granaries, probably from Muʿawiya. The ports cited in the geographers' itineraries as of the ninth century, particularly in the works of Ibn Khurradadhbih, were the departure and arrival points for Muslim ships and Christian pilgrims, if we are to believe the account by Willibald, an English bishop who left to make the pilgrimage to Jerusalem in 726. Willibald was faced with meticulous customs officials who searched luggage to ensure no commercial tax revenue was lost.[59] As shown in al-Bakri's maritime rutter, these maritime routes ran along the coast to the north and crossed over the border into Byzantium. Similarly, the map of the Mediterranean in the *Book of Curiosities* includes the Byzantine port of Antalya.

When Ibn Tulun found himself unable to control Tarsus, which was in the hands of Baghdad financial groups composed of those in power and their inner circle, he changed methods by financing razzias carried out by three thousand soldiers from Cilicia. Khumarawayh, Ibn Tulun's son and successor, bought the allegiance of Yazman, Tarsus's governor. Probably pushed by groups of merchants with ties to Baghdad, the city's inhabitants appealed to Caliph al-Muʿtadid, who sent a new governor in 898, before his successor, al-Muktafi, came to take possession of the city in 902. The reconstruction of the fleet, which had been burned before the caliph's eyes but immediately reassembled, allowed Damian to join forces with Leo of Tripoli and regularly carry out lucrative expeditions on the Aegean Sea, guaranteeing the city and the caliphate significant resources. By appointing these renegades as commanders, the caliph offset the influence of the Atrak, the Turks who were then all-powerful on the border. The Atrak also claimed to be in the caliph's service, but they aimed to control border traffic for their own benefit, with the support of the caliph's entourage.

As can be seen, the installation of defensive measures on the coast was a key issue that extended far beyond the framework of jihad. Those in power were able to hold sway over groups of professional fighters and sailors invited to settle with their families to defend the marches through control of the frontier regions' tax administration, the share deducted from the booty brought back from Christian land and maritime zones, and, more generally, the upholding of sultanate authority. Al-Muqaddasi's account of the activities of Palestinian ribats around the year 1000 reveals the inextricable links between jihad and business on Muslim shores, in this case concerning the ransoming of prisoners and, on a larger scale, maritime commerce with Byzantium, calling on even the most modest purses:

> Al-Ramla is, [as I have said], located in the middle of the fertile districts, surrounded by extraordinary district centers and ribats. . . . The capital [al-Ramla] oversees several coastal ribats, which are always ready to go into battle, to which the Greek barges and galleys sail, carrying Muslim prisoners, who are handed over at a price of 100 dinars for three. In each ribat, there are people who know the language of the Greeks and who are sent to them as representatives. The people of the ribat are provided with all kinds of food. When the Greeks' ships appear, the alarm is raised; if it is at night, [the signal] is lit at the ribat tower; if it is by day, smoke is produced. Each ribat is connected to the capital by a series of tall towers, with special personnel. [The signal] is lit at the ribat tower, then the following and so on, in such a way that not an hour goes by before the alarm has been raised in the capital. Then the drum is beaten on the tower [in the city], [the inhabitants] are exhorted to [go to] the ribat, and they go off in force and in arms, while the country youth gather; then the ransoms are paid: one person buys a man, another sacrifices a dirham or a small coin, so long as by the end all the prisoners brought have been bought back. The ribats in this district where the ransoms are paid are: Gaza, Mimas, Ashkelon, Mahuz Ashud [the port of Ashdod], Mahuz Jubna, Jaffa, Arsuf.[60]

The frontier allowed clans, generally close to those in power, to develop their own business through razzia warfare, land colonization, and land, sea, and especially cross-border trade. The Banu Salih at the beginning of the Abbasid period; the governors, generals, and admirals; and, in particular, officers of Turkic origin, allied to members of the dynasty, such as the Tulunids or the admirals of Greek origin, sometimes controlled actual conglomerates on the frontier, taking advantage of their position or their alliances at the court of Baghdad or Samarra. As of 750, only the caliphs could handle organization on such a scale. The regional emirates picked up the torch, following the example of the Aghlabids and the Tulunids. In short, the presence of sufficiently strong powers was indispensable to guarantee the stability of the fronts and to allow sailors and soldiers on the frontier free access to the sea, both to launch offensives and to finance defenses and expeditions and support the maritime commerce from which they themselves benefited.

Once the Abbasids were no longer in a position to ensure the defense of the countries bordering the Mediterranean, the Hamdanids of Aleppo took over. Despite the efforts of Sayf al-Dawla (945–967), celebrated by the great poet al-Mutanabbi (d. 965), the Hamdanids could not match Greek power the way the caliphs had.

When the crusaders captured the coasts of the Near East beginning in 1097, the Syrian ulema sent a delegation to Caliph al-Mustazhir (1094–1118), despite the fact that he had lost actual power to the Seljuq sultanate. The ulema still believed that only the heir to the ghazi sovereigns, who had led the jihad and stood up to the Christians, could head the armies of believers and chase away the crusaders: begun in the middle of the eighth century, both the formidable material mobilization for jihad and the remarkably effective propaganda continued to be operative until the beginning of the twelfth century.

10

THE MARITIME AWAKENING OF THE MUSLIM WEST

BEGINNING IN THE NINTH CENTURY, the western part of the Mediterranean Sea came to life, spurred on by the Muslims: in Ifriqiya, then under the domination of the Aghlabid emirs; and in al-Andalus, beginning in 798 with the arrival of a Berber fleet led by the Umayyad emir al-Hakam I's two uncles, and with the help of the Rustamids of Tahert and the Idrisids of Fez. Concise references to this marine activity reveal an overall trend that cannot be explained as the initiatives of a spontaneous generation of communities of sailors deciding, more or less at the same time, to make a living by going into piracy against the Latins and into trade with their compatriots.

THE DAWN OF A NEW MARITIME ERA: THE AGHLABID PERIOD

Appointed governor by Caliph al-Mansur, ʿAbd al-Rahman b. Habib had restored order to the western Maghreb, but his assassination in 754 put an end to the Tunisian fleet's activities for about half a century. Following his death, the unrest provoked by the *jund* lastingly compromised the program of naval attacks until 810, when Emir Ibrahim b. al-Aghlab restored peace and brought the Ifriqiyan contingent into line. However, it was Ziyadat Allah who was the first to devise a real plan to control the maritime space, taking advantage of favorable circumstances and a successful landing in Mazara in the east of Sicily in 827. He organized a permanent naval force to ensure the continuation of operations on the island. His system proved effective enough to keep up the war against Byzantium for seventy-five years, from Tunis and Sousse. Beginning in 831, Palermo served as a base for the fleet sailing from African shores to provide reinforcements and maintain authority over the island. This also allowed the Muslims to control the routes separating the central zone of the Mediterranean, stretching from Tripoli to Taranto, from the western basin zone. The taking of Malta in 869 and its subsequent complete depopulation brought to completion a plan that placed the central Mediterranean under Islam's lasting control.

Convoys to Sicily are mentioned, without any figures, in the context of major expeditions, beginning with the island's occupation in 827, though no further details are provided. Additionally, reports of dignitaries' frequent travels bear witness to the constant back and forth between the African continent and Sicily. According to a statement attributed to an admiral of the fleet, the crossing lasted a day and a half under normal conditions. Campaigns in the island's interior, made possible by reinforcements brought from Ifriqiya, and the numerous and sometimes months-long sieges of Syracuse, Palermo, Messina, and other coastal towns, required support from the fleets. Ifriqiya continued to be the departure point for these Sicilian expeditions. Though limited, this information suggests how frequently ships set sail from the two Ifriqiyan ports and the capital of Sicily. Attacks against Italy up to the mouth of the Po and the sieges of Salerno, Ragusa, and especially the island's Byzantine capital, which was blockaded for weeks at a time, clearly involved a capacity for significant logistical mobilization. The fleet's decisive part in the taking of Messina in 842–843 simultaneously gave the Muslims both control of the strait and the ability to provide reinforcements and reassurance to the troops laying siege to Bari, seized in 847. Similarly, the Ifriqiyan navy's ability to regain control of the maritime zone after suffering several defeats at the hands of the Byzantine fleet attests to the effectiveness of its administration. To put it mildly, the Aghlabids' naval organization was a decisive factor in the successful conquest of Sicily.

Ibrahim b. al-Aghlab had been able to relaunch the fleet as of 810. With the building of a port and a dockyard in Sousse, fifty kilometers (thirty miles) from Kairouan, the emirs now had a naval base they controlled directly, without having to depend on the whims of the Tunis *jund*. The information reported about the construction of the port and dockyard, which was protected by the city's rampart, does not provide any specific details on the layout of the premises: "Sousse has eight gates, one of which is very large and is located on the east of the building called *Dar al-sina'a:* this is where the ships come through. . . . It was Ziyadat Allah who erected these ramparts. . . . Inside the city there is a second fort called the Qasaba, it is located north of the medina, right next to the dockyard."[1]

The Fleet and Jihad

The Aghlabids proved themselves through the organization of their naval force, which provided them with the nearly constant ability to keep up their insular jihad from 827 to 902. According to the Egyptian historian al-Nuwayri (d. 1332), they landed ten thousand men from one hundred ships at Mazara in 827; describing the same event, al-Maliki reports ten thousand cavalrymen. Ibn 'Idhari reports seventy ships and seven hundred cavalrymen.[2] Though it is impossible to accurately assess the number of people and boats involved, the thirty-two expeditions that sailed from Ifriqiya and certainly mobilized large fleets for the conquest of Sicily, not to mention the innumerable crossings toward the island and the European continent, provide an idea of the naval resources available. In 827–828, during Asad b. al-Furat's first assault on Syracuse, the fleet fought off reinforcements sent from Venice and Greece; the capital was ultimately saved by the arrival of another Byzantine squadron, which forced the Muslims to burn their ships on the spot and disappear into the island's interior.

In 831, Palermo was surrounded on land and from the sea and forced to surrender; in 835, the Muslim fleet freed its ad hoc ally Naples from the grip of Sicard, prince of Benevento, who was seeking to take control of the region's ports. In 840, rivalries between Christians in Calabria provided the Arabs with an opportunity to seize Taranto, which then became the hub of Muslim activity in southern Italy. The same year, Ancona was pillaged. In 843, the fleet's entry into the port of Messina gave the Muslims control of the strait. Bari fell in 849, despite the presence in the region of the armies of Louis II, emperor of the Romans; lacking a fleet, Louis II was unable to save the city. The Christians soon became aware of the gifted general al-'Abbas b. al-Fadl, particularly following a large expedition launched from the island's capital against the south of the peninsula in 852 or 853; no Christian naval force could stop him. He repeated this campaign every year from 855 to 858. In 859, after a defeat on the open sea, al-'Abbas's brother 'Ali won a major naval victory and, if the Arabic texts are to be believed, sank one hundred Greek ships. After a period of respite, the new governor, Khafaja, resumed attacks against the capital and the cities of Val di Noto, in the southeast; in 865, during the same campaign, the fleet defeated the Greek squadron, which had arrived from Palermo. The city was again blockaded in 868: with Khafaja on land and his son on the sea, the Muslims repelled the reinforcements sent from Byzantium. The same fleet then set sail to attack Gaeta, devastating the entire region over the course of three months. When Malta was taken in 869, the Christian fleet beat back the squadron sent by Basileus Basil I (867–886), founder of the Macedonian dynasty. The early 870s saw the Muslims use troops brought from Taranto to launch a series of offensives in the region of Salerno, while Bari fell back into the hands of the Christians.

In 875, the war of conquest was revived by the arrival in Sicily's capital of a new Aghlabid governor, accompanied by fresh troops. However, it was his successor who would succeed in seizing Syracuse in 878. Once again, the fleet repelled reinforcements sent by the emperor, with the blockade of the port preventing fishermen and sailors from resupplying the city, which eventually surrendered. Also under the reign of Ibrahim II, the Byzantine fleet, though victorious in 879, lost control of the Strait of Otranto for a decade after suffering a total defeat in 889. Until that point, unrest in Ifriqiya had prevented the Muslims from sending new squadrons. The emir had had to wait ten years for the return to calm in Kairouan before he could send a fleet to Mazara and resume the conquest on the island and in Calabria. After using the Sousse fleet to take back the capital of Sicily from his rebellious relatives, he sent the same fleet to Messina and from there to Reggio Calabria, winning an important victory over the Greek squadron sent as reinforcements. With the maritime space back under his control, the emir could now consider personally leading the jihad on Italian soil.[3]

Jihad, a Necessary Outlet for Violence against the Regime

This impressive maritime track record was not solely due to good management of naval resources. The emirs had to head the jihad in order to keep armies standing at the ready and justify their title of "emir," given to those who governed in the name of the Abbasids and exercised military command; with the Maghreb Islamized, the sea, Sicily, and the south of the Italian Peninsula had become the emirs' new battlefields and their targets for lucrative razzias. Once Palermo was conquered, the Aghlabid clan took full control of operations on the island and took the helm of jihad in the south of the Peninsula. Having put an end to internal dissent, Emir Ibrahim II followed his role to its logical conclusion by personally leading the jihad. In 902, he landed at the head of his troops and seized Taormina, reducing the small Greek zone to the area of Rometta. With the Strait of Messina now reopened to Muslims, Ibrahim II landed in Calabria in September 902. His death in October put an end to the jihad.

The emirs had turned this large island and southern Italy into a frontier march and the battlefield of their jihad. While they officially saw themselves as the representatives of the caliphate, they kept war profits for their own clan. It seems likely that this was the mind-set of the last Aghlabid sovereign after he brutally regained control of the emirate and decided to follow the example of the caliphs, particularly Caliph al-Ma'mun, who had chosen to personally head the jihad from the ribat-city of Tarsus in Cilicia. Johannes Hymonides, our principal source, reports the threats made by the emir when he addressed the representatives of the Frankish and Byzantine sovereigns who had come to propose a truce in Calabria: "Let them [the Christian sovereigns] at least know for certain that I will not only destroy their cities, but also the city of that miserable old Peter. There will be nothing else for me to do then but to reach Constantinople and to tear it down with the momentum of my power."[4]

Whether it was actually spoken or not, this statement, drawing heavily from eschatology, echoed a persistent tradition that reached back to the time of the first Umayyads and had continued until the defeat of 717. Ibrahim II now borrowed it for his own use.

However, the founding principles of sultanate legitimacy, which was tied to jihad and formalized by the jurists of Baghdad, required above all that the holy territory of the Dar al-Islam be defended. As with the accounts of the caliphs' military endeavors, most references to Aghlabid jihad, found in the chronicles and biographies of the ulema, deal with the defense of the coasts of Ifriqiya.

THE ADVENT OF MUSLIM NAVIGATION IN THE MAGHREB AND AL-ANDALUS

The occupation and development of the Iberian Peninsula had required boats to transport thousands of Berber and Arab soldiers across the Strait of Gibraltar from 710 to 712. According to certain sources, Julian, the governor of Ceuta, incited Musa b. Nusayr to attack Roderic, king of the Visigoths. According to other opinions, the alliance was made once Musa b. Nusayr was in a position to threaten the Count of Ceuta in his city.[5] The late regional traditions have left a few indications regarding the methods of transportation the governor made available to the invaders to cross the strait. From these, we can deduce that the port had the necessary harbor facilities and ships to provide the Muslims with the best crossing point to Spain, used by the estimated five hundred soldiers under Tarif in 710; the forces of Tariq b. Ziyad in 711, estimated at seventeen thousand men by the most optimistic of the traditionists; and the up to eighteen thousand men said to have embarked with the Arab conqueror to join the Berber chief in 712.[6] Tarif "crossed the strait [with four hundred footmen and one hundred cavalrymen] using four ships" and took possession of Tarifa, which was described as the Visigoths' dockyard. The following season, Tariq and his seven thousand men "crossed the strait on the [same] boats, the only ones in their possession, which went back and forth to transport the infantry and cavalry [until] Musa, who after Tariq's departure had ordered boats to be built and now had a good number of them, sent him 5000 men."[7]

For his part, Ibn 'Idhari specifies that "to transport [Tariq b. Ziyad's] troops without the Visigoths' knowledge, Julian used trading ships that regularly coasted between the two shores, so that it was believed they were carrying merchants. All these soldiers were thus introduced little by little."[8]

The facilities and seamen left on site by the Byzantines since 680 had made it possible to transport Berber and Arab troops to the European continent. Subsequent references to crossings—essentially by participants in Arab political and military life, most often between Algeciras and Africa—reveal that relations continued between the two shores, now both under Islam's control. In light of events such as the Berber Revolt, crossing the strait seemed easy: in 741, after facing severe setbacks in the Maghreb, the survivors of the Syrian contingent sent by Caliph Hisham to put down the Berber uprising, estimated at five thousand men, landed in al-Andalus to go defeat the Peninsula's insurgents. They had earlier found refuge in Ceuta, where they had succeeded in resisting Berber assaults for a relatively long time, probably in the al-Mina' fortress, a vestige from the period of Justinian II. Emir Idris I's seizure of the port city in 789–790 marked a new stage in the growth of traffic between the two shores. Under the supervision of the two emirates established in Córdoba and Fez, the two capitals were now regularly connected by greater commercial traffic.[9]

The strait was not the only area open to maritime traffic prior to the arrival of Musa b. Nusayr and the Muslims; in fact, the entire coast of the Maghreb on the Mediterranean seaboard was concerned. The ports of the Moroccan Rif, in operation thanks to Berber sailors, were "discovered" once the Arab authorities integrated them into an Islamic framework, as attested to in this account of the founding of the emirate of Nekor: "Saleh conquered this land under the reign of al-Walid b. 'Abd al-Malik. Having arrived in the Maghreb at the time of the first Muslim conquest, he settled in the port of Tamsaman, near Bakdun, on the Wadi al-Baqar. The port of Tamsaman is 20 miles from the city of Nekor.

The Sanhaja and the Ghomaras, Berbers of this locality, allowed themselves to be converted to Islam."[10]

Commercial navigation, fishing, and possibly local piracy were practiced before the Muslims, but these activities are only revealed to us from the point when Muslim authorities took control of them, at least nominally. At the same time, by taking responsibility for conducting jihad, these emirate dynasties stimulated navigation all the way to the Latin coasts.[11]

The east coast of the Iberian Peninsula was also not devoid of maritime activity in the Visigoth period, as attested to by a retaliatory measure taken by the first Umayyad emir: "In 162 / 778–779, Imam ʿAbd al-Rahman ibn Muʿawiya (756–785) ordered the destruction of the boats (*marakib*) of the district of Tudmir and of all the sailing equipment."[12] Since the conquest in 714, this region, which basically corresponds to the present-day region of Murcia, had enjoyed a treaty of capitulation signed by ʿAbd al-ʿAziz b. Musa and Count Theudimer, lord of the principality that took his name. The principality's autonomy and the activity of its sailors are confirmed by the fact that the governor of al-Andalus had to tell Syrian soldiers wanting to go home from one of the region's ports after putting down the Berber Revolt of 741 to embark in Algeciras because the eastern coasts were not under Muslim control.[13] It appears that Emir ʿAbd al-Rahman I sought to challenge this freedom of navigation by having Tudmir's ships destroyed. Even long-distance crossings were possible. Thus, according to the tenth-century Andalusian man of letters Ibn al-Qutiyya (whose name means "son of the Gothic woman"), Sara the Goth, a descendant of the Visigothic king Wittiza, whose heirs had joined the Muslims to fight Roderic, "had a boat built for herself in Seville, which was the city where her father [Alamundo] had taken up residence. . . . Sara the Goth embarked with her brothers and headed for Syria. She landed in Ashkelon and continued her journey to arrive at the gates of the palace of Hisham b. ʿAbd al-Malik."[14]

While this story can be met with skepticism, long-distance sailing, including from the Iberian Peninsula, is repeatedly attested to in the first centuries of the Middle Ages and throughout the Mediterranean basin.[15]

The Confrontation between Christians and Muslims in the Western Mediterranean

The revolt of the emir of Córdoba's uncles against Emir al-Hakam I is reported to have provoked the first maritime attacks against Christians, launched on the Andalusian emir's order: "[In 798] ʿAbd Allah b. ʿAbd al-Rahman b. Muʿawiya al-Balansi irrupted into al-Andalus, coming from the African coast of Tahert."[16] The Rustamids had made crews available to back the two dissident uncles in the ports of the central Maghreb, particularly in ʿAin al-Farruj, Hunayn, and Ténès. Sulayman b. ʿAbd al-Rahman b. Muʿawiya and his brother ʿAbd Allah al-Balansi, "the Valencian," began by attempting to seize the Balearic Islands in 798. The Carolingians took the opportunity to send a squadron to the islands, the size of which is impossible to gauge. This initiative was not to bear fruit. The two uncles then landed on the east coast, very likely in the area of Valencia, of which ʿAbd Allah took command after visiting the court of Charlemagne in a failed attempt to gain support. In 802, after his brother had been killed in combat, he submitted to the emir and took over the government of the city and its region.[17]

After the uncles' failure to take control of the Balearics, the crews in the eastern ports of al-Andalus launched a series of attacks on the Carolingian coasts. These raids were only reported by the Latin sources. Given that the emir did not personally lead these expeditions, and in the absence of any sign of his having ordered them, it appears that they were planned by the coastal governor, which would also explain the Umayyad historians' silence. In 806, the emperor sent a squadron to Corsica in response to an expedition of "Moors" from the eastern coasts—in other words, of Berbers who had settled on eastern shores. The Carolingians entrusted Count Burchard of Lucca with the command of a fleet that intervened on the island several times, "the Moors having gotten in the habit of pillaging it in the previous years."[18] For their part, the Andalusian sailors set upon Sardinia. While they sustained losses inflicted by the Carolingian fleet on their return journey, they were able to reach Pantelleria and to leave with sixty monks as prisoners. After another attack on Corsica in 809, a fleet "from nearly all of Spain" successively attacked both islands' coasts, where a Muslim community took root, as had been the case with a group of sailors from Ifriqiya on the Sardinian coast to the south.[19]

The Carolingian annals report a joint attack by "Andalusian and African sailors" in 812, just before the beginning of negotiations between Idrisid emissaries and the Byzantine patrician of Syracuse. The two sides signed a truce between 813 and 815. Several attacks had already been launched against Sicily from Idrisid coasts. In the meantime, Andalusian vessels returning from Corsica were intercepted in Mallorcan waters and defeated by the Tuscans, who freed five hundred prisoners intended for the slave markets. The following year, the same Moors attacked Civitavecchia and Nice. Other Andalusian sailors were defeated off the coast of Sardinia. After several short-lived truces, the land victory over the Franks at Barcelona in 815, the year after Charlemagne's death, finally brought an end, on land and at sea, to a war that had begun in 801 with the Carolingian conquest of the Catalan capital. While the Latins were in a position of strength in Catalonia, they did not have the naval resources to put a stop to Andalusian and Maghrebi raids, except for the fleet commanded by Burchard of Lucca, which was probably based in Pisa.

This was a war between regional powers, not between the Provençal and starving pirates. These naval attacks on Christian shores must be seen in the context of the war between the two universalisms separated by the sea, which allowed the Maghrebi emirates to continue the jihad, a source of legitimacy, by assaulting Christian coasts. At the same time, the increase in the number of references to maritime traffic implies an expansion of both commercial and military shipping.[20] People at the time certainly saw piracy and trade as two separate things, as shown by several fatwas beginning in the ninth century and, especially, the treaty of 813, which was signed by Sicily's Greek authorities and the Aghlabid and Idrisid emirates. According to the jurists, the increase in piracy was a result of the authorities' inability to control maritime populations, despite the fact that attacks on Christian shores had actually begun once Muslim regional powers took control of ports and sailors. Maghrebi and Andalusian crews amply benefited from the situation thanks to the prospects offered by good relations with the emirs' capitals; their vigor was put in the service of the cause of jihad. For their part, like the Aghlabids and the Andalusian Umayyads, the Idrisid, Salihid, and probably Rustamid emirs opened a new space for jihad for themselves by encouraging raids on Christian shores now that the Maghreb was considered an Islamized land, and thus off limits to razzias outside of pockets of infidelity. The sea had become the only place for Maghrebi emirates seeking legitimacy to wage institutional jihad.

On this basis, the Salihid emirs, presenting themselves as Himyarite Arabs descended from one of the companions of ʿUqba b. Nafiʿ, succeeded in establishing a principality along the coast of the Rif, where the Ghomaras and other tribes had long lived off the sea. This small state rose out of obscurity after Saʿid b. Idris founded the city of Nekor close to the coast in 761.[21] However, it was not until the ninth century, and particularly under the government of Salih b. Idris (804–864), that the emirate would become known for its maritime dynamism. Salih had traveled to al-Andalus to wage jihad with Emir ʿAbd al-Rahman II, but it was by turning to the sea, a source of revenue, that the prince became able to present himself as the worthy defender of Islam. As on all the coastlines undergoing Islamization, these commitments stimulated the construction of coastal defenses and the practice of ribat. Similarly, the Idrisids of Fez seized on this expansion of coastal defenses and took over the places of ribat founded by coastal tribes seeking to protect themselves from the Vikings.[22]

Like the other emirs, they encouraged the pious practices inseparable from jihad. This gave them the opportunity to secure control of the coastal zones where donations and the enlistment of volunteers—in this case, from the tribes—financed the defense of the *sahil* and promoted the development of trade and other lucrative activities, especially as of the middle of the ninth century. At the same time and in the same area, Berber cities such as Basra, located on the Wadi Loukkos, exported local goods such as linen by crossing the Strait of Gibraltar to Mediterranean ports, evidence of an expansion that geographers such as Ibn Hawqal would bear witness to a century later. The success of jihad at sea, against the Christians, rested on the same principles, with the Maghrebis now able to reach the shores of infidelity and present themselves as other initiators of maritime jihad. There are few traditions reported about this movement from the central and western coasts of the Maghreb, but those that are known reveal an overall consistency in the expansion of maritime activity, driven by the societies of sailors of the Maghrebi coasts and, as of the ninth century, supervised by the region's emirs, who sought both to channel the tribes' combative energy on land and at sea and to prove their legitimacy by taking the initiative of jihad. The economic context, which remains difficult to grasp, and the military situation, which is only a little clearer, provide an understanding of the actions of these sailors who exclusively preyed on the enemies of Islam, outside the usual acts of local piracy and plunder. The simultaneous nature of the awakening of the Andalusian coasts and the reinforcement of the Maghrebi powers is certainly no coincidence.

THE FIRST ANDALUSIAN NAVY (NINTH CENTURY)

Before 844, al-Andalus's only border was the one that ran across the Iberian Peninsula from the mouth of the Ebro in Porto to the Douro. Aside from the Strait of Gibraltar, the eastern coast came to life—at least from a military perspective—with the war against Charlemagne. The Vikings can be credited with violently rousing the rest of the vast seaboard, which had previously remained tranquil.

The Aftereffects of Viking Attacks: The Umayyads Take Control of the Sea and Its Shores

Even after several crews left the eastern coasts for Egypt around 818, the Andalusian emirs did not lack for sailors when they needed them. Outside the constantly active zone of the strait, the settling of the Maghrebi Berbers on the east coast seems to have provided new blood to serve beside native sailors, both on the coast of Tudmir and in the regions of Almería and Cartagena.[23] Thanks to this potential, ʿAbd al-Rahman II was able to react immediately to the sack of Seville in 844. He brought these sailors from eastern coasts, at good wages, to lead the fleet built on the dockyards of Seville, which had been laid out shortly after the attack of the Norsemen.[24]

The irruption of the Vikings revealed the extent to which the coastal regions had previously been neglected by Umayyad governors and emirs. On the west coast, only the city of Lisbon was able to repel the invaders; after having saved his city, its governor Wahb Allah b. Hazm was the first to raise the alarm.[25] After being pillaged by the soldiers of the Asturian king Alfonso II (791–842) in 798, Lisbon had been fortified once the emir's troops reconquered it in 812. However, no measures were taken to protect the coastlines and coastal cities against an unlikely threat from the western sea. Niebla, Huelva, and the ports of the Guadalquivir, like the lower valley of the Guadiana, the coast of Cádiz, and the region of Medina-Sidonia, were within reach of these formidable sailors. Algeciras was spared in 844 but pillaged during a second incursion in 859. On the east coast, which was also targeted, only Tortosa was nominally designated an Umayyad fortress and military port. This absence of sultanate power on the shores is nowhere more apparent than in a laughable order sent by the emir to the coastal authorities after he received a letter from the governor of Lisbon: he recommended they "be vigilant."[26] The Andalusians' helplessness also shows through in several reports reproduced in the tenth century by men of letters such as Ibn al-Qutiyya: "Since no man from the Gharb al-Andalus had risked fighting them, [the emir] had to recruit people in Córdoba and the neighboring provinces. . . . Naturally, those who served on the frontiers had already been called to arms, from the beginning of the *majus* movement, when they landed in the West."[27]

The measures taken by the emir were felt when the sailors from the north returned in 858–859. While the Norsemen succeeded in pillaging several strongholds, the troops and fleet serving Muhammad, who had carried on with his father's policy, provided a more effective defense of the coast:

> The same year [858], the *majus* reappeared with sixty-two ships off the western seaboard; but they found the sea guarded by Muslim vessels that were cruising along the coastline of the Franks [Catalonia] and the Galicians. [After two ships were captured off the coast of Beja (Alentejo) and the *majus* were prevented from sailing up the Guadalquivir], the enemy fleet

> moved to Algeciras, where it landed, took control of the city, and set fire to its great mosque. [When the Frankish forces returned the following year,] Emir Muhammad's fleet advanced against them and captured two richly laden [ships] off the coast of Medina-Sidonia; the rest of the enemy vessels moved away.[28]

Though they did not succeed in protecting the entire coast, the defensive measures implemented along the vast seaboard yielded results described by the thirteenth-century Maghrebi chronicler Ibn 'Idhari, based on reports from the period of the Umayyad caliphate. The emir borrowed both the Abbasids' strategy and their terminology to describe the steps taken. As shown by the account of the attack in 858, the most effective preventive measures were maritime. From the three ports of Seville, Algeciras, and Tortosa, all equipped with dockyards, the fleets would set sail to intercept hostile ships. On the Atlantic, ships patrolling along the west coast of present-day Portugal could rely on finding havens in the harbor of Rado, the future site of Alcácer do Sal, and, farther south, Sines, along with Lisbon and Silves, the embarkation point for al-Ghazal, a poet and emissary sent by the emir to the court of Denmark. Once a ship rounded Cape Saint Vincent, Silves, Ocsonoba, Saltes, the mouth of the Guadiana, the river islands near the mouth of the Guadalquivir, the anchorage at Cádiz, and other shelters offered a multitude of stops up to Tarifa, which was fortified in the tenth century. On the eastern seaboard, references to unrest (*fitna*) during the last quarter of the ninth century reveal a dense occupation of the coast up to the Ebro at the beginning of 'Abd al-Rahman III's reign.

Beginning in 844, the Umayyad administration created administrative defense zones, referred to with the term *tarf* (cape): Sintra and Cabo da Roca, north of the Tagus; the Setúbal Peninsula, between the Portuguese capital and the Mondego; and Cape Saint Vincent, which was dominated by the monastery housing the relics of the saint, now served as lookout posts in which volunteers were stationed. Another such post was in Arrábida (al-Rabita), south of the Tagus. According to the scattered information provided, the coastal administration now covered the entire coast of al-Andalus (*sahil*) and was dedicated to surveillance and, if necessary, organizing defenses against enemies arriving by sea. As in Syria, this coastal administration was under the responsibility of the governors of the inland and coastal districts; along with the Portuguese capital, Coimbra, Beja, Ocsonoba, Niebla, Seville, and Shaduna, capital of the region of Cádiz, were all monitoring the ocean.

The Andalusian Ribat, an Imported Model

The first volunteer fighters appeared during the same period, on the coasts and on the land fronts, against the Latins, particularly in the region of Catalonia.[29] Ibn Hayyan's account of the *fitna* in the last third of the ninth century also identifies the mouth of the Douro as a "ribat zone." The same chronicler's lists of districts attest to the presence of *murabitun* in the locality of Arrábida (al-Rabita). Since 848, the Bay of Almería had been the site of towers serving as ribats, which doubled as sources of revenue generated by donations and taxes paid by the inhabitants of the Andarax valley for protection. The prospect of a similar practice probably led to the building of the Sant Carles de la Ràpita ribat at the mouth of the Ebro, at around the same time.[30]

After the Umayyad embassy to the king of the Danes and two further naval victories over Danish troops from 858–859 to 861, a squadron was placed under the command of admiral Khashkhash al-Bahri—most likely a relative of one of the leaders who had defeated the Danes—and charged with exploring the ocean north of the familiar waters of the Portuguese coast. The expedition's success may have led to the first Muslim attempt to attack the Atlantic coast north of the Douro from the sea, which ended prematurely with a shipwreck in the ever-perilous waters of the Gulf of Cádiz:

> [In 266 / 879–880] Emir Muhammad ordered the building of ships [on the river in] Córdoba, which al-Ru'ayti, known by the name of Ibn Mughith, was to lead onto the ocean, given that a spy had reported that Galicia's seafront lacked fortifications and that its inhabitants would be unable to defend themselves if they were surprised by an attack coming from that side. Once construction was finished, the command of this fleet was entrusted to 'Abd al-Hamid b. Mughith; but once they arrived on the sea, the ships all broke apart and were dispersed and could not be reassembled.[31]

The dynasty's budding ambition was not limited to expeditions against Christians and the defense of the coastline; maritime expansion had become an important territorial and economic concern, in a space increasingly frequented by merchants and from which the sovereigns of Córdoba fully intended to reap the benefits: "The reason for which the sailors settled in the city of Pechina was that, once the power of the Banu Hasan Idris b. Idris was reinforced in the Maghreb, the Umayyad 'caliphs' ordered the coasts to be controlled so that no boat could sail there without being monitored and controlled. No one could leave al-Andalus without authorization and no one could enter it before [the authorities] had made inquiries and knew where he was coming from and what he was transporting."[32]

'Abd al-Rahman II took advantage of the naval resources at his disposal to resume offensives against Latin shores during the period when he was undertaking a series of campaigns on the territory of Álava against King Ordoño I (850–866) and in Catalonia. Beginning in 838, Andalusian sailors carried out several expeditions against the Italian coast, the western islands, and, especially, Provence: the Latin annals, which are primarily monastic, report raids against Saint-Victor in Marseille in 838 and 848; Arles and Saint-Césaire in 842, 850, 859, and 869; Nimes in 859; and as far as Valence on the Rhône in 860.[33]

These razzias against Christian coastlines and islands, the growing intensity of maritime relations with the Maghreb since the beginning of the ninth century, and the desire to control the maritime routes passing the islands reveal the maritime space's strategic importance for the emirate of Córdoba. The attempted seizure in 848 of the Balearic Islands, which had been under Muslim control since 709, exemplifies the Mediterranean's change of military and economic status in the minds of the Andalusian authorities—long before the advent of the caliphate in 929.

Fitna and Maritime Development in Andalusia (875–912): A False Paradox?

The political crisis that rocked al-Andalus from 875 to 912, exclusively known to us through Ahmad al-Razi's account, highlights the divisions and weaknesses of the Umayyad government before the resounding recovery that took place under the reign of ʿAbd al-Rahman III and the proclamation of the caliphate in 929.[34] Yet the caliphal chronicle reveals indications of strong economic growth in the same period, of which regional elites and populations were both the architects and beneficiaries. The chronicle mentions the reconstruction of numerous cities that had apparently been previously abandoned. In particular, the founding of fortified villages (*husun*), also erected by the regional aristocracies, confirms a territorial reorganization of the provinces during the second half of the ninth century, of which the caliph would take advantage half a century later in administering the flourishing caliphal territory.[35]

Coastal regions seem to have particularly benefited from this trend, long before the advent of the caliphate. For example, Ibn Hayyan indicates that "Bakr b. Yahya b. Bakr settled in the city of Shant Mariyya in the canton of Ocsonoba, built structures there and turned it into a stronghold which he equipped with iron doors."[36] Bakr, whose background remains unclear, took advantage of the *fitna* that began in 875 to take control of the city—present-day Faro, in the Algarve—backed by Mozarabs and local Muslims. He had the venerable ancient city rebuilt and reinforced. The port's maritime activities, particularly fishing, and the exploitation of coastal forests for marine lumber became important resources, under the protection of the statue of Mary, the patron saint of fishermen who combined the two religions. The revenue generated allowed the Banu Bakr to escape the hold of the Yemenis who had previously dominated the region.[37]

The descriptions of maritime activities oriented toward trade report a new momentum in maritime exploitation from Umayyad shores. This is also evidenced by the regular relations established between ports on the east coast and those of the Maghreb, from the Strait of Gibraltar to the Algiers region. The beginning of this activity coincided precisely with the beginning of the *fitna* in 875, the year Ténès was founded through the efforts of Arab and Berber sailors from Iberian shores. These lasting ties extending to both sides of the Alboran Sea constantly grew in scope, as attested to by the founding of Oran in 902–903, the year the Balearic Islands bowed to the sultan's authority. Ibn Khaldun indicates that the initiative to invade the islands came from a private individual, ʿIsam al-Jawlani, who proposed to Emir ʿAbd Allah to subdue the archipelago, presenting it as an easy target upon his return from a pilgrimage to Mecca. While the initial impetus for the invasion may have come from the rich pilgrim's request, such an operation could never have been launched without the prince's agreement, particularly since Pechina had become the principal port of the emirate, with which he now had close ties. Appointed governor of Mallorca, al-Jawlani ordered the construction of mosques, baths, and *funduqs* (inns), "the fundamental elements that define an Islamic city."[38] The Muslims' control of the archipelago, after numerous failed attempts, can probably be attributed to the development of economic relations with the continent, which may have convinced the islanders to accept their tutelage. Several regional capitals, such as Seville, which was governed by the Banu Hajjaj, one of the rich Arab families that controlled the city, took advantage of the naval and port infrastructures built during the Viking attacks to turn themselves into prosperous trading posts where boats from the entire Mediterranean landed.[39] The best-documented and most significant example of this boom in the middle of the *fitna* period is Pechina.

Berber sailors are often presented as having taken the initiative that paved the way to the maritime city's naval fortune, before the caliphate became involved. Under the reign of Muhammad, probably shortly before 875, the sailors originating from communities that had participated in naval operations against Christians under the reigns of al-Hakam I and 'Abd al-Rahman II were accused of pillaging the Muslim port of Marchena, which is otherwise unknown to us. Angered by their actions, the emir ordered the dismantling of Tortosa's naval forces, which were primarily composed of Berber crews. Consequently, this act of piracy seems to have led these sailors, the *bahriyyun,* to settle in southern ports, and particularly in Águilas, Pechina, and Ashkubirash, which has also proved impossible to locate. Some of these Berber and Arab sailors chose to return to their homelands, but most put down roots on the south coast of al-Andalus and contributed to founding the city, with the authorization of the Andalusian emir. These experienced sailors expanded maritime business, though we do not know whether they did so in association with the Yemenis or after edging them out. In any case, they took advantage of their close ties with the communities in ports of the Maghreb, particularly in Ténès, which had become a prosperous trading post, and Oran, on the coast of the emirate of Tahert.[40]

The success of the city located next to the Bay of Almería rested on a favorable economic context and the privileged ties it had formed with the Umayyad caliphs since its founding. The clearest proof of its growth was in ʿAbd al-Rahman III's choice to make it the headquarters of the Umayyad admiralty, when he decided to take control of maritime affairs in 931. By taking over this fine instrument that would allow him to realize his maritime ambitions, the caliph was therefore only continuing and expanding on an initiative that had begun around 884. Yet the caliphal histories were able to give the impression that the caliph was the one truly responsible for the port's fortune by sidestepping the emirate period of its economic development and foregrounding the caliph's decision to take control of the fleet beginning in 931—the year Ceuta was occupied. The construction of a new city after the Fatimid razzia of 954 and the resettlement of Pechina's population in this city marked the final act of the idyll between Umayyad power and the sailors of the Bay of Almería.[41]

While the ninth century was unquestionably the period of the Muslim drive into the western Mediterranean, as it was in the eastern zone, the ideological framework imposed by the Abbasid caliphate, then the censorship exercised by the Mediterranean caliphates in the following century, determined temporal borders that served the caliphates' interests in setting historical memory. The title taken by the Umayyads and the Fatimids required them above all to conquer the Muslim world in its entirety and, in particular, Baghdad, while continuing to pursue jihad against Christians and to fight each other. In this new context, the Mediterranean was more than ever before the center of the three caliphates' concerns.

11

THE MARITIME IMPERIALISM OF THE CALIPHS IN THE TENTH CENTURY

The End of Jihad?

The literary manipulation and elimination of earlier traditions by men of letters in the service of the caliphs raise the question of whether there really was an economic rupture between the ninth century of the emirates and the tenth century of the caliphates in the Islamic West. If such a divide did exist, it would primarily have been in the Iberian Peninsula and Ifriqiya, areas where the caliphal states flourished. Yet it was precisely in these regions that the two major Mediterranean emirates seem to have made their most significant investments in the ninth century. Consequently, the two caliphates were in a position to make use of the effects of economic growth started in a previous era, as was the case on the shores of Byzantium, but also along Latin coasts. This overall trend is confirmed by the emergence of commercial networks that covered the entire space of the inner sea, such as the trade in *bacini* ceramics produced by Muslims and bought by Pisans or the business of Jewish merchants of the Geniza, networks that witnessed and participated in the general growth of commerce on a Mediterranean scale.[1]

FROM THE SEA OF JIHAD TO THE IMPERIAL SPACE

An assessment of the evolution of caliphal policies in the Mediterranean reveals a relative consistency in the strategy of the Fatimid and Umayyad caliphates, insofar as both states shared the goal of reaching Baghdad. The proclamation of the two caliphates at the beginning of the tenth century was to mark a major change in military objectives, with the conquest of the caliphal seat becoming necessary to realize the claim to govern all of Islam. The Fatimid conquest of Egypt and Syria as far as Damascus and the Andalusian objective to take control of the Maghreb, thus getting closer to the Middle East while annexing the Shiite caliphate, were the first stages of a conquest that was to last until the taking of Baghdad and the fall of the Abbasids. This reevaluation of the space of conquest, determined from Kairouan, Cairo, and Córdoba, gave the Mediterranean a different role from the one it had been assigned at the heart of the Dar al-Islam by Iraqi caliphs focused on the West.

This required an evolution of propaganda, which for the first time since the advent of Islam reversed the direction of legal war, now aimed no longer at the conquest of the infidel's territories but at the heart of the imperial domain. This profoundly changed the profile of the Mediterranean, as presented by the chronographs of the region's two caliphates. The Mediterranean's status shifted from that of an intermediary, frontier space facing the infidel, to that of a sea conquered and governed by Islam. With this established, no one was fooled by the few stirrings in favor of jihad against the Christians, for the rivalries between the two dynasties quickly appeared as the strategic stakes in the land and sea campaigns carried out by the region's two major powers.

Supposed to replace the use of force and implemented after the caliphs' land campaigns failed to alter the borders with the Iberian Peninsula's Christian states, the diplomacy of intimidation that the caliphs adopted with these Christian sovereignties often proved more effective. However, on several occasions the chronicles report that the African troops were sometimes hurriedly called to arms to deal with the Christian threat, such as when Gormaz, a military capital on the upper Douro, was attacked by the Count of Castile and his allies in 975. This situation reveals the limits of Umayyad military ambitions.[2] Similarly, the jihad against the Latins at sea lasted a relatively short time before being replaced by a naval policy entirely dedicated to fighting the Fatimids and increasingly favorable to the Mediterranean's commercial development.

The Fatimid caliphs' commitment to jihad, both on the water and on the continent, ended with the conquest of Sicily in 965 and their recovery of control of the straits, which had briefly been compromised by the Byzantines' naval initiatives. However, as of the reign of ʿUbayd Allah al-Mahdi, the conquest of Egypt became the Ifriqiyan caliphs' primary goal. The conquest required four offensives, in 915, 919, 935, and 969–971, the last of which proved decisive.[3] After the sack of Genoa in 934, the other event commented on by the party's "ideologue" Qadi Nuʿman was a punitive expedition against Pechina in 954, launched in retaliation for the capture of one of his ships off the coast of Sicily. Like the Umayyad naval expedition against Sousse and Marsa al-Kharaz, in the north of Ifriqiya, after the sack of Pechina, these events show that what was at stake in the Mediterranean was no longer jihad against the infidel but the control and division of maritime waters among Muslim sovereignties.[4]

Umayyad Fleets in the Service of Caliphal Ambitions

The accession of Caliph ʿAbd al-Rahman III in 929 is thought to have marked the beginning of the Andalusians' maritime jihad against the Latin infidel. Indeed, for the first time since the conquest of al-Andalus, the caliphate's men of letters listed the razzias launched against Latin shores. Though the loss of several passages of Ibn Hayyan's chronicle deprives us of several parts of this maritime history, the presentation of the facts leaves no doubt regarding the master of Medina Azahara's intention to suppress knowledge of naval expeditions carried out by his ancestors and predecessors. This omission could lead one to believe that the emirs of Córdoba never sponsored sea expeditions outside of those against the Vikings. On the contrary, the mention of naval raids against the Christians as of 933 meant that the advent of maritime jihad coincided with the advent of the caliphate.[5] This historical manipulation proved all the more necessary given that the Fatimid imams imposed the same rupture with regard to the Aghlabid period.

Beyond declarations made for propaganda purposes, the various episodes involving the navy of the caliph, master of the seas and the two shores (or *al-ʿidwatayn,* the name given to the administrative region of the Strait of Gibraltar and the adjacent coastal and maritime zones after the taking of Ceuta), show that the fleet, one of the most substantial on the Mediterranean, was primarily used for the conquest of North Africa.

In 913, the future caliph's first act of maritime policy had been to gather the available crews in Algeciras and build a dockyard with the aim of taking control of the maritime zone extending to the Alboran Sea, at the expense of the dissident Ibn Hafsun and the Idrisids who supplied him. The publicity given to this reassertion of control primarily aimed to serve as a reminder of the Umayyads' rights over the maritime zone separating the two continents. Reports on the first African campaigns revealed new intentions for a military conquest of the Maghreb's western territories. Following the failure of direct domination over the region beyond Ceuta and its surroundings, a new phase of Umayyad policy in the Maghreb was inaugurated by the alliance with the Zenata emirates, who divided up the government of a large part of the regions of present-day Morocco in the name of the sovereign, and the formal submission of the chiefs of the powerful Barghawata confederation. In fact, one of the principal reasons for the Umayyads' failure was that it had proved impossible to simultaneously mobilize enough troops on the fronts of the Christian frontier and the Maghreb al-Aqsa:

> [In 321 / 933] the caliph ordered the sending of help, with valiant men-at-arms and skillful archers with their provisions of arrows and bows, and against the enemies of God he sent by sea [to Ceuta] a squadron of carefully chosen ships and their crews, which were in large enough numbers and well equipped. But [this measure] appeared belated given the stated urgency, which did not give the ruler the time necessary [to react]: knowing nothing of [the admiral of the fleet's] situation and having had no news on the subject, [the caliph] had already sent his principal squadron to fight the country of the Franks—may God strike them down—at the very moment when he had sent his

> generals and his elite troops to fight the infidel to the east and to the north, so that he could only send what was left in the capital and that stood ready.[6]

On more than one occasion, Christian attacks on the northern front or land expeditions in the Maghreb al-Aqsa by the Zirid emirs, generals for the Fatimids, impeded the caliph's military plans and ultimately made it impossible to establish his direct sovereignty beyond the area of the strait. However, thanks to the fortification of the port city of Ceuta and the caliph's complete domination of the Maghreb's western waters, he had control over traffic between Europe and Africa. Additionally, the submission of the Idrisid ports, the conquest of Melilla, and the solid support of the emirs of Nekor, who dominated the ports of the Rif, offered control of ports of call up to the region of Algiers.[7] Consequently, the squadron that regularly patrolled these shores could have Umayyad troops intervene in Africa at any moment, which made it an essential link in Mediterranean and African policy. It was also necessary to secure the Latin maritime front, which stretched from Catalonia to the islands and coasts of the Carolingian empire (or what remained of it) and was a potential source of danger.

It is no coincidence that the first raid against Christian shores following 'Abd al-Rahman III's accession to power was launched in 933, just as the caliph was organizing the first great ceremony in Córdoba to mark the official birth of the caliphal fleet based in Almería. In the capital, the generals and admirals received the insignia of command from representatives of the sovereign drawn from his inner circle. With the sovereign in attendance, they then headed for the bay to embark on the ships built in the yards of Pechina. In fact, due to inclement weather, the fifteen ships chartered would go no farther than Torotosa. On the other hand, 935 was a prosperous year for Andalusian sailors. The fleet, composed of forty units, sailed to Mallorca to be completely fitted out, then continued on to pillage the port of Nice, where it destroyed the ships and dockyard, and Marseille. On the return journey, the squadron made a display of the Umayyad caliphate's maritime supremacy off Barcelona.

The squadron returned to threaten the Catalan capital in 940 to pressure Count Sunier to agree to the treaty brought by the caliph's envoy, the doctor and ambassador Hasday b. Shaprut. It should be noted that agreements on the freedom of maritime commerce were also made on this occasion.[8] At the same time, admiral of the fleet Muhammad b. al-Rumahis personally headed the maritime *sayfa* of 943, leading thirty-six ships to pillage Agde, despite a strong gale that drove several ships aground on the coast of Languedoc; he then attacked Marseille and safely returned to his point of departure. These are the only raids launched from the flagship port against Latin shores to have been reported in the Andalusian chronicles, though the chronicles often mention more modest razzias such as the one Ibn Khaldun attributes to the governor of the Balearic Islands, al-Muwaffaq, after he was appointed in 961.[9]

According to the same logic, the Arabic texts only mention the Muslim settlement at Fraxinetum when negotiations initiated by Hugh of Arles, Count of Provence, in 940 led to the caliph's direct involvement in the affairs of Provence. The presence of a military leader (*qa'id*) and representative of the caliph in the stronghold of Fraxinetum shows that the sovereign considered the fortress a land of Islam, under his authority. He intended to direct naval operations, deciding when Muslim sailors should stop carrying out acts of piracy at sea, in keeping with the agreements reached with the count.[10]

The Catalan coast and the adjacent islands up to Corsica were the top Christian targets of the caliphal fleet that cruised along these Latin coasts from 933 to 943, at the very moment when the caliph's emissary was obtaining a truce from the Catalan count, which involved the recognition of Umayyad supremacy. The truce was renewed the following year by the Catalan count's ambassador, who was received in Medina Azahara.[11] Ibn Hayyan specifies that the caliph ordered his sailors to stop attacking the coasts under the count's rule. The peace lasted, more or less, until the end of al-Hakam III's reign. The same period also saw the launch of a major policy of diplomacy, particularly with the Holy Roman Empire, which was represented in Córdoba by John of Gorze, and the Byzantines, who were fighting the Shiite caliph, an enemy shared by the Umayyads, in the central Mediterranean.[12] Within the framework of good internal communication, this diplomatic offensive designated the sovereign of Medina Azahara as the region's strongman, responsible for launching ground attacks against the Iberian kingdoms of Navarre and León and making peace with the Catalonians and the great Christian empires. At the same time, the end of maritime jihad freed up crews who could now potentially be directed against the Fatimids. After 955, the agreement between Córdoba and Constantinople, at the expense of the Shiite caliphs, dispensed the Umayyad caliph from risking a maritime commitment in dangerous Ismaili waters. Consequently, he was able to concentrate naval forces on the Strait of Gibraltar and the west coast of the Maghreb.

The real confrontation between the two caliphates did not take place at sea but rather on Maghrebi soil. On several occasions, the troops under Buluggin (972–984), the future Zirid emir who led the Berber armies of the caliph of Sabra-Mansuriyya, pushed far toward the West, briefly occupied Fez, and were even in a position to threaten Ceuta. The caliphs therefore needed to concentrate their efforts on Africa and mobilize the fleet to transport reinforcements across the sea or patrol along African coastlines. Aside from a few inconsequential alerts of Viking raids in 956 and 970–971, which nonetheless led to two launches of the Seville squadron, the Andalusian coast was never really threatened.

After having taken power from the caliphate's established military leaders, Ghalib and Admiral Muhammad b. al-Rumahis, and neutralized the authority of Caliph Hisham II (976–1009), Ibn Abi ʿAmir al-Mansur launched a series of about fifty military campaigns to push into Christian lands, sometimes as far as the foot of the Pyrenees. Since al-Mansur lacked the titles necessary to personally take on responsibility for caliphal jihad, the presentation of jihad totally changed, insofar as the claim of universal jihad, entailing the conquest of Baghdad, was pushed aside in favor of systematic war against the Christians on the Peninsula. While the squadrons were used heavily, first and foremost to guard routes to Africa but also as a means of logistics support, against Barcelona in 985 and Santiago de Compostela in 997, the sea was not a real field of legitimization now that the conquest of the East was no longer on the agenda.[13]

The Fatimids' Maritime Jihads, from Sicily to the Bilad al-Sham

After the proclamation of the caliphate in 909, Caliph ʿUbayd Allah and his son al-Qa'im owed a great deal to the Aghlabid emirs, particularly for the naval organization they had left behind. This legacy allowed father and son to launch a series of maritime campaigns against Byzantine territories in Sicily and southern Italy after pacifying their new domain. After a difficult struggle, they succeeded in taking Palermo and Tripoli by force. It was at this stage, in 915, that the Egyptian campaigns began, without any involvement of the fleet. During the second campaign, in 919, the squadron anchored at Rosetta to back the troops on land but was taken by surprise by the Muslim fleet arriving from Tarsus of Cilicia and destroyed by its Greek fire.[14]

Once Muslim Sicily was pacified in 917, the sovereign no longer encountered naval opposition from Aghlabid dissidents in the caliphate's territorial waters. He was now able to resume jihad on the island and on the continent: Reggio was taken in 918. In 916, Mahdia, which had been founded by the caliph, became the squadrons' principal port. After another pause in 919, troops were sent to Calabria: Oria was pillaged, but the Muslims failed to overcome the inhabitants of Brindisi. From 927 to 930, Otranto, Taranto, and the regions of Salerno and Naples were repeatedly attacked. Even the Adriatic was invaded, with Termoli bearing the brunt of the Fatimids' naval superiority. After the fleet's triumphant return to Mahdia in 930, emissaries sent by Basileus Romanos Lekapenos (920–944) agreed to the regular payment of a tribute supposed to guarantee Calabria's safety.

During the caliphate of al-Qa'im, the Ismaili imams' maritime and eastern ambitions were impeded by another failed attempt at conquering Egypt in 937, the Sicilian government's autonomist leanings until 941, and especially the Kharijite rebellion under the leadership of Abu Yazid, "the Man on the Donkey," which ended in 948. Regarding the revolt, one must underline the essential role played by the fleet, which literally saved the dynasty: besieged in 946 but protected by the formidable defensive wall closing off the isthmus, Mahdia held out for two years thanks to the supplies brought by the caliph's ships. The fresh troops sent by sea from Mahdia to Sousse repelled Kharijite assaults, in a victory that marked the beginning of a reversal in favor of Caliph al-Mansur.[15]

It was the quality of the maritime organization that allowed the caliph to have at his disposal the best naval force on the Mediterranean. The fleet, crews, dockyards, and military ports were under the direct control of the imam, through the intermediary of the eunuch Jawdhar, who was responsible for the navy's management. The results in the field lived up to the naval organization's widely publicized qualities.

Al-Muʿizz was to lead the caliphate's naval power to its peak, on a path opened by the fleet's victories over the Umayyads and Macedonians in 971. In 955, however, the fleet had sunk during a storm after the pillaging of Almería, losing a large number of crewmen and soldiers. This disaster forced the sovereign to negotiate a truce with Byzantium, which was respected until 963. At this time, the Greeks were busy on the Aegean Sea and the Anatolian front, which made it possible to launch another attack in Corsica in 957. The caliph of Sabra-Mansuriyya was then able to complete the conquest of Sicily, which he achieved in 965, at the same time the Byzantines were seizing Cyprus, after taking Crete in 961.

After the caliphs' departure, the Zirid emirs and the Kalbids maintained the fleet, enabling attacks against the coasts of Italy and the maintenance of a naval presence in the zone of the straits separating the Mediterranean's two basins, still in the name of the Ismaili imam.[16] Indeed, the caliphs strove to maintain their authority over Ifriqiya's naval jewel until the rejection of caliphal tutelage in the middle of the eleventh century.[17] Subsequently, the naval reinforcement of Italian ports made it possible for Christians to venture farther and farther into Africa's Muslim waters, until the sack of Mahdia by the Pisans and Genoese in 1087.[18] At this point, the two emirates, unlike the caliphs, were unable to keep control of the straits. Meanwhile, the caliphs concentrated their maritime efforts on the Aegean Sea and, especially, the Red Sea.

Despite a few naval operations, such as the seasonal razzias from Syrian ports, Fatimid naval forces were less often put to use in the name of jihad. Border dwellers, who were now under the domination of Shiite sovereigns, renewed the tradition of raids from the Syrian border, though these never equaled the major expeditions of the early tenth century. The Muslim squadrons' range of operations was considerably limited by the loss of the strategic islands of Crete and Cyprus in 971, before the Shiite imams were put in place, and the effectiveness of the Macedonian emperors' fleet. Nonetheless, the fleet remained a force to be reckoned with, as seen in Nasir Khusraw's report on the city of Tripoli. According to Khusraw, the port could hold up to one thousand ships, a figure one has to assume is exaggerated for promotional purposes. Most of the naval force was concentrated in Fustat and Cairo, while the Syrian ports were forbidden to build ships without the caliph's approval. However, the Fatimids were no longer masters of the sea's fate, as Abbasid sailors had been; naval installations were primarily maintained to ward off Greek attacks on the Egyptian coast, which was easily accessible from Crete.

With the crusade in the twelfth century, the Egyptian emirs were forced to resume the maritime jihad to attempt to delay the conquest of the Bilad al-Sham's seaboard (1097–1154). As long as their squadrons were able to hold the crusaders' fleets at bay off of Tyre, the city resisted and provided the Egyptian fleets with supplies and safe passage to sail up the Syrian coast. Once the squadron was defeated by Venetian naval forces in 1124, the crusaders were able to seize Tyre, but the struggle for control over the route between the valley of the Nile and the Palestinian coast only came to an end after extensive resistance and the taking of Ashkelon in 1153. The effectiveness of the Shiite sovereigns' fleet was evident in the difficulties the Italians faced in imposing themselves on the Aegean Sea, but the loss of naval control along the Syrian coast opened the path to Egypt to Christian war fleets.[19]

THE "COMMERCIAL REVOLUTION" IN THE MEDITERRANEAN IN THE TENTH CENTURY, A MAJOR STRATEGIC CHANGE

One cannot avoid noticing the new vigor of economic activities in the tenth century, as seen in contemporary sources from the Islamic world and Byzantium and, even more so, the Latin texts.[20] One of the principal indicators of this trend is the increase in commercial relations between Christians and Muslims. Historians such as Maurice Lombard long traced the impetus for Muslim commerce in the Mediterranean to the Indian Ocean and East Asia: spices, precious goods, ceramics, silk, and other products with high added value, mentioned or discovered in ports from the Persian Gulf to the Red Sea, wound up in the souks of the major Muslim capitals and ports of the Mediterranean. Similarly, the Sahara provided gold brought from Sijilmasa in the tenth century to coin the caliphate of Córdoba's currency and, in even greater quantities, gold that the Fatimids siphoned to Ifriqiya, then the valley of the Nile between the tenth and twelfth centuries, turning Cairo into the principal gold supplier on the Mediterranean, at the expense of the Eastern caliphate's territories.[21]

However, geographers' accounts and archeological material provide a growing amount of evidence of a specifically Mediterranean boom, which appears to be the real foundation for the lasting development of commercial exchanges in the region. Indeed, Arab geographers' accounts of land development by Berber village communities and tribes and Egyptian and Syrian farmers bring us back to the heart of the Mediterranean, where we find signs of trade networks on the African continent, controlled by tribal groups that could own up to twenty thousand dromedaries used to transport goods from the black kingdoms of the Niger, which could also be carried by sea, as of the ninth century. As formal as al-Bakri's descriptions of the Maghreb may be, they are unambiguous in showing that the ninth and tenth centuries marked a decisive stage in the region's economic development, driven by Berber farmers and tribes.[22] The other regions, particularly the Christian regions, present a far better documented scenario, but one that follows the same outlines and credits farmers and small communities of sailors and merchants with the initiative for an economic momentum on the scale of the village and its surroundings or the castle's territory or coastal cabotage. According to archeological evidence, tribal organization and the organization of "village" communities appear in al-Andalus as of this period—at the latest in the second half of the ninth century.

Pierre Toubert's *Latium* and other regional studies of Italy have opened the way for a study of the mutations and capacity for adaptation of populations combining peasant families and regional aristocracy. Yet whether in the Latin zone, which has been more closely studied, or in the Muslim and Byzantine regions, and more specifically in those areas where regional rulers supervise or protect these populations with increasing effectiveness, these socioeconomic mutations are accompanied by signs of the development of commercial exchanges.[23] In a second phase, in both the most powerful and best organized Muslim states and Byzantium, one finds convincing indications of more sophisticated economic organization, promoted and supervised by the three great imperial and economic powers of the tenth century. These powers gave a decisive push to the economy, now on the scale of the entire Mediterranean. The lasting war that followed the Arab invasions had a constant impact on these Mediterranean transformations, not in the sense of systematic financial ruin but as an imposed framework from which societies and economies were adapted by coastal populations under the supervision of the authorities.

Commercial Organization on the Scale of the Mediterranean?

Alluded to by Ibn Hawqal, the organization of markets in Umayyad, Fatimid, and Byzantine zones resulted from a long-established practice that had made it possible to reconcile conflicts and commercial exchanges from at least the ninth century. After this long, often chaotic, and little-documented maturation, the economic situation and consolidation of the three empires were favorable to the emergence of the great trade networks of the tenth century, in particular the network by which the Pisans imported the Muslim ceramics known as *bacini* and the one that, at the invitation of the Egyptian authorities, prompted the Jewish merchants of Cairo to develop a commercial network stretching from the shores of the Indian Ocean to the Iberian Peninsula.[24]

The discovery of the provenance of the *bacini* ceramics, which can be admired on the apses of Pisan churches and were also found in excavations of the medieval city, has revealed the existence of regular commercial traffic that was maintained until the twelfth century.[25] The Pisans were long presented as the initiators and sole middlemen of this business, which saw them traveling to Islam's richest regions—initially

Ifriqiya, then Egypt, and later al-Andalus—to buy the ceramics, whose quality was highly appreciated by Italians around Pisa until at least the twelfth century, when the Pisans started making lower-quality copies to sell in the port cities of the Tyrrhenian coast.[26] However, the Italian documents, particularly several hagiographies, reveal that, during the same period, Muslim merchants were regularly found in the port cities of the Gulf of Lion and the Tyrrhenian Sea, as well as in Byzantium. The presence of Muslim sailors and merchants in ports where they were warmly welcomed in the tenth century indicates that they had developed their own trade networks between Muslim and Christian shores.

Better yet, the letters found in the storehouses of the Ben Ezra Synagogue in Fustat revealed the existence of networks of Jewish merchants, whose modus operandi is reminiscent of that of the back rooms of Amalfi, Genoa, Venice, and Pisa. The root of this structure is to be found in the area of the Sea of the Arabs, where the development of trade was then far more advanced than in the maritime regions of the Muslim Mediterranean.[27] The Geniza's networks in the Mediterranean grew steadily until the twelfth century, with central headquarters in Cairo, until they reached all of the trading centers on the Muslim shores of the Mediterranean. The ports of the Maghreb, Sicily, and the Iberian Peninsula (particularly Almería) regularly hosted these merchants, which confirms the existence of Mediterranean networks within the Islamic zone.

Once they controlled Egypt, the Fatimid authorities played a decisive role. The caliphs were responsible for the Jewish merchants lastingly establishing their principal base in the Egyptian capital. Early in the eleventh century, for instance, the Shiite caliphate took control of the Red Sea and the traffic of merchant ship convoys, which during the shipping season (later known by the term *karim*) sailed from their port of call in Aden to the ports of Qusayr and Aydhab, among others. On the Mediterranean side, these same merchants benefited from the vast maritime space under the control of the Fatimids, but also from the opening of the ports along all the Muslim coasts, including the territory of the caliphate of Córdoba. Even during phases of nearly permanent confrontation, agreements with Christian countries also enabled Jewish merchants from the Islamic world to make lasting ties with merchants in Latin and probably Greek countries.[28] The expansion of the empire to a significant part of the Mediterranean's shores, in particular to coastal Syria, which led to the marches and routes of the Asian world, as well as the commercial agreements reached with the Byzantines shortly after the Fatimids came to power in Egypt, opened the economic space of the Greek empire to Muslim merchants and vice versa, according to a system that had proved itself under Abbasid domination.

At the same time, the siphoning of Saharan gold and the striking of the gold dinar competed with the Byzantine *nomisma*. Long-standing ties with southern Italy, particularly Amalfi, favored the development of lasting exchanges in an economic area that, whether directly or through intermediaries, grew to reach from the south of Italy to Saharan zones, with the sea at its center. The organization of the customs in the dockyards of ports on the Egyptian coast and in the country's capital attracted a growing number of Latin merchants, thus consolidating Egypt's central role in a now "global" medieval commerce, rather than the Latin ports: the sovereigns could rightly assert that the nerve center of Mediterranean commerce was the valley of the Nile, located between the two major trading seas and the Sahara and the Asian continent.[29]

Administrative literature, particularly of the Ismaili era, began to include more references to trade activities and maritime itineraries. Already in Ifriqiya, the activity in ports had been one of the subjects regularly discussed by the chronographers, as seen in the collection of letters by the eunuch Jawdhar.[30] Far from happenstance, the preservation of these extraordinary documents, like the treatise on chartering mentioned earlier or the Arab geographers' references to navigation, naval construction, and caliphal administration of the port and dockyards, show that the Ifriqiyans were highly familiar with business and seafaring, activities widely encouraged by the caliphal initiative. The heavy presence of Jewish merchants is another indication of the importance of Ifriqiyan ports up to the Norman conquest, as was the production of texts on commerce by their administrators, especially in Cairo.

The fiscal treatise by the Egyptian al-Makhzumi fits into this tradition of an administrative production between the Fatimid and Ayyubid periods, starting in 1171. The treatise covered the tax system used in the

Egyptian coast's ports and dockyards.[31] Entitled *Nuzhat al-Muqlatayn fi Akhbar al-Dawlatayn* (The history of the two dynasties), the text left by Ibn al-Tuwayr (d. 1220) is of a different nature, but it also illustrates the desire to pass on to the Ayyubid sultan a tried and proven system elaborated by the Shiite sovereigns' administrators. Saladin and his successors had every intention to make the most of the Ismaili administration's excellence and to preserve the writers' know-how to properly train future managers of the Egyptian administration. Similar motives drove several Egyptian men of letters of the Mamluk period, particularly al-Qalqashandi (d. 1418) and al-Maqrizi, working in different genres, to save the administrative treatises and other works of the Fatimid era from oblivion. The enormous didactic treatise by al-Qalqashandi ("The Art of the Chancellery") contains a large quantity of documents from the Ismaili period, which the Sunni man of letters collected to show his gratitude for the Shiite administration's competence. Among the most important fields that drew Ayyubid and Mamluk scribes' attention after 1250, the navy was given a more than respectable place, despite the fact that the sultans showed little affinity for the sea and all that was related to it.[32]

Economic competition between the two caliphates of Baghdad and Cairo was a significant factor in provoking the Fatimids' vigorous efforts to divert traffic between the Indian and Mediterranean area.

The Commercial Opening of al-Andalus

The discovery of potters' ovens in the coastal cities of southeast al-Andalus has made it possible to determine the area of origin of ceramics that were highly appreciated by the Andalusian caliphs. This pottery, identified by its characteristic decoration, which uses the *cuerda seca* technique originally developed in China, was produced in the ports of the Peninsula's east coast beginning in the tenth century and intended for caliphal circles.[33] This type of design was obtained by using specific firing techniques that had spread along the coasts of the Indian Ocean and the eastern shores of the Mediterranean beginning in the ninth century, then circulated in the Muslim West at the time of the caliphate of Córdoba.[34] A growing number of archeological digs carried out in all of the Peninsula's regions have confirmed the spread of ceramics of the same type, though more commonplace, discovered in many villages and in the Andalusian and Maghrebi secondary localities, in this case beginning in the second half of the eleventh century.[35] This coarser production's commercial distribution reveals the reach of commercial circuits that extended to the most remote rural areas, at the same time—the twelfth century—that Pisans were coming to the very same ports to buy *bacini* ceramics. The wealth of Almería, the former port of the caliphs and the western Mediterranean's most active port, at least in the Muslim area, until its destruction by the Genoese in 1147, offers an equally remarkable example of the economic development of the coastal regions of al-Andalus, the roots of which go back to the ninth century.

At the very moment when the Umayyads were launching a large-scale charm offensive on the imperial Christian courts and deploying their all-powerful squadron to the walls of Barcelona, they authorized the Catalan and Amalfitan merchants, or more generally the Italian traders, to come trade on Andalusian soil. In 942, these traders were invited to display luxury goods such as Byzantine silks, which they spread out before Caliph 'Abd al-Rahman III. Ahmad al-Razi's chronicle gives pride of place to the account of this ceremony, which was on a par with the most splendid audiences granted to the ambassadors of the Mediterranean empires. This account also indicates how eager the sovereign was to let the entire Mediterranean know about the change in his policy toward the Latins, no matter the merchants' origins. To allow them to reach Medina Azahara, the caliph had had to authorize the opening of the island route that passed via Sardinia and the Balearic Islands, a route by which travelers could also reach Almería and from there safely continue to Córdoba. The Sardinians were therefore associated with the opening of the route. We do not know whether the agreement this symbolized was tacit or official, but it was surely a first step in developing lasting relations.

During the same period, the status of the Muslim stronghold in Provence evolved under pressure from the caliph. Here too, the embassy sent by Count Hugh, a candidate for the crown of Italy who had come looking for support in Medina Azahara in 941, inaugurated a change in the caliphate's policy, as shown by the title of the relevant paragraph in the caliphal chronicle: "Peace with the Franks."[36] The chronicler specified that the caliph had ordered his sailors to stop attacking Catalan coasts, while the Latin chronicles reveal that the people of Fraxinetum put themselves in the service of Hugh of Arles against his rival Berengar (d. 924) by taking control of the Alpine passes. Peace with the Catalan counts basically lasted until the end of al-Hakam II's reign and favored the development of commercial relations that would have major consequences in Catalonia.[37] The presence of Muslim merchant vessels, revealed by underwater excavations at the wreck of the Bataguier and in the Bay of Cannes, confirms that the Muslim stronghold in the heart of the garrigue of Provence also had a commercial purpose, probably subsequent to the passage of merchants from the Islamic world, including ships from the Fatimid area, which were reported in the ports of Marseille and Montpellier on several occasions.[38] Thus, before the incident provoked by the spectacular kidnapping of Abbot Majolus in 972, the west coast of the Mediterranean had become a more peaceful area, a space of exchanges rather than a field for the race between Muslim powers, through the will of the all-powerful caliph who had won the war at sea and imposed a peace symbolized by maritime commerce.

One therefore has to reexamine the systematic opposition between "empires" denounced as archaic economic structures said to have slowed economic development through cumbersome administrations and taxation (used to strengthen armed forces) and what appeared in the writings of Latin historians as the beginnings of a capitalism that would only be promoted by the reformed Catholic society that was to become open to the mercantile spirit as of the twelfth century. The imperial circles of Byzantium and Islam were responsible for putting in place an initial system of exchanges on a significantly expanded Mediterranean scale—for their own benefit. Behind an impalpable economic situation, it appears as early as the ninth century that it was the authorities of the empires, emirs, and counts that put in place the material, fiscal, and legal conditions for an expansion of Mediterranean exchanges.[39] For their part, the Byzantine and Muslim merchants took advantage of their strategic space, from the routes crossing Central Asia and the Indian Ocean to those of the Sahara, but also of the needs of the Latins, who were themselves attracted to the sophisticated organization of the two imperial spaces' administrations, to develop their own networks in the imperial space that sheltered them. However, except for the Geniza documents and material traces such as the seals of Byzantine merchants, currency throughout the basin, and typical ceramics from a handful of production circuits, the evidence of these networks remains far less visible than that of the Latin ports, for which we have archives as of the twelfth century.

12

ISLAM'S MARITIME SOVEREIGNTY IN THE FACE OF LATIN EXPANSION

IT IS LIKELY THAT the Almohad caliphs of Marrakech commanded the largest naval force of medieval Islam in the Mediterranean. The fleet was often deployed to seize Muslim territories, first from the Almoravids, then from the Hammadids of Béjaïa and the Zirids in Ifriqiya, up to Tripoli (1152–1161). The empire's formation ended in 1161 with the successful conquest of the Ifriqiyan ports that Roger II of Sicily had seized from the Ifriqiyan emirs, including Mahdia. The caliphate was subsequently faced with Latin naval forces—Italian, Catalan, Portuguese—and its objective shifted to preserving its maritime domain. Until the first signs of the dynastic crisis that followed the disaster at Las Navas de Tolosa, which would drive the caliphate to slowly collapse, the fleet succeeded in containing Latin assaults and protecting the western Muslim coasts.

Beyond the weakening of Islam in the Mediterranean, questions arise about the Muslim powers' strategy regarding the commercial and maritime forces of the Latin world at a time when these interests were taking hold of the maritime space. The Almohad example is particularly interesting in that the caliphate was a naval power that successfully held off the Latin states' navies until the 1220s, simultaneously attracting Latin merchants to its ports, yet it could hardly ignore the considerable risks entailed in allowing the Italians total control of western Mediterranean trade routes. This is what al-Zuhri had to say on the power of Pisa in the twelfth century:

> Its inhabitants are very brave at war and are for the most part skillful sailors. . . . They are formidable combatants on the sea, experts at launching naphtha. They are devious and harmful people, full of violence and cruelty. They have an abundance of [shipping] timber, but they also work iron, of which they make all sorts of quality equipment such as coats of mail, helmets, and spears. . . . They are also merchants on land and at sea, who go as far as the boundaries of Syria, to Alexandria and Egypt, and to the outer limits of the Maghreb and to al-Andalus.[1]

THE ALMOHAD MAGHREB AND AL-ANDALUS, A GREAT MEDITERRANEAN POWER IN THE TWELFTH CENTURY

> In the year 1162, Abd al-Mu'min had squadrons built on all the coasts of his empire, having decided to attack the Christians on land and at sea. 400 ships were fitted out, including 120 at the delta of al-Ma'mura and its port, 100 in Tangier, Ceuta, Badis, and the ports of the Rif, 100 on the coasts of Ifriqiya, in Oran, and in the ports of Hunayn, 80 in al-Andalus.[2]

Once the Almoravid emirate of Marrakech was eliminated in 1147, Abd al-Mu'min took advantage of the rallying of the Banu Maymun, the admirals then commanding the Almoravid fleet, and took control of the naval installations, crews, and ships to turn them into tools to conquer the western coasts of Africa, from Tripoli to Libya. In 1147, Seville was blockaded on land and from the river and surrendered without any resistance. Tangier and Ceuta were besieged on land and at sea and submitted in 1148–1149. In 1151, the still-modest port of Algiers was opened

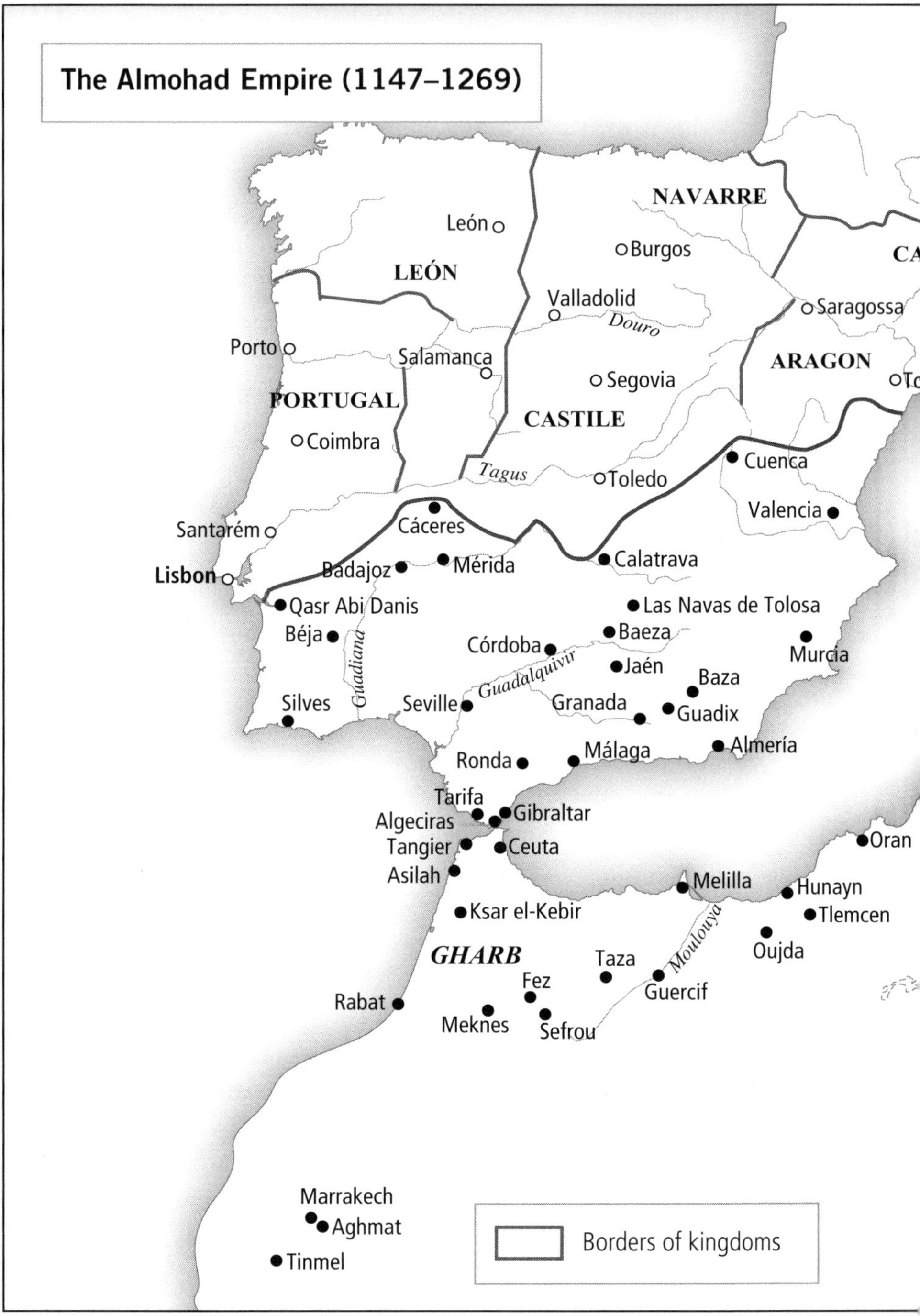

The Almohad Empire (1147–1269)

Genoa
Marseille
Corsica
Rome
Naples
Sardinia
Mayurqa
Mediterranean Sea
Palermo
Sicily
Béjaïa
Tunis
Sétif
Constantine
Al Qal'a of Beni Hammad
Kairouan
Hodna
Mahdia
MZAB
Biskra
Sfax
Gafsa
Tozeur
Gabès
Djerba
Tripoli
NAFUSA
MOUNTAINS

to the Almohad squadron. In 1157, Almería was taken from the Christians after a long land and sea blockade. The conquest of the eastern territories, at the expense of the Hammadids and the Zirid emirs of Ifriqiya, was followed by that of all the seaside cities on the Tunisian coast and the island of Djerba, which had fallen into the hands of Roger II of Sicily in the 1140s.[3] The fleet often played a decisive part in these operations, notably during the taking of Béjaïa in 1151 and especially that of Mahdia in 1160, with the squadron blocking the city off from the sea and repelling Christian ships sent to the rescue. The chancellery letters report on several of these expeditions, highlighting the importance the Almohad sovereigns placed on the fleet's actions and, more generally, the maritime space, which was treated as a military territory as important as the vast empire's land regions.[4]

The campaign against Bejaïa led to a reorganization of the fleet's command. The admiralty was headquartered at Ceuta and headed by a close relative of the caliph (*sayyid*), while the port became the gathering place for squadrons about to leave on an expedition, whether on the Mediterranean or the ocean. The empire's vast seaboard had numerous dockyards, but this did not prevent the Almohads from building new dockyards or having others expanded: a covered, closed dockyard, protected by a solid *qasaba,* was built in Saltes, a modest port located on the Odiel estuary, near Huelva, that was recognized for its specialization in ironwork.[5] The largest dockyard in the caliphate was built on the Sebou River at al-Maʿmura, northeast of Rabat-Salé, to prepare the campaign of 1151. A forest overlooking the estuary provided naval timber. The anchorage here was safer than the one on the Bou Regreg, the river at Salé, whose mouth was considered dangerous for ships due to shifting sandbars. Having been reorganized, the fleet cast off from the ports solicited, sailing to the admiral port before continuing to their target.

The Almohads had to enlist the best admirals to contain the first Portuguese squadron, commanded by Admiral Dom Fuas Roupinho. Ali b. Mardanish, a member of the caliphal family of Murcia, was appointed to head the Seville fleet but was captured by Portuguese sailors in 1179. Admiral Ahmad al-Siqilli took over from him and distinguished himself by vanquishing the Portuguese squadron one year after Ibn Mardanish's defeat; he was so celebrated that two centuries later, Ibn Khaldun would make him the central hero of the Almohads' maritime success. The caliph's sailors were able to hold off the maritime assaults of King Afonso I's ships. What could be seen as the first "battle of the Atlantic," according to Ibn 'Idhari's report, had begun in 1179 at the latest. The following year, having repelled the Christian squadron, al-Siqilli pillaged the coast north of the Portuguese capital. Dom Fuas Roupinho is said to have launched one or two attacks against Ceuta in 1180 and 1182. The first was presented as a victory for the Portuguese admiral, despite the fact that he was unable to reach the strait's port. The second cost him his life. His fleet was wiped out with him, due to either a storm or a defeat at the hands of the Almohad squadron, or possibly both at once.[6]

This victory allowed Caliph Abu Ya'qub Yusuf to carry out the expedition his father had planned but been unable to launch before his death in 1163. In 1184, Abu Ya'qub Yusuf ordered the fleet to cast off to attack two key positions of the Gharb al-Andalus on the Tagus: Santarém and Lisbon. The naval siege of the Portuguese capital failed, while the city of Setúbal was saved by the arrow that mortally wounded the caliph.[7] Nonetheless, Portugal was then forced to call in crusader ships traveling to the Holy Land on the North Sea to reinforce its own squadrons and counter the Almohads' naval initiatives—proof of the efficiency of the caliphs' sailors. In 1189, an English squadron intending to join Richard the Lionheart (1189–1199) in the Mediterranean provided decisive support to the Portuguese during the assault on Silves, the largest Muslim city to the west of the capital of Andalusia. Caliph al-Mansur now had to mobilize considerable land and naval forces to take back Silves and part of the Alentejo in 1190–1191.[8] After this victory, the Muslim navy kept control of the Gulf of Cádiz from its bases in the numerous ports, forming a string of anchorages from Cape Saint Vincent to Gibraltar. As late as 1217, the galleys of Alcácer do Sal succeeded in repelling a German squadron that had come to support the Portuguese, but they were unable to prevent the city from falling once it was attacked by land. This strategic loss permanently opened the Alentejo to the Portuguese.[9]

The naval war machine worked as effectively on the Mediterranean as on the Atlantic, though the taking of the Balearic Islands in 1203 from the Banu Ghaniya, the Almoravid emirs, came too late to allow the

Almohads to regain control of the maritime routes between the north and south shores of the western Mediterranean.[10] At least the Strait of Gibraltar, the Alboran Sea, and the Ifriqiyan zone were still out of reach of Latin squadrons.

The Almohads' maritime supremacy crumbled after Las Navas de Tolosa. This collapse was not due to the Latins, however, but primarily to dissension among the members of the dynasty after the death of Caliph al-Nasir. In 1260, the Latins assaulted Salé. Despite the fact that the Marinids, then in the midst of claiming power, chased off the attackers, the assault showed that every maritime zone in the crumbling empire was now within reach of the Christian galleys. The Hafsid and Marinid sultanates continued to handle the caliphs' naval legacy, retaining the means to intervene locally on the sea until the crises of the fourteenth century, but were unable to prevent the Latin fleets from gradually taking control of all the maritime routes. The opening of a regular line between Genoa and the North Sea beginning in the last years of the thirteenth century was due above all to the Muslims' inability to control traffic to the ocean.

The Almohad capital of Seville had experienced extraordinary growth stimulated by the Abbadids in the eleventh century and again when it became the Almoravid capital in al-Andalus, which resulted in the building of a new quarter in the north. The produce from the large estates of the Aljarafe to the west of the Andalusian capital were in the hands of local families of notables, such as the Banu Khaldun, who owned several properties and hundreds of hectares of wheat, olive trees, and fig trees. Much of the yield was intended to be exported to Egypt and sometimes as far as the Indian Ocean.[11] The area experienced an agricultural golden age, with the Andalusian capital carrying on with Toledo's advances and reaching a level of agronomic sophistication that would be put to use by Italian agronomists centuries later. The region's commercial practices, on a par with those of the great Italian ports of the twelfth century, were characterized by capital accumulated by great families that had grown wealthy through their service to the state; progress in agriculture, with yields reaching twentieth-century levels; commercial networks with connections in Egypt and as far as Yemen; and the availability of the ships in the dockyard, whose crews were rented to merchants during peacetime.

The description of the banks of the Guadalquivir, which served as a port, already heralded the peak of the Almohad period, marked by the vigor of port traffic.[12] The city shone most brightly under the authority of the Almohad caliphs and their governors—generally the caliph's son and designated successor—a period during which it was profoundly transformed and expanded: the Giralda and the great mosque now stood right next to al-Buhayra, the vast palatial zone built for the caliphs.[13] The river's meandering course and catastrophic flooding, particularly in 1184, led to a redevelopment of the banks of the Guadalquivir, including the building of a protective embankment and the partial reconstruction of its fortifications. The city's economic activity and military requirements called for a new dockyard to be built close to the bridge and the palace, the layout of which is thought to have served as a model for those built by the kings of Castile in Seville and the Catalans in Barcelona. The boat bridge built at the foot of the Torre del Oro located at the tip of the palace, where ships paid a tax to enter the city, protected access to the port, which was sealed off by a chain strung across the river in case of danger. The enlarged and embellished city handled colossal amounts of money, much of it generated by trade. During the same period, coastal cities such as Silves, Saltes, Algeciras, Málaga, Salé, and Rabat benefited from peace in an imperial space that extended up to Tripoli of Libya.

The Sea, a Major Area of Almohad Wealth

The commercial treaty between the Almoravids and the Pisans, the leading agents of Italian commercial involvement in the Maghreb, allowed for Tuscan sailors to be established in Mallorca by 1133. However, it was during the period of the Marrakech caliphate and until the crisis of the fourteenth century that Latin trade was to experience its greatest expansion, through the regular signing of treaties with Pisa, Venice, and Genoa. Outside of the general economic situation, which was then at an absolute peak, this golden age was due to Italian initiatives. Nonetheless, the role of the caliphal authorities needs to be reevaluated to provide a view different from the long-held idea of a one-way relationship, entirely initiated by the Latins, in which Maghrebi sovereigns and business circles were subjected to a system of exchanges.[14] In some years, the three Italian ports' profits from Maghrebi trade exceeded those from the Mediterranean East. The extension of the truces from ten to forty years was for the most part respected by both parties. The establishment of *funduks,* which were basically comparable to consulates and provided lodgings for communities of merchants from the Italian cities in the major large ports of the Maghreb, as was the case in Egypt and later in Syria, would continue until at least the crisis of the fourteenth century.[15] These commercial exchanges so desired by sultanate and Latin leaders were only temporarily hampered by periods of tension, such as those that paralyzed activity in Ceuta from 1222 to 1235 and Salé in 1260. Even the crisis, which was exacerbated by the Great Plague and heavily affected the region, did not permanently hinder trade.

The Collapse of Almohad Power and Latin Economic Domination: The Illuminating Example of Ceuta

The fate of Ceuta perfectly encapsulates the connection between the political evolution of the caliphal dynasty and the collapse of Muslim sea power. Since 1160, the Genoese had called at this port on the strait and were authorized to trade in the port of Salé, which opened the rich hinterland of the Atlantic plains to the Ligurians' trading appetites: known as Garbo in the Latin documents, the western area comprising the Strait of Gibraltar and the Atlantic seaboard of present-day Morocco and Portugal became one of the most lucrative stops for Genoese merchants. Several treaties were signed beginning at the end of the twelfth century, then in 1208, 1223, and 1235. However, as of the 1220s, with Ceuta having become a key strategic position, the seat of the admiralty, and an economic power made rich by maritime activity, the port city was frequently the focus of rivalries between Latins and Muslims, who were often allies, because it controlled maritime traffic. The accounts by Ibn Khaldun and Ibn 'Idhari, among others, report attempts on the part of the city's notables, including sailors, merchants, and jurists, to take control of their city's fate. Supported by the people of Ceuta, Admiral al-Randahi; Abu l-'Abbas al-Yanashti, a rich merchant who governed the city from 1233 to 1236; and especially Abu l-Qasim al-ʿAzafi, heir to a family of renowned and prosperous jurists, took advantage of the dynastic crisis to provide the city with an independent but unstable government until 1328.

The city drew its power from the sea. Beyond its walls was a relatively barren inland region lacking water sources outside of a few small patches like Belyounech. Unlike the Italian powers, Ceuta suffered from the lack of a hinterland. Aside from a few wealthy families that owned ships or were in the caliphate's service, the powerful communities of sailors, fishermen, coral harvesters, craftsmen, laborers, and especially dockyard ship workers provide a vague but suggestive idea of a society whose resources came from the sea. Seville, Béjaïa, and later Tunis also became rich thanks to the maritime space, but their notables' fortunes came above all from serving the state. The fortunes accumulated by merchants like al-Yanashti and sailors like al-Randahi, the admiral of the fleet who led the dockyard's uprising and took control of the city at the head of his crews, were built using the same assets as Italian merchants and sailors. However, unlike the great dynasties of the Latin port cities, the most prestigious Ceuta families were those that had renowned jurists in their ancestry rather than ship owners or merchants.[16]

Ceuta was always a focus for the ambitions of far stronger external powers: rivalries between regional dynasties successively turned pretenders from the Almohad, Marinid, Nasrid, and later Abd al-Wadid and even Hafsid dynasties into the city's allies or adversaries, for Ceuta's elites were generally unable to govern without the support of one of these sultanate sovereignties. Ceuta was also not in a position to compete with the large Italian ports' naval forces, particularly the "Calcurini" force, which was probably composed of Catalans and attacked the city in 1231 to damage Genoese interests. In 1235, the Ligurian city sent a fleet to protect its interests and did not encounter any resistance. Under the reign of Alfonso X (1252–1284), the Castilians attacked the port cities that had come under the control of the people of Ceuta, in particular Tangier. The Aragonese, who were then allied with the sultan of Fez and asked the Christian fleet for support, were unable to overtake the city itself in 1274, but they paralyzed business for an extensive period.[17] Finally, the Portuguese seized the city on the strait from the Muslims in 1415.

EGYPT, THE HUB OF WORLD COMMERCE

In a letter addressed to the Abbasid caliph al-Mustadi (1170–1180) regarding the attack launched on Alexandria in 1174 at the order of King William II, Saladin shows that the Muslim authorities considered it in their interest to attract Christian merchant vessels, to the point that they were prepared to deal with the Latins' aggressiveness and maintain commercial ties whatever the cost, including when they attacked Egyptian ports or sought to invade the country:

> [In 1174, the king of Sicily, William II,] made an imposing, terrible display in front of Alexandria. Never had the sea carried so many vessels, never had it been covered with such a number of foot soldiers and cavalrymen. It was an entire province, no, entire provinces that it carried, an army like no king has ever led; but God inflicted a shameful defeat upon him. Among our enemies, there were also soldiers of Venice, Pisa, and Genoa, but all of them behaved at one moment as warriors causing serious damages and burning with an inextinguishable hatred, and at the next as travelers who imposed themselves upon Islam through trade and escaped the rigor of regulations. Well, there is not a single one of them who does not now come to bring us the weapons with which he fights his fight and his jihad, not one who does not seek our favor by offering us his most precious products and goods. We have established good relations with them all and concluded advantageous peace treaties, despite their resistance and while placing our interests above theirs.[18]

Commercial exchanges with the Christians were restricted by rigorous legislation established by the jurists of the Shiite imams but rested largely on long-established rules, particularly those of the Maliki. Qadi Nu‘man, a jurist of the first four Fatimid caliphs (909–975), set the conditions for exchanges between the Christian infidel and Muslims, particularly in regard to taxation. He adopted the principle that the tax collected from the Latins, the *khum* or *quint,* should be paid to the caliph since it was considered equivalent to booty taken from the infidel: "Booty (*ghanima*) was to be understood not as what was taken from the polytheists by force, but any kind of earnings [taken from them]."[19] At least since that period, the establishment of commercial relations with the Latins had a legal basis, with a convenient lack of distinction between booty and the tax rate paid by Christian merchants from abroad, normally higher than that paid by Muslims and the *dhimmi.* Saladin plays on the same ambiguities in the letter to his Almohad rival, despite the fact that as soon as he came to power, he had claimed to do away with eighty-eight taxes instituted by the caliphs and now deemed illegal. On the other hand, the *maks,* which generally refers to an illegal tax levy, was retained as taxation on transactions with Latins. The sovereigns therefore considered trade with the infidel—and thus Latins' visits to Muslim soil—a sign of Islam's superiority over Christianity, de facto legalizing the commercial treaties. Like most medieval rulers, the Muslim sovereigns considered that importing goods impoverished exporting countries and enriched the buyer, precisely because of the taxes collected and the appropriation of goods such as weapons.[20] The amount of the *maks* and the *khums*—the taxes paid by Christians from abroad—was generally one-tenth of the value, evaluated by number of units or weight, according to the product, and was generally charged on both the sale and the purchase. Usually, the *dhimmi,* Christian and Jewish subjects under the rule of Islam, paid one-twentieth, while the Muslims paid one-fiftieth. However, it seems that in certain ports such as Tinnis, the tax paid by the Latin merchants was equivalent to that paid by the Muslims, at least in the case of bilateral partnerships.[21]

What remains of al-Makhzumi's fiscal treatise provides the most precise information about the organization of Latin imports and exports in Egypt. The text mentions a *khums rumi,* a term that refers to both the tax and the administration that collected it. However, a close look at the stages of clearing customs—the inspection of merchandise on board ship, the sale at auction (*halqa*), and the payment of taxes decided on by the inspector—reveals a wide variety of amounts, with the tax deduced reaching 10, 20, and 30 percent of the stock's value, according to the merchandise, as was the case in the Maghreb. The conditions for taxation and merchants' stays on Muslim soil evolved according to place and circumstance, as shown for instance by the treaty between Genoa and the Mamluks in 1291.[22] While the treaty was very favorable to the Ligurians, it was also indispensable to the sultans, who needed it to bring in the soldier slaves filling the holds of the big Genoese ships at the moment that they were about to permanently chase the crusaders out of the Holy Land. However, the average amount of tax paid for imported and locally bought goods remained stable at around 10 percent. On the other hand, each port had specific rules determining how these payments were used: in Tripoli of Lebanon, the tax was assessed so that it could be used to pay the garrison.[23]

One of the economic risks tied to these exchanges, well known today with the vigor of "emerging markets," was in the ability of Italians and other Latins to appropriate the know-how of craftsmen and producers from exporting countries such as Egypt. The history of sugarcane provides a good illustration of this problem.[24] Similarly, Genoa became the place for specialists working with gold wire, which was reexported to the Muslim countries, and the skills of Cairo's artisans contributed a great deal to Murano glass and other local specialties. Sometimes, competition in raw materials, such as alum, discovered on the island of Kos in the thirteenth century, then two centuries later in the Papal States, put an end to the Egyptian monopoly and exporting of the material. At the same time, the Fatimid policy to develop activities on the Red Sea, which was kept up by the Fatimids' successors in cooperation or competition with the sultans of Aden, preventing any Latin intrusion into the Indian space, allowed Egypt to remain a stop for transloading between the Mediterranean and the Red Sea, which was indispensable to the Latins as long as they were unable to reach the Indian Ocean.[25] Consequently, Saladin's statement was not off the mark.

CONCLUSION

The Medieval Mediterranean and Islamic Memory

> I am but one of you; my profession is the sea, and to that I owe my fame. I will be with you against any enemy who comes from the sea.
>
> —*Admiral Muhammad b. Maymun, addressing the people of Almería, ca. 1147*

MANY ARABIC TEXTS of the Middle Ages relate the fame of celebrated sailors—admirals (*sahib al-bahr*) and "leaders [*ra'is*] of sailors"—acquired on the waters of the Mediterranean. The remarks attributed to one of the most glorious of these sailors, Muhammad b. Maymun, an admiral of the Almoravid, then Almohad fleets, as well as a member of a family originally from Denia that produced five admirals who served Islam, show the extent to which the profession had gained prestige and recognition in the port cities of Islam, as well as in Constantinople, Venice, Pisa, Genoa, and Barcelona. As early as the period of the Medina caliphate, the figure of 'Abd Allah b. Qays al-Jasi, the man who led fifty maritime campaigns and the first Muslim martyr to win glory at the head of the caliph's fleet by landing in Cyprus in the middle of the seventh century, occupies an important place in the collective memory passed down by the historians of Baghdad. Several Abbasid admirals were similarly honored. Among them, the two commanders of the caliphal squadrons based in Tarsus in Cilicia and Tripoli of Lebanon, Damian and Leo, became famous in 904 after pillaging Thessaloniki. Their Greek origins, which made them "renegades," as well as the obscure background of Ahmad al-Siqilli, who defeated the Portuguese admiral Fuas Roupinho in 1181, showed the advantages of assimilating all those who joined Islam, no matter their origins, by serving the caliph. Other admirals, such as the Banu Kalbi, in the service of the Fatimids; the Banu l-Rumahis, favorites of the Umayyad caliphs of Córdoba; and the Banu Maymun, admirals of the Almoravids and Almohads, but also Ghanim b. Mardanish, one of the sons of the emir of Murcia, who had joined the Almohads in 1172, and even one of the members of the caliphal dynasty, 'Abd Allah b. Ishaq al-Jami', were often from high-ranking clans and families, a sign of the prestige attached to the position. Some maritime lives were even recounted in narratives honoring the heroes who fought the Christians at sea. Thus the eleventh-century emirs of Denia, al-Mujahid and his son 'Ali, distinguished themselves by their commitment to jihad on the sea: they undertook the conquest of Sardinia, an initiative doomed to failure, but which brought them immortality through the Arabic chronicles. During the Almoravid collapse in 1147, 'Ali b. Maymun, nephew of the admiral of Almería, turned Cádiz, then a mere anchorage, into the capital of his principality. These glorious deeds recalled those found throughout the accounts of the heroes of the Arab conquest celebrated for having pushed back the boundaries of the Dar al-Islam.

The Mediterranean of the Arabic texts was thus distinguished, among the seas of Islam, as the place where the caliph's jihad was accomplished, even if the caliph did not participate in person. The presence of the Prophet's successor on the Basileus's border between Cappadocia and Syria was enough to associate all the regions, both land and maritime, with jihad. As a space of war, the Sea of the Romans had become the vast and terrifying stage for the display of Islamic universality under the guidance of the caliph. The Mediterranean embodied the ultimate hostile space for the believer, which therefore also became the sea of the martyr, the conquest of which was to be achieved with the taking of Constantinople and Rome and would precede the beginning of the time of salvation. Consequently, the saga of the great sailors of Islam, who represented the caliph at sea, singled out the Mediterranean among the seas of the Dar al-Islam as the only maritime space of caliphal jihad. This is a far cry from the Latin pragmatism attributed to Benedetto Zaccaria, the great Genoese admiral who defeated the Pisans at the Battle of Meloria in 1284 and a shrewd businessman who embodied the Genoese spirit: *Ianuensis ergo Mercator,* "a Genoese, therefore a merchant."[1]

Nonetheless, when ʿAli b. Maymun turned Cádiz into a real port city and launched razzias against the coasts of Galicia, he fully intended to make a financial profit from his maritime activity. The Muslims always considered Islamization, war on the land and maritime borders, and commercial profits as part of a single movement combining the spirit of conquest, resistance to Christian attacks, and profitable business dealings. As of 634, the first Arabs of the Mediterranean certainly did not associate the Arab conquest with an economic disaster but rather viewed it as a way of expanding and enriching nascent Islam. In a later era, the idea of profit held by Louis IX (1226–1270) was probably closer to Saladin's than that of the doges of Venice as they prepared for the *muda* season, when the convoy of Venetian ships left to trade in the Mediterranean. Thus, the barrier between Muslims and Byzantines on the one hand and the Latins of the Italian, Provençal, and Catalan ports on the other was not so much the product of a mental gulf separating "pre-capitalists" seeking markets and conquerors seeking martyrdom, insofar as Islam, like Byzantium, was able to develop the tools of a Mediterranean commerce, while the Latins also practiced abnegation in taking up the cross to deliver the tomb of Christ.

According to Fernand Braudel and Jacques Le Goff, the gulf between the two worlds was due to the ability of the maritime republics of Italy and the Crown of Aragon to organize a structure favoring the business of merchants, thanks, above all, to their capacity to mobilize capital for a world commerce and to use maritime resources to create the means to take financial and technical risks.[2] This was accompanied by a new state of mind, ultimately supported by the church, which was the only force capable of creating the conditions for the kind of capitalism that would appear on the shores of the North Sea in the modern era. Perhaps this turn of mind made the Capetian palace on the Île de la Cité as foreign to the ways of thinking of Italy and Barcelona as those of Medina Azahara? During the same long time span of the medieval Mediterranean, the Jewish merchants of the Geniza and the rich Muslim families of Seville who ran large agricultural estates were prosperous, even adventurous, businessmen who financed commercial networks whose model was found in the ports of the Indian Ocean, the seat of a civilization that had reached China while basically wielding the same tools as merchants at the Champagne fairs. The length of maritime commitments and the ability to insure against commercial risk, through both maritime insurance and the invention of sustainable commercial practices through improvements in shipbuilding, made the difference in the long time span of the Middle Ages, tipping the scales in favor of the great maritime cities of the Latin world, in a prelude to the development of capitalism on the North Sea.

Ultimately, successive caliphs imposed an Islamic Mediterranean through the prism of the values disseminated through the texts and maps they commissioned in large quantities from the best men of letters of the Islamic world, even if it meant remodeling and erasing the memory of their predecessors. Perhaps this explains why most historians of a triumphant Latin Europe long stayed away from a medieval Mediterranean that spoke in three voices?

Despite the fact that Islam remained the only universality he recognized, al-Idrisi, a Muslim Arab who lived in the middle of a formerly Greek, then Islamic, land that became Latin in 1063, was convinced he lived in the heart of the ecumene, not because his homeland of Sicily was under Norman and Christian control but because in the twelfth century it was a prosperous world born of the admittedly violent cohabitation of three great civilizations, visible in places such as the palatial chapel of the Norman kings. In his unrivaled descriptions of innumerable communities, such as Sicily's fishing villages and their timeless fishing techniques,[3] this Muslim in the service of the Norman king reveals the richness of this world in its totality, no longer from the perspective of the kingdom or the caliphate but from that of the villager, the fisherman, or the sailor. More than war, whose damaging effects on

Ifriqiya are described in his work, al-Idrisi renders a complex Mediterranean civilization, in which prosperity constantly existed side by side with the disasters of violence and destruction. The Sicilian geographer's map and its commentary are the peak of the art of Arab geography, a discipline born in Baghdad, which for a time was alone in its constant task of discovering and measuring the Mediterranean.

One generation later, Ibn Jubayr left us the account of his first journey (1184–1185) to the East in the form of a travel journal (*rihla*) in which he expresses his doubts and hopes regarding the confrontation between the two universalisms.[4] The Mediterranean Sea he describes was now Christian. During his trip to the Hejaz, which was initially a pilgrimage, he searched for the places from which Islam's salvation could spring. He first found hope in the original land of Islam, that of the Companions of the Prophet and the first conquerors, located between Cairo, Mecca, Medina, and Damascus. His spirits were lifted even higher when he saw Saladin coming out of the Syrian capital at the head of his troops on his way to fight the crusaders at Shaizar. Later, he would find hope for the reconquest of lost territory in the Almohad caliph al-Mansur and his fleet.[5]

In the writings of many authors, such as al-Harawi (d. 1215), the Mediterranean and its Muslim territories come alive not as a space reconfigured by a nostalgic memory but as an Islamic territory to be reconquered, spurred on by new forces, new *'asabiyya,* or solidarity based on kinship, according to Ibn Khaldun, which should be inspired by the example of the first Arabs.

Ibn Khaldun took this logic to its natural conclusion in his masterpiece, *The Book of Examples.* He has the period of Muslim domination over the Mediterranean coincide with the period of the region's Fatimid and Umayyad caliphates in the tenth century. He assigns the sea the role of a border, controlled by the most powerful rulers in Islam, whether caliphs or sultans, not as an end unto itself but as a prelude to other conquests, under the guidance of the most virtuous princes and conquering tribal forces driven by the spirit of Islam. When Ibn Khaldun met Tamerlane in the capital of Syria, he gave him a signed copy of his book, thinking he had found the Muslim sovereign able to subject the world—including the Christian world and its seas—to Islam. Like his peers, he was not looking for a particular place in the Islamic world from which the conquest would be launched but rather for an army and its guide, who would be able to revive the conquering spirit of their Arab ancestors. The lost Mediterranean had not become a place of useless nostalgia but an area to be taken back from the Christians thanks to the spirit of Islam.

Finally, the Mediterranean has a singular place in the *rihla* of Ibn Battuta (1304–ca. 1377), but not in the way one would expect from a Maghrebi and native of Tangier.[6] In this redistribution of the world's spatial hierarchy, it is the new spaces, the lands and seas of expansion and Islamization that most attracted the Moroccan traveler's attention: India and its oceanic extension, the steppes of Central Asia, the Mali of Mansa Suleyman (1335–1358), and the southeast of Africa between Mogadishu and Kilwa are presented as models of government, some of which were still poorly integrated but prosperous and filled with hope for Islam's future. For Ibn Battuta, the sea that embodies Islam's maritime space is no longer his own but instead the Red Sea, and more specifically the maritime route of the pilgrimage to Jeddah, Islam's maritime center stretching from Rabat to Delhi.

Paradoxically, a "peaceful" sea like the Indian Ocean, a sea of the Arabs, that is, a sea without enemies of Islam, could not become the caliph's sea. One has to wait for another era—the period of the ascendancy of the Egyptian caliphate and sultanates or that of the Rasulid dynasty of Aden (1229–1454)—for maritime commerce to become an instrument of the display of sultanate domination over Arab seas.[7] Under the authority of the caliphs of Baghdad, only the Sea of the Romans—in other words, the enemy sea—could be the stage on which caliphal jihad was displayed, bringing together every form of expansion, whether through religious conversion or military and commercial means, despite the fact that neither the caliphs of the conquest, nor the Abbasids and Umayyads, nor even the Fatimids and Almohads ever "straddled" the sea of caliphs, other than to cross the Strait of Gibraltar.

NOTES

GLOSSARY

CHRONOLOGIES

SELECTED BIBLIOGRAPHY

INDEX

NOTES

INTRODUCTION

Chapter title: "Moorish and Saracen" comes from Eginhard, a chronicler of Charlemagne.

Epigraph: Al-Tabari (1879–1901), 1:2821; English trans. (1985–1999), 15:26.

1. F. Braudel (1995), 1:17.
2. H. Pirenne (2005).
3. A. R. Lewis (1951).
4. Definition of "pirate" from the *Dictionnaire de l'Académie française:* "n. borrowed, via the Latin *pirata,* from the Greek *peirâtes,* 'brigand, pirate,' itself derived from *peirân,* 'to try, to attempt,' then 'to attempt the adventure, to devote one's self to brigandage.' An adventurer who commits brigandage on the seas, a member of a crew that attacks and robs merchant ships."
5. P. Brown (1971); C. Wickham (2005).
6. L. Musset (1994).
7. A. Schaube (1906); S. D. Goitein (1967).
8. P. Horden and N. Purcell (2000).
9. G. Martinez-Gros (1992).
10. M. Balard (1978); D. Coulon (2004); D. Coulon, C. Picard, and D. Valérian (2007); M. Tangheroni (1996); A. L. Udovitch (1978); D. Valérian (2006); A. E. Laiou (2002); J.-P. Sodini (2000).
11. P. Brown (1971); R. Hodges and D. Whitehouse (1996); C. Wickham (2005). On Byzantium, see A. E. Laiou (2002) and M. McCormick (2001). On the Islamic world, see F. Micheau (2012).
12. M. Whittow (2009); A. G. Walmsley (2007); C. Wickham (2005).
13. P. Toubert (1973); L. Feller (1998); J.-M. Poisson (1992); J.-M. Martin (2001).
14. P. Horden and N. Purcell (2000).
15. Al-Muqaddasi (1906, 1950, 1963); A. Miquel (1973–1984); S. D. Goitein (1967).
16. Li Guo (2000).

17. A. Miquel (1973–1984), 1:323.
18. N. Michel (2000).
19. A. Miquel (1973–1984), 1:1–3.
20. G. Martinez-Gros (1992).
21. J.-M. Poisson (1992); J.-M. Martin (2001).
22. F. Menant (2005), 193 and following.
23. M. Ouerfelli (2009); C. Picard (2009).
24. Almohad text, cited below, pp. 214–216.
25. Al-Idrisi (1975, 1999).
26. Al-Tabari (1879–1901, 1985–1999); H. Kennedy (2003a); M. Bonner (1996).
27. D. Ayalon (1996); A. Fuess (2001).
28. A.-M. Eddé (2008).

1. THE ARAB DISCOVERY OF THE MEDITERRANEAN

1. F. Donner (1998); F. Micheau (2012).
2. Ibn Habib (1991); Ibn ʿAbd al-Hakam (1922, 1948).
3. L. I. Conrad (1992); A. M. Fahmy (1966).
4. Y. Ragheb (2006).
5. S. D. Goitein (1967).
6. F. Donner (1998); G. Schoeler (2002).
7. H. Kennedy (2003a, 2003b).
8. Y. Kamal (1987).
9. J. B. Harley and D. Woodward (1992).
10. A. Borrut (2011).
11. J. Schiettecatte (2011); P. Baujeard (2012).
12. A. Galland (1965), 1:230. While it is highly likely that these tales were written later, during the Ottoman period (see J. C. Garcin [2013]), ninth- and tenth-century Arabic descriptions of the Indian Ocean confirm such initiatives.
13. É. Vallet (2012).
14. H. Kennedy (1981).
15. V. Déroche et al. (2007), 21–80.
16. P. Gautier Dalché (1997); N. Bouloux (2004); E. Vagnon (2013); C. Hofmann, H. Richard, E. Vagnon (2012).
17. P. Zumthor (1993), 317–344; J. Richard (1981).
18. E. Savage-Smith and Y. Rapoport (2007); Ibn Hawqal (1938–1939, 1964).
19. Ibn Jubayr (1907, 1949); Y. Dejugnat (2010).
20. Al-Idrisi (1975, 1999).
21. A. Miquel (1973–1984), vols. I and II; vol. 1, chs. VII and VIII.

22. Nasir-i Kushraw (1881).
23. A. Miquel (1973–1984), vol. 1, 204: *Muruj al-dhahab* [The meadows of gold] and *Kitab al-Tanbih wa l-Ishraf* [The book of notification and verification].
24. C. Pellat, "Al-Masʿudi," in *Encyclopédie de l'Islam,* 2nd ed., 6:773–778; T. Khalidi (1975); A. Shboul (1979).
25. F. Gabrieli, "Adab," in *Encyclopédie de l'Islam,* 3rd ed., 1:175–176.
26. Ibn al-Nadim, *al-Fihrist,* made a list of the books he found in the most prestigious libraries of Baghdad. See H. Touati (2003).
27. H. Touati (2000).
28. C. Pellat, "Al-Masʿudi," 6:774; J. Sauvaget (1948); F. X. Fauvelle-Aymar and B. Hirsch (2003).
29. Al-Masʿudi (1861–1877), 1:234; French trans. (1962–1965), 94.
30. A. Miquel (1973–1984), 1:173, 313–330.
31. J. Sauvaget (1948); V. Minorsky (1955).
32. Ibn al-Faqih al-Hamadhani (1885), 48; French trans. (1973), 59.
33. Al-Masʿudi (1861–1877), 1:243–244; French trans. (1962–1965), 98.
34. A. Miquel (1973–1984), 1:35–68, 202–212.
35. Al-Masʿudi (1861–1877), 1:281–283; French trans. (1962–1965), 115–116. See also analysis of Al-Masʿudi in H. Touati (2000).
36. Ibn al-Nadim (1871, 1970); G. Martinez-Gros (1992, 1997).
37. Al-Masʿudi (1861–1877), 1:369; French trans. (1962–1965), 149.
38. Al-Masʿudi (1861–1877), 1:258–259; French trans. (1962–1965), 106.
39. H. Touati (2003).
40. A. Amara and A. Nef (2000).
41. H. Bresc and A. Nef, introduction to al-Idrisi (1999), 13–53; G. Martinez-Gros (2006).
42. J. Jones (1995).
43. H. Bresc (1981).
44. Al-Idrisi (1999), 309.
45. Ibid., 270.
46. H. Bresc, "Le choc des reconquêtes et de la Croisade," in J. C. Garcin et al. (1995–2000), 1:173–203.
47. H. Bresc and A. Nef, introduction to al-Idrisi (1999), 52.
48. Al-Idrisi (1975, 1989, 1999); J.-C. Ducène (2010).
49. A. Amara and A. Nef (2000).
50. CD Rom of al-Idrisi's map, produced by the Bibliothèque nationale de France, Cartes et Plans section.
51. G. Martinez-Gros (2006), 116; Ibn Khaldun (2002), bk. 1, 270.
52. G. Martinez (2006), 110.
53. Ibid., 66 and following.

54. Ibn Khaldun (2002), bk. 1, ch. 2, 264–313: "The spread of civilization on earth. A few indications on the seas, rivers, and climates."
55. Ibn Khaldun (2002), 563–569.
56. Ibid., bk. 1, 569.
57. Ibid., bk. 1, 564.
58. P. Horden and N. Purcell (2000); T. Bianquis, P. Guichard, and M. Tillier (2012).

2. ARAB WRITING ON THE CONQUEST OF THE MEDITERRANEAN

1. Koran 17:62. 18:59, 25:55.
2. Ibn Khaldun (2002), 5.
3. F. Donner (1998); Ch. Décobert (1991); A.-L. de Prémare (2002).
4. F. Donner (1998), 299–306 (table).
5. G. Schoeler (2002). For the example of the conquest of al-Andalus, see P. Chalmeta (2003).
6. A. Borrut (2009).
7. D. Sourdel (1999); T. El-Hibri (1999).
8. Al-Mas'udi (1861–1877), 1:15–16, French trans. (1962–1965), 6–7; H. Kennedy (2003b); C. Gilliot (1988); F. Rosenthal, "General Introduction," in al-Tabari (1985–1999), 1:3–154; A. Borrut (2011), 9–55.
9. F. Rosenthal (1968); A. Cheddadi (2004); F. Donner (1998); A. Elad (2003); A.-L. de Prémare (2002); C. Décobert (1991).
10. M. Tillier (2009).
11. S. Bouderbala (2008).
12. M. Muranyi (1999).
13. H. Kennedy (1997).
14. H. Kennedy (2003b); Al-Tabari (1879–1901, 1985–1999).
15. F. Donner (1998), 132–138; H. Kennedy (1997).
16. Al-Tabari (1879–1901), 1:2580–2581; French trans. (1985–1999) 13:163.
17. C. F. Robinson (2003); G. Schoeler (2002); A. Borrut (2011), pp. 45–48 and no. 164.
18. Al-Ya'qubi (1960), 2:262; French translation by A.-L. de Prémare (2002), 462–463.
19. J. M. Fiey (1980); S. K. Samir (2003); D. Gutas (2005); R. G. Hoyland (1997).
20. T. El-Hibri (1999).
21. A. Borrut (2011).
22. H. Djaït (1986).
23. H. Djaït (2004).

24. P. Cobb (2001); A. Borrut (2011).
25. F. Donner (1981), 91–155, 157–220.
26. A. Borrut (2011), 389–393, 446–450; P. Cobb (2001), 21 and following; H. Kennedy (1981), 74 and following.
27. M. Bonner (2004); A. Borrut (2004).
28. D. Sourdel (1980); P. Cobb (1999).
29. The expression "ghazi-caliph" was coined by C. E. Bosworth (1992), derived from the Turkish title that appeared in the eleventh century.
30. A. M. Fahmy (1966).
31. L. I. Conrad (1992); M. Canard (1926); R. Guilland (1955).
32. Al-Mawardi (1984), 76.
33. D. Cook (2002).
34. K. Y. Blankinship (1994); G. R. Hawting (2000); P. Cobb, "'Umar II," in *Encyclopédie de l'Islam,* 2nd ed., 10:886–887; A. Borrut (2005), 201–281; A. Borrut (2011).
35. A. Borrut (2011), 229–282; J.-L. Bacqué-Grammont, F. de Polignac, and G. Bohas (2000); F. de Polignac (1982, 1999).
36. Ibn Khurradadhbih (1889), 169.
37. The phrase "the end of the jihadist caliphate" is a paraphrase of the title of the book by K. Y. Blankinship (1994), *The End of the Jihâd State.*
38. R. G. Khoury (2004).
39. Agapius (1901); R. G. Khoury (2004); C. Décobert and J.-Y. Empereur (1998).
40. Y. Ragheb (1996).
41. F. Donner (1998), 214–229.
42. S. Bouderbala (2008), 183–247; H. Kennedy (1997), 72 and following.
43. A. Miquel (1973–1984), 1:253–257.
44. "'Amr," "Adruh," in *Encyclopédie de l'Islam,* 2nd ed.
45. A.-L. de Prémare (2002), 79–81.
46. H. Kennedy (1997), 65.
47. M. Tillier (2009).
48. Ibn Khallikan (1948), 1:349.
49. M. Gil (1992), 126; P. Cobb (1995).
50. F. Rosenthal (1968), 590.
51. Al-Suyuti (1997).
52. Al-Khushani (1914, 1922, 1982); Al-Maqqari (1840–1843, 1967, 1968).
53. M. Talbi, "Sahnun," in *Encyclopédie de l'Islam,* 2nd ed., 8:843–845; J. Schacht (1999); Y. Dutton (1999), J. Brockopp (1998); M. Muranyi (1984, 1999).
54. A. Othman (1999).

55. Particularly al-Maliki. See N. Amri (2011).
56. Ibn Sa'd (1917–1940), 2:213; French trans. M. Canard (1926), 71.
57. Al-Zuhri, § 117. See Abu 'Ubayda b. al-Jarrah, in *Encyclopédie de l'Islam,* 3rd ed.
58. J. Chabbi, "Shahid," in *Encyclopédie de l'Islam,* 2nd ed.
59. P. Sénac (2006); Ibn 'Abd al-Hakam (1922), 120, French trans. (1948), 121.
60. A tribe that had rallied behind Islam after the revolt against the Muslims following the death of Muhammad, under the caliphate of Abu Bakr (632–634).
61. Al-Tabari (1879–1901), 2:2824; French trans., 15:29.
62. Al-Baladhuri (1863–1866), 152, 154; French trans., 235, 237. According to an Egyptian tradition, the first expedition on the Mediterranean actually took place in 643.
63. Ibn 'Abd al-Hakam (1922), 34–36; French trans. (1948), 35–37.
64. Ibn 'Abd al-Hakam (1922), 76–78, French trans. (1948), 79–80; Ibn 'Idhari (1948–1951), 1:22–24, French trans. (1901–1904), 28–31; H. Djaït (2004).
65. H. Djaït (2004).
66. Ibn 'Abd al-Hakam (1922), 60–62; French trans. (1948), 61–63.
67. H. Djaït (2004).
68. Ibn 'Abd al-Hakam (1922), 64; French trans. (1948), 65.
69. Ibn al-Athir (1965–1967), 4:88; French trans. (1901), 20–22, including the encounter between 'Uqba and Julian.
70. H. Djaït (2004).
71. Secondary pilgrimage sites.
72. Ibn 'Abd al-Hakam (1922), 96; French trans. (1948), 97.
73. Ibn al-Athir (1965–1967), 4:444–445; French trans. (1901), 42–43.
74. Ibn Habib (1991), 137; French trans. M. Wilk (2008), 26.
75. G. Martinez-Gros (1992).
76. Ibn al-Athir (1965–1967), 4:448; French trans. (1901), 48.
77. Al-Idrisi (1999), 130.
78. A.-M. Eddé, F. Micheau, and C. Picard (1997).

3. THE SILENCES OF THE SEA

1. F. Donner (1991).
2. M. Canard (1973a); A. Kaplony (2002); M. Bonner (2004).
3. D. Gutas (2005); H. Touati (2003), 125–203.
4. Ibn al-Faqih al-Hamadhani (1885), 108; French trans. (1973), 132–133.
5. On 'Abd al-Malik's policy, see C. F. Robinson (2005). On the mosque of Damascus, see F. B. Flood (2000).

6. Al-Muqaddasi (1906), 107; French trans. (1963), 170.
7. Ibn al-Faqih al-Hamadhani (1885), 106–108, French trans. (1973), 127–133; A. Borrut (2011), 339–344.
8. M. Canard (1973a).
9. Ibn al-Faqih al-Hamadhani (1885), 136–139; French trans. (1973), 163–166.
10. Sa'id al-Andalusi (1913, 1966); G. Martinez-Gros (1984).
11. D. Gutas (2005), 95 and following.
12. A.-M. Eddé, F. Micheau, and C. Picard (1997).
13. Ibn al-Nadim (1871, 1970).
14. Ibn al-Nadim (1871), 245; French trans. D. Jacquart and F. Micheau (1990), 33.
15. S. Bouderbala (2008), 278–279.
16. R. Hodges and D. Whitehouse (1996).
17. M. Bonner (1996).
18. A. Morabia (1993); A. Borrut (2004).
19. The expression "armed scholars" was coined by M. Bonner (1996).
20. H. Kennedy (2003a), 35.
21. A. M. Fahmy (1966).
22. S. Bouderbala (2008); A. Borrut (1999–2000, 2001).
23. Principally, M. Bonner (1996); C. E. Bosworth (1992); M. Canard (1973b); V. Christides (1982); P. Cobb (2001); P. Crone (1980); T. El-Hibri (1999); A. M. Fahmy (1966); H. Kennedy (2001, 2003a); and P. Von Sievers (1982).
24. D. Gimaret, "Mu'tazila," in *Encyclopédie de l'Islam,* 2nd ed., 7:783–787.
25. Ibn Shaddad (1980–1981, 1984).
26. A. Borrut (1999–2000, 2001); H. Kennedy (2001).
27. Abu Yusuf Ya'qub (1921); M. Bonner (1996).
28. J.-M. Poisson (1992); J.-M. Martin (2001).
29. Ibn Shaddad (1984). See introduction, xi–xlv.
30. Terminology borrowed from A. Borrut (2011). Of the many works on the subject, see A. Borrut (2004); F. Donner (2008); and R. Firestone (1999).
31. A. Morabia (1993); A. Borrut (2004).
32. *Sahib sunna wa-ghazwa:* the expression was coined by Ibn Sa'd, a historian of the first half of the ninth century: M. Bonner (1996), 110.
33. Ibid., 127.
34. F. Donner (2008).
35. C. Décobert (1991).
36. V. Christides (1982).
37. Al-Mawardi, French trans. of the passage from *Kitab al-Ahkam al-Sultaniyya* by A. Morabia (1993), 207–209.
38. Qudama ibn Ja'far (1967).

39. Al-Mawardi (1909), 23; French trans. (1984), 30–31.
40. Al-Mawardi (1909), 61; French trans. (1984), 75–76.
41. J. Chabbi (1995); C. Picard and A. Borrut (2003).
42. Ibn Shaddad (1980–1981), 316–367; French trans. (1984), 232. See J. Chabbi (1995); H. S. Khalilieh (1999); and C. Picard and A. Borrut (2003).
43. L. Caetani (1912).
44. Al-Tabari (1879–1901), 3:631; English trans. (1985–1999), 144. On the ribat in the empire's eastern zone, see E. de la Vaissière (2008), the first to mention this "coincidence." On Ifriqiya, see C. Picard and A. Borrut (2003).
45. C. E. Bosworth (1992); M. Bonner (1996).
46. Al-Maliki (1983); N. Amri (2011).
47. Qudama Ibn Ja'far, *Khitab al-Kharaj,* ed. 255; French trans. 195–196.
48. Al-Ya'qubi (1967), 115; French trans. (1937), 179.
49. T. El-Hibri (1999); H. Kennedy (2003a); M. Bonner (1996).
50. A. Nef (2011b), 205.
51. H. Kennedy (1997). On Syria in the first Abbasid century, see P. Cobb (2001), and A. Borrut (2011), 389–392.

4. THE GEOGRAPHERS' MEDITERRANEAN

1. Al-Mas'udi (1894), 33, French trans. (1896), 53; H. Touati (2003), 161–203.
2. Definition of "geography" from the *Oxford American Dictionary.*
3. A. Miquel (1973–1984), 1:7–14; I. J. Kratchkovsky (1957); Maqbul, "Jughrafiya," in *Encyclopédie de l'Islam,* 2nd ed.
4. H. Touati (2003), based on a reference by al-Nadim in the *Fihrist* (1871), 342.
5. A. Borrut (2011), 357 and following.
6. A. Miquel (1973–1984), 1:87.
7. Ibid., 1:35–68.
8. P. Beaujard (2012).
9. É. Vallet (2012).
10. A. Miquel (1973–1984), 1:87–92.
11. Ibn Khurradadhbih (1889), 8–10; French trans. (1949), 9–11.
12. C. Picard (2011b).
13. The land of the Khazars, west of the Caspian Sea and north of the Caucasus.
14. Al-Faqih al-Hamadhani (1885), 3–4, French trans. (1973), 5–6; Ibn 'Abd al-Hakam, French trans. (1948), 1. See G. R. Tibbets (1992b), 90–93.
15. A. Miquel (1973–1984), 1:322.
16. G. R. Tibbets (1992b).

17. G. Martinez-Gros (1998), 317–322.
18. Al-Muqaddasi (1906), 36; French trans. (1963), 81.
19. Al-Muqaddasi (1906), 15–16; French trans. (1963), 43–44.
20. Al-Muqaddasi (1906), 15; French trans. (1963), 41–43.
21. See A. Miquel (1973–1984), 1:299–309; G. Martinez-Gros (1998), 325–328; and J.-C. Garcin (1983).
22. C. Picard (2000).
23. Ibn Hawqal, ed. p. 201, French trans. pp. 195–196.
24. Ibid., ed. p. 190, French trans. p. 187.
25. C. Picard (1997b).
26. Ibn Hawqal (1938–1939), 108; French trans. (1964), 107–108.
27. Ibn Hawqal (1938–1939), 153; French trans. (1964), 150. The vizier was Christian.
28. Ibn Hawqal (1938–1939), 190–205; French trans. (1964), 187–200.
29. Ibn Hawqal (1938–1939), 205; French trans. (1964), 199.
30. Vassiliev (1935), 2:411.
31. Ibn Hawqal (1938–1939), 201; French trans. (1964), 195.

5. MUSLIM CENTERS OF THE WESTERN MEDITERRANEAN

1. J. Lirola Delgado (1995); E. Tixier du Mesnil (2014), 521–567.
2. J. Vernet (1985).
3. M. Talbi (1966); H. Djaït (2004); V. Prévost (2010).
4. M. Talbi (1966), 71–87.
5. The same approach was followed on the eastern side: E. de La Vaissière (2008).
6. A. Lezine (1956, 1965); N. Djelloul (1999); F. Mahfoudh (2003); G. Marçais (1957); M. Hassen (2001).
7. Al-Maliki (1983), 2:28; J. Chabbi (1995), 523; C. Picard and A. Borrut (2003).
8. Al-Maliki (1983), 1:487; French trans. N. Amri (2011).
9. Al-Ya'qubi (1967), 350; French trans. (1937), 213.
10. M. Hassen (2001); N. Djelloul (1999).
11. Al-Wansharisi (1981–1983), 7:31; French trans. V. Lagardère (1995), 212.
12. M. Talbi (1985); N. Amri (2011).
13. R. Azuar Ruiz (1991), 7–72.
14. Al-Idrisi (1975), 562, French trans. (1999), 281; E. Erbati (2002), 287.
15. V. Prigent (2007).
16. The name of one of Kairouan's gates. See M. Talbi (1966), 182–185.
17. Ibn 'Idhari (1948–1951), 1:99; French trans. (1901–1904), 1:135.

18. Ibn al-Athir (1965–1967), 5:263; French trans. M. Talbi (1966), 251.
19. Ibn al-Athir (1965–1967), 4:195; French trans. M. Talbi (1966), 248.
20. M. Amari (1933–1938), 1:145; A. Nef (2008).
21. H. S. Khalilieh (2006).
22. In M. Talbi (1966), 534–535. On maritime commerce in the Aghlabid period, see ibid., 529–538.
23. H. Halm (1992).
24. Al-Maliki (1983), 2:37–38; French trans. N. Amri (2011).
25. Al-Maliki (1983), 2:222, French trans. N. Amri (2011); H. Halm (1996), 221–235.
26. Ibn Hawqal (1938–1939), 121.
27. M. Talbi (1966), 431, no. 1, 432–433.
28. Y. Benhima (2011).
29. É. Lévi-Provençal (1959–1967), 1:34–64; P. Chalmeta (2003), 97–250.
30. P. Sénac (2000a); E. Manzano Moreno (1991).
31. J. L. Delgado and J. M. Puerta Vilchez (2002–); M. J. Viguera Molíns (1995); G. Martinez-Gros (1997); E. Fricaud (1994); Ibn al-Athir.
32. J. L. Delgado and J. M. Puerta Vilchez (2002–); M. J. Viguera Molíns (1995); G. Martinez-Gros (1997).
33. E. Fricaud (1994); Ibn al-Athir (1901, 1965–1967).
34. P. Guichard (1983, 1995b); J. P. Poly (1976).
35. E. Manzano Moreno (1991); P. Sénac (2000a).
36. P. Guichard (2001); C. De La Puente (1999); C. Picard (2006b).
37. These expeditions have all been mentioned by É. Lévi-Provençal (1959–1967), vol. 1.
38. Ibid., 1:193–225.
39. C. Picard (1997a).
40. R. Dozy (1965); J. Bosch Vilá (1984), 43–51.
41. Ibn al-Qutiya (1868), 66; Spanish trans. (1926), 53.
42. Ibn ʿIdhari (1948–1951), 2:88, French trans. (1901–1904), 2:145; G. Rosselló Bordoy (1968); P. Guichard (1987). The conquest failed.
43. J. P. Poly (1976), 4–13; C. Picard (2007a).
44. C. Picard (2000), 194–196.
45. Al-Himyari (1970), Spanish trans. (2005), 145–147.
46. Al-Bakri (1965), 111; French trans. ibid., 220.

6. THE MEDITERRANEAN OF THE WESTERN CALIPHS

1. Ibn Khaldun (2002), 565–567.
2. G. Martinez-Gros (1992); E. Tixier du Mesnil (2014).

3. A. Miquel (1973–1984), 1:259–262; J. Lirola Delgado (1995).
4. A. Miquel (1973–1984), 1:243–265.
5. Quoted by É. Lévi-Provençal (1959–1967), 3:504, from the *Muqtabis* by Ibn Hayyan.
6. H. Kennedy (2003b).
7. É. Lévi-Provençal (1953).
8. Ibn Hayyan (1979), 301; Spanish trans. (1981), 228.
9. E. Molina López (1983).
10. É. Lévi-Provençal (1959–1967), 1:348–356; J. Lirola Delgado (1993), 137–150; C. Picard (1997a), 9–20.
11. Al-Himyari (1938), 188, French trans., ibid., 228; G. Rosselló Bordoy (1968).
12. M. Acién Almensa (1997).
13. Ibn Hayyan (1979), 87–88; Spanish trans. (1981), 76–77.
14. J. Lirola Delgado (1993), 389–392. The Alboran Sea lies between the southern coast of Spain and the shores of the Maghreb.
15. G. Martinez Gros (1992, 1997).
16. É. Lévi-Provençal (1932); L. Torres Balbas (1957b).
17. C. Barceló Torres, "Los escritos árabes de las rábita de Guardamar," in R. Azuar Ruiz (2004), 131–135; S. Guttierrez Lloret, "El *ribât* antes del *ribât*: El contexto material y social del *ribât* antiguo," in ibid., 73–87.
18. É. Lévi-Provençal (1953), 90.
19. A. Sidarus (1990); C. Picard and I. C. Ferreira Fernandes (1999).
20. Ibn 'Idhari (1948–1951), 2:220; French trans. (1901–1904) (revised by author), 2:265. See C. Picard (2000), 141–142.
21. See M. Talbi (1966), 431–432; and P. Guichard (1995b).
22. M. J. Viguera, "Turtusha," in *Encyclopédie de l'Islam,* 2nd ed., 10:738–739; A. Ben Abdesselem, "Al-Turtushi," in *Encyclopédie de l'Islam,* 3rd ed., 10:739.
23. É. Lévi-Provençal (1931), 83–84.
24. Al-Himyari (1938), 124; French trans., ibid., 151–152.
25. Al-'Udhri (1965), Spanish trans. (1975–1976) in J. Lirola Delgado (2005), 32–33.
26. J. Lirola Delgado (1993), 271–275.
27. Ibn Hayyan (1979), 312; Spanish trans. (1981), 220.
28. J. Lirola Delgado (2005).
29. J. Lirola Delgado (1993), 198–203.
30. Al-'Udhri (1965), Spanish trans. (1975–1976) in J. Lirola Delgado (2005), 32–33.
31. Al-Himyari (1938), 73; French trans., ibid., 91–92.
32. C. Picard (2010a).

33. M. I. Calero Secall (1995).
34. É. Lévi-Provençal (1959–1967), 2:236–238; T. Bruce (2013).
35. Ibn ʻIdhari (1948–1951), 2:245, French trans. (1901–1904), 405; C. Picard (1997b), 270–271.
36. Expression used by Gabriel Martinez-Gros (1992), 1.
37. Ibn Hayyan (1965, 1967, 1979, 1981).
38. Ibn Hayyan, *Muqtabis* VII, Spanish trans. (1967), 104.
39. G. Martinez-Gros (1992); J. Dakhlia (1998).
40. Ibn Hayyan (1979), § 211–212; Spanish trans. (1981), 236–237.
41. Ibn Hawqal (1938–1939), 198–199; French trans. P. Sénac (2001), 120.
42. Ibn Hayyan (1979), 454–455; Spanish trans. (1981), 342.
43. J.-P. Poly (1976).
44. D. Bramoullé (2011).
45. S. D. Goitein (1967, 1973).
46. Al-Makhzumi (1986); C. Cahen (1964, 1977a, 1986).
47. A. Fuess (2001).
48. S. Denoix (1992); J. Loiseau (2010).
49. A.-M. Eddé (2008), 501–508; S. Denoix (1992); J. Loiseau (2010).
50. Al-Maqrizi (2002–2004), 3:618–619; French trans. D. Bramoullé (2011), 275.
51. Abu l-Fida' (1840); Yaqut (1866–1873).
52. E. Savage-Smith and Y. Rapoport (2007); A. Miquel (1973–1984), 1:309–312.
53. Al-Maqrizi (2002–2004), 2:379.
54. É. Vallet (2012).
55. A. Nanji, "Nasir-i Kushraw," in *Encyclopédie de l'Islam*, 3rd ed., 7:1006–1007.
56. Y. Dejugnat (2010).
57. Nasir-i Kushraw (1881), French trans., 120–126.
58. Ibid., French trans., 40–41.
59. Al-Raqiq (1990).
60. C. Cahen (1983), 37–38; D. Jacoby (1995).
61. Insofar as this pavilion already existed under the same name in Mahdia, it seems difficult to associate the term "al-bahr" with the Nile rather than the Mediterranean. It is absolutely conceivable that the ambiguity was intentional.
62. D. Bramoullé (2011), 308–309.
63. C. Cahen (1964). One must also include the references in the Geniza letters and Latin letters.
64. H. Halm (1996); F. Dachraoui (1981), 402–403; A.-M. Eddé (2008), 498–508; A. S. Ehrenkreutz (1955); Y. Lev (1991), 168–184.

65. C. Cahen (1977a).
66. Al-Nu'man (1975), 327–328; French trans. F. Mahfoudh (2003), 243. See H. Halm (1996), 214–221.
67. F. Mahfoudh (2003), 243–249.
68. F. Dachraoui (1981), 188–189; H. Halm (1996), 298–325; H. Halm (1992).
69. C. Picard (2009a).
70. Al-Bakri (1965), 30; French trans., ibid., 67–68.
71. A. Bazzana (2011).
72. M. Kamil Husayn, and M. A. Sha'ira (1954), 102–103; French trans. M. Canard (1958), 154–155.
73. M. Kamil Husayn, and M. A. Sha'ira (1954), 103–104; French trans. M. Canard (1958), 156.
74. Ibn Duqmaq (1893–1896), 12.
75. D. Bramoullé (2011), 287–318.
76. M. Canard (1947).
77. Ibn Hani' (n.d.), 161; M. Yalaoui (1976).
78. Ibn Hani', quoted by M. Canard (1947), 161.
79. Ibid., 188–189.
80. Ibid.
81. B. Z. Kedar (1997).
82. Al-Nu'man (1978), 164–165; Spanish trans. J. Lirola Delgado (1993), 198–199.
83. M. Canard (1973a); H. Bresc, in J.-C. Garcin et al. (1995–2000), 1:173–203.
84. J. Jones (1987, 1995); A. Nef (2011b), 119–176.
85. M. Barrucand (1999); C. Tonghini (1999).
86. M. Canard (1973a).
87. A. Nef (2011b).
88. Ibn Jubayr (1907), 330–334; French trans. (1949), 389–392.
89. Ibn Jubayr (1907), 325; French trans. (1949), 380–381.
90. Al-Maqrizi (1991). His history of the Fatimids was lost, but a summary can be found in the *Itti'az*.
91. Al-Maqrizi (1991), 20; French trans. A. Nef (2011b), 122.
92. J. Jones (1987).
93. M. Canard (1973a). On the ceremonial of Muslim sovereigns, see J. Dakhlia (1998).
94. Land and naval.
95. A. Nef (2008), 33–44, esp. 36–38.
96. S. Mazot (1999).
97. V. Christides (1982, 1984a); H. S. Khalilieh (2006).

7. THE WESTERN MEDITERRANEAN

1. P. Guichard (1999a).
2. On the Andalusian emirates of the eleventh century, see F. Clément (1997).
3. C. Picard (1997a); T. Bruce (2013); H. Ferhat (1993b).
4. C. Picard (1997b, 2006a).
5. Al-Zuhri (1968, 1991); Al-Gharnati (1993); J. Arbach (1995); H. Ferhat (1993b); M. Cherif (2005).
6. F. Clément (1997), 272.
7. P. Guichard (1990–1991), 53–63; T. Bruce (2013); C. Picard (2000), 65–84.
8. C. Picard (1997a), 31–42.
9. P. Guichard and V. Lagardère (1990).
10. Ibn 'Abdun (1947), 30, French trans. (1955), 65; P. Chalmeta (1973).
11. T. Bruce (2013).
12. D. Wasserstein (1985).
13. B. Foulon and E. Tixier du Mesnil (2008), 241–245.
14. P. Guichard (1995b).
15. T. Bruce (2013).
16. Al-Himyari (1938), 184; French trans., ibid., 222, which largely reproduces al-Idrisi's text, French trans. 282–286.
17. C. Picard (1997a), 57–74; C. Picard (1998).
18. V. Lagardère (1989b, 1998b); E. Tixier du Mesnil (2011).
19. Al-Bakri (1968).
20. "Ecological" in the sense given by P. Horden and N. Purcell (2000).
21. C. Picard (2011a); G. Martinez-Gros (2006).
22. G. Camps (1980).
23. P. Guichard (1990–1991), 19–24.
24. P. Guichard (1977).
25. Ibn 'Idhari (1948–1951), 2:107–108; French trans. (1901–1904), 210, 213.
26. Y. Benhima (2011).
27. Ibid.
28. V. Lagardère (1989a), 17–60.
29. Al-Bakri (1965), 166; French trans., ibid., 314.
30. M. J. Viguera Molíns (1977); French trans. V. Lagardère (1998b), 15.
31. P. Sénac (2006), 84–91.
32. H. Ahrweiler (1966), 40, 60; E. Tixier du Mesnil (2014).
33. A.-M. Eddé (2008), 505.
34. C. Picard (2003).
35. M. De Epalza (1986).
36. R. Mauny (1960); C. Picard (1997b), 377–416.

37. P. Guichard (1983); C. Picard (2007a, 2007b); C. Aillet (2010), 55–57.
38. Al-Bakri (1965), 61–62; French trans., ibid., 128–129. On Asilah, see ibid., 111; French trans., ibid., 220.
39. J. Lirola Delgado (1993), 120–131; M. De Epalza (1986, 1987).
40. R. Azuar Ruiz (2005); P. Cressier (2004).
41. C. Picard (2003).
42. Al-Bakri (1965), 81; French trans., ibid., 163.
43. Al-Idrisi (1989), introduction to the translation, 39–40.
44. Al-Bakri (1965), 90; French trans., ibid., 182.
45. Ibid., 101; French trans., ibid., 199.
46. C. Aillet (2010), 52–59.
47. Al-Badisi (1926, 1982).
48. E. Tixier du Mesnil (2014).
49. Ibn Abi Zar' (1973), 201; Spanish trans. (1964), 400.
50. J. Arbach (1995); C. Picard (1997a).
51. P. Guichard (1990), 181–183.
52. A. Huici Miranda (1956–1957a, 1956–1957b).
53. C. Picard (1997b), 167–169, 477–478.
54. Al-Baydhaq (1928), 107.
55. A. Amara (2003); D. Valérian (2006a).
56. P. Buresi (2004).
57. Y. Benhima (2003); C. Picard (1997b), 476–481; J. Arbach (1995), 103–111.
58. P. Buresi and H. El Allaoui (2012).
59. É. Lévi-Provençal, ed., *Trente-sept lettres officielles almohades* (1941).
60. Ibn 'Idhari (1985); Ibn Sahib al-Sala (1969); Al-Marrakushi (1955, 1968).
61. Ibn al-Qattan (1964).
62. Ibn 'Idhari (1985), 185.
63. M. Vegua, S. Peña, and M. C. Feria (2006), 1035.
64. É. Lévi-Provençal, ed., *Trente-sept lettres officielles almohades* (1941), 37; French trans. J. Arbach (1995), 80.
65. M. Cherif (1996).
66. Ibn Khaldun (1983), 4:63; French trans. (2002), 81.
67. A. Ettahiri, A. Filli, and J. P. Van Staevel (2008).
68. J. Arbach (1995).
69. É. Lévi-Provençal, ed., *Trente-sept lettres officielles almohades* (1941), 68. A more detailed account is provided in Al-Himyari (1938), 188–189; French trans., ibid., 228–230.
70. On the siege and the taking of Mahdia, see H. R. Idris (1962), 1:384–394.
71. J. Arbach (1995, 1997).
72. "Catechism" setting out Almohad doctrine, written by Ibn Tumart.

73. Ibn al-Qattan (1964), 139–149; Ibn Simak (1979), 150–151, French trans. J. Arbach (1995), 191.
74. Koran 17 (The Night Journey), 66: "It is your Lord who drives your ships across the ocean, so that you may sail in them in quest of his abundance." See also 5:96; English trans. by N. J. Dawood.
75. Al-Balawi (n.d.); French trans. J. Arbach (1995), 441–442.
76. O. R. Constable (1994); H. Touati (2000).
77. Ibn Jubayr (1907, 1949). See Y. Dejugnat (2010).
78. J. Arbach (1995), 1:311–314.
79. Al-Tadili (1984, 1994).
80. Ibn ʿIdhari (1985), 344; Ibn Sahib al-Sala (1964), 129–130; A. Huici Miranda (1956–1957a), 184.
81. Al-Idrisi (1999), 191; Al-Zuhri (1968), 198–200; S. Zaglul, (1958), 125.
82. Al-Idrisi (1999), 192–193.
83. On marine fauna, see M. P. Torres (1995).
84. H. Bresc and A. Nef, introduction to the translation, in Al-Idrisi (1999), 31.
85. Al-Idrisi (1989).
86. C. Picard (1997b), 193–194.
87. C. Dubler (1949).
88. This subsection is informed by H. R. Idris (1961) and H. S. Khalilieh (2006). For the *Treatise*, see Al-Kinani (1983, 2006); A. L. Udovitch (1993).
89. H. R. Idris (1961), 230.
90. A. Nef (2001).
91. V. Lagardère (1989b), 127 and following.
92. On Ibn Rushd, see P. Guichard and V. Lagardère (1990). On Qadi Iyad, see H. Ferhat (1993b), 146–161.
93. Al-Badisi (1926, 1982); M. Cherif (2000).
94. H. Ferhat (1993a).
95. Al-Tadili (1984, 1994); Al-Tamimi (2002); H. Ferhat (1998); H. Ferhat (1993b), 399–417; M. Cherif (2000). On al-Tadili, see P. Guichard and V. Lagardère (1990).
96. M. Cherif (2005), 7.
97. D. Valérian (2006a).

8. THE MEDITERRANEAN OF THE TWO EMPIRES

1. C. Picard (2010b).
2. A.-L. de Prémare (2002), 151–172.
3. T. Bianquis, P. Guichard, and M. Tillier (2012); F. Micheau (2012), 72–73.
4. F. Donner (1998).

5. Al-Tabari (1879–1901), 4:64, English trans. (1985–1999), 13:10; F. Donner (1998), 153–155; A. Borrut (1999–2000), 29.
6. Al-Baladhuri (1863–1866), 117; English trans. (1968), 180.
7. H. Ahrweiler (1966); C. Morrisson, in J.-C. Cheynet (2004).
8. Ibn ʻAbd Al Hakam (1922), 36 38; French trans. (1948), 37 39.
9. Al-Tabari (1879–1901), 2821–2822, English trans. (1985–1999), 15:26–27; R. S. Humphreys (2006), 53–54.
10. F. Donner (1998), 153–155.
11. On the difficulties of sailing on the Aegean Sea, see G. de Saint-Guillain (2005). For a more general discussion of the technical aspects of sailing on the Mediterranean, see J. H. Pryor (1988, 2006).
12. H. Ahrweiler (1966), 31–35.
13. Al-Tabari (1879–1901), 1:2822; English trans. (1985–1999), 15:26–27.
14. Al-Baladhuri (1863–1866), 117; English trans. (1985–1999), 180.
15. Ibn ʻAbd al-Hakam (1922), 279; Ibn Yunus (2000), 1:503; S. Bouderbala (2008), 278–282.
16. F. Donner (1998).
17. P. Sijpesteijn (2007).
18. J.-C. Cheynet (2004), 3–8.
19. V. Prigent (2007).
20. J. Durliat (1990).
21. Al-Tabari (1879–1901), 2:2867–2871, 2927, English trans. (1985–1999) 15:74–77, 131–132; Ibn ʻAbd al-Hakam (1922), 189–191; A. Fahmy (1966), 82 and following. For the Christian versions, particularly Agapius and Theophanes, see A. N. Stratos (1980).
22. F. Trombley (2004).
23. A. Fahmy (1966), 35–38.
24. S. Bouderbala (2008), 287–291, 328.
25. A. Fahmy (1966).
26. H. Ahrweiler (1966).
27. J.-C. Cheynet (2006), 3–8; A. Kaplony (2002); M. Bonner (2004).
28. A. Fahmy (1966), 35; S. Bouderbala (2008), 283, 290.
29. Al-Baladhuri (1863–1866), 153; English trans. (1968), 236. The same account is given by al-Tabari (1879–1901), 1:2826–2827; English trans. (1985–1999), 15:30–31.
30. L. I. Conrad (1992); H. Bresc (2004).
31. G. R. Hawting (2000), 40–45.
32. M. Canard (1926); R. Guilland (1955); L. I. Conrad (1992); A. M. Fahmy (1966), 91–110; A. Kaplony (2002). On Maslama, see A. Borrut (2011), 201–247.
33. J. H. Mordtmann, "Kustantiniya," in *Encyclopédie de l'Islam*, 3rd ed., 5:532b.
34. Al-Tabari (1879–1901), 2:86; Al-Yaʻqubi (1960), 2:271, 285.

35. Al-Tabari (1879–1901), 2:86; Al-Yaʿqubi (1960), 2:285; Ibn al-Athir (1965–1967), 3:383, 392.
36. Theophanes (1883), 353–354.
37. Al-Baladhuri, English trans. (1985–1999), 236; Al-Tabari (1879–1901), 2:163; Ibn al-Athir (1965–1967), 3:413.
38. See "Maslama Ibn ʿAbd al-Malik," in *Encyclopédie de l'Islam,* 2nd ed. (CD-ROM ed.), 6:740.
39. V. Prigent (2007).
40. P. Chalmeta (2003).
41. P. Sénac (2006); P. Guichard (1995b).
42. Khalifa b. Khayyat al-Usfuri (1967).
43. Al-Bakri (1965), 38–39; French trans. (revised by author), ibid., 84.
44. See the discussion earlier in this chapter: Musa b. Nusayr did not attempt to seize control of the coastal cities of Mauretania Caesariensis, nor those of Mauretania Tingitana, with the exception of those in the area of the Strait of Gibraltar.
45. P. Chalmeta (2003), 80–86.
46. Ibn al-Qutiya (1926), 135.
47. Ibid.
48. Khalifa b. Khayyat al-Usfuri (1967), 1:303; French trans. P. Fois (2012), 179–180.
49. P. Fois (2012).

9. CONTROLLING THE MEDITERRANEAN

1. H. Kennedy (1981); P. Crone (1980); A. Northedge (2005); E. de La Vaissière (2007); M. Gordon (2001).
2. H. Ahrweiler (1971).
3. J.-C. Cheynet (2004), 13–22.
4. C. E. Bosworth, "Taraz," in *Encyclopédie de l'Islam,* 3rd ed., 10:222–223.
5. P. Sénac (2006).
6. A. Borrut (2011), 354–450.
7. P. Cobb (2001); H. Kennedy (1981).
8. V. Christides (1984a).
9. H. Ahrweiler (1966).
10. V. Prigent (2007).
11. Ibn al-Athir (1965–1967), 5:575, French trans. (1901), 106; C. Picard (2000), 30–32.
12. C. Picard (2000), 30–32.
13. É. Lévi-Provençal (1959–1967), 1:263–276.

14. Severus, *History of the Patriarchs;* C. Picard (2011d).
15. B. Kubiak (1970).
16. M. McCormick (2001, 2004); N. Drocourt (2004).
17. A. Vassiliev (1935), 2:1.
18. M. Compagnolo-Pothitou (1995).
19. M. Canard (1964); N. Drocourt (2004).
20. P. Sénac (2006), 43–66, bibliography (item 2), 44.
21. G. Levi della Vida (1954).
22. H. Ahrweiler (1966), 31–40.
23. Ibn Khurradadhbih (1889), 77–78; French trans. (1949), 56–57.
24. Qudama b. Jaʿfar (1967), 255; French trans., ibid., 195–196.
25. J.-C. Cheynet (2006), 13–16.
26. Ibn Duqmaq (1893–1896), 80–81; Al-Kindi (1912), 202. On the recruiting of oarsmen, see G. Levi della Vida (1944–1945), and A. Fahmy (1966).
27. V. Christides (1984a), 39–40.
28. Al-Muqaddasi (1906), 162–163; French trans. (1963), 181–182.
29. Al-Baladhuri (1863–1866), 236; English trans. (1968), 376.
30. V. Christides (1984a), 85.
31. Al-Tabari (1879–1901), 9:276; Al-Baladhuri (1863–1866), 236, English trans. (1968), 376.
32. B. Kubiak (1970).
33. Al-Baladhuri (1863–1866), 163; English trans. M. Bonner (1996), 105. [*Translator's Note:* The quote is taken from the English source.]
34. M. Bonner (1996), 153–154.
35. D. Sourdel (1999), 167 and following.
36. S. Bouderbala (2008).
37. C. Picard (2004).
38. P. Guichard (1983).
39. V. Christides (1984a); É. Lévi-Provençal (1959–1967), 1:150–191; P. Guichard (1999a), 53–55.
40. G. Tate, in C. Morrisson and J.-C. Cheynet (2005–2006), 395–401.
41. Al-Baladhuri (1863–1866), 116–118, English trans. (1968), 178–181; M. Sharon (1997).
42. M. Hassen (2001).
43. C. Picard (1997a, 1997b); P. Cressier (2004).
44. R. Azuar Ruiz (2004); M. Hassen (2001); F. Mahfoudh (2003).
45. M. Hassen (2001).
46. P. Toubert (1973).
47. Al-Kindi (1912), 418–419; French trans. and analysis, S. Bouderbala (2008), 292. This subsection draws on A. Morabia (1993) and A. Borrut (2004).

48. R. G. Khoury (1986), 250.
49. H. S. Khalilieh (1999); A. Borrut (2004), 123–144; S. Bouderbala (2008), 292–293.
50. S. Garnier (2012).
51. N. Amri (2011).
52. J. Lirola Delgado (1993), 114. On the emirate of al-Hakam I, see Chapter 6.
53. P. Toubert (1973); J.-M. Poisson (1992), 9–17.
54. J.-C. Cheynet (2005–2006); J. F. Haldon (1999).
55. P. Bonnassie (1975–1976).
56. H. Lammens (1926).
57. P. Crone (1980).
58. Ibn Shaddad (1980–1981, 1984); P. Von Sievers (1982).
59. A. Borrut (1999–2000).
60. Al-Muqaddasi (1906), 164, 177; French trans. (1963), 184, 209–210.

10. THE MARITIME AWAKENING OF THE MUSLIM WEST

1. Al-Bakri (1982), 102; French trans. F. Mahfoudh (2003), 227–228.
2. M. Talbi (1966), 419n2. The figures are rough but give an idea of the size of the troops.
3. J.-C. Cheynet (2006), 482–483.
4. Johannes Hymonides, quoted by M. Talbi (1966), 525.
5. P. Chalmeta (2003), 112–119.
6. Ibid., 123–126; C. Picard (1997b), 64–66.
7. *Akhbar Majmu'a*, ed. 2–3; Spanish trans. (1897), 10–12.
8. Ibn 'Idhari (1948–1951), 2:6; French trans. (1901–1904), 2:9.
9. H. Ferhat (1993b), 42–55.
10. Al-Bakri (1965), 91–92; French trans., ibid., 183–185.
11. C. Picard (1997b), 246.
12. Al-'Udhri (1965), 11; Spanish trans. (1975–1976), 76.
13. Ibn 'Idhari (1948–1951), 2:31; French trans. (1901–1904), 2:45.
14. Ibn al-Qutiya (1868), 1; Spanish trans. (1926), 2.
15. M. McCormick (2001).
16. Ibn Hayyan (1999), 89v; Spanish trans. (2001), 19.
17. Ibn Hayyan, Spanish trans. (2001), 21–22.
18. *Monumenta Germaniae Historica,* 1:193–194.
19. Ibid., 1:197. The Carolingian sources are in P. Guichard (1983), but they are used to reach different conclusions.
20. A. R. Lewis (1951) already sensed this development; D. Abulafia (1985).
21. Al-Bakri (1965), 90–99; French trans., ibid., 180–196.

22. Ibid., 111–112; French trans., ibid., 221–222.
23. S. Gutiérrez Lloret (1996).
24. J. Bosch Vilá (1984).
25. C. Picard (1997b), 71–76.
26. Ibn 'Idhari (1948–1951), 2:87–88; French trans. (1901–1904), 2:141–144.
27. Ibn al-Qutiya (1868), 62; Spanish trans. (1926), 49. The *Majus* or "magus" refers to those populations that practice religions not of the "Book."
28. Ibn 'Idhari (1948–1951), 2:96–97; French trans. (1901–1904), 2:157–158.
29. P. Sénac (2000a).
30. R. Azuar Ruiz (2004); A. Bazzana (2011).
31. Ibn 'Idhari (1948–1951), 2:103–104; French trans. (1901–1904), 2:170.
32. Al-Himyari (1970), 33; Spanish trans. (2005), 388.
33. J.-P. Poly (1976), 4–13.
34. Ibn Hayyan (1973, 1979, 1981); M. Acién Almensa (1997); M. Fierro (1995, 2005).
35. H. Catarino (1997–1998).
36. Quoted by Ibn 'Idhari (1948–1951), 2:137, French trans. (1901–1904), 2:228; Ibn Hayyan (1937, 1950–1959, 1973, 1979, 1981).
37. C. Picard (2000), 48–50, 183.
38. J. L. Delgado (1993), 154–158.
39. J. Bosch Vilá (1984).
40. J. L. Delgado (1993), 139–140.
41. G. Martinez-Gros (1992).

11. THE MARITIME IMPERIALISM OF THE CALIPHS IN THE TENTH CENTURY

1. G. Berti (2000).
2. P. Sénac (2001); E. Manzano Moreno (1991); C. Picard (1997a).
3. D. Bramoullé (2011).
4. F. Dachraoui (1981); D. Bramoullé (2011), 89–157; Y. Lev (1991).
5. C. Picard (2010a); G. Martinez-Gros (1992).
6. Ibn Hayyan (1979), 328–329; Spanish trans. (1981), 248.
7. É. Lévi-Provençal (1959–1967).
8. P. Sénac (2001), 121–122.
9. Ibid., 126. We are lacking the principal source, Ibn Hayyan's *Muqtabis,* which breaks off for the years 942–971.
10. P. Sénac (2001).
11. P. Bonnassie (1975–1976).
12. P. Sénac (2000a).

13. On Santiago, see C. Picard (1990, 1997a, 1998, 2010a).
14. D. Bramoullé (2011).
15. F. Dachraoui (1981), 165–187; H. Halm (1996), 298–309.
16. H. R. Idris (1962).
17. S. D. Goitein (1962).
18. See H. E. J. Cowdrey (1977).
19. D. Bramoullé (2011).
20. M. Barrucand (1999).
21. M. Lombard (1947).
22. P. Horden and N. Purcell (2000).
23. P. Toubert (1973); L. Feller (1998).
24. G. Berti and L. Tongiorgi (1981); S. D. Goitein (1967).
25. G. Berti (2000).
26. G. Berti and L. Tongiorgi (1981).
27. É. Vallet (2012).
28. D. Bramoullé (2011); A. Nef (2007); É. Vallet (2010, 2012).
29. C. Cahen (1977a, 1983, 1986); M. Balard (1999); A. L. Udovitch (1999).
30. *Jawdhar.*
31. C. Cahen (1977a).
32. A. Fuess (2001).
33. C. Delery (2006).
34. A. Rougeulle (1990); C. Delery (2006).
35. P. Cressier (1998).
36. Ibn Hayyan (1979), 454.
37. P. Bonnassie (1975–1976); P. Sénac (2000a).
38. P. Sénac (2001).
39. P. Bonnassie (1975–1976).

12. ISLAM'S MARITIME SOVEREIGNTY IN THE FACE OF LATIN EXPANSION

1. Al-Zuhri (1968), 229; Spanish trans. (1991), 92–93.
2. Ibn Abi Zar (1964), 201; Spanish trans. (1973), 400. The chronicler's information is not always reliable.
3. A. Amara (2003).
4. É. Lévi-Provençal (1941).
5. C. Picard (2010b).
6. J. Arbach (1995).
7. A. Huici Miranda (1956–1957a); P. Buresi (2004).
8. C. Picard (2000).

9. C. Picard (1997b).
10. A. Bel (1903); P. Guichard (1990–1991); D. Abulafia (1994, 1996); A. Campaner y Fuertes (1984).
11. C. Picard (1992).
12. Ibn ʿAbdun (1947, 1955).
13. P. Buresi (2004).
14. D. Valérian (2006a).
15. O. R. Constable (2003).
16. M. Cherif (1996).
17. C.-E. Dufourcq (1965).
18. Abu Shama (1898), 177–181.
19. Al-Nuʿman (1951–1961), 308, English trans. (2002–2004), 451; D. Bramoullé (2011), 438.
20. C. Cahen (1983).
21. M. Balard (1999); A. L. Udovitch (1999).
22. O. R. Constable (2003).
23. D. Bramoullé (2011).
24. M. Ouerfelli (2008).
25. É. Vallet (2007, 2010, 2012).

CONCLUSION

Epigraph: Quoted by P. Guichard (1990–1991), from Ibn al-Abbar, 114.

1. R. Lopez (1974).
2. F. Braudel (1995); J. Le Goff (1986).
3. H. Bresc (1986).
4. Y. Dejugnat (2010).
5. A.-M. Eddé (2008), 240–241; L. Pouzet (1975).
6. F.-X. Fauvelle-Aymar and B. Hirsch (2003); A. Miquel (1977).
7. D. Bramoullé (2011); É. Vallet (2010).

GLOSSARY

abna': Members of the family of the Abbasid caliph.

adab: "Good manners" taught during the first centuries of Islam, based on Iranian treatises translated into Arabic and welcomed by educated circles of Baghdad, before being circulated throughout the Muslim world. The *adab* also refers to a literary current found in Baghdad as of the ninth century and comparable to the encyclopedic spirit of the French seventeenth century.

'aja'ib: (Book of) Wonders.

akhbar: "Reports" or "stories"; plural of *khabar,* which refers to news in a more general sense. The first *akhbar* recounted the life of Muhammad. They later covered the lives of the Shiite imams, before providing the first historical works of Islam.

'asabiyya: Solidarity based on kinship and especially tribal solidarity, which according to Ibn Khaldun was the essential virtue of the tribes and gave them the advantage over "sedentary" peoples.

atraf (sing. *tarf*): Capes (headlands or promontories). In administrative books, these were autonomously administered strategic sites on Muslim coastlines.

Al-'Awasim: Fortified cities on the Syrian border, the seats of the frontier governors and bases for troops (*jund*) away from the front lines.

barid: Mail, postal service, and, by extension, strategic routes of the empire.

Bayt al-Hikma: "House of Wisdom," name given to the "academy" where Abbasid caliph al-Ma'mun brought scholarly works and scholars.

dar al-sina'a: Dockyard.

dhimma: "Pact of protection" that defined *dhimmi* status.

dhimmi: "Tributaries" or "protected persons" featured in the Koran as "people of the Book" (*ahl al-Kitab*): Jews, Christians, and Zoroastrians who were granted freedom of worship, on condition of paying a special tax, the *jizya,* entailing an inferior status.

diwan: Administrative services; originally financial registers.

fay' (*ghanima*): Booty from a conquest or razzia, specifically defined by the jurists of the Muslim authorities based on information in the Koran and the hadiths.

fitna: Unrest or revolts within the Dar al-Islam; illegal war as opposed to jihad (legal war).

fuqaha' (pl. of *faqih*): Jurist(s), specialists in religious jurisprudence (*fiqh*). The qadis (judges) played an essential role as supervisors; those who reached the highest positions enjoyed great renown.

futuh (pl. of *fath*): Victory, term used to refer to Islam's conquests.

ghanima: See *fay'*.

ghazwa: Razzia and, by extension, conquest.

habus (*waqf*): Mortmain property, inalienable.

Hadith: Words or narrative attributed to Muhammad, passed down by the Companions of the Prophet. They were collected in the canonical texts.

hajib: The equivalent of the chamberlain, a dignitary in the caliph's immediate circle, particularly in the entourage of the Umayyad caliph of Córdoba.

halqa: Auction.

hisn (pl. *husun*): Fortified area, ranging in size from that of a fortress to that of a small city.

huffaz: Eminent members of the Berber tribes, recruited to become "officers" of the caliphate.

'idwatayn: "The two shores," name given to the Strait of Gibraltar.

iqlim: "Climate," term derived from the Greek (Ptolemy's seven climates) and used to refer to the different provinces of the Islamic world, beginning in the tenth century.

isnad: The chain of authorities attesting to the authenticity of the Prophet's sayings, and their transmission by those who had heard him speak.

jund: Army of Arab conquerors, later the army in general.

jundi (pl. of *junud*): An individual soldier.

khums (*quint*): Tax levied on the Latins.

khutba: The sermon given in Friday prayer.

kitab al-siyar: Texts on legal war (jihad).

kura: Administrative district.

madhhab: Islamic legal school.

madina (pl. *mudun*): City, capital.

maghazi: War expeditions (see *sira*).

maharis: Watchtowers.

Majus: Vikings.

maks: Illegal excise tax.

Mamlaka: The Islamic empire.

masalik wa l-mamalik: (Book of) routes and kingdoms.

mawsim (*moussem*): A large annual gathering to celebrate a city or region's saint.

Mihna: Inquisition.

misr: (Military) camp and, by extension, Misr: Egypt.

Mudawanna: Title of Sahnun's work on the law.

qaid: General.

qaid al-bahr: Admiral.

qarya (pl. *qura*): Village.

qasaba: Citadel (generally urban).

qasr (pl. *qusur*): Fort.

qaysariyya: Sultanate edifice devoted to trade in precious goods (derived from "Caesarian").

ra'is: Chief.

rihla: Journey; travel narrative.

risala: Message, dispatch, or report.

rusiyya: "Like a taut rope," a maritime leg in a straight line.

sahib al-bahr: Admiral.

sahil (pl. *sawahil*): Shore; maritime district or border.

Saqaliba: Slaves (generally military).

sayfa: Summer expedition.

sayyids: The highest members of the Almohad administration.

shahid: Martyr.

sina'a: See *dar al-sina'a.*

sira: Behavior, conduct; particularly used in reference to Muhammad.

siyar: Legal text on jihad.

sufun: Ships.

sulak al-sufun: Ship itineraries.

tabaqat: "Classes" and, by extension, biographical dictionaries, primarily comprising the lives of ulema (scholars), organized in alphabetical or chronological order.

Taktika: Byzantine military treatise; plural of *taktikon,* a list of precedence at the Byzantine court.

talaba (*tullab*): The elite of the government entourage.

taqwiran: "In a curve," a maritime leg following the coast.

ta'rikh: History.

tariq: Path, itinerary, by land (*al-barr*) or by sea (*al-bahr*).

thaghr (pl. *thughur*): Frontier, with the same meaning as in English: the frontiers of a state.

wali: Governor.

Terms are primarily based on J. Sourdel and D. Sourdel, *Dictionnaire historique de l'Islam* (Paris: Presses universitaires de France, 1996).

CHRONOLOGIES

References to Muslim naval expeditions in the western Mediterranean in the period of the Arab conquest (Greek, Latin, and Arabic sources):

664	raid against Sicily from Barca with ships from Egypt
703	raid against Sardinia from Egypt
704–705	raid against Sicily from Ifriqiya; raid against Sardinia and the Balearic Islands
705–706	raid against Syracuse from Ifriqiya
706	raid against Sardinia (point of departure not mentioned)
707–708	raid against Sardinia
710–711	raid against Sardinia from Ifriqiya
720	raid against Sicily from Ifriqiya
728–729	raid against Sicily from Ifriqiya
729–730	raid against Sicily from Ifriqiya
730–731	raid against Sicily from Ifriqiya
732–733	raid against Sicily and Sardinia
733–734	raid against Sicily from Ifriqiya
734–735	raid against Sicily from Ifriqiya
735	raid against Sardinia
737	raid against Sardinia
739	siege of Syracuse from Ifriqiya
752–753	raid against Sicily and Sardinia from Ifriqiya

Raids mentioned leaving from al-Andalus during the period of "Saracen piracy" (Latin and Muslim sources):

798	raid against the Balearic Islands
799	raid against the Balearic Islands
800–805	mentions of Muslim pirates near the coasts of Provence and Italy

806 raid against Pantelleria and Corsica
807–808 raid against Sardinia and Corsica
809 raid against Corsica
810 raid against Sardinia and Corsica
812 raid against Sardinia and Corsica
813 raid against Corsica, Sardinia, the bay of Naples, Ponza, Lampedusa, Civitavecchia, and the region of Reggio; the Count of Ampurias captures eight Muslim ships near Mallorca (treaty between al-Hakam I and Charlemagne)
816–817 raid against Sardinia
830 three hundred ships from Tortosa sent as reinforcements to Sicily
834 raid against southern Italy
839 raid against southern Italy
850 the sack of the abbey of Saint-Césaire
869 the sack of Arles
c. 890–892 Andalusians in La Garde-Freinet (Fraxinetum)
933–934 raid against Sardinia
934–935 raid against Sardinia
972 abduction of Majolus, abbot of Cluny; end of Fraxinetum
1014 raid against Sardinia
1015 raid against Sardinia
1054 raid against Sardinia

SELECTED BIBLIOGRAPHY

PRIMARY SOURCES

Abu l-Fida'. (1840). *Kitâb taqwîm al-Buldân*. Edited by M. Reinaud and W. Mac Guckin de Slane. Paris. Translated by M. Reinaud (Paris, 1848) and Guyard (Paris, 1883).

Abu Shama. (1898). *Livre des deux jardins, ou histoire des deux règnes*. In *Recueil des historiens des Croisades*. Vol. 2, *Historiens orientaux*. Paris.

Abu Yusuf Ya'qub. (1921). *Le livre de l'impôt foncier*. Translated by E. Fagnan. Paris: Librairie orientaliste Paul Geuthner. French translation of *Kitâb al-Kharâj*.

Al-Abyari, ed. (1981). *Akhbâr Majmû'a fî fath al-Andalus*. New ed. Cairo.

Agapius. (1901). *Kitâb al-'Unwân*. Edited and translated by A. Vasiliev. Patrologia orientalis, vols. 5, 7, 8, and 11. Paris.

Amari, M., ed. (1863). *I diplomi arabi del Archivio fiorentino*. Florence.

Azzawi, A., ed. (1996). *Rasâ'il Muwahhidiyya: Majmû'a jadida*. Kenitra, Morocco: Université Ibn Tofayll.

———, ed. (2006). *Rasâ'il diwâniyya Muwahhidiyya*. Rabat.

Al-Badisi. (1926). *Vie des saints du Rif*. Translated by G. S. Colin. Paris: Librairie ancienne Honoré Champion. French translation of *Al-maqsad al-Sharîf wa l-manza' al-latif fî l-ta'rîf bi sulahâ' al-Rîf*.

———. (1982). *Al-maqsad al-Sharîf wa l-manza' al-latif fî l-ta'rîf bi sulahâ' al-Rîf*. Edited by S. A. A'rab. Rabat.

Al-Bakri. (1965). *Description de l'Afrique septentrionale par Abou Obeïd el-Bekri [Kitâb l-masâlik wa l-Mamâlik]*. New ed. Edited and with partial French translations by Mac Guckin de Slane. Paris: Maisonneuve.

———. (1968). *Jughrâfiyatu l-Andalus wa l-Urûbbâ min Kitâbi l-masâlik wa l-Mamâlik li Abi 'Ubaydi l-Bakrî*. Edited by Al-Hajji. Beirut.

———. (1982). *Geografía de España de Abû 'Ubayd al-Bakri*. Translated by E. Vidal. Saragossa, Spain. Partial French translation of *Jughrâfiyatu l-Andalus wa l-Urûbbâ min Kitâbi l-masâlik wa l-Mamâlik li Abi ʿUbaydi l-Bakrî.*

———. (1993). *Kitâb al-masâlik wa l-mamâlik de Abû ʿUbayd al-Bakri (XIe siècle).* Partial critical edition with introduction, French translation, and notes by S. Bouamrane. PhD diss., Université Paris-I.

Al-Baladhuri. (1863–1866). *Kitâb futûh al-buldân.* Edited by M. J. De Goeje. Leiden: Brill.

———. (1968). *The Origins of the Islamic State.* Translated by P. K. Hitti and F. C. Murgotten. New York. English translation of *Kitâb futûh al-buldân.* Originally published 1916.

Al-Balawi, ed. (n.d.). *Al-ʿAtâ' al-jazil fi fann al-Tarsil: Lettres almohades.* Manuscript no. 6148. Rabat: Bibliothèque royale de Rabat.

Al-Baydhaq. (1928). *L'Histoire des Almohades d'Abû Bakr b. ʿAlî al-Sanhâjî, surnommé al-Baydhaq: Documents inédits d'histoire almohade: Fragments manuscrits du "Legajo" 1919 du Fonds arabe de l'Escurial* [*Kitâb akhbâr al-Mâhdi Ibn Tûmart wa bidâyat dawlat al-muwahhidîn*]. Edited and with French translations by É. Lévi-Provençal. Paris: Geuthner.

Al-Biruni. (1929). *Kitâb al-Hind.* Edited by C. E. Sachau. Leiden.

———. (1996). *Le Livre de l'Inde.* Translated by V. Monteil. Paris: Sindbad. Partial French translation of *Kitâb al-Hind.*

Canard, M., trans. (1958). *Vie de l'Ustadh Jaudhar (contenant sermons, lettres et rescrits des premiers califes fatimides écrits par Mansûr le secrétaire à l'époque du calife al-ʿAzîz billâh, 365–386/975–996).* 2nd series, vol. 20. Algiers: Publications de l'Institut d'études orientales d'Algiers. French translation of *Sîrat Ustadh Jawdhar.*

Al-Dabbi. (1989). *Kitâb Bughyat al-Multamis fî ta'rîkh rijâl al-Andalus.* New ed. Edited by Al-Abyari. Cairo. Originally published in Madrid in 1885, edited by F. Codera and J. Ribera.

De Gonzalez, E. J., ed. and trans. (1889). *Fath al-Andalus.* Spanish translation. Algiers.

Ducène, J.-C., ed. (2010). *L'Afrique dans le Uns al-muhâj wa rawd al-furaj, d'al-Idrîsî.* Leuven, Belgium: Peeters.

Eddé, A.-M., and F. Micheau, eds. (2002). *L'Orient au temps des croisades: Textes arabes.* Paris: GF-Flammarion.

Fagnan, E., trans. (1993). *L'Afrique septentrionale au XIIe siècle de notre ère: Description extraite du "Kitâb al-Istibsâr."* Frankfurt am Main, Germany: Goethe Universität. French translation of *Kitâb al-Istibsâr fî ʿajâ'ib al-amsâr.* Originally published 1900.

Foulon, B., and E. Tixier du Mesnil, eds. (2008). *Al-Andalus: Anthologie.* Paris: Garnier-Flammarion.

Gabrieli, F., ed. (1996). *Chroniques arabes des croisades.* Paris: Sindbad.

Galland, A., trans. (1965). *Les Mille et Une Nuits.* Paris: Garnier-Flammarion.

Gautier Dalché, P., ed. (1996). *Carte marine et portulan au XIIe siècle: Le Liber de existencia riveriarum et forma maris nostri Mediterranei.* Collection of the École française de Rome, no. 203. Rome: École française de Rome.

Al-Gharnati. (1993). *Tuhfat al-albâb wa nukhbat al-i'jab.* Edited by I. Al-Arbi. Casablanca, Morocco: Dâr al-Afâq al-jadida.

Goitein, S. D., ed. (1973). *Letters of Medieval Jewish Traders, Translated from the Arabic with Introduction and Notes.* Princeton, NJ: Princeton University Press.

Goitein, S. D., and M. A. Friedman, eds. (2007). *India Traders of the Middle Ages.* Leiden: Brill.

Al-Harawi. (1953). *Kitâb al-isharât ilâ ma'rifat al-ziyârât.* Edited by J. Sourdel-Thomine. Damascus.

———. (1957). *Guide des lieux de pèlerinages.* Translated by J. Sourdel-Thomine. Damascus. French translation of *Kitâb al-isharât ilâ ma'rifat al-ziyârât.*

———. (2004). *A Lonely Wayfarer's Guide to Pilgrimage: 'Ali ibn Abi Bakr al-Harawi's Kitâb al-ishârât ilâ ma'rifat al-ziyârât.* Princeton, NJ: Darwin.

Al-Himyari. (1938). *La Péninsule Ibérique au Moyen Âge d'après le "Kitâb al-Rawd al-Mi'târ": Texte arabe des notices relatives à l'Espagne, au Portugal et au sud-ouest de la France.* Edited and with French translations by É. Lévi-Provençal. Leiden: Brill.

———. (1970). In I. 'Abbas, "Ittihâd al-bahriyyîn fî Bajjâna bi-l-Andalus." *Abhâth* 23:3–14 (Arabic section).

———. (2005). In *Almería andalusí y su territorio,* edited and translated by J. Lirola Delgado, 135–150. Almería, Spain. Spanish translation.

Hoffmann, H., ed. (1980). *Die Chronik von Montecassino.* Vol. 1 of *Chronique du Mont-Cassin: Chronica Monasterii Casinensis.* Monumenta Germaniae Historica, Scriptores, no. 34. Hanover, Germany: Hahn.

Ibn al-Abbar. (1964). *Kitâb al-hulla al-siyâra.* Edited by H. Monés. 2 vols. Cairo.

Ibn 'Abd al-Hakam. (1922). *History of the Conquest of Egypt, North Africa and Spain [Kitâb futûh Misr wa akhbârruhâ].* Edited by C. Torrey. New Haven, CT: Yale University Press.

———. (1948). Edited and translated by A. Gateau. Algiers: Carbonel. French translation of *Kitâb futûh Misr wa akhbârruhâ.*

Ibn 'Abdun. (1947). *Séville musulmane au début du XIIe siècle: Le traité d'Ibn 'Abdûn sur la vie urbaine et les corps de métiers.* Paris: Maisonneuve. French translation of *Risâlâ fi l-qadâ wa l-hisba.*

———. (1955). *Documents inédits sur la vie sociale et économique en Occident musulman au Moyen Âge, 1re série: Trois traités hispaniques de hisba [Risâlâ fi l-qadâ wa l-hisba].* Edited and with French translations by É. Lévi-Provençal, 1–65. Cairo: Institut français d'archéologie orientale.

Ibn Abi Firas. (n.d.). *Kitâb akriyat al-sufun wa-l-nizâ'bayna ahlihâ.* Edited by Mustafa Anwar Tahir. *Les Cahiers de Tunisie* 123–124:5–52.

Ibn Abi Zar'. (1964). *Textos Medievales.* 2nd ed. Translated by A. Huici Miranda. Valencia. Spanish translation of *Kitâb al-anîs al-mutrib bi rawd al-qirtâs.*

———. (1973). *Kitâb al-anîs al-mutrib bi rawd al-qirtâs.* Rabat.

Ibn 'Asakir. (1959). *Description de la ville de Damas d'Ibn 'Asâkir.* Translated by N. Elisséeff. Damascus. French translation of vol. 1 of *Ta'rîkh madînat Dimashq.*

———. (1995–2000). *Ta'rîkh madînat Dimashq.* Edited by al-'Amrawi and Dar al-Fikr. 80 vols. Beirut. ed. Arab Academy of Damascus, 10 vols. since 1965.

Ibn al-Athir. (1901). *Annales du Maghreb et de l'Espagne.* Translated by E. Fagnan. Algiers. Partial French translation of *Kitâb al-Kâmil fî ta'rîkh.*

———. (1965–1967). *Kitâb al-Kâmil fî ta'rîkh.* New ed. Edited by C. J. Tornberg. 13 vols. Beirut. Originally published in Leiden in 1851–1876.

Ibn Bashkuwal. (1966). *Kitâb al-Sila.* Edited by Khalaf. Cairo.

Ibn Bassam al-Shantarini. (2000). *Al-Dhakîra fî mahâsin ahl al-Jazîra.* Edited by I. 'Abbas. 4 vols. Beirut.

Ibn Battuta. (1853–1859). *Tuhfat al-nuzzâr fi gharâ'ib al-amsâr wa 'ajâ'ib al-asfar.* Edited by C. Defrémery and B. R. Sanguinetti. 4 vols. Paris; new ed. Beirut: Dâr Sâdir-Dâr, 1960.

———. (1991). In *Voyageurs arabes: Ibn Fadlân, Ibn Jubayr, Ibn Battûta et un auteur anonyme,* translated by P. Charles-Dominique. Bibliothèque de la Pléiade. Paris: Gallimard. French translation of *Tuhfat al-nuzzâr fi gharâ'ib al-amsâr wa 'ajâ'ib al-asfar.*

Ibn Duqmaq. (1893–1896). *Kitâb al-Intisâr lî wâsitat 'Aqd al-Amsâr.* Edited by K. Vollers. Cairo: Bûlâq.

Ibn Fadlan. (1956). *Voyage chez les Bulgares de la Volga.* Edited by A. P. Kovalesky, *Le Livre d'Ahmed ibn Fadlân sur son voyage vers la Volga dans les années 921–922, articles, traductions et commentaires.* Kharkov, Ukraine: Gorky National University.

———. (1991). *Ibn Fadlân: Récit de voyage.* In *Voyageurs arabes: Ibn Fadlân, Ibn Jubayr, Ibn Battûta et un auteur anonyme,* translated by P. Charles-Dominique. Bibliothèque de la Pléiade. Paris: Gallimard.

Ibn al-Faqih al-Hamadhani. (1885). *Mukhtasar kitâb al-buldân.* Edited by M. J. De Goeje. Leiden: Brill.

———. (1973). *Abrégé du Livre des pays.* Translated by H. Massé. Damascus. French translation of *Mukhtasar kitâb al-buldân.*

Ibn al-Faradi. (1954). *Ta'rîkh 'ulamâ' l-Andalus.* Edited by al-Husayni. Cairo.

Ibn Habib. (1991). *Kitâb al-Ta'rîkh.* Edited by J. Aguadé. Madrid.

Ibn Hani'. (n.d.). *Dîwân.* Edited by A. Zâhid. Partial French translation in M. Canard, "L'impérialisme des Fatimides et leur propaganda," *Annales de l'Institut d'études orientales* 6 (1942–1947): 106–136.

Ibn Hawqal. (1938–1939). *Viae et regna: Descriptio ditionis moslemicae* [*Kitâb surat al-ard*]. Edited by G. H. Kramers. Leiden.

———. (1964). *Configuration de la Terre.* Translated by G. H. Kramers and G. Wiet. 2 vols. Paris. French translation of *Kitâb surat al-ard.*

Ibn Hayyan. (1937). *Al-Muqtabis: Chronique du règne du calife umaiyade 'Abd Allah à Cordoue.* Edited by M. M. Antuña. Paris.

———. (1950–1959). *Cuadernos de Historia de España.* Vols. 12–30. Translated by J. Guraieb. French translation of *Al-Muqtabis: Chronique du règne du calife umaiyade 'Abd Allah à Cordoue.*

———. (1965). *Al-Muqtabis fi Akhbâr balad al-Andalus.* Edited by A. Hajji. Beirut.

———. (1967). *Anales Palatinos del Califa de Cordoba al-Hakam II.* Translated by J. García Gomez. Madrid. Spanish translation of *Al-Muqtabis fi Akhbâr balad al-Andalus.*

———. (1973). *Al-Muqtabis min anba: Ahl al-Andalus.* Edited by M. A. Makki. Beirut.

Crónica del califa 'Abd al-Rahmân III al-Nâsir entre los años 912–942, ed. Chalmeta. Madrid: Corriente, Subh, 1979; Spanish trans. Viguera, Corriente. Saragossa, "Textos Medievales," no. 64, 1981 (Ibn Hayyan, *Muqtabis* V).

———. (1999). *Kitâb al-Muqtabis fi ta'rîkh rijal al-Andalus: Muqtabis II: Anales de los Emires de Córdoba Alhaqam I (180–206H/796–822 J.-C.) y Abderramán II (206–232/822–847).* Edited by J. Vallvé Bermejo. Madrid.

———. (2001). *Crónica de los emires Alhakam I y Abdarrahmân II entre los años 796 y 847.* Translated by M. A. Makki and F. Corriente. Saragossa. Spanish translation of *Kitâb al-Muqtabis fi ta'rîkh rijal al-Andalus: Muqtabis II.*

Ibn Hazm. (1948). *Kitâb Jamharat ansâb al-'arab.* Edited by É. Lévi-Provençal. Cairo. Spanish translation of passages about Spanish Arabs by E. Teres in "Linajes Arabes en al-Andalus," *Al-Andalus* 22 (1957).

Ibn 'Idhari. (1901–1904). *Histoire de l'Afrique et de l'Espagne intitulée al-bayano l-mogrib.* Translated by E. Fagnan. 2 vols. Algiers. French translation of *Kitâb al-Bayân al-Mugrib fî Akhbâr mulûk al-Andalus wa l-Magrib.*

———. (1930). *Kitâb al-Bayân al-Mugrib fî Akhbâr mulûk al-Andalus wa l-Magrib.* Edited by É. Lévi-Provençal. Vol. 3, *Histoire de l'Espagne musulmane au XIe siècle, texte arabe publié pour la première fois d'après un manuscrit de Fès.* Paris: Geuthner.

———. (1948–1951). *Kitâb al-Bayân al-Mugrib fî Akhbâr mulûk al-Andalus wa l-Magrib: Texte arabe des parties relatives au Maghreb et à l'Espagne de la conquête au XIe siècle.* Edited by G. S. Colin and É. Lévi-Provençal. 2 vols. Leiden.

———. (1961). "Un Fragmento inédito de Ibn 'Idhârî sobre los Almorávides." Edited by A. Huici Miranda. *Hespéris-Tamuda* 2:43–111.

———. (1976). *Kitâb al-Bayân al-Mughrib.* Edited by I. 'Abbas. Beirut.

———. (1985). *Kitâb al-Bayân al-Mughrib.* New ed. (Almohad period). Rabat.

———. (1993). *La caída del califato de Córdoba y los reyes de taifas.* Translated by F. Maillo Salgado. Salamanca. Spanish translation of *Kitâb al-Bayân al-Mugrib fî Akhbâr mulûk al-Andalus wa l-Magrib* (1930 ed.).

Ibn Jubayr. (1907). *The Travels of Ibn Jubayr.* Arabic text of *Tadhkira li akhbâr 'an ittifâqât al-afar,* with English glossary and notes. Edited by W. Wright and M. J. De Goeje. Leiden: Gibb Memorial Series, 1907.

———. (1949). *Voyages.* Translated by M. Godefroy-Demombynes. 3 vols. Paris: Geuthner. French translation of *Tadhkira li akhbâr 'an ittifâqât al-afar.*

Ibn Khaldun. (1983). *Ta'rîkh al-'allâma Ibn Khaldûn.* Beirut: Dâr al-Kitâb al-Lubnâni.

———. (2002). *Le Livre des exemples.* Vol. 1, *Autobiographie, Muqaddima.* Translated by A. Cheddadi. Bibliothèque de la Pléiade. Paris: Gallimard. Partial French translation of *Ta'rîkh al-'allâma Ibn Khaldûn.*

———. (2012). *Le Livre des exemples.* Vol. 2, *Histoire des Arabes et des Berbères du Maghreb.* Translated by A. Cheddadi. Bibliothèque de la Pléiade. Paris: Gallimard. Partial French translation of *Ta'rîkh al-'allâma Ibn Khaldûn.*

Ibn Khallikan. (1948). *Wafayât al-a'yyân.* 6 vols. Cairo.

Ibn al-Khatib. (1934). *Histoire de l'Espagne musulmane extraite du "Kitâb a'mâl al-a'lâm."* Edited by É. Lévi-Provençal. Rabat. Partial edition of *Kitâb a'mâl al-a'lâm fî ta'rîkh.*

Ibn Khurradadhbih. (1889). *Kitâb al-masâlik wa l-mamâlik* [885?]. Bibliotheca geographorum arabicorum 6. Leiden: Brill.

———. (1949). *Description du Maghreb et de l'Europe au IIIe/IXe siècle.* Edited and translated for the western area by M. Hadj-Sadok. Algiers. French translation of *Kitâb al-masâlik wa l-mamâlik.*

Ibn Mammati. (1943). *Kitâb qawânîn al-dawânîn.* Edited by A. S. Atiya. Cairo.

Ibn al-Nadim. (1871). *al-Fihrist.* Edited by G. Flügel. Leipzig.

———. (1970). Translated by B. Dodge. 2 vols. New York. English translation of *al-Fihrist.*

Ibn al-Qattan. (1964). *Nazm al-Jumân li tartib mâ salafa min akhbâr al-zamân.* Edited by M. A. Makki. Beirut.

Ibn Qutayba al-Dinawari. (1904). *Kitâb al-imâma wa-al-siyâsa.* Edited by Maktabat al-Halabî. 2 vols. Cairo.

Ibn al-Qutiyya. (1868). *Ta'rîkh iftitâh l-Andalus.* Edited by P. de Gayangos, E. Saavedra, and F. Codera. Madrid.

———. (1926). *Historia de la conquista de España de Abnelcotia el Cordobés.* Translated by J. Ribeira. De obras arábigas de Historia y geografía de la Real Academia de la Historia 2. Madrid. Spanish translation of *Ta'rîkh iftitâh l-Andalus.*

Ibn Rushd, Abu l-Walid. (1987). *Kitâb al-Fatâwâ.* Edited by Ibn al-Tahir al-Talili. 3 vols. Beirut.

Ibn Rustah. (1967). *Kitâb al-A'lâq al-nafîsa.* Edited by M. J. De Goeje. Bibliotheca geographorum arabicorum 7. Leiden: Brill. Originally published 1882.

———. (1949). *Ibn Khurradâdhbih, Ibn al-Faqîh al-Hamadhânî et Ibn Rustah: Description du Maghreb et de l'Europe au IIIe–IXe siècle: Extraits du "Kitâb al-Masâlik wa l-Mamâlik," du "Kitâb al-Buldân" et du "Kitâb al-A'lâq al-nafîsa."* Edited and translated by M. Hadj-Sadok. Algiers: Carbonel. Partial French translation of *Kitâb al-A'lâq al-nafîsa.*

———. (1967). *Les Atours précieux.* Translated by G. Wiet. Cairo. French translation of *Kitâb al-A'lâq al-nafîsa.*

Ibn Sa'd Muhammad. (1917–1940). *Kitâb al-Tabaqât al-kabîr.* Edited by E. Sachau *et alii.* 9 vols. Leiden: Brill.

———. (1969). Translated by A. Huici Miranda. Valencia. Spanish translation of *Al-mann bi l-imâma.*

———. (1998). Edited by I. 'Abbas. 9 vols. Beirut.

Ibn Sahib al-Sala. (1964). *Al-mann bi l-imâma.* Edited by Abd al-Rahman al-Tazi. Beirut.

Ibn Shaddad, 'Izz al-Din. (1980–1981). *Al-a'lâq al-khatîra fî dhikr umarâ' al-Shâm wa-al-Jazîra.* Partial ed. Edited by A.-M. Eddé. *Bulletin d'études orientales* 32–33:316–367.

———. (1984). *Description de la Syrie du Nord.* Translated by A.-M. Eddé. Damascus. French translation of *Al-a'lâq al-khatîra fî dhikr umarâ' al-Shâm wa-al-Jazîra.*

Ibn Simak. (1951). *Al-hulâl al-Mawshiyya: Crónica árabe de las dinastías almorávide, almohade y benimerín.* Translated by A. Huici Miranda. Tétouan, Morocco. Spanish translation of *Kitâb al-hulâl al-Mawshiyya fi dhikr al-akhbâr al-Marrâkushiya.*

———. (1979). *Kitâb al-hulâl al-Mawshiyya fi dhikr al-akhbâr al-Marrâkushiya.* Edited by S. Zakkar and A. Zamama. Casablanca, Morocco.

Ibn al-Tuwayr. (1992). *Nuzhat al-Muqlatayn fi akhbâr al-dawlatayn.* Edited by A. F. Sayyid. Beirut: F. Steiner Verlag.

Ibn Wasif Shah. (1898a). *Abrégé des Merveilles.* Translated by B. Carra de Vaux. Paris. French translation of *Mukhtasar al-'ajâ'ib.*

———. (1898b). *Mukhtasar al-'ajâ'ib.* With commentary by C. F. Seybold. *Orientalistische Literaturzeitung* 1:146–150.

Ibn Yunus. (2000). *Ta'rîkh Ibn Yûnus al-Misrî.* Edited by 'Abd al-Fattah. 2 vols. Beirut.

Al-Idrisi. (1975). *Al-Idrisi, Opus Geographicum* [*Nuzhat al-mushtâq fi Ikhtirâk al-afak*]. Edited by Istituto Universitario di Napoli e Istituto per il Medio e Estremo Oriente. Naples.

———. (1989). *Los caminos de al-Andalus en el siglo XII* [*Uns al-muhâj wa rawd al-fura*]. Edited and with Spanish translations by M. J. Mizal. Madrid: Consejo Superior de Investigaciones Científicas, Instituto de Filología.

———. (1999). *La Première Géographie de l'Occident.* Translated by H. Bresc and A. Nef. Paris: GF-Flammarion. French translation of *Nuzhat al-mushtâq fi Ikhtirâk al-afak.*

Al-Istakhri. (1961). *Kitâb al-masâlik wa l-mamâlik.* Edited by A. al-Hînî. Cairo. Previously published in an edition edited by M. J. De Goeje, Bibliotheca geographorum arabicorum (Leiden: Brill, 1927).

'Iyad, Qadi. (1981–1984). *Tartîb al-madârik.* 8 vols. Rabat: Varios.

———. (1991). *Madhâhib al-hukkâm fî nawâzil al-ahkam.* Edited by M. Bensherifa. Rabat.

———. (1998). *Madhâhib al-hukkâm fî nawâzil al-ahkam.* Translated into Spanish by D. Serrano. Madrid.

Kamal, Y., ed. (1987). *Monumenta cartografica Africae et Aegypti.* New ed. Frankfurt: Sezgin. Originally published 1926–1952.

Kamil Husayn, M., and M. A. Sha'ira, eds. (1954). *Sîrat Ustadh Jawdhar.* Cairo.

Khalifa b. Khayyat al-Usfuri. (1967). *Ta'rîkh.* Edited by A. D. al-'Umari. Najaf, Iraq.

Al-Khushani [Ibn Harith]. (1914). *Historia de los jueces de Córdoba.* Edited and translated by J. Riberay Tarragó. Madrid. Spanish translation of *Qudât Qurtuba.*

———. (1922). *Ajbâr al-Fuqâhâ'.* Edited by M. L. Avila and L. Molina. Madrid: Consejo Superior de Investigaciones Científicas-AECIA.

———(1982). *Qudât Qurtuba.* Edited by I. al-Abyâri. Cairo.

Al-Kinani. (1983). *Kitâb akriyat al-sufun wa l-nazâ bayna ahlihâ.* Edited by M. A. Tahir. *Cahiers de Tunisie* 31, no. 123–124:5–52.

———. (2006). *Admiralty and Maritime Laws in the Mediterranean Sea (ca. 800–1500): The* Kitâb *Akriyat al-sufun vis-à-vis the Nomos Rhodion Nautikos*. Translated by H. S. Khalilieh. Leiden: Brill. 273–330. English translation of *Kitâb akriyat al-sufun wa l-nazâ bayna ahlihâ*.

Kindi, 'Umar b. Muhammad al-. (1912). *Kitâb al-wulât wa kitâb al-Qudât*. Edited by R. Guest. London.

———. (1971). *Fada'il Misr*. Edited by I. A. Adawi and A. M. Umar. Cairo.

———. (2012). *Histoire des cadis égyptiens*. Translated by M. Tillier. Cairo: Institut français d'archéologie orientale. French translation of *Kitâb al-wulât wa kitâb al-Qudât*.

Lafuente y Alcantara, D. E., ed. and trans. (1897). *Akhbâr Majmû'a fî fath al-Andalus, Ajbar Machmûa (colección de tradiciones): Crónica Anónima del siglo XI*. Madrid: Colección de Historia y Geografía, Real Academia 1.

Lévi-Provençal, É., ed. (1929). *Documents inédits d'histoire almohade: Fragments manuscrit du "Legajo" 1919 arabe de l'Escurial*. Paris: Geuthner.

———. (1941). *Trente-sept lettres officielles almohades*. Rabat: Collection of Arabic texts of the Institut des hautes études marocaines

———. (1942). *Un recueil de lettres officielles almohades: Étude diplomatique, analyse et commentaire historique*. Paris: Larose.

———. (1953). "La description de l'Espagne d'Ahmad al-Râzî." French translation from texts in Castilian and Portuguese. *Al-Andalus* 8.

Lévi-Provençal, É., and E. Garcia Gomez, eds. and trans. (1950). *Una crónica anónima de 'Abd al-Rahmân III al-Nâsir*. Madrid.

Lirola Delgado, J., ed. (2005). *Almería andalusí y su território: Textos geográficos*. Almería, Spain.

Al-Makhzumi. (1986). *Kitâb al-minhâj fi 'ilm kharâj Misr*. Edited by C. Cahen and Y. Ragib. Supplément aux Annales islamologiques, cahier no. 8. Cairo: Institut français d'archéologie orientale.

Al-Maliki. (1983). *Kitâb riyâd al-Nufûs*. Edited by B. al-Bakkush. 3 vols. Beirut.

Malik b. Anas. (1971). *Kitâb al-Muwatta', recension de Yahyâ b. Yahyâ al-Laythi*. Edited by A. R. 'Armus. Beirut.

Al-Maqqari. (1840–1843). *The History of the Mohammedan Dynasties in Spain*. Translated by P. de Gayangos. 2 vols. London. English translation of *Kitâb Nafh al-Tîb*.

———. (1967). *Analectes sur l'Histoire et la littérature des Arabes d'Espagne*. Edited by R. Dozy. Amsterdam. Originally published 1855–1861.

———. (1968). *Kitâb Nafh al-Tîb*. Edited by I. 'Abbas. 8 vols. Beirut.

Al-Maqrizi. (1967–1973). *Itti'az al-Hunafâ' bi-akhbâr al-A'imma al-Fatimiyyîn al-khulafâ'*. Vol. 1 (1967) edited by M. Ata'. Vols. 2–3 (1971–1973) edited by M. H. M. Ahmad. Cairo.

———. (1991). *Kitâb al-Muqaffâ' al-Kabîr.* Edited by M. Yalaoui. 3 vols. Beirut.

———. (2002–2004). *Kitâb al-mawâ'iz wa l-i'tiba'âr fî dhikr al-khitât wa l-athâr.* Edited by A. F. Sayyid. 5 vols. London.

———. (2009). *Toward a shi'i Mediterranean Empire: Fatimid Egypt and the Founding of Cairo: The Reign of the Imam-Caliph al-Mu'izz from al-Maqrîzî's Itti'az al-Hunafâ'*. Translated by S. Jiwa. London: I. B. Tauris. Partial translation of *Itti'az al-Hunafâ' bi-akhbâr al-A'imma al-Fatimiyyîn al-khulafâ'*.

Al-Marrakushi 'Abd al-Wahid. (1955). *Lo admirable en el resumen de las noticias del Maghrib.* Translated by A. Huici Miranda. Tétouan, Morocco. Spanish translation of *Kitâb al-Mu'jib fî talkhîs akhbâr al-Maghrib.*

———. (1968). *Kitâb al-Mu'jib fî talkhîs akhbâr al-Maghrib.* Edited by R. Dozy. New ed. Amsterdam. Originally published 1881.

Mas Latrie, L. de, ed. (1866). *Traités de paix et de commerce et documents concernant les relations des Chrétiens avec les Arabes de l'Afrique septentrionale au Moyen Âge.* 2 vols. Paris.

Al-Mas'udi. (1861–1877). *Murûj al-dhahab.* Edited and translated by C. Barbier de Meynard and J. Pavet de Courteille. 2 vols. Paris.

———. (1894). *Kitâb al-Tanbih wa l-Ishrâf.* Bibliotheca geographorum arabicorum 8. Leiden: Brill.

———. (1896). *Le Livre de l'avertissement et de la révision.* Translated by B. Carra de Vaux. Paris. French translation of *Kitâb al-Tanbih wa l-Ishrâf.*

———. (1962–1965). *Les Prairies d'or.* Translated by C. Pellat. Paris: Société asiatique. French translation of *Murûj al-dhahab.*

Al-Mawardi. (1909). *Kitâb al-Ahkâm al-Sultâniyya.* Cairo.

———. (1984). *Les Statuts gouvernementaux.* New ed. Translated by E. Fagnan. Algiers: Office des traductions universitaires. French translation of *Kitâb al-Ahkâm al-Sultâniyya.*

Monumenta Germaniae Historica: Scriptores. Hanover, 1879.

Al-Muqaddasi. (1906). *Ahsan al-taqâsîm fî ma'rifat al-aqalîm.* Edited by M. J. De Goeje. Leiden: Brill.

———. (1950). *Al-Muqaddasî (vers 375–985): Description de l'Occident musulman au IVe–Xe siècle.* Edited and translated by C. Pellat. Algiers: Carbonel. Partial translation of *Ahsan al-taqâsîm fî ma'rifat al-aqalîm.*

———. (1963). *La Meilleure Répartition pour la connaissance des provinces.* Translated by A. Miquel. Damascus. French translation of *Ahsan al-taqâsîm fî ma'rifat al-aqalîm.*

Nasir-i Kushraw. (1881). *Sefer Nameh*. Edited and translated by C. Schefer. Paris.

Al-Nu'man, al-Qadi. (1951–1961). *Da'â'im al-Islâm*. Edited by A. Fyzee. Cairo.

———. (1975). *Iftitâh al-Da'wa*. Edited by F. Dachraoui. Tunis.

———. (1978). *Kitâb al-Majâlis wa l-musârayât*. Edited by al-Habib al-Faqi Ibrahim Shabbuh and Muhammad al-Ya'lawi. Tunis.

———. (2002–2004). *Pillars of Islam*. Translated by A. Fyzee. New Delhi. English translation of *Da'â'im al-Islâm*.

———. (2006). *Founding the Fatimid State: The Rise of an Early Islamic Empire*. Translated by H. Haji. London: I. B. Tauris. English translation of *Iftitâh al-Da'wa*.

Al-Nuwayri. (1917). *Historia de los musulmanes de España y África*. Translated by E. Gaspar Remiro. Granada. Partial Spanish translation of *Nihâyat al-'arab fi funun al-adab*.

———. (1963). *Nihâyat al-'arab fi funun al-adab*. New ed. Edited by Ahmad Zaki Pacha. 18 vols. Cairo. Originally published 1923–1944.

Al-Qalqashandi. (1987). *Subh al-A' shâ fî sinâ'a al-Inshâ'*. Edited by N. al-Khatib. 14 vols. Beirut.

Al-Qazwini. (1848). *Kitâb athâr al-bilâd*. Edited by F. Wustenfeld. Leipzig.

———. (1849). *Kitâb 'ajâ'ib al-makhlûqât*. Edited by F. Wustenfeld. Göttingen, Germany.

———. (1990). *Kitâb athâr al-bilâd* [partial translation]. In F. R. Castro, *El Occidente de al-Andalus en el Athâr al-bilâd de al-Qazwînî (1203–1283)*, translated by F. R. Castro.

Qudama b. Ja'far. (1967). *Kitâb al-Kharâj wa âinâ' ât al-kitâba*. New ed. Edited and with partial translations by M. J. De Goeje. Leiden: Brill. Originally published 1889.

Raghib, Y., ed. (1981). "Lettres nouvelles de Qurrâ b. Sharîk." *Journal of Near Eastern Studies* 40, no. 3:173–187.

———. (1982–1992). *Marchands d'étoffes du Fayyoum au IIIe/IXe siècle d'après leurs archives (actes et lettres)*. 2 vols. Cairo: Institut français d'archéologie orientale.

Al-Raqiq. (1990). *Ta'rîkh Ifrîqiyya wal-Maghrib*. Edited by A. A. al-Zaydân and I. U. A. Musa. Beirut: Dâr al-Gharb al-Islâmî.

Sa'id al-Andalusi. (1913). *Kitâb taqât al-umam*. Edited by P. Cheikho. Beirut.

———. (1966). *Les Catégories des nations*. Translated by R. Blachère. Paris. French translation of *Kitâb taqât al-umam*.

Al-Saqati. (1931). *Un manuel hispanique de hisba* [*Kitâb fî adâb al-hisba*]. Edited by G. S. Colin and É. Lévi-Provençal. Paris.

———. (1967–1968). "Libro del buen gobierno del zoco." Translated by P. Chalmeta. *Al-Andalus* 31, no. 1 (1967): 125–162; 32, no. 2 (1967): 359–397; 33, no. 1 (1968): 143–195; 33, no. 2 (1968): 367–434. Spanish translation of *Kitâb fî adâb al-hisba.*

Sauvaget, J., ed. and trans. (1948). *Relation de la Chine et de l'Inde.* Paris: Les Belles Lettres. French translation of *Akhbâr al-Sîn wa l-Hind* [ca. 851].

Savage-Smith, E., and Y. Rapoport, eds. and trans. (2007). *Book of Curiosities: Kitâb Gharâ'ib al-funûn wa milah al-'uyûn.* Critical ed. Oxford: Bodleian Library. http://www.bodley.ox.ac.uk/bookofcuriosities.

Sayf b. 'Umar al-Tamimi. (1995). *Kitâb al-Ridda wa l-futûh and Kitâb al-Jamal wa masir 'Â'isha wa 'Ali: A Facsimile of the Fragments Preserved in the University Library of Imâm Muhammad b. Sa'ûd Islamic University in Riyadh, Sa'udi Arabia.* Edited by Q. Al-Samarrai. 2 vols. Leiden: Smitskamp Oriental Antiquarium.

Severus. (1904–). *History of the Patriarchs of the Coptic Church of Alexandria.* Patrologia orientalis. Paris.

Al-Suyuti. (1997). *Ta'rîkh al-khulafâ'.* Edited by I. Salih. Beirut: Dâr Sâdir; Damascus: Dûr la-Bashâ'ir.

Al-Tabari. (1879–1901). *Ta'rîkh al-rusul wa l-mulûk.* Edited by M. J. De Goeje *et alii.* 15 vols. Leiden: Brill.

———. (1985–1999). *The History of al-Tabari.* 38 vols. Bibliotheca Persica. Albany: State University of New York Press. English translation of *Ta'rîkh al-rusul wa l-mulûk.*

Al-Tadili. (1984). *Kitâb al-Tasawwuf ilâ rijâl al-Tasawwuf.* Edited by A. Toufiq. Rabat: Faculty of Letters and Human Sciences of Rabat.

———. (1994). *Regard sur le temps des Soufis: Vie des saints du Sud marocain des Ve, VIe, VIIe siècles de l'hégire.* Translated by M. de Feynol. Casablanca, Morocco: Eddif, Unesco. Partial French translation of *Kitâb al-Tasawwuf ilâ rijâl al-Tasawwuf.*

Tamimi, Muhammad al-. (2002). *Al-Mustafâda fi manaqib al-ubbad bi-madînat Fas wa ma yaliha min al-bilâd.* Edited by M. Cherif. Tétouan, Morocco.

Theophanes. (1883). *Chronographia.* Edited by C. de Boor. Leipzig: Teubner.

———. (1963). *Chronographia.* New ed. Edited by G. Olms.

———. (1997). *The Chronicle of Theophanes Confessor: Byzantine and Near Eastern History, AD 284–813.* Translated by C. Mango. Oxford: Clarendon. English translation of *Chronographia.*

Toëlle, H., ed. (2009). *Les Suspendues: Al-mu'allaqât.* Paris: Flammarion.

Al-'Udhri. (1965). *Fragmentos geográfico-históricos de ilâ jami'a l-mamâlik wa -l-masâlik* [*Tarsi' al-akhbâr*]. Edited by A. Al-Ahwani. Madrid.

———. (1975–1976). "La Cora de Ilbira (Granada y Almería) en los siglos X y XI, según al-'Udhrî (1003–1085)." Translated by M. Sánchez Martínez. *Cuadernos de Historia del Islam* 7. Spanish translation of *Tarsi' al-akhbâr.*

Al-'Umari. (1927). *L'Afrique moins l'Égypte.* Translated by J. Gaudefroy-Demombynes. Paris. French translation of *Masâlik al-Absâr fi mamâlik al-Amsâr.*

———. (1985). *Masâlik al-Absâr fî mamâlik al-Amsâr.* Edited by M. Ahmad. Casablanca, Morocco.

Al-Wansharisi. (1981–1983). *Al-Mi'yâr al-mughrib wa l-jâmi' al-mu'rib 'an fatâwâ ahl Ifrîqiya wa l-Andalus wa l-Maghrib.* 13 vols. Rabat: Ministère de la Culture et des Affaires religieuses.

Al-Ya'qubi. (1937). *Le Livre des pays.* Translated by G. Wiet. Cairo. French translation of *Kitâb al-Buldân.*

———. (1960). *Ta'rîkh, Historiae.* 2 vols. Beirut: Dar Sadir. Originally published in Leiden in 1883.

———. (1962). *Mushâkalat al-nâs li-zamânihim.* Edited by W. G. Millward. Beirut.

———. (1964). "The Adapation of Men to Their Times: An Historical Essay by al-Ya'qûbi." Translated by W. G. Millward. *Journal of the American Oriental Society* 84:329–344. English translation of *Mushâkalat al-nâs li-zamânihim.*

———. (1967). *Kitâb al-Buldân.* Edited by M. J. De Goeje. Leiden: Brill. Originally published 1892.

Yaqut. (1866–1873). *Mu'jâm al-Buldân.* Edited by F. Wustenfeld. 6 vols. Leipzig: Jacuts geographisches Wörterbuch.

Zaglul, S., ed. (1958). *Kitâb al-Istibsâr fî 'ajâ'ib al-amsâr.* Alexandria.

Al-Zuhri. (1968). *Kitâb al-Ja'râfiya.* Edited by M. Hadj Sadok. *Bulletin d'études orientales* 21:9–312.

———. (1991). *El mundo en el siglo XII.* Translated by D. Bramon. Barcelona. Spanish translation of *Kitâb al-Ja'râfiya.*

WORKS CITED

'Abbadi, A. Salim al-. (1981). *Ta'rîkh al-bahriyya al-islâmiyya fi hawz al-bahr al-abyad al-mutawassit.* Beirut.

Abulafia, D. (1985). "The Pisan *Bacini* and the Medieval Mediterranean Economy: A Historian's View Point." *Papers in Italian Archeology* 5:287–302.

———. (1994). *A Mediterranean Emporium: The Catalan Kingdom of Majorca.* Cambridge: Cambridge University Press.

———. (1995). *Commerce and Conquest in the Mediterranean, 1100–1500.* Aldershot, UK: Variorum Reprints.

———. (1996). "El comercio y el Reino de Mallorca, 1150–1450." In *En las costas del Mediterráneo occidental: Les ciudades de la Península Ibérica y del renno de Mallorca y el comercio mediterráneo en la Edad Media,* edited by D. Abulafia, B. Garí, 115–154.

———. (2012). *The Great Sea: A Human History of the Mediterranean.* London: Penguin Books.

Acién Almensa, M. (1997). *Entre el feudalismo y el Islam: 'Umar Ibn Hafsûn en los historiadores, en las fuentes y en la historia.* Jaén, Spain: Universidad de Jaén.

Ageil, M. A. (1985). "Naval Policy and the Rise of the Fleet of Ifrîqiyyah from the 1st to 3d Centuries A.H. (7th to 9th Centuries A.D.)." PhD diss., University of Michigan.

Agius, D. (2008). *Classic Ships of Islam.* Leiden: Brill.

Ahrweiler, H. (1966). *Byzance et la mer.* Paris: Presses universitaires de France.

———. (1971). *Études sur les structures administratives et sociales de Byzance.* London: Variorum Reprints.

———. (1978). "Les ports byzantins (VIe–Xe siècles)." In Centro italiano di studi sull'alto medioevo, *La navigazione mediterranea nell'Alto Medioevo,* 269–285. Settimane di studio del Centro italiano di studi sull'Alto Medioevo 25. Spoleto, Italy: Presso la sede del Centro.

Aillet, C. (2010). *Les Mozarabes: Christianisme, islamisation et arabisation en péninsule Ibérique (IXe–XIIe siècle).* Madrid: Casa de Velázquez.

———, ed. (2012). "L'Ibadisme, une minorité au coeur de l'Islam." Special issue, *Revue des mondes musulmans et de la Méditerranée* 132.

Al-Andalus y el Mediterráneo. (1995). Madrid: El Legado Andalusí; Barcelona: Lunwerg Editores. Exhibition catalog.

'Allaoui, H. al-, and P. Buresi. (2006). "La chancellerie almohade." In *Los Almohades: Problemas y perspectivas,* edited by P. Cressier, M. Fierro, and L. Molina, 2:477–503. Madrid: Consejo Superior de Investigaciones Científicas.

Amara, A. (2003). "Pouvoir, économie et société dans le Maghreb hammadide (395 / 1004–547 / 1152)." PhD diss., Université Paris-I.

———. (2012). "La mer et les milieux mystiques d'après la production hagiographique du Maghreb occidental (XIIe–XVe s.)." In "La Mer et le sacré en Islam médiéval," edited by C. Picard, special issue, *Revue des mondes musulmans et de la Méditerranée* 130:33–52.

Amara, A., and A. Nef. (2000). "Al-Idrîsî et les Hammûdides de Sicile: Nouvelles données biographiques sur l'auteur du *Livre de Roger.*" *Arabica* 47:1–7.

Amari, M. (1933–1938). *Storia dei Musulmani di Sicilia.* 3 vols. Catania, Italy: C. A. Nallino.

Amri, N. (2008). *Les Saints en Islam, les messagers de l'espérance: Sainteté et eschatologie au Maghreb aux XIVe et XVe siècles.* Paris: Éditions du Cerf.

———. (2011). "*Ribât* et idéal de sainteté à Kairouan et sur le littoral ifrîqiyen du IIe / VIIIe au ive / xe siècle d'après le *Riyâd al-nufûs* d'al-Mâlikî." In *Islamisation et arabisation de l'Occident musulman médiéval (VIIIe–XIIe siècle),* edited by D. Valérian, 331–368. Paris: Publications de la Sorbonne.

Apellaniz, F. J. (2009). *Pouvoir et finance en Méditerranée pré-moderne: Le deuxième État mamelouk et le commerce des épices, 1382–1517.* Barcelona: Consejo Superior de Investigaciones Científicas.

Arbach, J. (1995). "Le domaine maritime en Occident musulman à l'époque almohade (XIIe–XIIIe siècles)." PhD diss., Université Toulouse–Le Mirail.

———. (1997). "Une 'école navale' à Marrakesh au temps des Almohades." *Mélanges pour le 25e anniversaire de l'UFR d'arabe de l'Université Toulouse–Le Mirail,* 4–15. Toulouse.

Arnaldez, R. (1962). "La guerre sainte selon Ibn Hazm de Cordoue." In *Études d'orientalisme dédiées à la mémoire de Lévi-Provençal,* 2:445–459. Paris: Maisonneuve et Larose.

Ashtor, E. (1969). *Histoire des prix et des salaires dans l'Orient médiéval.* Paris: SEVPEN.

———. (1978). *The Medieval Near-East: Social and Economic History.* Princeton, NJ: Princeton University Press; London: Variorum Reprints.

———. (1986). *East-West Trade in the Medieval Mediterranean.* London: Variorum Reprints.

Ayalon, D. (1996). *Le Phénomène mamelouk dans l'Orient islamique.* Paris: Presses universitaires de France.

Azuar Ruiz, R. (1989). *Denia islámica: Arqueología y poblamiento.* Alicante, Spain: Instituto de Cultura Juan Gil-Albert.

———. (1991). "Una Rábita hispanomusulmana del siglo X (Guardamar del Segura, Alicante, España)." *Archéologie islamique* 1:109–122.

———. (1992–1993). "La taifa de Denia en el comercio Mediterráneo del siglo XI." *Historia Medieval: Anales de la Universidad de Alicante* 9:39–52.

———, ed. (2004). *Fouilles de la Rábita de Guardamar.* Vol 1, *El ribât califal: Excavaciones e investigaciones (1984–1992).* Collection of the Casa de Velázquez 85. Madrid: Casa de Velázquez.

———. (2005). "Piratería y rábitas en la formación del Sharq al-Andalus." In "Portos Antigos do Mediterrâneo, Colloque de Mértola, 2003," edited by S. Macias and S. Gomez Martinez, special issue, *Arqueologia Medieval* 9:147–159.

Bacqué-Grammont, J.-L., F. de Polignac, and G. Bohas. (2000). "Monstres et murailles, Alexandre le bicornu, mythes et bon sens." In "Figures mythiques de l'Orient musulman," edited by D. Aigle, special issue, *Revue des mondes musulmans et de la Méditerranée* 89–90:109–127.

Balard, M. (1978). *La Romanie génoise (XIIe–début du XVe siècle).* 2 vols. Genoa: École française de Rome.

———. (1999). "Notes sur le commerce entre l'Italie et l'Égypte sous les Fatimides." In *L'Égypte fatimide: Son art et son histoire: Actes du colloque de mai 1998 de Paris,* edited by M. Barrucand, 627–633. Paris: Presses universitaires de Paris-Sorbonne.

———. (2005–2006). "Bilan de la quatrième croisade." In *1204, la quatrième croisade de Blois à Constantinople: Éclats d'empires,* edited by I. Villela-Petit, 79–85. Paris: Société française d'héraldique et de sigillographie, Blois-Paris. Exhibition catalog.

———. (2006). *Les Latins en Orient, XIe–XVe siècle.* Paris: Presses universitaires de France.

Bariani, L. (2003). *Almanzor.* Madrid: Nerea.

Barrucand, M., ed. (1999). *L'Égypte fatimide: Son art et son histoire: Actes du colloque de mai 1998 de Paris.* Paris: Presses universitaires de Paris-Sorbonne.

Beaujard, P. (2012). *Les mondes de l'océan Indien.* 2 vols. Paris: Armand Colin.

Bautier, R. H. (1953–1954). "Les relations commerciales entre l'Europe et l'Afrique du Nord et l'équilibre économique méditerranéen du XIIe au XIVe siècle." *Bulletin philologique et historique,* 399–416.

Bazzana, A., ed. (2011). *Madînat Shaltîsh: Une ville islamique dans les marécages de l'Odiel (Huelva, Andalousie) du IXe au XIIIe siècle.* Archéologie 14. Namur, Belgium: Institut du patrimoine wallon.

Bazzana, A., P. Cressier, and P. Guichard. (1988). *Les châteaux ruraux d'al-Andalus: Histoire et archéologie des husûn du sud-est de l'Espagne.* Madrid: Casa de Velázquez.

Bel, A. (1903). *Les Banou Ghânya, derniers représentants de l'Empire almoravide et leur lutte contre l'Empire almohade.* Paris: E. Leroux.

Benhima, Y. (2003). "Espace et société rurale au Maroc médiéval: Stratégies territoriales et structures de l'habitat: L'exemple de Safi." PhD diss., Université Lumière Lyon-II.

———. (2006). “L’évolution du peuplement et l’organisation du territoire de la région de Safi à l’époque almohade.” In *Los Almohades: Problemas y perspectivas,* edited by P. Cressier, M. Fierro, and L. Molina, 2:651–684. Madrid: Consejo Superior de Investigaciones Científicas.

———. (2011). “Quelques remarques sur les conditions de l’islamisation du Magrib al-Aqsâ: Aspects religieux et linguistiques.” in *Islamisation et arabisation de l’Occident musulman médiéval (VIIe–XIIe siècle),* edited by D. Valérian, 315–330. Paris: Publications de la Sorbonne.

Berti, G. (2000). “Pisa: Ceramiche e commerci (2° metà X–1° metà XIV s.).” In *I Congresso nazionale di archeologia medievale, Pisa, 29–31 maggio 1997,* edited by S. Gelichi, 346–351. Florence: All’Insegna del Giglio.

Berti, G., and T. Mannoni. (1998). “Pisa—A Seafaring Republic: Trading Relations with Islamic Countries in the Light of Ceramic Testimonies (2nd Half of 10th to Middle 13th c.), with a Report on Mineralogical Analysis.” In *Colloque international d’archéologie islamique—Le Caire, 1993,* edited by R. P. Gayraud, 301–317. Textes arabes et études islamiques 36. Cairo: Institut français d’archéologie orientale.

Berti, G., and L. Tongiorgi. (1981). *I bacini ceramici medievali delle chiese di Pisa.* Cuaderni di cultura materiale 3. Rome: L’Erma di Bretschneider.

Bianquis, T. (1989). *Damas et la Syrie sous la domination fatimide.* 2 vols. Damascus: Institut français.

Bianquis, T., P. Guichard, and M. Tillier, eds. (2012). *Les débuts du monde musulman, VIIe–Xe siècle.* 2 vols. Paris: Presses universitaires de France.

Blankinship, K. Y. (1994). *The End of the Jihâd State: The Reign of Hishâm Ibn ʿAbd al-Malik and the Collapse of the Umayyads.* New York: State University of New York Press.

Bonnassie, P. (1975–1976). *La Catalogne du milieu du Xe à la fin du XIe siècle.* 2 vols. Toulouse: Association des Publications de l’Université Toulouse–Le Mirail.

———. (2001). “Le littoral catalan durant le haut Moyen Âge.” In *Castrum 7: Zones côtières littorales dans le monde méditerranéen au Moyen Âge: Défense, peuplement, mise en valeur, Rome, 23–26 October 1996,* edited by J.-M. Martin, 251–271. Rome: École française de Rome; Madrid: Casa de Velázquez.

Bonner, M. (1996). *Aristocratic Violence and Holy War: Studies in the Jihad and the Arab-Byzantine Frontier.* New Haven, CT: American Oriental Society.

———. (2004). *Arab-Byzantine Relations in Early Islamic Times.* Aldershot, UK: Ashgate.

Borrut, A. (1999–2000). “L’espace maritime syrien au cours des premiers siècles de l’Islam (VIIe–Xe siècle): Le cas de la région entre Acre et Tripoli.” *Tempora: Annales d’histoire et d’archéologie* 10–11:1–33.

———. (2001). “Architecture des espaces portuaires et réseaux défensifs du littoral syro-palestinien dans les sources arabes (VIIe–XIe s.).” *Archéologie islamique* 11:21–46.

———. (2004). *Le Jihad: Origines, interprétations, combats.* Paris: Téraèdre.

———. (2005). “Entre tradition et histoire: Genèse et diffusion de l’image de Umar II.” In *Regards croisés sur le Moyen Âge arabe: Mélanges à la mémoire de Louis Pouzet s.j. (1928–2002),* edited by A.-M. Eddé and E. Gannagé, 58:329–378. Mélanges de l’Université Saint-Joseph. Beirut: Université Saint-Joseph Dar El-Machreq.

———. (2009). “La circulation de l’information historique entre les sources arabo-musulmanes et syriaques: Élie de Nisibe et ses sources.” In *Historiographie syriaque I,* edited by M. Debié, 137–159. Études syriaques 6. Paris: Geuthner.

———. (2011). *Entre mémoire et oubli: La Syrie sous les derniers omeyyades et les premiers Abbassides (v. 692–809).* Leiden: Brill.

Borrut, A., and P. Cobb, eds. (2010). *Umayyad Legacies: Medieval Memories from Syria to Spain.* Leiden: Brill.

Borrut, A., M. Debié, and A. Papaconstantinou, eds. (2007). *Peuplement et dynamiques spatiales: Actes du colloque “Continuités de l’occupation entre les périodes byzantine et abbasside au Proche-Orient, VIIe–IXe siècles,” Paris, 18–20 October 2007.* Turnhout, Belgium: Brepols.

Bosch Vilá, J. (1984). *La Sevilla Islámica, 712–1248.* Seville: Publications of the University of Seville.

Bosworth, C. E. (1992). “The City of Tarsus and the Arab-Byzantine Frontiers in Early and Middle ʿAbbâsid Times.” *Oriens* 33:268–286.

Boucheron, P., ed. (2009). *Histoire du monde au xve siècle.* Paris: Fayard.

Bouderbala, S. (2008). “Jund Misr: Étude de l’administration militaire dans l’Égypte des débuts de l’Islam (21 / 642–218 / 833).” PhD diss., Université Paris-I Panthéon-Sorbonne.

Bouloux, N. (2004). “Les îles dans les descriptions géographiques et les cartes du Moyen Âge.” *Médiévales* 47:47–62.

Bourdieu, P., and J.-C. Passeron. (1970). *La Reproduction: Éléments pour une théorie du système d’enseignement.* Paris: Minuit.

Bourin-Derruau, M., D. Le Blevec, C. Raynaud, and L. Schneider. (2001). “Le littoral languedocien au Moyen Âge.” In *Castrum 7: Zones côtières littorales dans le monde méditerranéen au Moyen Âge: Défense, peuplement, mise en valeur, Rome, 23–26 October 1996,* edited by J.-M. Martin, 345–423. Rome: École française de Rome; Madrid: Casa de Velázquez.

Bramoullé, D. (2007a). “Composing and Recruiting the Crew in the Fatimid Navy (909–1171).” *Medieval Encounters* 13:4–31.

———. (2007b). "Les villes fatimides en Méditerranée orientale (969–1171)." *Histoire urbaine* 19:93–116.

———. (2010). "Les populations littorales du *Bilâd al-Shâm* fatimide et la guerre (X[e]–XIIe siècles)." *Annales islamologiques* 43:303–336.

———. (2011). "Les Fatimides et la mer (341–567 / 953–1171): Du rêve mystique à l'empire du large." PhD diss., Université Paris-I.

Braudel, F. (1995). *The Mediterranean and the Mediterranean World in the Age of Philip II*. Translated by Siân Reynolds. 2 vols. Berkeley: University of California Press. First French edition published 1949.

Bray, J., ed. (2006). *Writing and Representation in Medieval Islam: Muslim Horizons*. London: Routledge.

Bresc, H. (1981). "La Sicile et la mer: Marins, navires et routes maritimes (XIe–XVe siècles)." In *Navigation et gens de mer en Méditerranée, de la préhistoire à nos jours*, 59–67. Paris: Editions du Centre national de la recherche scientifique.

———. (1986). *Un monde méditerranéen, économie et société en Sicile, 1300–1450*. Rome: École française de Rome.

———. (1998). "Le royaume normand d'Afrique et l'archevêché de Mahdiyya." In *Le Partage du monde: Échanges et colonisation dans la Méditerranée médiévale*, edited by M. Balard and A. Ducellier, 347–361. Paris: Publications de la Sorbonne.

———. *et alii* (2000). *La Méditerranée entre pays d'Islam et monde latin (milieu Xe–milieu XIIIe siècle): Textes et documents*. Paris: Sedes.

———. (2004). "Îles et 'tissus connectifs' de la Méditerranée médiévale." *Îles du Moyen Âge, Médiévales* 47:123–138.

Bresc, H., and G. Bresc-Bautier, eds. (1993). *Palerme, 1070–1492: Mosaïque de peuples, nation rebelle: La naissance violente de l'identité sicilienne*. Autrement 21. Paris: Autrement.

Bresc, H., A.-M. Eddé, and P. Guichard. (1990). "Les autonomismes urbains des cités islamiques." In *Les Origines des libertés urbaines: XVIe congrès de la Société des historiens médiévistes de l'enseignement supérieur public, Rouen, 1985*, 97–119. Rouen: Publications de l'Université de Rouen.

Brett, M. (2001). *The Rise of the Fatimids: The World of the Mediterranean and the Middle East in the Fourth Century of the Hijra, Tenth Century CE*. Leiden: Brill.

Brockopp, J. (1998). "Rereading the History of Early Mâlikî Jurisprudence." *Journal of the American Oriental Society* 118:233–238.

Brown, P. (1971). *The World of Late Antiquity from Marcus Aurelius to Muhammad*. New York: Norton.

Bruce, T. (2013). *La Taifa de Denia et la Méditerranée au Ve/XIe siècle.* Toulouse: Presses du Mirail.

Brunschvig, R. (1940–1947). *La Berbérie orientale sous les Hafsides, des origines au XVe siècle.* 2 vols. Paris: A. Maisonneuve.

———. (1942–1947). "Ibn ʿAbd al-Hakam et la conquête de l'Afrique du Nord par les Arabes." *Annales de l'Institut d'études orientales* 6:108–155. Published in English in *The Expansion of the Early Islamic State,* edited by F. Donner, 189–228, Formation of the Classical Islamic World, vol. 5 (Aldershot, UK: Ashgate Variorum, 2008).

Buchet, C., J. Meyer, and J.-P. Poussou, eds. (2004). *La Puissance maritime: Actes du colloque international tenu à l'Institut catholique de Paris, 13–15 décembre 2001.* Paris: Presses de l'Université de Paris-Sorbonne.

Buresi, P. (2004). *Une frontière entre chrétienté et Islam: La région entre Tage et Sierra Morena (Espagne fin XIe s.–milieu XIIIe s.).* Paris: Publibook.

Buresi, P., and H. El Allaoui. (2012). *Governing the Empire: Appointing Provincial Officials in the Almohad Caliphate.* Leiden: Brill.

Caetani, L. (1912). *Chronographia Islamica.* 5 vols. Paris, first period, installment III, year 45–65 H=13 March 666–7 August 685 E.V.

Cahen, C. (1964). "Douanes et commerce dans les ports méditerranéens de l'Égypte médiévale d'après le *Minhâdj* d'al-Makhzûmî." *Journal of Economic and Social History of the Orient* 7: 217–313.

———. (1973). "Les marchands étrangers au Caire sous les Fatimides et les Ayyubides," *Millénaire du Caire. Colloque international sur l'histoire du Caire,* 97–101. Gräfenhanichen.

———. (1977a). "Le commerce d'Amalfi dans le Proche-Orient musulman avant et après la croisade." *Compte-rendu des séances de l'année 1977 de l'Académie des inscriptions et belles-lettres,* 291–301. Paris.

———. (1977b). *Les peuples musulmans dans l'histoire médiévale.* Paris: A. Maisonneuve.

———. (1977c). *Makhzûmiyyât: Études sur l'histoire économique et financière de l'Égypte médiévale.* Leiden: Brill.

———. (1979). "Pour l'interprétation des trouvailles monétaires arabes en Europe orientale." *Occident et Orient au Xe siècle: Actes du IXe congrès de la Société des historiens médiévistes de l'enseignement supérieur public, Dijon, 2–4 juin 1978,* 113–119. Paris: Les Belles Lettres.

———. (1983). *Orient et Occident à l'époque des croisades.* Paris: Aubier.

———. (1986). *Makhzûmiyyât: Supplément aux Annales islamologiques,* cahier no. 8. Cairo: Institut français d'archéologie orientale.

Calder, N. (1993). *Studies in Early Muslim Jurisprudence.* Oxford: Clarendon.

Calero Secall, M. I. (1995). "Málaga y Ceuta en el siglo xi." In *Actas del II Congreso Internacional "El Estrecho de Gibraltar," Ceuta, noviembre 1990,* edited by E. Ripoll Perelló and M. F. Ladero Quesada, vol. 3, *Historia medieval, geografía y varia,* 39–48. Madrid: Universidad nacional de educación a distancia.

Cameron, M. E. (2001). "Sayf at First: The Transmission of Sayf ibn 'Umar in al-Tabari and Ibn 'Asâkir." In *Ibn 'Asâkir and the Early Islamic History,* edited by J. Lindsay, 62–77. Princeton, NJ: Darwin.

Campaner y Fuertes, A. (1987). *Bosquejo histórico de la dominación islamita en las islas Baleares.* Palma de Mallorca.

Camps, G. (1980). *Berbères aux marges de l'histoire.* Paris: Hespérides.

Canard, M. (1926). "Les expéditions des Arabes contre Constantinople dans l'histoire et dans *la légende.*" *Journal asiatique* 208:61–121.

———. (1947). "L'impérialisme des Fatimides et leur propaganda." *Annales de l'Institut d'études orientales* 6:156–193.

———. (1951). "Le cérémonial fatimide et le cérémonial byzantin: Essai de comparaison." *Byzantion* 21:355–420.

———. (1962). "Ibrâhîm b. Ya'qûb et sa relation de voyage en Europe." In *Études d'orientalisme dédiées à la mémoire de Lévi-Provençal,* 2:503–508. Paris: Maisonneuve et Larose.

———. (1964). "Les relations politiques et sociales entre Byzance et les Arabes." *Dumbarton Oaks Papers* 18:33–56.

———. (1973a). *Byzance et les musulmans du Proche-Orient.* London: Variorum Reprints.

———. (1973b). "Une lettre du calife fatimide al-Hâfiz (524–544/11130–1149) à Roger II." In *Miscellanea Orientalia,* London: Variorum Reprints. Originally appeared in *VIII Centenario della morte de Ruggero II: Atti del Convegno Internazionale di Studi Ruggeriani (Palerme, 1954),* 125–146 (Palermo, 1955).

Catarino, H. (1997–1998). *O Algarve Oriental durante a ocupação islâmica.* 3 vols. Coimbra.

Centro italiano di studi sull'alto medioevo. (1977). *Les Ports de la Méditerranée médiévale.* Settimane di studio del Centro italiano di studi sull'Alto Medioevo 15. Spoleto, Italy: Presso la sede del Centro.

———. (1978). *La navigazione mediterranea nell'Alto Medioevo.* Settimane di studio del Centro italiano di studi sull'Alto Medioevo 25. Spoleto, Italy: Presso la sede del Centro.

Chabbi, J. (1995). "Ribât." In *Encyclopédie de l'Islam,* 2nd ed., 8:510–523. Leiden: Brill.

Chalmeta, P. (1973). *El señor del zoco en España.* Madrid: Instituto hispano-árabe de cultura.

———. (2003). *Invasión e Islamización: La sumisión de Hispania y la formación de al-Andalus.* Jaén, Spain: Universidad de Jaén.

Chamberlain, M. (1994). *Knowledge and Social Practice in Medieval Damascus, 1190–1350.* Cambridge: Cambridge University Press.

Chaunu, P. (1969). *L'Expansion européenne du XIIIe au XVe siècle.* Paris: Presses universitaires de France.

Cheddadi, A. (2004). *Les Arabes et l'appropriation de l'histoire: Émergence et premiers développements de l'historiographie musulmane jusqu'au IIe/VIIIe siècle.* Arles, France: Sindbad-Actes Sud.

———. (2006). *Ibn Khaldûn, l'homme et le théoricien de la civilisation.* Paris: Gallimard.

Cherif, M. (1991). "L'importance de Ceuta dans le réseau du commerce méditerranéen (XIIe–XIIIe siècles)." *Revue de la Faculté des lettres de Tétouan* 5:89–93.

———. (1996). *Ceuta aux époques almohade et mérinide.* Paris: L'Harmattan.

———. (2000). "L'homme et l'espace maritime dans la région du Rif d'après *Al-Maqsad al-Sharîf.*" *Arab Historical Review for Ottoman Studies* (Zaghouan) 21:103–113.

———. (2005). "Quand les saints protègent les pèlerins en Méditerranée médiévale." In "Portos Antigos do Mediterrâneo, Colloque de Mértola, 2003," edited by S. Macias and S. Gomez Martinez, special issue, *Arqueologia Medieval* 9:5–11.

Cheynet, J.-C. (2004). *Byzance: L'Empire romain d'Orient.* Paris: Armand Colin.

———. (2005–2006). "Les États grecs après la chute de Constantinople." In *1204, la quatrième croisade de Blois à Constantinople: Éclats d'empires,* edited by I. Villela-Petit, 121–127. Paris: Société française d'héraldique et de sigillographie, Blois-Paris. Exhibition catalog.

———, ed. (2006). *Le Monde byzantin.* Vol. 2, *L'Empire byzantin (641–1204).* Paris: Presses universitaires de France.

Christ, G. (2012). *Trading Conflicts: Venitian Merchants and Mamluk Officials in Late Medieval Alexandria.* Leiden: Brill.

Christides, V. (1982). "Two Parallel Naval Guides of the Tenth Century: Qudama's Document and Leo VI's Naumachica; A Study on Byzantine and Moslem Naval Preparedness." *Graeco-Arabica* 1:51–103.

———. (1984a). *The Conquest of Crete by the Arabs (ca 824): A Turning Point in the Struggle between Byzantium and Islam.* Athens: Athens Academy.

———. (1984b). "Naval Warfare in the Eastern Mediterranean (6th–14th Centuries): An Arabic Translation of Leo VI's Naumachica." *Graeco-Arabica* 3:137–143.

Citarella, A. O. (1977). *Il commercio di Amalfi nell'alto Medioevo.* Salerno, Italy: Centro Raffaele Guariglia.

———. (1983). *The Ninth-Century Treasure of Monte Cassino in the Context of Political and Economic Developments in South Italy.* Archivio di Montecassino.

Clément, F. (1997). *Pouvoir et légitimité en Espagne musulmane à l'époque des Taifas (Ve–XIe siècle): L'imam fictif.* Paris: L'Harmattan.

Cobb, P. (1995). "Scholars and Society at Early Islamic Eyla." *Journal of Economic and Social History of Orient* 38, no. 4:417–428.

———. (1999). "Al-Mutawakkil Damascus: A New 'Abbasid Capital?" *Journal of Near-East Studies* 58, no. 4:241–257.

———. (2001). *The White Banners: Contention in Abbassid Syria (750–880).* Albany: State University of New York Press.

Compagnolo-Pothitou, M. (1995). "Les échanges de prisonniers entre Byzance et Islam aux IXe et Xe siècles." *Journal of Oriental and African Studies* 7:1–56.

Conrad, L. I. (1992). "The Conquest of Arwâd: A Source-Critical Study in the Historiography of the Early Medieval Near-East." In *The Byzantine and Early Islamic Near East,* edited by A. Cameron and L. I. Conrad, vol. 1, *Problems in Literary Source Material,* 317–401. Princeton, NJ: Darwin.

Constable, O. R. (1992). "Muslim Merchants in Andalusi International Trade." In *The Legacy of Islam,* edited by K. Jayyusi, 759–773. Leiden: Brill.

———. (1994). *Trade and Traders in Muslim Spain: Commercial Realignment of the Iberian Peninsula, 900–1500.* Cambridge: Cambridge University Press.

———. (2003). *Housing the Stranger in the Mediterranean World: Lodging, Trade, and Travel in Late Antiquity and the Middle Ages.* Cambridge: Cambridge University Press.

Contamine, P. (2003). *La Guerre au Moyen Âge.* Paris: Presses universitaires de France.

Cook, D. (2002). *Studies in Muslim Apocalyptic.* Princeton, NJ: Darwin.

Cornette, J. (1993). *Le Roi de guerre: Essai sur la souveraineté dans la France du Grand Siècle.* Paris: Payot.

Coulon, D. (2004). *Barcelone et le grand commerce d'Orient au Moyen Âge: Un siècle de relations avec l'Égypte et la Syrie-Palestine (ca. 1330–ca. 1430).* Madrid: Casa de Velázquez; Barcelona: Institut europeu de la Mediterrània.

Coulon, D., C. Picard, and D. Valérian, eds. (2007). *Espaces et réseaux en Méditerranée.* Vol. 1, *La configuration des réseaux.* Paris: Bouchène.

Coutau-Bégarie, H., ed. (1991). *L'Évolution de la pensée navale.* Paris: Documentation française.

———, ed. (2004). *La Puissance maritime: Actes du colloque international tenu à l'Institut catholique de Paris, 13–15 décembre 2001.* Paris: Presses de l'Université de Paris-Sorbonne.

———. (2006). *Traité de stratégie.* Paris: Institut de stratégie comparée.

Coutau-Bégarie, H., and A. Bru, eds. (1995). *La Lutte pour l'empire de la mer: Histoire et géostratégie maritimes.* Paris: Institut de stratégie comparée, Economica.

Cowdrey, H. E. J. (1977). "The Mahdia Campaign of 1087." *English Historical Review* 92:24–29.

Cressier, P. (1998). "Urbanisation, arabisation, islamisation au Maroc du Nord: Quelques remarques depuis l'archéologie." In *Peuplement et arabisation au Maghreb occidental: Dialectologie et histoire,* edited by J. Aguadé, P. Cressier, and A. Vicente, 27–38. Madrid: Casa de Velázquez; Saragossa, Spain: University of Saragossa.

———. (2004). "De un *ribât* a otro: Una hipotesis sobre los ribât-s del Magrib al-Aqsâ (siglo IX-inicios del siglo XI)." In *Fouilles de la Rabita de Guardamar,* edited by R. Azuar Ruiz, vol. 1, *El* ribât *califal: Excavaciones e investigaciones (1984–1992),* 73–87. Madrid: Casa de Velázquez.

Cressier, P., M. Fierro, and J.-P. Van Staëvel, eds. (2000). *L'Urbanisme dans l'Occident musulman au Moyen Âge: Aspects juridiques.* Madrid: Casa de Velázquez.

Crone, P. (1980). *Slaves and Horses: The Evolution of the Islamic Polity.* Cambridge: Cambridge University Press.

———. (1987). *Mekkan Trade and the Rise of Islam.* Princeton, NJ: Princeton University Press.

Crone, P., and M. Cook. (1977). *Hagarism: The Making of the Islamic World.* Cambridge: Cambridge University Press.

Crouzet-Pavant, É. (2004). *Venise triomphante: Les horizons d'un mythe.* Paris: Albin Michel.

Dachraoui, F. (1959). "La Crète dans le conflit entre Byzance et al-Mu'izz." *Cahiers de Tunisie* 7:307–318.

———. (1981). *Le Califat fatimide au Maghreb (296–362/909–973): Histoire politique et institutions.* Tunis: Société tunisienne de diffusion.

Daftary, F. (2004). *Ismaili Literature: A Bibliography of Sources and Studies.* London: Intitute of Ismaili Studies.

Dakhlia, J. (1998). *Le Divan des rois: Le politique et le religieux en l'Islam.* Paris: Aubier.

Dars, J. (1992). *La Marine chinoise du Xe au XIVe siècle.* Paris: Commission française d'histoire maritime–Economica.

Declercq, A. (2008). "L'Océan Environnant aux confins de la terre: Comparaison des perceptions grecque et arabe des limites du monde connu." PhD diss., Université de Toulouse.

Décobert, C. (1991). *Le mendiant et le combattant: L'institution de l'islam.* Paris: Seuil.

———. (1998). "Alexandrie au XIIIe siècle: Une nouvelle topographie." In *Alexandrie médiévale,* edited by C. Décobert and J.-Y. Empereur, 1:71–100. Cairo: Institut français d'archéologie orientale.

———. (2004). "L'autorité religieuse aux premiers siècles de l'Islam." *Archives des sciences sociales des religions* 125:23–44.

Décobert, C., and J.-Y. Empereur, eds. (1998). *Alexandrie médiévale.* 2 vols. Alexandria: Centre d'études alexandrines.

Décobert, C., J.-Y. Empereur, and C. Picard, eds. (2011). *Alexandrie et le commerce de la Méditerranée de la fin de l'Antiquité.* Vol. 4 of *Alexandrie médiévale.* Alexandria: Centre d'études alexandrines.

De Epalza, M. (1986). "Costas alicantinas y costas magrebíes: El espacio marítimo musulmán según los textos árabes." *Sharq al-Andalus* 3:25–31.

———. (1987). "Costas alicantinas y costas magrebíes: El espacio marítimo musulmán según los textos árabes." *Sharq al-Andalus* 4:45–48.

Dejugnat, Y. (2010). "Le Voyage d'Occident et d'Orient des lettrés d'al-Andalus: Genèse et affirmation d'une culture du voyage (XIe–XIIIe siècle)." PhD diss., Université Paris-I.

De La Puente, C. (1999). "El *ŷyhâd* en el califato omeya de al-Andalus y su culminación bajo Hishâm II." In *La Península Ibérica y el Mediterráneo durante los siglos XI y XII,* edited by F. Valdés Fernández and Aguilar de Campo, vol. 2, *Almanzor y los terrores del milenio,* 25–38.

Delery, C. (2006). "Dynamiques économiques, sociales et culturelles d'al-Andalus à partir d'une étude de la céramique de cuerda seca (seconde moitié du Xe siècle–première moitié du XIIIe siècle)." PhD diss., Université Toulouse-Le-Mirail.

Delgado, J. L., and J. M. Puerta Vilchez, eds. (2002–). *Enciclopedia de al-Andalus: Diccionario de autores y obras andalusíes.* Granada: El Legado Andalusí, Junta de Andalucía.

De Libera, A. (1993). *La Philosophie médiévale.* Paris: Presses universitaires de France.

Den Heijer, J. (1989). *Mawhûd Ibn Mansûr Ibn Mufarrig et l'historiographie copto-arabe: Étude sur la composition de l'Histoire des Patriarches d'Alexandrie.* Leuven, Belgium: Peeters.

Denoix, S. (1992). *Décrire Cairo: Fustât-Misr d'après Ibn Duqmâq et Maqrîzî.* Cairo: Institut français d'archéologie orientale.

Denoix, S., J.-C. Depaule, and M. Tuchscherer. (1997). *Le Khan al-Khalili et ses environs, un centre commercial et artisanal au Caire.* Cairo: Institut français d'archéologie orientale.

Déroche, V., S. Métivier, V. Puech, and G. Saint-Guillain. (2007). *Le Monde byzantin (750–1204): Économie et société.* Neuilly-sur-Seine, France: Atlande.

Devisse, J. (1972). "Routes de commerce et échanges en Afrique occidentale en relation avec la Méditerranée: Un essai sur le commerce africain médiéval du XIe au XVIe siècle." *Revue d'histoire économique et sociale* 50:42–73, 357–397.

Devrim Atauz, A. (2004). "Trade, Piracy, and Naval Warfare in the Central Mediterranean: The Maritime History and Archaeology of Malta." PhD diss., Texas A&M University.

Djaït, H. (1986). *Al-Kûfa: Naissance de la ville islamique.* Paris: Maisonneuve et Larose.

———. (1989). *La Grande Discorde: Religion et politique dans l'Islam des origines.* Paris: Gallimard.

———. (2004). *La Fondation du Maghreb islamique.* Sfax, Tunisia: Amal éditions.

Djaït, H., M. Talbi, F. Dachraoui, *et alii* (1972). *Histoire de la Tunisie: Le Moyen Âge.* Tunis: Société tunisienne de diffusion.

Djebbar, A. (2001). *Une histoire de la science arabe: Introduction à la connaissance du patrimoine scientifique des pays d'Islam.* Paris: Seuil.

Djelloul, N. (1999). *Al-ribâtât al-bahriyya bi-Ifrîqiya fî l-'asr al-wasit.* Tunis.

———. (2011). *La Voile et l'Épée: Les côtes du Maghreb à l'époque médiévale.* Tunis: Faculté des lettres, des arts et des humanités de la Manouba.

Donner, F. (1981). *The Early Islamic Conquests.* Princeton, NJ: Princeton University Press, 1981.

———. (1991). "The Sources of Islamic Conceptions of War." In *Just War and Jihad: Historical Perspectives on War and Peace in Western and Islamic Traditions,* edited by J. Kelsay and J. Turner Johnson, 31–69. New York: Greenwood Press.

———. (1998). *Narratives of Islamic Origins: The Beginnings of Historical Writing.* Princeton, NJ: Darwin.

———. (2008). "Centralized Authority and Military Autonomy in the Early Islamic Conquest." In *The Expansion of the Early Islamic State,* edited by F. Donner, 263–286. Formation of the Classical Islamic World, vol. 5. Aldershot, UK: Ashgate Variorum.

Doumerc, B. (1999). *Venise et l'État hafside, 1231–1535.* Paris: L'Harmattan.

Dozy, R. (1881). *Suppléments aux dictionnaires arabes.* 2 vols. Leiden: Brill.

———. (1965). *Recherches sur l'histoire et la littérature de l'Espagne pendant le Moyen Âge.* Amsterdam: Oriental Press. First edition published 1860.

Drocourt, N. (2004). "Ambassades latines et musulmanes à Byzance: Une situation contrastée (VIIIe–XIe siècles)." *Byzantion* 74, no. 2:348–381.

Dubler, C. (1949). "Los caminos a Compostela en la obra de al-Idrîsî." *Al-Andalus* 14, no. 1:59–122.

Ducellier, A. (1996). *Chrétiens d'Orient et Islam au Moyen Âge*. Paris: Armand Colin.

Ducène, J.-C. (2010). *L'Afrique dans le Uns al-muhâj wa rawd al-furâj d'al-Idrîsî*. Brussels: Peteers.

Dufourcq, C.-E. (1965). *L'Espagne catalane et le Maghrib aux XIIIe et XIVe siècles: De la bataille de Las Navas de Tolosa (1212) à l'avènement du sultan mérinide Abou-l-Hasan (1331)*. Paris: Presses universitaires de France.

Durliat, J. (1990). *De la ville antique à la ville byzantine: Les problèmes de subsistence*. Rome: École française de Rome.

———. (2002). *De l'Antiquité au Moyen Âge: l'Occident de 313 à 800*. Paris: Ellipses.

Dutton, Y. (1999). *The Origins of Islamic Law: The Qur'an, the Muwatta' and Madinan 'Amal*. London: Curzon.

Eddé, A.-M. (1996). "Saint Louis et la Septième Croisade vus par les auteurs arabes." *Cahiers de recherches médiévales (XIIIe–XVe s.)* 1:65–92.

———. (1999). *La Principauté ayyoubide d'Alep (579/1183–658/1260)*. Stuttgart, Germany: Franz Steiner Verlag.

———. (2008). *Saladin*. Paris: Flammarion.

Eddé, A.-M., F. Micheau, and C. Picard. (1997). *Communautés chrétiennes en pays d'Islam du début du VIIe siècle au milieu du XIe siècle*. Paris: Société d'édition d'enseignement supérieur.

Ehrenkreutz, A. S. (1955). "The Place of Saladin in the Naval History of the Mediterranean in the Middle Ages." *Journal of the American Oriental Society* 75:100–116.

Eickhoff, E. (1966), *Seekrieg und Seepolitik zwischen Islam und Abendland*. Berlin: De Gruyter.

Elad, A. (2002). "Community of Believers of 'Holy Men and Saints' or Community of Muslims? The Rise and Development of Early Muslim Historiography." *Journal of Semitic Studies* 47:241–308.

———. (2003). "The Beginnings of Historiographical Writing by the Arabs: The Earliest Syrian Writers on the Conquests." *Jerusalem Studies in Arabic and Islam* 281:65–152.

El-Hajji, A. (1967). "The Andalusian Diplomatic Relations with the Vikings during the Umayyad Period (H. 138–366/A.D. 755–976)." *Hespéris-Tamada* 8:67–110.

———. (1970). *Andalusian Diplomatic Relations with Western Europe during the Umayyad Period (H. 138–366/A.D. 755–976)*. Beirut: Dar al-Irshâd.

El-Hibri, T. (1999). *Reinterpreting Islamic Historiography, Hârûn al-Rashîd and the Narrative of the Abbâsid Caliphate*. Cambridge: Cambridge University Press.

———. (2010). *Parable and Politics in Early Islamic History: The Rashidun Caliphs.* New York: Columbia University Press.

Encyclopédie de l'Islam. (1954–). 2nd ed. 11 vols. Leiden: Brill.

———. (n.d.). 3rd ed. Leiden: Brill.

Erbati, E. (2002). "Deux sites urbains (IXe–XIe siècles): Casba des Oudayas et Aghmat: Approche comparative." In *Du nord au sud du Sahara: Bilan et perspectives de cinquante ans d'archéologie française, 13–14 mai 2002,* 285–293. Paris: Sépia.

Ettahiri, A., A. Filli, and J.-P. Van Staevel. (2008). "Nouvelles recherches archéologiques sur la période islamique du Maroc: Fez, Aghmât, Igîlîz." In *Histoire et archéologie de l'Occident musulman (VIIe–XVe s. Al-Andalus, Maghreb, Sicile),* edited by P. Sénac, 157–181. Villa 4. Toulouse: Presses Universitaires du Midi.

Fahmy, A. M. (1948). *Muslim Naval Organisation in the Eastern Mediterranean from the Seventh to the Tenth Century.* Cairo. Arabic ed. 1973.

———. (1966). *Muslim Sea Power in the Eastern Mediterranean from the Seventh to the Tenth Century.* Cairo: National Publication and Printing House.

Fauvelle-Aymar, F.-X., and B. Hirsch. (2003). "Voyage aux frontières du monde: Topologie, narration et jeux de miroir dans la *rihla* d'Ibn Battûta." *Afrique et histoire* 1:75–122.

Feller, L. (1998). *Les Abruzzes médiévales: Territoire, économie et société en Italie centrale du IXe au XIIe siècle.* Rome: Bibliothèque des écoles françaises d'Athènes et de Rome.

Fentress, E., and H. Limane. (2007). "Excavations in Medieval Settlements at Volubilis, 2000–2004." In *Le Maghreb, al-Andalus et la Méditerranée occidentale (VIIIe–XIIIe siècles),* edited by P. Sénac, 37–56. Toulouse: Presses Universitaires du Midi.

Ferhat, H. (1992). "Démons et merveilles: l'Atlantique dans l'imaginaire marocain médiéval." In *Le Maroc et l'Atlantique,* edited by A. Kaddouri, 31–49. Rabat: Université Mohammed-V.

———, ed. (1993a). *Le Maghreb aux XIIe et XIIIe siècles: Les siècles de la foi.* Casablanca, Morocco: Wallada.

———. (1993b). *Sabta, des origines au XIVe siècle.* Rabat: Ministeère des Affaires culturelles.

———. (1998). "L'évolution de l'écriture hagiographique entre les XIIe et XIVe siècles au Maroc." in *Le Maghreb aux XIIe et XIIIe siècles: Les siècles de la foi,* 13–28. Casablanca, Morocco: Wallada.

Ferrand, G. (1928). *Instructions nautiques et routiers arabes et portugais des XVe et XVIe siècles.* 3 vols. Paris: Geuthner.

Ferreira Fernandes, I. C. (2004). *O castelo de Palmela do Islâmico ao Cristão.* Lisbon: Colibri.

Fierro, M. (1989). "La obra histórica de Ibn al-Qûtiyya." *Al-Qantara* X-2: 485–512.

———. (1991). "El derecho mâliki en al-Andalus. Siglos II / VIII–V / XI." *Al Qantara* 12:119–132.

———. (1995). "Cuatro preguntas en torno a Ibn Hafsûn." *Al-Qantara* 16:222–257.

———. (2005). "*Mawali* and *Muwalladun,* in al-Andalus (Second / Eighth–Fourth / Tenth Centuries)." In *Patronate and Patronage in Early and Classical Islam,* edited by M. Bernards and J. Nawas, 195–245. Leiden: Brill.

Fiey, J. M. (1980). *Chrétiens syriaques sous les Abbassides.* Leuven, Belgium: Corpus Scriptorum Christianorum Orientalium.

Firestone, R. (1999). *Jihâd: The Origin of Holy War in Islam.* Oxford: Oxford University Press.

Flood, F. B. (2000). *The Great Mosque of Damascus: Studies on the Making of an Umayyad Visual Culture.* Leiden: Brill.

Fois, P. (2012). "La Sardaigne et l'Islam (VIIe–XIe siècle)." PhD diss., Université Paris-I.

Fossier, R., ed. (1982). *Le Moyen Âge.* 3 vols. Paris: Armand Colin.

Fowden, G. (2004). *Qusayr 'Amra: Art and the Umayyad Elite in Late Antique Syria.* Berkeley: University of California Press.

Fricaud, E. (1994). *Ibn 'Idhârî al-Marrâkushî (m. début XIVe s.) historien marocain du Maghrib et d'al-Andalus, bilan d'un siècle et demi de recherches sur al-Bayân al-Mughrib.* Lille, France: Atelier National de Reproduction des Thèses.

Fuess, A. (2001). *Verbranntes Ufer: Auswirkungen mamlukischer Seepolitik auf Beirut und die syro-palästinensische Küste (1250–1517).* Leiden: Brill.

Fukuyama, F. (1992). *La Fin de l'histoire et le dernier homme.* Paris: Flammarion.

Garcin, J.-C. (1973–1974). "La Méditerranéisation de l'empire mamluk sous les sultans Bahrides." *Rivista degli Studi Orientali* 48:109–116.

———. (1976). *Un centre musulman de la Haute-Égypte médiévale: Qûs.* Cairo: Institut français d'archéologie orientale.

———. (1980). "Pour un recours à l'histoire de l'espace vécu dans l'étude de l'Égypte arabe." *Annales: Économies, Sociétés, Civilisations* 35:436–451.

———. (1983). "Ibn Hawqal: L'Orient et le Maghreb." *Revue de l'Occident musulman et de la Méditerranée* 35, no. 1:77–91.

———, ed. (2000). *Grandes Villes méditerranéennes du monde musulman médiéval.* Rome: École française de Rome.

———. (2013). *Pour une lecture historique des "Mille et Une Nuits": Essai sur l'édition de Bûlâq (1835).* Arles, France: Sindbad-Actes Sud.

Garcin, J.-C., *et alii* (1995–2000). *États, sociétés et cultures du monde musulman médiéval.* 3 vols. Paris: Presses universitaires de France.

Garnier, S. (2012). "La sacralisation du littoral ifrîqiyen à l'époque hafside: Les sites de Radès et Monastir dans la *Rihla* d'al-Tijânî." *Revue des mondes musulmans et de la Méditerranée* 130:103–130.

Gaudefroy-Demombynes, M. (1925). "Lettre de Saladin au calife almohade." In *Mélanges René Basset: Études nord-africaines et orientales,* 2:281–289. Rabat: Institut des hautes études marocaines.

Gautier Dalché, P. (1997). *Géographie et culture: La représentation de l'espace du vie au XIIe siècle.* Aldershot, UK: Ashgate.

———. (2005). *Du Yorkshire à l'Inde, une "géographie" urbaine et maritime de la fin du XIIe siècle (Roger de Howden?).* Paris: Droz.

Gayraud, R. P. (1998). "Fostat: Évolution d'une capitale arabe du VIIe au XIIe siècle d'après les fouilles d'Istabl ʿAntar." In *Colloque international d'archéologie islamique,* edited by R. P. Gayraud. Cairo: Institut français d'archéologie orientale.

Geary, P. J. (1996). *La Mémoire et l'oubli à la fin du premier millénaire.* Paris: Aubier.

Genequand, D. (2010). "Formation et devenir du paysage architectural omeyyade: L'apport de l'archéologie." In *Umayyad Legacies: Medieval Memories from Syria to Spain,* edited by A. Borrut and P. Cobb, 417–473. Leiden: Brill.

Ghouirgate, M. (2007). "Les processions, un instrument de gouvernement: Quelques remarques sur le cérémonial califal almohade." In *Le Maghreb, al-Andalus et la Méditerranée occidentale (VIIIe–XIIIe siècle),* edited by P. Sénac, 285–307. Toulouse: Presses Universitaires du Midi.

Gil, M. (1992). *A History of Palestine, 634–1099.* Translated by E. Broido. Cambridge: Cambridge University Press.

———. (2004). *Jews in Islamic Countries in the Middle Ages.* Leiden: Brill.

———. (2008). "Shipping in the Mediterranean in the Eleventh Century A.D." *Journal of Near-East Studies* 67:247–292.

Gilliot, C. (1988). "La formation intellectuelle de Tabari (224/5–310/839/923)." *Journal asiatique* 276, no. 3–4:203–244.

Goitein, S. D. (1962). "La Tunisie du XIe siècle à la lumière des documents de la Geniza du Caire." In *Études d'orientalisme dédiées à la mémoire de Lévi-Provençal,* 2:559–579. Paris: Maisonneuve et Larose.

———. (1964). "The Commercial Mail Service in Medieval Islam." *Journal of the American Oriental Society* 48:118–123.

———. (1967). *A Mediterranean Society: The Jewish Communities of the Arab World as Portrayed in the Documents of the Geniza.* 4 vols., reprinted 6 vols. Princeton, NJ: Princeton University Press.

Goldberg, J. (2012). *Trade and Institutions in the Medieval Mediterranean: The Geniza Merchants and Their Business World.* New York: Cambridge University Press.

Golvin, L. (1957). *Le Maghreb central à l'époque des Zirides.* Paris: Arts et Métiers graphiques.

Gómez Martínez, S. (2006). "Cerámica islámica de Mértola: Producción y comercio." PhD diss., Universidad Complutense de Madrid. http://biblioteca.ucm.es/tesis/ghi/ucm-t27826.pdf.

Gordon, M. (2001). *The Breaking of a Thousand Swords: A History of the Turkish Military of Samarra (A.H. 200–275/C.E. 815–889).* Albany: State University of New York Press.

Grabar, O. (1987). *The Formation of Islamic Art.* New ed. New Haven, CT: Yale University Press.

Greatex, G., C. Mango, and R. Scott. (1997). *The Chronicle of Theophanes Confessor: Byzantine and Near Eastern History, AD 284–813.* Oxford: Clarendon.

Guichard, P. (1977). *Structures sociales "orientales" et "occidentales" dans l'Espagne musulmane.* Paris: Mouton.

———. (1979). "Animation maritime et développement urbain des côtes de l'Espagne orientale et du Languedoc au Xe siècle." In *Occident et Orient au Xe siècle: Actes du IXe congrès de la Société des historiens médiévistes de l'enseignement supérieur public, Dijon, 2–4 juin 1978,* 187–207. Paris: Les Belles Lettres.

———. (1983). "Les débuts de la piraterie andalouse en Méditerranée occidentale (798–813)." *Revue de l'Occident musulman et de la Méditerranée* 35:55–76.

———. (1987). "L'intégration des Baléares au pouvoir des Omeyyades de Cordoue." In *Les Illes orientals d'al-Andalus,* 5:55–71. Jornades d'estudis hitòrics locals. Palma de Mallorca: Institut d'Estudis Baleàrics.

———. (1989). "Recherche onomastique à propos des Banû Maymûn de Denia." *Cahiers d'onomastique arabe.* Paris.

———. (1990). *L'Espagne et la Sicile musulmanes aux XIe et XIIe siècles.* Lyon: Presses universitaires de Lyon.

———. (1990–1991). *Les Musulmans de Valence et la Reconquête, XIe–XIIIe siècles.* 2 vols. Damascus: Institut Français du Proche-Orient.

———. (1995a). "Les pays de la Méditerranée occidentale entre le Ve et le Xe siècle: Retour sur la problématique pirennienne." In *L'Occident musulman et l'Occident chrétien au Moyen Âge,* 75–90. Rabat: Université Mohammed-V.

———. (1995b). "L'Islam e l'Europa." In *Storia d'Europa,* edited by G. Ortalli, vol. 3, *Il Medioevo,* 295–340. Turin, Italy: Einaudi.

———. (1999a). *Al-Andalous.* Paris: Hachette.

———. (1999b). "Littérature jurisprudentielle de l'Espagne musulmane: La lente intégration des *fatwâ/s* malikites à l'historiographie d'al-Andalus." *Comptes rendus de l'Académie des inscriptions et belles-lettres* 2:757–799.

———. (1999c). "Omeyyades et Fatimides au Maghreb: Problématique d'un conflit politico-idéologique (vers 929–vers 980)." In *L'Égypte fatimide: Son art et son histoire; Actes du colloque de mai 1998 de Paris,* edited by M. Barrucand, 55–67. Paris: Presses universitaires de Paris-Sorbonne.

———. (2001). "Combattants de l'Occident chrétien et de l'Islam: Quelques remarques sur leurs images réciproques (fin Xe s.–XIIe s.)." In *Identidad y representación de la frontera en la España medieval,* 223–251. Madrid: Casa de Velázquez.

———. (2002). *De la conquête arabe à la Reconquête: Grandeur et fragilité d'al-Andalus.* Granada: El Legado Andalusí.

Guichard, P., and V. Lagardère. (1990). "La vie sociale et économique de l'Espagne musulmane aux XIe–XIIe siècles à travers les *fatwa/s* du *Mi'yâr* d'al-Wansharîsî." *Mélanges de la Casa de Velázquez* 26, no. 1:197–236.

Guilland, R. (1955). "L'expédition de Maslama contre Constantinople (717–718)." *Al-Mashriq* 49:89–112.

Gutas, D. (2005). *Pensée grecque, culture arabe, le mouvement de traduction gréco-arabe à Bagdad et la société abbasside primitive (IIe–IVe / VIIIe–Xe siècles).* Translated by A. Cheddadi. Paris: Aubier. English edition published 1998.

Gutiérrez Lloret, S. (1996). *La Cora de Tudmir de la antigüedad tardia al mundo islámico: Poblamiento y cultura material.* Madrid: Casa de Velázquez.

Hajari, M. al-. (1981). "Hayât al-nâs fi mudun al-thughûr: Madînat Tarsûs." *Dirâsât Ta'rîkhîya* 5:85–95.

Haldon, J. F. (1999). *Warfare, State and Society in the Byzantine World, 565–1204.* London: Routledge.

Halm, H. (1992). "Nachrichten zu Bauten der Aglabiden und Fatimiden in Libyen und Tunesien." *Die Welt des Orients* 23:129–157.

———. (1995). *Le Chiisme.* Paris: Presses universitaires de France.

———. (1996). *The Empire of the Mâhdi: The Rise of the Fatimids.* Translated by M. Bonner. Leiden: Brill.

Hamblin, W. J. (1986). "The Fatimid Navy during the Early Crusades, 1099–1124." *American Neptune* 46:77–83.

Harley, J. B., and D. Woodward, eds. (1992). *The History of Cartography.* Vol. 2, *Cartography in the Traditional Islamic and South Asian Societies.* Chicago: University of Chicago Press.

Hassen, M. (2001). "Les ribâts du sahel d'Ifrîqiya: Peuplement et évolution du territoire au Moyen Âge." In *Castrum 7: Zones côtières littorales dans le monde méditerranéen au Moyen Âge: Défense, peuplement, mise en valeur, Rome, 23–26 October 1996,* edited by J.-M. Martin, 147–162. Rome: École française de Rome; Madrid: Casa de Velázquez.

———, ed. (2005). *Byzacium antique et Sâhil médiéval: Urbanisme et occupation du sol.* Tunis: Université de Tunis.

Hawting, G. R. (2000). *The First Dynasty of Islam: The Umayyad Caliphate, AD 661–750.* Carbondale: Southern Illinois University Press.

Heyd, W. (1959). *Histoire du commerce du Levant au Moyen Âge.* 2 vols. Amsterdam: Adolf M. Hakkert. First edition published 1886.

Hillenbrand, C. (1999). *The Crusades: Islamic Perspectives.* Edinburgh: Edinburgh University Press.

Hodges, R., and D. Whitehouse. (1996). *Mahomet, Charlemagne et les origines de l'Europe.* Paris: P. Lethielleux.

Hodgson, M. G. S. (1974). *The Venture of Islam: Conscience and History in a World Civilization.* 3 vols. Chicago: University of Chicago Press.

Hofmann, C., H. Richard, and E. Vagnon, eds. (2012). *L'Âge d'or des cartes marines: Quand l'Europe découvrait le monde.* Paris: Bibliothèque nationale de France.

Horden, P., and N. Purcell. (2000). *The Corrupting Sea: A Study of Mediterranean History.* Oxford: Oxford University Press.

Hourani, G. F. (1995). *Arab Seafaring in the Indian Ocean in Ancient and Early Medieval Times.* Rev. ed. Edited by J. Carswell. Princeton, NJ: Princeton University Press. First edition published 1951.

Hoyland, R. G. (1997). *Seing Islam as Others Saw It: A Survey and Evaluation of Christian, Jewish and Zoroastrian Writings on Early Islam.* Princeton, NJ: Darwin.

Huici Miranda, A. (1956–1957a). *Historia política del imperio almohade.* 2 vols. Tétouan, Morocco: Editora Marroqui.

———. (1956–1957b). *Las grandes batallas de la Reconquista durante las invasiones africanas (Almorávides, Almohades y Benimerines).* Madrid: Consejo Superior de Investigaciones Científicas.

Humphreys, R. S. (1991). *Islamic History: A Framework for Inquiry.* London: Tauris.

———. (2006). *Mu'awiya Ibn Abi Sufyan.* Oxford: Oneworld.

Idris, H. R. (1935–1936). "Contribution à l'histoire de l'Ifrîqiya: Tableau de la vie intellectuelle et administrative à Kairouan sous les Aghlabides et les Fatimides d'après le *Riyâd al-Nufus* de Abû Bakr al-Mâlikî." *Revue des études islamiques* 1935:105–177, 273–305; 1936:45–103.

———. (1961). "Commerce maritime et *qirâd* en Berbérie orientale, d'après un recueil inédit de fatwas médiévales." *Journal of Economic and Social History of Orient* 4:223–239.

———. (1962). *La Berbérie orientale sous les Zirides, X^e–XIIIe siècles.* 2 vols. Paris: Maisonneuve et Larose.

Jacoby, D. (1995), "Les Italiens en Égypte du XIe au XIIIe siècle: Du comptoir à la colonie." In *Coloniser au Moyen Âge,* edited by M. Balard and A. Ducellier, 76–89. Paris: Armand Colin.

Jacquart, D., and F. Micheau. (1990). *La Médecine arabe et l'Occident médiéval.* Paris: Maisonneuve et Larose.

Jalabert, C. (2004). "Hommes et lieux dans l'islamisation de l'espace syrien (Ier / VIIe–VIIe / XIIIe siècle)." PhD diss., Université Paris-I.

Jansen, P., A. Nef, and C. Picard. (2000). *La Méditerranée entre pays d'Islam et monde latin (milieu X^e–milieu XIIIe siècle).* Paris: Sedes.

Jehel, G. (2001). *L'Italie et le Maghreb au Moyen Âge: Conflits et échanges du VIIe au XVe siècle.* Paris: Presses universitaires de France.

Jones, J. (1987). "*Malik Ifrikiya:* The Norman Kingdom of Africa and the Fatimids." *Libyan Studies* 18:89–101.

———. (1995). "I re normanni e i califfi fatimiti: Nuove prospettive su vecchi materiali." In *Del nuovo sulla Sicilia musulmana (Giornata di studio del'Accademia nazionale dei Lincei, Rome, 3 mai 1993),* 9–50. Rome: Accademia nazionale dei Lincei.

Kably, M. (1986). *Société, pouvoir et religion au Maroc à la fin du Moyen Âge.* Paris: Maisonneuve et Larose.

Kaplony, A. (2002). *Konstantinopel und Damaskus: Gesandtschaften und Verträge zwischen Kaisern und Kalifen, 639–750: Untersuchungen zum Gewohnheits-Völkerrecht und zur interkulturellen Diplomatie.* Berlin: K. Schwarz.

Kedar, B. Z. (1997). "Una nuova fonte per l'incursione musulmana del 934–935 e le sue implicazione per la storia genovese." In *Oriente e Occidente tra Medioevo ed Età Moderna: Studi in onore di Geo Pistarino,* 608–609. Genoa, Italy: Brigati.

Kennedy, H. (1981). *The Early Abbassid Caliphate: A Political History.* London: Croom Helm.

———. (1994). *The Prophet and the Age of the Caliphates: The Islamic Near East from the Sixth Century to the Eleventh Century.* London: Longman. First edition published 1986.

———. (1997). "Egypt as a Province in the Early Islamic Caliphate, 641–868." In *The Cambridge History of Egypt,* edited by C. Petry, 1:62–85. Cambridge: Cambridge University Press.

———. (2001). *The Armies of the Caliphs: Military and Society in the Early Islamic State.* London: Routledge.

———. (2003a). "Caliphs and Their Chroniclers in the Middle Abbassid Period (3th / 9th Century)." In *Texts, Documents and Arterfacts: Islamic Studies in Honor of D. S. Richards,* edited by C. Robinson, 17–35. Leiden: Brill.

———, ed. (2003b). *Al-Tabarî: A Muslim Historian and His Work.* Studies in Late Antiquity and Early Islam. Princeton, NJ: Darwin.

Khalidi, T. (1975). *Islamic Historiography: The Histories of Mas'ûdi.* Albany: State University of New York Press.

———. (1994). *Arabic Historical Thought in the Classical Period.* Cambridge: Cambridge University Press.

Khalilieh, H. S. (1999). "The Ribât System and Its Role in Coastal Navigation." *Journal of Economic and Social History of Orient* 42, no. 2:212–225.

———. (2006). *Admiralty and Maritime Laws in the Mediterranean Sea (ca. 800–1500): The "Kitâb Akriyat al-sufun" vis-à-vis the "Nomos Rhodion Nautikos."* Leiden: Brill.

Khoury, R. G. (1986). *'Abd Allâh ibn Lahi'a (97–174 / 715–790), juge et grand maître de l'école égyptienne: Avec édition critique de l'unique rouleau de papyrus arabe conservé à Heidelberg.* Wiesbaden, Germany: Otto Harrassowitz.

———. (2004). "L'apport spécialement important de la papyrologie et de la codification des plus anciennes versions des *Mille et Une Nuits* et d'autres livres des deux premiers siècles islamiques." In *Papyrology and the History of Early Islamic Egypt,* edited by M. Sijpesteijn and L. Sundelin, 63–95. Islamic History and Civilization, vol. 55. Leiden, Brill.

Kratchkovsky, I. J. (1957). *Arabskaïa geografitcheskaïa literature.* Moscow.

Krueger, M. C. (1933). "Genoese Trade with Northwest Africa in the Twelfth Century." *Speculum* 8:377–395.

———. (1937). "The Wares of Exchange in the Genoese-African Traffic of the Twelfth Century." *Speculum* 12:57–71.

Kubiak, B. (1970). "The Byzantine Attack on Damietta in 853 and the Egyptian Navy in the 9th Century." *Byzantion* 40:45–66.

Lagardère, V. (1989a). *Les Almoravides jusqu'au règne de Yûsuf b. Tâshfîn (1039–1063).* Paris: L'Harmattan.

———. (1989b). *Le Vendredi de Zallâqa, 23 octobre 1086.* Paris: L'Harmattan.

———. (1995). *Histoire et Société en Occident musulman au Moyen Âge: Analyse du Mi'yâr d'al-Wansharîsî.* Collection of the Casa de Velázquez 53. Madrid: Casa de Velázquez.

———. (1998a). "Évolution de la notion de djihad à l'époque almoravide (1039–1147)." *Cahiers de civilisation médiévale* 41:8–15.

———. (1998b). *Les Almoravides: Le djihâd andalou (1106–1143).* Paris: L'Harmattan.

———. (2006). "Le *djihâd* almohade: Théorie et pratique." In *Los Almohades: Problemas y Perspectivas,* edited by P. Cressier, M. Fierro, and L. Molina, 2:617–631. Madrid: Consejo Superior de Investigaciones Científicas.

Laiou, A. E., ed. (2002). *Economic History of Byzantium, from the Seventh through the Fifteenth Century.* Washington, DC: Dumbarton Oaks Research Library and Collection. https://www.doaks.org/research/publications/books/the-economic-history-of-byzantium.

Lammens, H. (1926). "Les 'Perses' du Liban et l'origine des Métoualis." In *Congrès archéologique de Syrie et de Palestine,* 23–39. Beirut.

Landau-Tasseron, A. (1990). "Sayf ibn 'Umar in Medieval and Modern Scholarship." *Der Islam* 67, no. 1:1–26.

La Vaissière, E. de. (2007). *Samarcande et Samarra: Élites d'Asie centrale dans l'Empire abbasside.* Paris: Association pour l'avancement des études iraniennes.

———. (2008). "Le *ribât* d'Asie centrale." *Cahiers de Studia Iranica* 39:71–94.

Le Goff, J. (1986). *La Bourse et la Vie.* Paris: Hachette.

Le Strange, G. (1965). *Palestine under the Muslims: A Description of Syria and the Holy Land from* A.D. *650 to 1500.* Beirut: Kahyats. First edition published 1890.

Lev, Y. (1984). "The Fatimid Navy, Byzantium, and the Mediterranean Sea, 996–1036." *Byzantion* 54:220–252.

———. (1991). *State and Society in Fatimid Egypt.* Leiden: Brill.

Levi della Vida, G. (1944–1945). "A Papyrus Reference to the Damietta Raid of 853 A.D." *Byzantion* 17:212–222.

———. (1954). "La corrispondenza di Berta di Toscana col califfo Muktafi." *Rivista storica italiana* 46:21–38.

Lévi-Provençal, É. (1931). *Les Inscriptions arabes d'Espagne.* 2 vols. Leiden: Brill; Paris: Larose.

———. (1932). *L'Espagne musulmane au Xe siècle: Institutions et vie sociale.* Paris: Larose; repr. Paris: Maisonneuve et Larose, 1996.

———. (1937). "Un échange d'ambassadeurs entre Cordoue et Byzance au IXe siècle." *Byzantion* 12:1–24.

———. (1959–1967). *Histoire de l'Espagne musulmane.* 3 vols. Paris: Maisonneuve et Larose; repr. 1999.

Lewicki, T. (1969). *Arabic External Sources for the History of Africa to the South of Sahara.* Wroclaw: Zaklad Narodowy Imienia Ossolinskich.

———. (1973). "Le monde berbère vu par les écrivains arabes du Moyen Âge." In *Actes du Premier Congrès d'études des cultures méditerranéennes d'influence arabo-berbère,* 31–42. Algiers: Société nationale d'édition et de diffusion.

———. (1978). "Les voies maritimes de la Méditerranée dans le haut Moyen Âge d'après les sources arabes." In *La navigazione mediterranea nell'Alto Medioevo,* 2:439–471. Settimane di studio del Centro italiano di studi sull'Alto Medioevo 25. Spoleto, Italy: Presso la sede del Centro.

Lewis, A. R. (1951). *Naval Power and Trade in the Mediterranean,* A.D. *500–1100.* Princeton, NJ: Princeton University. (reprint 1971).

Lezine, A. (1956). *Le Ribat de Sousse, suivi de notes sur le ribat de Monastir.* Tunis: La Rapide.

———. (1965). *Mahdiyya, recherches d'archéologie musulmane.* Paris: Klincksieck.

Li Guo (2004). *Commerce, Culture, and Community in a Red Sea Port in the Thirteenth Century: The Arabic Documents from Quseir.* Leiden: Brill.

Lindsay, J., ed. (2001). *Ibn 'Asâkir and Early Islamic History.* Princeton, NJ: Darwin.

Lirola Delgado, J. (1993). *El poder naval de al-Andalus en la época del califato omeya.* Granada: Universidad de Granada.

———. (1995). "Al-Bakri, Abû 'Ubayd." In *Enciclopedia de al-Andalus: Diccionario de autores y obras andalusíes,* edited by J. L. Delgado and J. M. Puerta Vilchez, 1:92–97. Granada: El Legado Andalusí, Junta de Andalucía.

Loiseau, J. (2010). *Reconstruire la maison du sultan: Ruine et recomposition de l'ordre urbain au Caire (1350–1450).* Cairo: Institut français d'archéologie orientale.

Lombard, M. (1947). "Les bases monétaires d'une suprématie économique: L'or musulman du VIIe au XIe siècle." *Annales: Économies, Sociétés, Civilisations* 2:143–160.

———. (1958). "Arsenaux et bois de marine dans la Méditerranée musulmane (VIIe–XIe siècles)." In *Le Navire et l'Économie maritime du Moyen Âge au XVIIIe siècle, principalement en Méditerranée, 2e colloque international d'histoire maritime.* Paris: Académie de marine.

———. (1969). *L'Islam dans sa première grandeur.* Paris: Flammarion.

Lopez, R. (1974). *La Révolution commerciale dans l'Europe médiévale.* Paris: Aubier-Montaigne.

Lopez, R., and I. Raymond. (1973). *Medieval Trade in the Mediterranean World.* New York: Columbia University Press.

López Pérez, M. D. (1995). *La Corona de Aragón y el Magreb en el siglo XIV (1331–1410).* Barcelona: Consejo Superior de Investigaciones Científicas.

Macias, S. (2006). *Mértola, le dernier port de la Méditerranée.* 3 vols. Mértola, Portugual: Campo Arqueológico de Mértola.

Mahfoudh, F. (2003). *Architecture et urbanisme en Ifrîqiya médiévale: Proposition pour une nouvelle approche.* Tunis: Faculté des Lettres de la Manouba.

Mâhir, S. (1967). *Al-Bahriyya fî Misr al-Islâmiyya wa athâruhâ al-bâqiya.* Cairo.

Maire Vigueur, J.-C. (2003). *Cavaliers et citoyens: Guerres, conflits et société dans l'Italie communale, XIIe–XIIIe siècles.* Paris: École des hautes études en sciences sociales.

Manzano Moreno, E. (1991). *La frontera de al-Andalus en época de los Omeyas.* Madrid: Consejo Superior de Investigaciones Científicas.

Marçais, G. (1957). "Notes sur les ribâts en Berbérie." In *Mélanges d'histoire et d'archéologie de l'Occident musulman,* 1:23–36. Paris. First edition published 1925.

Maréchal, R., and P. Sénac. (2007). "Ruscino, un établissement musulman du VIIIe siècle." In *Villes et campagnes de Tarraconnaise et d'al-Andalus (VIe–XIe siècle): La transition,* edited by P. Sénac, 67–94. Villa 2. Toulouse: Presses Universitaires du Midi.

Margariti, R. E. (2007). *Aden and the Indian Ocean Trade: 150 Years in the Life of a Medieval Arabian Port.* Chapel Hill: University of North Carolina Press.

Marin, M. (1994). "El ribat en al-Andalus y el Norte de Africa." In *La Ràpita islàmica: Història institucional i altres estudis regionals,* 121–130. Sant Carles de la Ràpita, Spain.

———. (1995). "Ifrîqiya et al-Andalus, à propos de la transmission des sciences islamiques aux premiers siècles de l'Islam." *Revue de l'Occident musulman et de la Méditerranée* 40, no. 2:45–53.

Martin, J.-M., ed. (2001). *Castrum 7: Zones côtières littorales dans le monde méditerranéen au Moyen Âge: Défense, peuplement, mise en valeur, Rome, 23–26 October 1996.* Rome: École française de Rome; Madrid: Casa de Velázquez.

———. (2006). "L'Italie byzantine (641–1071)." In *Le Monde byzantine,* vol. 2, *L'Empire byzantin (641–1204),* edited by J.-C. Cheynet, 473–494. Paris: Presses universitaires de France.

Martinez-Gros, G. (1984). "Classification des sciences et classification des nations." *Mélanges de la Casa de Velázquez* 20:83–114.

———. (1992). *L'Idéologie omeyyade: La construction de la légitimité du Califat de Cordoue (Xe–XIe siècles).* Madrid: Casa de Velázquez.

———. (1997). *Identité andalouse.* Arles, France: Sindbad-Actes Sud.

———. (1998). "La division du monde selon Idrîsî." In *Le Partage du monde,* edited by M. Balard and A. Ducellier, 315–334. Paris: Publications de la Sorbonne.

———. (2006). *Ibn Khaldun, les sept vies de l'Islam.* Arles, France: Sindbad-Actes Sud.

———. (2010). "Le califat omeyyade selon Ibn Khaldûn: Revanche des impies ou fondation de l'empire." In *Umayyad Legacies: Medieval Memories from Syria to Spain,* edited by A. Borrut and P. Cobb, 167–183. Leiden: Brill.

Martinez Lillo, S. (1995). "La arqueología y el mar." In *Al-Andalus y el Mediterráneo,* 215–241. Madrid: Lunwerg.

Mauny, R. (1960). *Les Navigations médiévales sur les côtes sahariennes antérieures à la découverte portugaise (1434).* Lisbon: Centro des Estudos Históricos Ultramarinos.

Maurici, F. (1992). *Castelli medievali in Sicilia: Dai Bizantini ai Normanni.* Palermo, Italy: Sellerio.

Mazot, S. (1999). "L'architecture d'influence nord-africaine à Palerme." In *L'Égypte fatimide: Son art et son histoire: Actes du colloque de mai 1998 de Paris,* edited by M. Barrucand, 665–679. Paris: Presses universitaires de Paris-Sorbonne.

McCormick, M. (2001). *Origins of the European Economy: Communications and Commerce—A.D. 300–900.* Cambridge: Cambridge University Press.

———. (2004). "Pepin III, the Embassy of Caliph al-Mansur and the Mediterranean World." In *Der Dynastiewechsel von 751: Vorgeschichte, Legitimationsstrategien und Erinnerung,* edited by M. Becker and J. Jarunts, 221–241. Münster, Germany: Scriptorium.

Meloy, J. L. (2010). *Imperial Power and Maritime Trade: Mecca and Cairo in the Later Middle Ages.* Chicago: University of Chicago Press.

Menant, F. (2005). *L'Italie des communes, 1100–1350.* Paris: Armand Colin.

Menéndez Pidal, R., ed. (coll. 1969–1997). *Historia de España.* 2nd ed. Vols. 5 (1969), 8-1 (1995), and 8-2 (1997). Madrid: Espasa-Calpe.

Metcalfe, A. (2009). *The Muslims of Medieval Italy.* Edinburgh: Edinburgh University Press.

Micheau, F. (2012). *Les Débuts de l'Islam: Jalons pour une nouvelle histoire.* Paris: Téraèdre.

Michel, N. (2000). "Devoirs fiscaux et droits foncier: La condition des fellahs égyptiens (XIIIe–XVIe siècle)." *Journal of the Economic and Social History of the Orient* 43, no. 4:521–578.

Minorsky, V. (1955). *Abû Dulaf Mis'ar Travels in Iran.* Cairo: Cairo University Press.

Miquel, A. (1973–1984). *La Géographie humaine du monde musulman jusqu'au milieu du XIe siècle.* 4 vols. Paris: Mouton.

———. (1977). "Ibn Battûta: Trente années de voyages de Pékin au Niger." In *Les Africains,* edited by C.-A. Julien *et alii,* 1:113–140. Paris: Jeune Afrique.

Moderan, Y. (2003). *Les Maures et l'Afrique romaine, IVe–VIIe siècle.* Rome: École française de Rome.

Molina López, E. (1983). "Algunas consideraciones sobre la vida socioeconómica de Almería en el siglo y primera mitad del XII." In *Actas IV Coloquio Hispano-Tunecino,* 181–196. Madrid: Instituto hispano-árabe de cultura.

———. (1986). "Almería islámica: 'Puerta de Oriente,' objetivo militar (nuevos datos para su estudio en el *Kitâb Iqtibâs al-anwâr* de al-Rushâti)." In *Actas del XII Congresso de la U.E.A.I. (Málaga, 1984),* 559–608. Madrid: Instituto hispano-árabe de cultura.

Morabia, A. (1993). *Le Gihad dans l'Islam médiéval, le "combat sacré" des origines au XIIe siècle.* Paris: Albin Michel.

Morimoto, K. (1981). *The Fiscal Administration of Egypt in the Early Islamic Period.* Kyoto: Dohosha.

Morrisson, C., and J.-C. Cheynet, eds. (2004). *Le Monde byzantin.* Vol. 1, *L'Empire romain d'Orient (330–641).* Paris: Presses universitaires de France.

———. (2006). *Le Monde byzantin.* Vol. 2, *L'Empire byzantin (641–1204).* Paris: Presses universitaires de France.

Motzki, H. (1998). "The Prophet and the Cat: On Datins Malik's *Muwatta'* and Legal Traditions." *Jerusalem Studies in Arabic and Islam* 22:18–83.

Moukarzel, P. (2010). "La qualité bien rare de Salîh b. Yahyâ Salîh b. Yahyâ parmi les historiens orientaux au Moyen Âge: Écrire l'histoire des émirs Buhtur en utilisant les archives familiales." *Revue des mondes musulmans et de la Méditerranée* 127:239–257.

Muranyi, M. (1984). *Materialien zur Mâlikitischen Rechtsliteratur.* Wiesbaden, Germany: O. Harrassowitz.

———. (1997). "Die Frühe Rechtsliteratur zwischen Quelle Analyse und Fiktion." *Islamic Law and Society* 4:224–241.

———. (1999). *Die Rechtsbücher des Qairawaners Sahnûn b. Sa'id, Entstehungsgeschichte und Werküberlieferung.* Stuttgart, Germany: Franz Steiner Verlag.

Musset, L. (1994). *Les Invasions: Le second assaut contre l'Europe chrétienne (VIIe–XIe siècle).* Nouvelle Clio. Paris: Presses universitaires de France. First edition published 1965.

Nef, A. (2007). "La Sicile dans la documentation de la Geniza cairote (fin X[e]–XIIIe siècle): Les réseaux attestés et leur nature." In *Espaces et réseaux en Méditerranée,* edited by D. Coulon, C. Picard, and D. Valérian, 273–292. Paris: Bouchène.

———. (2008). "Instruments de la légitimation politique et légitimité religieuse dans l'Ifrîqiya de la fin du IXe siècle: L'exemple d'Ibrâhîm II." In *La Légitimation du pouvoir au Maghreb médiéval: De l'orientalisation à l'émancipation politique,* studies collected by A. Nef and É. Voguet, 127:75–91. Collection of the Casa de Velázquez 127. Madrid: Casa de Velázquez.

———. (2011a). "Comment les Aghlabides ont décidé de conquérir la Sicile." In *Le polycentrisme dans l'Islam médiéval: Les dynamiques régionales de l'innovation,* 191–211. Annales islamologiques 45. Cairo: Institut français d'archéologie orientale.

———. (2011b). *Conquérir et gouverner la Sicile islamique aux XIe et XIIe siècles.* Rome: Bibliothèque des écoles françaises d'Athènes et de Rome.

Nichanian, M., and V. Prigent. (2003). "Les stratèges de Sicile: De la naissance du thème au règne de Léon V." *Revue des études byzantines* 61:97–141.

Nora, P., ed. (1997). *Les Lieux de mémoire.* Paris: Gallimard.

Northedge, A. (2005). *The Historical Topography of Samarra, Samarra Studies I.* London: British School of Archaeology in Irak.

Noth, A. (1971). "Der Charakter der ersten großen Sammlungen von Nachrichten zur frühen Kalifenzeit." *Der Islam* 47:168–199.

———. (1973). *Quellenkritische Studien zu Themen, Formen und Tendenzen, frühislamische Geschichtsüberlieferung.* Bonn, Germany: Selbstverlag des Orientalischen Seminars der Universität Bonn.

Noth, A., and L. I. Conrad. (1994). *The Early Arabic Historical Tradition: A Source-Critical Study.* Princeton, NJ: Darwin.

Othman, A. (1999). "*Sahâba* et *tâbi'ûn* au Maghreb d'après les sources biographiques d'Abûl-'Arab, de Mâliki et d'Ibn Nadji." PhD diss., Université Paris-IV Sorbonne.

Ouerfelli, M. (2004). "Les relations entre le royaume de Chypre et le sultanat mamelouk au XVe siècle." *Le Moyen Âge* vol. 110, no. 2:327–344.

———. (2008). *Le Sucre: Production, commercialisation et usages dans la Méditerranée médiévale.* Leiden: Brill.

———. (2009). "Les traités de paix et de commerce entre Pise et l'Égypte au Moyen Âge." In *L'Autorité de l'écrit au Moyen Âge (Orient-Occident)*, 39th Symposium of the Société des historiens médiévistes de l'enseignement supérieur public, Cairo, 30 April–5 May 2008, 45–57. Paris: Publications de la Sorbonne.

Parkin, D., and R. Barnes, eds. (2002). *Ships and the Development of Maritime Technology in the Indian Ocean.* London: Routledge Curzon.

Patlagean, E. (1993). "Byzance et les marchés du grand commerce, vers 830–vers 1030: Entre Pirenne et Polanyi." In *Mercati e mercanti nell'alto medioevo: L'area euroasiatica e l'area mediterranea, 23–29 aprile 1992*, 429–460. Settimane di studio del Centro italiano di studi sull'Alto Medioevo 40. Spoleto, Italy: Presso la sede del Centro.

Pellat, C. (1964). "La España musulmana en las obras de al-Mas'ûdi." In *Actas del primer congreso de estudios árabes e islámicos*, 257–264. Madrid: Comite permanente del Congreso de Estudios Arabes e Islamicos.

———. (1995). "al-Râdhâniyya." In *Encyclopédie de l'Islam*, 2nd ed., 8:376–380. Leiden: Brill.

Pérès, H. (1953). *La Poésie andalouse en arabe classique au XIe siècle.* Paris: Maisonneuve et Larose.

Picard, C. (1990). "Quelques aspects des relations entre chrétiens et musulmans dans les zones de confins du nord-ouest de la péninsule Ibérique (IXe–XIe siècle)." In *Études d'histoire de l'Université de Saint-Étienne*, 5–26. Saint-Etienne, France: Centre de recherches historiques.

———. (1992). "Quelques remarques sur la propriété du sol dans le Gharb al-Andalus pendant la période musulmane." *Revue des études islamiques* 60, no. 2:471–519.

———. (1993). "Le renouveau urbain en Occident ibérique aux IXe–Xe siècles, sous l'impulsion de seigneurs *muwalladûn*." In *Princes et Pouvoirs au Moyen Âge*, 23rd Symposium of the Société des historiens médiévistes de l'enseignement supérieur public, 49–67. Paris: Publications de la Sorbonne.

———. (1995a). "Récits merveilleux et réalité d'une navigation en océan Atlantique chez les auteurs musulmans." In *Miracles, prodiges et merveilles au Moyen Âge*, 25th Symposium of the Société des historiens médiévistes de l'enseignement supérieur public, Orléans, 1994, 75–87. Paris: Publications de la Sorbonne.

———. (1995b). "Sanctuaires et pèlerinages chrétiens en terre musulmane: L'Occident de l'Andalus (XIe–XIIe siècle)." In *Pèlerinages et Croisades: 118e Congrès des Sociétés historiques et scientifiques (Pau, 1993)*, 235–247. Paris: Éditions du Comité des travaux historiques et scientifiques.

———. (1997a). *La Mer et les Musulmans d'Occident au Moyen Âge (VIIIe–XIIIe siècle).* Paris: Presses universitaires de France.

———. (1997b). *L'Océan Atlantique musulman de la conquête arabe à l'époque almohade. Navigation et mise en valeur des côtes d'al-Andalus et du Maghreb occidental (Portugal, Espagne, Maroc).* Paris: Maisonneuve et Larose.

———. (1998). "La 'piraterie' musulmane sur l'océan Atlantique." *Qurtuba: Estudios andalusíes* 3:153–169.

———. (2000). *Le Portugal musulman (VIIIe–XIIIe siècle): L'Occident d'al-Andalus sous domination islamique.* Paris: Maisonneuve et Larose.

———. (2001). "Les défenses côtières de la façade atlantique d'al-Andalus." In *Castrum 7: Zones côtières littorales dans le monde méditerranéen au Moyen Âge: Défense, peuplement, mise en valeur, Rome, 23–26 October 1996,* edited by J.-M. Martin, 163–176. Rome: École française de Rome; Madrid: Casa de Velázquez.

———. (2002). "Les ribats au Portugal à l'époque musulmane: Sources et définitions." In *Mil anos de fortificações na Península Ibérica e no Magreb (500–1500): Actas do Simpósio Internacional sobre Castelos,* 203–212. Lisbon: Colibri-Câmara Municipal de Palmela.

———. (2003). "L'inventaire des ports et de la navigation du Maghreb, d'après les relations des auteurs arabes médiévaux." *Compte-rendu des séances de l'Académie des inscriptions et belles-lettres,* 65–89.

———. (2004). "Les arsenaux musulmans de la Méditerranée et de l'océan Atlantique (VIIe–XVe siècle)." *Chemins d'outre-mer: Études sur la Méditerranée médiévale offertes à Michel Balard.* 2 vols. 691–710. Paris: Publications de la Sorbonne.

———. (2005). "La navigation médiévale des musulmans entre Méditerranée et océan Atlantique (IXe–XIIe siècle)." In "Portos Antigos do Mediterrâneo, Colloque de Mértola, 2003," edited by S. Macias and S. Gomez Martinez, special issue, *Arqueologia Medieval* 9:13–20.

———. (2006a). "La politique navale des premiers califes almohades." In *Los Almohades: Problemas y Perspectivas,* edited by P. Cressier, M. Fierro, and L. Molina, 1:567–584. Madrid: Consejo Superior de Investigaciones Científicas.

———. (2006b). "Regards croisés sur l'élaboration du jihad entre Occident et Orient musulman (VIIIe–XIIe siècle): Perspectives et réflexion sur une origine commune." In *Regards croisés sur la guerre sainte: Guerre, religion et idéologie dans l'espace méditerranéen latin (XIe–XIIIe siècle),* edited by D. Baloup and P. Josserand, 33–66. Toulouse: Méridiennes.

———. (2007a). "*Bahriyyûn,* émirs et califes: L'origine des équipages des flottes musulmanes en Méditerranée occidentale." *Medieval Encounters* 13:413–451.

———. (2007b). "Retour sur la piraterie sarrasine d'al-Andalus contre le monde latin (Italie et Provence) au IXe et Xe siècle." In *Quel mar che la terra inghirlanda: In ricordo di Marco Tangheroni,* edited by F. Cardini and M. L. Ceccarelli Lemut, 576–596. Pisa: Pacini editore.

———. (2009a). "De l'usage de l'écrit documentaire en Islam." In *L'Autorité de l'écrit au Moyen Âge (Orient-Occident),* 39th Symposium of the Société des historiens médiévistes de l'enseignement supérieur public, Cairo, 30 April–5 May 2008. Paris: Publications de la Sorbonne.

———. (2009b). "Le port 'construit' sur les littoraux de l'Occident médiéval (VIIIe–XVe siècle), d'après les sources arabes." In *Les Ports et la navigation en Méditerranée au Moyen Âge: Actes du colloque de Lattes, 12–14 novembre 2004,* edited by G. Fabre, D. Le Blévec, and D. Menjot, 213–224. Paris: Éditions du Manuscrit.

———. (2010a). "La Méditerranée musulmane, un héritage omeyyade." In *Umayyad Legacies,* edited by A. Borrut and P. Cobb, 385–402. Leiden: Brill, 2010.

———. (2010b). "Le calife 'Umar interdit la Méditerranée aux Arabes: Peur de la mer ou raison d'État?" In *Un Moyen Âge pour aujourd'hui: Mélanges offerts à Claude Gauvard,* edited by J. Claustre, O. Mattéoni, and N. Offenstadt, 247–257. Paris: Presses universitaires de France.

———. (2011a). "Berbères du Maghreb al-Aqsâ et mise en valeur économique d'après les géographes arabes." In *La Légitimation du pouvoir au Maghreb médiéval: De l'orientalisation à l'émancipation politique,* edited by A. Nef and E. Voguet, 11–34. Madrid: Casa de Velázquez.

———. (2011b). "Espaces maritimes et polycentrisme dans l'Islam abbasside." In *Le Polycentrisme dans l'Islam médiéval: Les dynamiques régionales de l'innovation,* edited by A. Nef and M. Tillier, 23–46. Annales islamologiques 45. Cairo: Institut français d'archéologie orientale.

———. (2011c). "Saltés et l'Atlantique: Le rôle maritime de la ville dans l'essor de la navigation musulmane aux Xe-XIIIe siècles." In *Madînat Shaltîsh: Une ville islamique dans les marécages de l'Odiel (Huelva, Andalousie) du IXe au XIIIe siècle,* edited by A. Bazzana, 41–55. Namur, Belgium: Ministère de la Région wallonne.

———. (2012). "La Mer et le sacré en Islam médiéval." In "La Mer et le sacré en Islam médiéval," edited by C. Picard, special issue, *Revue des mondes musulmans et de la Méditerranée* 130:13–32.

Picard, C., and A. Borrut. (2003). "*Râbata, Ribât, Râbita:* Une institution à reconsidérer." In *Chrétiens et Musulmans en Méditerranée médiévale*

(VIIIe–XIIIe siècle): Échanges et contacts, Beirut Symposium, May 2002, coordinated by P. Sénac and N. Prouteau, 33–65. Poitiers, France: Centre d'études supérieures de civilisation médiévale.

Picard, C., and I. C. Ferreira Fernandes. (1999). "La défense côtière au Portugal à l'époque musulmane: L'exemple de la presqu'île de Setúbal." *Archéologie islamique* 8–9:67–94.

Pirenne, H. (2005). *Mahomet et Charlemagne.* New ed. Quadrige. Paris: Presses universitaires de France. First edition published 1936.

Poisson, J.-M., ed. (1992). *Castrum 4: Frontière et peuplement dans le monde méditerranéen au Moyen Âge.* Proceedings of the Erice-Trapani Conference, Italy, 18–25 September 1988. Rome: École française de Rome; Madrid: Casa de Velázquez.

Polignac, F. de (1982). "L'image d'Alexandre dans la littérature arabe." *Arabica* 29:296–306.

———. (1999). "Alexandre, maître des seuils et des passages: De la légende antique au mythe arabe." In *Alexandre le Grand dans les littératures occidentales et proche-orientales,* Proceedings of the Paris Symposium, 27–29 November 1999, collected by L. Harf-Lancner, C. Kappler, and F. Svard, 215–225. Nanterre, France: Université de Paris X-Nanterre.

Poly, J.-P. (1976). *La Provence et la société féodale, 879–1166.* Paris: Bordas.

Pons Boigues, F. (1898). *Ensayo bio-blibliográfico sobre los historiadores y geógrafos arábigo-españoles.* Madrid (new ed. Amsterdam, 1972).

Pouzet, L. (1975). "Maghrébins à Damas au VIIe–XIIIe siècle." *Bulletin d'études orientales* 28:167–199.

Prémare, A.-L. de. (2002). *Les Fondations de l'Islam entre écriture et histoire.* Paris: Seuil.

Prévost, V. (2010). *Les Ibâdites: De Djerba à Oman, la troisième voie de l'Islam.* Turnhout, Belgium: Brepols.

Prigent, V. (2007). *La Sicile byzantine (VIe–Xe siècle).* Lille, France: Atelier National de Reproduction des Thèses.

Pryor, J. H. (1988). *Geography, Technology and War Studies in the Maritime History of the Mediterranean, 649–1571.* Cambridge: Cambridge University Press.

———. (2006). *The Age of the Dromon: The Byzantine Navy, ca. 500–1204.* Leiden: Brill.

Ramírez del Río, J. (2002). *La orientalización de al-Andalus: Los días de los árabes en la Península Ibérica.* Seville: Universidad de Sevilla.

Ragheb, Y. (1996). "Les plus anciens papyrus arabes." *Annales islamologiques* 30:143–168.

Rashed, R., ed. (1997). *Histoire des sciences arabes.* 3 vols. Paris: Seuil.

Raymond, A. (1993). *Cairo.* Paris: Mazenod.

Reddé, M. (1986). *Mare nostrum: Les infrastructures, le dispositif et l'histoire de la marine militaire sous l'Empire romain.* Rome: Bibliothèque des écoles françaises d'Athènes et de Rome.

Richard, J. (1981). *Les Récits de voyage et de pèlerinage.* Tournai, Belgium: Brepols.

Ríos Saloma, M. (2006). "La Reconquista: Una invención historiográfica." In *Regards croisés sur la guerre sainte: Guerre, religion et idéologie dans l'espace méditerranéen latin (XIe–XIIIe siècle),* edited by D. Baloup and P. Josserand, 413–429. Toulouse: Méridiennes.

Robinson, C. F. (2003). *Islamic Historiography.* Cambridge: Cambridge University Press.

———. (2005). *'Abd al-Malik.* Oxford: Oneworld.

Rodinson, M. (1966). *Islam et capitalisme.* Paris: Seuil.

Roldán F. (1993). *Niebla musulmana.* Huelva, Spain: Diputación provincial de Huelva.

Rosenberger, B. (1995). "Le contrôle du détroit de Gibraltar aux XIIe–XIIIe siècles." In *L'Occident musulman et l'Occident chrétien au Moyen Âge,* edited by M. Hammam, 16–42. Rabat: Université Mohammed-V.

———. (2005). "Ports médiévaux de la côte méditerranéenne du Maroc: Guerre et commerce." In "Portos Antigos do Mediterrâneo, Colloque de Mértola, 2003," edited by S. Macias and S. Gomez Martinez, special issue, *Arqueologia Medieval* 9:21–40.

Rosenthal, F. (1968). *A History of Muslim Historiography.* Rev. 2nd ed. Leiden: Brill.

Rosselló Bordoy, G. (1968). *L'Islam a les Illes Balears.* Palma de Mallorca, Spain: Daedalus.

Rougeulle, A. (1990). "Les Importations extrêmes-orientales trouvées sur les sites de la période abbasside: Contribution à l'étude du commerce moyen-oriental au Moyen Âge." PhD diss., Université Paris-IV Sorbonne.

Said, E. (1978). *Orientalism.* London: Routledge and Kegan Paul.

Saint-Guillain, G. de (2005). "L'Archipel des seigneurs: Pouvoirs, société et insularité dans les Cyclades, à l'époque de la domination latine." PhD diss., Université Paris-I.

Salierno, V. (2010). *Il Mediterraneo nella cartografia ottomana (coste, porti, isole negli atlanti di Piri Reis).* Lecce, Italy: Capone.

Samir, S. K. (2003). "La transmission du savoir de Byzance à Bagdad." In *Chrétiens et Musulmans en Méditerranée médiévale (VIIIe–XIIIe siècle): Échanges et contacts,* Beirut symposium, May 2002, coord. P. Sénac and N. Prouteau, 125–183. Poitiers, France: Centre d'études supérieures de civilisation médiévale.

Sauvaget, J. (1941). *Alep, essai sur le développement d'une grande ville syrienne des origines au milieu du XIXe siècle.* 2 vols. Bibliothèque archéologique et historique, vol. 39. Paris: P. Geuthner.

Schacht, J. (1959). *The Origins of Muhammadan Jurisprudence.* Oxford: Clarendon.

———. (1999). *Introduction au droit musulman.* Paris: Maisonneuve et Larose. First edition published 1964.

Schatzmiller, M. (1994). *Labour in Medieval Islam.* Leiden: Brill.

Schaube, A. (1906). *Handelsgeschichte der romanischen Völker des Mittelmeergebiets bis zum Ende der Kreuzzüge.* Berlin.

Schiettecatte, J. (2011). *D'Aden à Zafar, villes de l'Arabie du Sud préislamique.* Paris: De Boccard.

Schoeler, G. (2002). *Écrire et transmettre dans les débuts de l'Islam.* Islamiques. Paris: Presses universitaires de France.

Sénac, P. (1982). *Provence et piraterie sarrasine.* Paris: Maisonneuve et Larose.

———. (2000a). *La Frontière et les hommes (VIIIe–XIIe siècle): Le peuplement musulman au nord de l'Èbre et les débuts de la reconquête aragonaise.* Paris: Maisonneuve et Larose.

———. (2000b). "Notes sur les relations diplomatiques entre les comtes de Barcelone et le califat de Cordoue au xe siècle." In *Les Relations des pays d'Islam avec le monde latin du milieu du xe siècle au milieu du XIIIe siècle,* edited by F. Micheau, 116–135. Paris: J. Marseille.

———. (2001). "Le califat de Cordoue et la Méditerranée occidentale au Xe siècle: Le Fraxinet des Maures." In *Castrum 7: Zones côtières littorales dans le monde méditerranéen au Moyen Âge: Défense, peuplement, mise en valeur, Rome, 23–26 October 1996,* edited by J.-M. Martin, 113–126. Rome: École française de Rome; Madrid: Casa de Velázquez.

———. (2002). *Les Carolingiens et al-Andalus (VIIIe–IXe siècles).* Paris: Maisonneuve et Larose.

———. (2006). *Le Monde carolingien et l'Islam.* Paris: L'Harmattan.

Sharon, M. (1997). *Corpus inscriptionum arabicarum Palaestinae.* Vol. A. Leiden: Brill.

Shaykha, J. (1981). "Al-Thawra al-Mayûrqiyyîn bi-Ifrîqiya wa athâruha fî tawâzun al-quwâ bayna l-Islâm wa l-Nasraniyya fi l-Maghrib wa l-Andalus." *Cahiers de Tunisie* 117–118:91–122.

Shboul, A. (1979). *Al-Mas'ûdî and His World: A Muslim Humanist and His Interest in Non-Muslims.* London: Ithaca.

Sidarus, A. (1990). "O Alentejo durante a grande dissidência luso-muçulmana do século IX–X." *Encontro Regional de História.* Évora, Portugual.

———. (1994). "Um texto arabe do século X relativo à nova fundação de Évora e aos movimentos muladi e berbere no Ocidente andaluz." *A Cidade de Evora*, no. 71–76, 45–50:7–37.

Sidarus, A., and F. Teichner. (1997). "Termas romanas no Garb al-Andalus: As inscrições árabes de Milreu." *Arqueologia Medieval* 5:177–189.

Sijpesteijn, P. (2004). "Travel and Trade on the River." In *Papyrology and the History of Early Islamic Egypt*, edited by M. Sijpesteijn and L. Sundelin, 115–152. Islamic History and Civilization, vol. 55. Leiden: Brill.

———. (2007). "New Rule over Old Structures: Egypt after the Muslim Conquest." *Proceedings of the British Academy* 136:183–200.

Sijpesteijn, P., and L. Sundelin, eds. (2004). *Papyrology and the History of Early Islamic Egypt*. Islamic History and Civilization, vol. 55. Leiden: Brill.

Silverstein, A. J. (2007). *Postal Systems in the Pre-modern Islamic World*. Cambridge: Cambridge University Press.

Siraj, A. (1995). *L'Image de la Tingitane: L'historiographie arabe médiévale et l'Antiquité nord-africaine*. Collection de l'École française de Rome, no. 209. Rome: École française de Rome.

Sivan, E. (1968). *L'Islam et la croisade: Idéologie et propagande dans les réactions musulmanes aux Croisades*. Paris: Adrien Maisonneuve.

Société des historiens médiévistes de l'enseignement supérieur public (SHMESP), ed. (2009). *L'Autorité de l'écrit au Moyen Âge (Orient-Occident)*, 39th Symposium of the SHMESP, Cairo, 30 April–5 May 2008. Paris: Publications de la Sorbonne.

Sodini, J.-P. (2000). "Productions et échanges dans le monde protobyzantin (IVe–VIIe siècles): Le cas de la céramique." In *Byzanz als Raum*, edited by K. Belke, F. Hild, J. Koder, and P. Soustal, 181–208. Vienna: Akademie der Wissenschaften.

Soravia, B. (1998). "Les Fonctionnaires épistoliers (Kuttâb al-insa') en Espagne musulmane à l'époque des roitelets (V^{e}/XIe siècle)." PhD diss., Université Paris-III Nouvelle Sorbonne.

Sourdel, D. (1980). "La Syrie au temps des premiers califes abbassides." *Revue des études islamiques* 48, no. 2:155–175.

———. (1999). *L'État impérial des califes abbassides, VIIIe–Xe siècle*. Paris: Presses universitaires de France.

Sourdel, D., and J. Sourdel. (1968). *La Civilisation de l'Islam classique*. Grandes Civilisations. Paris: Arthaud.

———. (1996). *Dictionnaire historique de l'Islam*. Paris: Presses universitaires de France.

Stratos, A. N. (1980). "The Naval Engagement at Phoenix." In *Charanis Studies: Essays in Honor of Peter Charanis*, edited by A. E. Laiou-Thomadakis, 229–247. New Brunswick, NJ: Rutgers University Press.

Subrahmanyam, S. (1995). "Of *Imârat* and *Tijârat:* Asian Merchants and State Power in the Western Indian Ocean, 1400 to 1750." *Comparative Studies in Society and History* 37:750–780.

———. (1999). *L'Empire portugais d'Asie, 1500–1700: Histoire politique et économique.* Paris: Maisonneuve et Larose.

Talbi, M. (1966). *L'Émirat aghlabide (184–296/800–909): Histoire politique.* Paris: A. M. Maisonneuve.

———. (1972). "Kairouan et le malikisme espagnol." In *Études d'orientalisme dédiées à la mémoire de Lévi-Provençal,* 317–337. Paris: Maisonneuve et Larose.

———. (1985). "Intérêt des oeuvres juridiques traitant de la guerre pour l'historien des armées médiévales ifrîqiyennes (d'après le *Kitâb al-nawâdir* d'Ibn Abi Zayd)." In *Études d'histoire et de civilisation musulmane en Ifrîqiya.* Tunis.

Tangheroni, M. (1996). *Commercio e navigazione nel Medioevo.* Rome: Laterza.

Tibbets, G. R. (1992a). "The Balkhi School of Geographers." In *The History of Cartography,* edited by J. B. Harley, D. Woodward, vol. 2, *Cartography in the Traditional Islamic and South Asian Societies,* 108–129. Chicago: University of Chicago Press.

———. (1992b). "The Beginnings of a Cartographic Tradition." In *The History of Cartography,* edited by J. B. Harley, D. Woodward, vol. 2, *Cartography in the Traditional Islamic and South Asian Societies,* 90–107. Chicago: University of Chicago Press.

Tillier, M. (2009). *Les Cadis d'Irak et l'État Abbasside.* Damascus: Institut Français du Proche-Orient.

Tixier du Mesnil, E. (2011). "Bakrî et le Maghreb." In *Islamisation et arabisation de l'Occident musulman médiéval, VIIe–XIIe siècle,* edited by D. Valérian, 369–384. Paris: Publications de la Sorbonne.

———. (2014). *Géographes d'al-Andalus: De l'inventaire d'un territoire à la construction d'une mémoire.* Paris: Publications de la Sorbonne.

Tonghini, C. (1999). "Fatimid Ceramics from Italy: The Archaeological Evidence." In *L'Égypte fatimide: Son art et son histoire: Actes du colloque de mai 1998 de Paris,* edited by M. Barrucand, 287–297. Paris: Presses universitaires de Paris-Sorbonne.

Tor, D. (2005). "Privatized Jihad and Public Order in the Pre-Seljuq Period: The Role of the *Mutatawwi'a.*" *Iranian Studies* 38, no. 4:555–573.

Torres, C. (1982). "A alcáçova de Mértola: História et arqueologia urbana." *Arqueologia* 6:86–95.

Torres, C., and S. Macias. (1998). *O legado islâmico em Portugal.* Lisbon: Fundação Círculo de Leitores.

Torres, M. P. (1995). "Ictionimia en glosarios andalusíes." In *Al-Andalus y el Mediterráneo,* 227–241. Madrid: El Legado Andalusí; Barcelona: Lunwerg Editores.

Torres Balbas, L. (1946). "Atarazanas hispanomusulmanas." *Al-Andalus* 11:175–209.

———. (1957a). "Almería islámica." *Al-Andalus* 22:411–455.

———. (1957b). *Ciudades hispanomusulmanes.* 2 vols. Madrid: Offprint of the Boletín de la Real Academia de la Historia.

Touati, H. (2000). *Islam et voyage au Moyen Âge: Histoire et anthropologie d'une pratique lettrée.* Paris: Seuil.

———. (2003). *L'Armoire à sagesse: Bibliothèques et collections en Islam.* Paris: Aubier.

Toubert, P. (1973). *Les Structures du Latium médiéval: Le Latium méridional et la Sabine du IX*e *à la fin du XIII*e *siècle.* 2 vols. Rome: Bibliothèque des écoles françaises d'Athènes et de Rome, 221.

Trombley, F. (2004). "Sawirus ibn al-Muqaffa' and the Christians of Umayyad Egypt: War and Society in Documentary Context." In *Papyrology and the History of Early Islamic Egypt,* edited by M. Sijpesteijn and L. Sundelin, 199–226. Islamic History and Civilization, vol. 55. Leiden: Brill.

Udovitch, A. L. (1978). *Partnership and Profit in Medieval Islam.* Princeton, NJ: Princeton University Press.

———. (1993). "An Eleventh Century Islamic Treatise on the Law of the Sea." *Annales islamologiques* 27:37–54.

———. (1999). "Fatimid Cairo: Crossroads of World Trade—From Spain to India." In *L'Égypte fatimide: Son art et son histoire: Actes du colloque de mai 1998 de Paris,* edited by M. Barrucand, 681–691. Paris: Presses universitaires de Paris-Sorbonne.

Urvoy, D. (1974). "La pensée d'Ibn Tûmart." *Bulletin d'études orientales* 27:19–44.

———. (1978). *Le Monde des oulémas andalous du V*e*–XI*e *au XI*e*-XIII*e *siècle.* Geneva: Droz.

———. (1990). *Pensers d'al-Andalus: La vie intellectuelle à Cordoue et Séville au temps des empires berbères (fin XI*e*–début XIII*e *siècle).* Toulouse: Presses Universitaires du Midi.

Vagnon, E. (2013). *Cartographie et représentations de l'Orient méditerranéen en Occident (milieu XIII*e*–fin du XV*e *siècle).* Turnhout, Belgium: Brepols.

Valérian, D. (2006a). *Bougie, port maghrébin, 1076–1510.* Rome: École française de Rome.

———. (2006b). *Les Sources italiennes du Maghreb médiéval.* Paris: Bouchène.

———. (2010). *Ports et réseaux d'échanges dans le Maghreb médiéval.* Paris: Université Paris-I.

———, ed. (2011). *Islamisation et arabisation de l'Occident musulman médiéval (VIIe XIIe siècle).* Paris: Publications de la Sorbonne.

Vallet, É. (1999). *Marchands vénitiens en Syrie à la fin du xve siècle: Pour l'honneur et le profit.* Paris: Association pour le développement de l'histoire économique.

———. (2006). "Yemeni 'Oceanic Policy' at the End of the Thirteenth Century." In *Proceedings of the Seminar for Arabian Studies,* 36:289–296. London: P. J. Parr.

———. (2007). "Entre deux mondes: Les produits du commerce égyptien à Aden, XIIIe–XIVe siècle." In *Espaces et réseaux en Méditerranée,* edited by D. Coulon, C. Picard, and D. Valérian, vol. 1, *La Configuration des réseaux,* 206–237. Paris: Bouchène.

———. (2010). *L'Arabie marchande: État et commerce sous les sultans rasûlides du Yémen (676–858/1229–1454).* Paris: Publications de la Sorbonne.

———. (2012). "Le périple au miroir des sources arabes médiévales: Le cas des produits du commerce." In *Autour de la mer Érythrée,* edited by M.-F. Boussac, J.-F. Salles, and J.-B. Yon, 359–380. Lyon: Maison de l'Orient et de la Méditerranée.

Vallvé Bermejo, J. (1967). "La intervención omeya en el Norte de África." *Cuadernos de la Biblioteca española de Tetuán* 4:7–39.

———. (1986). *La división territorial en la España musulmana.* Madrid: Consejo Superior de Investigaciones Científicas–Instituto Miguel Asín.

Vassiliev, A. (1935). *Byzance et les Arabes.* 3 vols. Brussels: Éditions de l'Institut de philologie et d'histoire orientales et slaves.

Vegua, M., S. Peña, and M. C. Feria. (2006). "La doctrina almohade a través de la numismática." In *Los Almohades: Problemas y Perspectivas,* edited by P. Cressier, M. Fierro, and L. Molina, 2:1013–1049. Madrid: Consejo Superior de Investigaciones Científicas.

Vernet, J. (1985). *Ce que la culture doit aux Arabes d'Espagne.* Paris: Sindbad.

Viguera Molíns, M. J. (1977). "Las cartas de al-Ghazâlî y al-Turtûshî al soberano almorávid Yûsuf b. Tâšfîn." *Al-Andalus* 42, no. 2:361–374.

———. (1995). auteur du vol. 8–1, in R. Menendez Pidal (coll.), *Historia de España.* 2nd ed. Madrid.

———. (1988). "La intervención de los Benimerines en al-Andalus." In *Relaciones de la Península Ibérica con el Magreb Siglos XIII–XVI: Actas del coloquio (Madrid, 17–18 diciembre 1987),* edited by M. Garcia-Arenal and M. J. Viguera, 237–247. Madrid: Consejo Superior de Investigaciones Científicas.

Von Sievers, P. (1979). "Military, Merchants and Nomads: The Social Evolution of the Syrian Cities and Countryside during the Classical Period, 780–962/133–358." *Der Islam* 56:212–244.

———. (1982). "Tax and Trade in the 'Abbassids Thughûr (750–962/133–951)." *Journal of Economic and Social History of Orient* 25, no. 1:71–99.

Walmsley, A. G. (2000). "The Islamic City: Archeological Experience in Jordan." *Mediterranean Archaeology* 13:1–9.

———. (2007). *Early Islamic Syria: An Archaeological Assessment.* London: Duckworth.

Wasserstein, D. (1985). *The Rise and Fall of the Party-Kings: Politics and Society in Islamic Spain, 1002–1086.* Princeton, NJ: Princeton University Press.

Watt, M. (1989). *Mahomet à La Mecque.* Paris: Payot. First edition published 1958.

Whittow, M. (2009). "The Middle Byzantine Economy." In *The Cambridge History of the Byzantine Empire,* edited by J. Shepard. Cambridge: Cambridge University Press.

Wickham, C. (2005). *Framing the Early Middle Ages: Europe and Mediterranean, 400–800.* Oxford: Oxford University Press.

Wilk, M. (2008). "Le Discours historique d'al-Andalus depuis la conquête arabe jusqu'à l'époque des Taifas." PhD diss., École des hautes études en sciences sociales, Paris.

Yalaoui, M. (1976). *Un poète shiite d'Occident au IVe/Xe siècle: Ibn Hâni' al-Andalûsî.* Tunis: Publications de l'Université de Tunis.

Zemouli, M. (2002). "La navigation maritime chez les Arabes à travers les textes du Coran et la poésie arabe: Une introduction." In *Aspects of Arab Seafaring: An Attempt to Fill in the Gaps of Maritime History.* Athens: Institute for Graeco-Oriental and African Studies.

Zouache, A., ed. (2009). "La guerre dans le monde arabo-musulman médiéval." *Annales islamologiques* 43.

Zumthor, P. (1993). *La Mesure du monde.* Paris: Seuil.

INDEX